AF328366

Lienhard von Monkiewitsch
Farbe und Raum

Lienhard von Monkiewitsch

Farbe und Raum | Color and Space

herausgegeben von
edited by
MICHAEL SCHWARZ

mit Textbeiträgen von | with texts by
ELKE BIPPUS, ULRIKE LEHMANN,
HEINO R. MÖLLER, MICHAEL SCHWARZ,
MICHAEL STOEBER und | and WALTER VITT

KERBER VERLAG

Diese Publikation erscheint aus Anlass
der Ausstellungen einzelner Werkgruppen in:
This catalogue is being published on
the occasion of the exhibitions of individual
groups of works in:

Wilhelm-Hack-Museum Ludwigshafen
4. 3. bis 7. 5. 2006 | March 4 – May 7, 2006

Marburger Kunstverein, Marburg
11. 3. bis 27. 4. 2006 | March 11 – April 27, 2006

Galerie vom Zufall und vom Glück und
Städtische Galerie Kubus, Hannover
24. 3. bis 23. 4. 2006 | March 24 – April 23, 2006

Galerie der Hochschule für Bildende Künste
Braunschweig
26. 4. bis 28. 5. 2006 | April 26 – May 28, 2006

Städtische Galerie Wolfsburg
26. 4. bis 5. 6. 2006 | April 26 – June 5, 2006

Die Publikation wurde gefördert durch
This publication was funded by

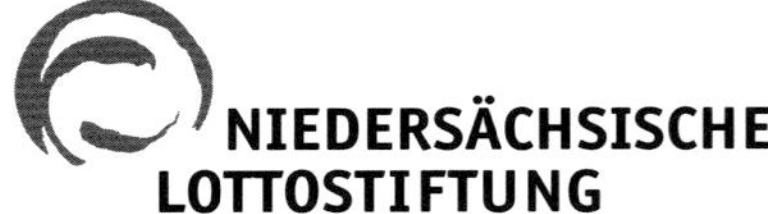

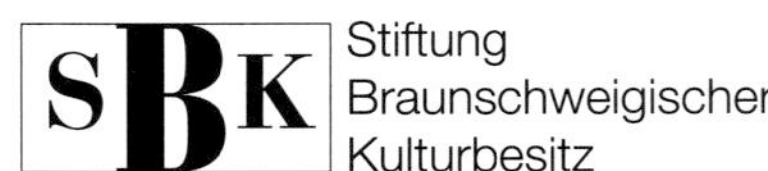

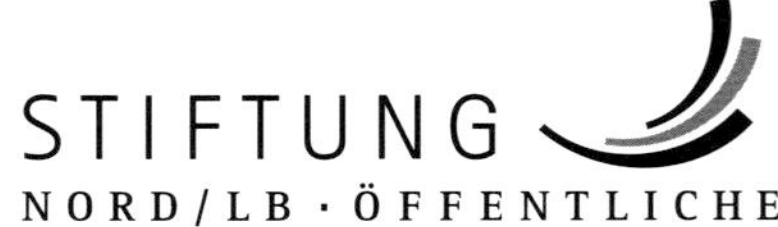

und durch Beiträge der beteiligten Aus-
stellungsinstitute | and by contributions
from the participating instititions

Inhalt | Contents

Vorwort | Foreword

Dieses Buch erscheint aus Anlass von Ausstellungen des Künstlers und Hochschullehrers Lienhard von Monkiewitsch in Ludwigshafen, Marburg, Hannover, Wolfsburg und Braunschweig. Die Ausstellungen werden nahezu gleichzeitig eröffnet und zeigen Werkentwicklungen oder einzelne Werkgruppen aus über 35 Jahren. Im Wilhelm-Hack-Museum Ludwigshafen ist eine Werkschau zu sehen, die den Bogen von den Zeichnungen der späten 6oer Jahre bis zu den aktuellen Farbkompositionen spannt. Im Marburger Kunstverein zeigt der Künstler eine Auswahl seiner großen Architekturbilder und in der Galerie vom Zufall und vom Glück in Hannover frühe Boden- und Fußleistenbilder, weil dies bis zum Umzug nach Berlin 1982 die Adresse der Galerie Brusberg war, die den Künstler mit eben diesen Arbeiten hier ausgestellt hatte. In den anderen Häusern, in der Städtischen Galerie Wolfsburg und der Hochschule für Bildende Künste Braunschweig, sind die Beiträge eher speziell und beziehen sich auf das Sammelprofil oder auf die besonderen Bedingungen der Räume. Weil die Ausstellungen in den einzelnen Institutionen autonom sind und in einem gemeinsamen Katalogbuch nicht hätten abgebildet werden können, folgt dieses der Arbeitsbiografie des Künstlers von den Anfängen bis in die unmittelbare Gegenwart.

Eine Werkphase wird allerdings nicht behandelt oder ausgestellt. Lienhard von Monkiewitsch hatte unter dem Eindruck realistischer Positionen der 7oer Jahre und der Erwartung einer damals politischen Studentenschaft an die gesellschaftliche Funktion der Kunst 1974 begonnen, figürlich-gegenständliche Bilder zu malen. Diese Werke schienen uns nur auf einer sehr hohen Abstraktionsebene mit den ab 1978 entstehenden Architekturbildern verbunden und wären im Kontext der Gesamtentwicklung schwer zu vermitteln gewesen.

Dafür wird das Œuvre des Künstlers nach der 1994 erschienenen und lange vergriffenen Monografie von Walter Vitt zum ersten Mal in einem ikonografischen Kontext und in seinen stilgeschichtlichen Ableitungen diskutiert und dargestellt. Die Reihe der Essays beginnt mit einem Beitrag von Heino R. Möller über die frühen Fußleisten- und Bodenarbeiten, die insbesondere für die Kategorie des Raumes im Werk des Künstlers von anhaltender Bedeutung sind. In weiteren Beiträgen wird dann der Bezug zur nachexpressionistischen Kunst der 6oer und 7oer Jahre in Amerika herausgearbeitet. Für Künstler wie Donald Judd ist das Rechteck des Bildes nicht länger das Fenster zur Welt, sondern eine eigenständige Form, die die Anordnung dessen begrenzt, was sich in ihr ereignet. Die konzeptionellen Parallelen zwischen den Architekturbildern und der Minimal Art eines Sol LeWitt und Robert Mangold oder den frühen Arbeiten Frank Stellas thematisiert Ulrike Lehmann in ihrem Aufsatz. Das Eigenständige dieser in Rom begonnenen Bildserie erkennt sie in der Erfindung von abbildhaften Shaped Canvases, „die den gemalten Raum mit dem realen Raum verbinden". In diesem Raum ist ein Betrachter zu denken,

This book is being published on the occasion of exhibitions by the artist and university teacher Lienhard von Monkiewitsch in Ludwigshafen, Marburg, Hannover, Wolfsburg, and Braunschweig. The exhibitions are being opened virtually simultaneously and show the development of his work or individual groups of works from more than thirty-five years. A retrospective is being shown in the Wilhelm Hack Museum in Ludwigshafen which includes works ranging from drawings produced in the 1960s to his current color compositions. In the Marburger Kunstverein, the artist is showing a selection of his large-format architecture paintings, and his early floor and baseboard pictures are being presented in the Galerie vom Zufall und vom Glück in Hannover. Until it moved to Berlin in 1982, the latter accommodated the Galerie Brusberg, where the artist once exhibited these same works. The other venues – the Städtische Galerie Wolfsburg and the Hochschule für Bildende Künste Braunschweig – are presenting contributions which make particular reference to the respective collection profile or the particular spatial conditions. Because the exhibitions in the individual institutions are autonomous and could not have been reproduced in a single catalogue, this book traces the biography of work by the artist from the beginning to the present day.

One work phase, however, is not being treated or represented. Under the impression of realist positions in the 1970s and the expectations of students at the time on the social function of art, in 1974 Lienhard von Monkiewitsch began to produce figurative-representational paintings. It appeared to us that these works were only associated with the architecture paintings produced after 1978 on a very high level of abstraction and that they would have been difficult to convey within the context of the artist's overall development.

Instead, for the first time since the publication in 1994 of the long since out-of-print monograph by Walter Vitt, the artist's œuvre is being discussed and presented within an iconographic context and in its derivations with regard to the history of style. The series of essays begins with a contribution by Heino R. Möller on the early baseboard and floor pieces, which are of particular importance for the category of space in the artist's work.

Further contributions bring out von Monkiewitsch's relationship to the post-Expressionist art of the 1960s and 1970s in America. For artists like Donald Judd, the square of the painting is no longer the window into the world, but an independent form which limits the arrangement of that which occurs within it. In another essay, Ulrike Lehmann thematicizes the conceptional parallels between the architecture paintings and the Minimal Art by someone such as Sol LeWitt or Robert Mangold, or early works by Frank Stella. She sees the independent quality of this series, which was begun in Rome, in the invention of picture-like Shaped Canvases, "that connect the painted space with the real space." The viewer, to whom Lienhard von Monkiewitsch has always assigned an important – and later an active – role, is to imagine himself in the space.

In her contribution on "Serial Deeds," Elke Bippus brings out the participatory approach of von Monkiewitsch's work when she points out that viewing serial works always has to be regarded as a process, and therefore as an act. Finally, Michael Stoeber inquires into the image behind von Monkiewitsch's paintings. Do we only see what we see? "No, we do not see things because they are visible, rather they become visible because we see them." In this regard, he calls the artist with his strategies derived from system and coincidence a structuralist artist, who in a movement contrary to the thought patterns of the Structuralists, creates complex worlds of images out of only several elements.

The exhibitions and the catalogue have been developed in a trusting and therefore consistently unstrained dialogue between the artist, the editor, the authors, and the partners in the respective institutions. I would like to thank Ulrike Lehmann and Richard W. Gassen from the Wilhelm Hack Museum in Ludwigshafen, Gerhard Paetzold from the Marburger Kunstverein, Ludwig Zerull from the Galerie vom Zufall und vom Glück in Hannover, Susanne Pfleger from the Städtische Galerie Wolfsburg, and Ellen Fischer, Heike Hümme, Christiane Preißler and Barbara Straka from the Hochschule für Bildende Künste Braunschweig for their valuable cooperation in the preparation of this project. I would also like to express my gratitude to the foundations for funding this publication, thus enabling it to be published at a reasonable cost by a respected publishing house and to achieve international distribution beyond the exhibition venues. Thanks also go out to those many people on whom larger-scale projects always rely.

My heartfelt and very personal thanks are due the artist Lienhard von Monkiewitsch, who became involved in this undertaking at just the right time.

dem Lienhard von Monkiewitsch eine wichtige und in späteren Werkgruppen dann auch aktive Rolle zugewiesen hat.

Elke Bippus arbeitet in ihrem Beitrag über „Serielle Taten" den partizipatorischen Ansatz des Werkes heraus, wenn sie darauf hinweist, dass die Betrachtung serieller Arbeiten immer als Prozess und somit als Handlung gesehen werden muss. Michael Stoeber fragt nach dem Bild hinter den Bildern von Lienhard von Monkiewitsch. Sehen wir nur das, was wir sehen? „Nein, wir sehen die Dinge nicht, weil sie sichtbar sind, sondern sie werden sichtbar, weil wir sie sehen". In diesem Sinne nennt er den Künstler mit seinen Strategien aus System und Zufall einen strukturalistischen Künstler, der in einer gegenläufigen Bewegung zu den Denkmodellen der Strukturalisten aus wenigen Bildelementen komplexe Bildwelten erschafft.

Ausstellungen und Katalog sind in einem vertrauensvollen und deshalb immer unangestrengten Dialog zwischen Künstler, Herausgeber, den Autoren und den Partnern in den Institutionen entwickelt worden. Ich danke Ulrike Lehmann und Richard W. Gassen vom Wilhelm-Hack-Museum in Ludwigshafen, Gerhard Paetzold vom Marburger Kunstverein, Ludwig Zerull von der Galerie vom Zufall und vom Glück Hannover, Susanne Pfleger von der Städtischen Galerie Wolfsburg und Ellen Fischer, Heike Hümme, Christiane Preißler und Barbara Straka von der Hochschule für Bildende Künste Braunschweig für die gute Kooperation bei der Vorbereitung des Projektes. Den Stiftungen sei nachdrücklich für die Förderung der vorliegenden Publikation gedankt, die dadurch zu einem raisonablen Preis in einem angesehenen Verlag erscheinen konnte und über die Verbreitung durch die Ausstellungshäuser hinaus in einen internationalen Vertrieb gelangt. Gedankt sei den Vielen, auf die größere Projekte immer angewiesen sind.

Mein herzlicher und ganz persönlicher Dank gilt dem Künstler Lienhard von Monkiewitsch, der sich auf dieses Unternehmen zur rechten Zeit eingelassen hat.

MICHAEL SCHWARZ

Heino R. Möller

Innenräume – Innenwelten. Arbeiten 1968 bis 1973

Interior Spaces – Interior Worlds: Works from 1968 to 1973

Im Œuvre Lienhard von Monkiewitschs zeichnet sich 1968 der Beginn einer themen-, motiv- und problemgebundenen Werkphase ab, die über Jahre mit großer Intensität verfolgt und schließlich 1973 abrupt beendet wird. Voraussetzungen der Werkphase und spätere Neuorientierungen hat Walter Vitt beschrieben.[1] Die Originalität und bildnerische Konsequenz dieser Werkphase brachten dem damals jungen Künstler internationale Anerkennung.

Die in den Jahren 1968 bis 1973 entstehenden Bilder, welche die genannte Werkphase konstituieren, sind ausnahmslos Interieurs und folgen der Tradition einer bedeutenden Gattung der Malereigeschichte. Die Darstellung der Innenräume beginnt im Werk von Monkiewitschs tastend mit der Einbindung skurril-surrealer Gestalten, wird aber schon 1969 nach deren Eliminierung auf eine Grundproblematik hin ausgerichtet, die der Thematik neue Aspekte erschließt. Die Tafelbilder und großformatigen Farbstiftzeichnungen auf Karton führen konzeptionell immer zwei kontradiktische Komponenten zusammen. Die eine Komponente figuriert im jeweils unteren Bildsektor einen Fußboden, der gegenständlich in perspektivisch und illusionistisch perfekter Weise gestaltet ist und dem Betrachter die realistische Erschließung vielfach komplexer Raumfolgen unter nachhaltiger Berücksichtigung von Lichtführungen verheißt. Dem widerspricht als zweite Komponente ein quantitativ dominanter oberer Bildsektor, der antiillusionistisch in früheren Arbeiten tapetenhaft aus vertikalen, gleichmäßig breiten Farbstreifen und in den nachfolgenden aus farbig monochromen oder weißen Bildfeldern besteht. Die Streifenbilder sind auf Markisenstoffe gemalt beziehungsweise auf entsprechend gemusterte Geschenkpapiere gezeichnet, in den Farbstiftzeichnungen steht die Fußbodenzone auf dem weißen Karton der Bildträger.

Für den Betrachter bedeutet das Zusammentreffen der antithetischen Komponenten von realistischer Raumdarstellung und realer Bildfläche eine irritierende Seherfahrung. Die intensivste Reizzone ist vordergründig jene, wo die divergenten Partien unvermittelt aufeinander stoßen. Dann jedoch wird deutlich, wie die Komponenten miteinander ins Spiel kommen, sich in ihren Wertigkeiten wechselseitig überstrahlen. Der mit großer Intensität illusionistisch ausgearbeitete Bereich mit Bodenfliesen und Fußleisten, Lichtreflexen und Schattenzonen wird in seinem verführenden Realismus durch die Flächenzone desillusioniert – diese aber durch den Illusionismus der Fußbodenzone als komplexer Illusionsraum fassbar, anders gesagt: Man kann ihn als Raumsystem denken. Solcherart entsteht, was Walter Vitt zutreffend als „Seh-Denk-Prozess" beschrieben hat.[2] Es ist ein Raumsystem, das sich zwischen Mauerzungen und hinter Wänden zu öffnen scheint und zugleich verschließt. Hierin lässt sich ungesagt ausformen, was man an Vorstellungen hineindenken möchte. Der „Seh-Denk-Prozess" evoziert die schöpferische Phantasie des Betrachters, macht ihn zum Mitgestalter oder temporären Vollender jeweili-

In Lienhard von Monkiewitsch's œuvre, 1968 marks the beginning of a theme-, motif- and problem-related work phase that he intensely pursued for years, finally ending abruptly in 1973. Walter Vitt has described the conditions of this work phase and von Monkiewitsch's later reorientations.[1] The originality and painterly consistency of this phase gained the young artist international recognition.

The paintings produced between 1968 and 1973, which constitute said work phase, are without exception interiors and adhere to the tradition of an important genre in the history of painting. In von Monkiewitsch's work, the depiction of interior rooms begins tentatively with the inclusion of bizarre-surreal shapes; however, after their elimination in 1969, it is oriented toward fundamental problems, which open up new aspects of the theme. With regard to their concept, the panels and large-format colored-pencil drawings on cardboard always bring together two contradictory components. In each of the lower sectors of the paintings, the one component figures a floor, the representation of which is perfect with regard to perspective and illusion and promises the viewer the realistic opening up of in many cases complex spatial sequences with sustained consideration of light distribution. This is contradicted by a second component – a quantitatively dominant upper sector of the painting, which in earlier works consisted of vertical, equally wide stripes of color, anti-illusionistic and wallpaper-like, and in later works of monochromatic color or white painting fields. The stripe paintings were painted on sunblind fabric or drawn on correspondingly patterned gift wrapping paper; in the colored-pencil drawings, the floor zone is on the white carrier material.

For the viewer, the meeting of the antithetical components of realistic spatial representation and real image surface amounts to an irritating visual experience. The most intense zone of irritation is ostensibly the one in which the divergent parties unexpectedly run against each other. Then, however, it becomes clear how the components come into play with one another, how they mutually illuminate each other in their valency. In its seductive realism, the intensely and illusionistically drawn-up area with floor tiles and baseboards, light reflexes and shadow

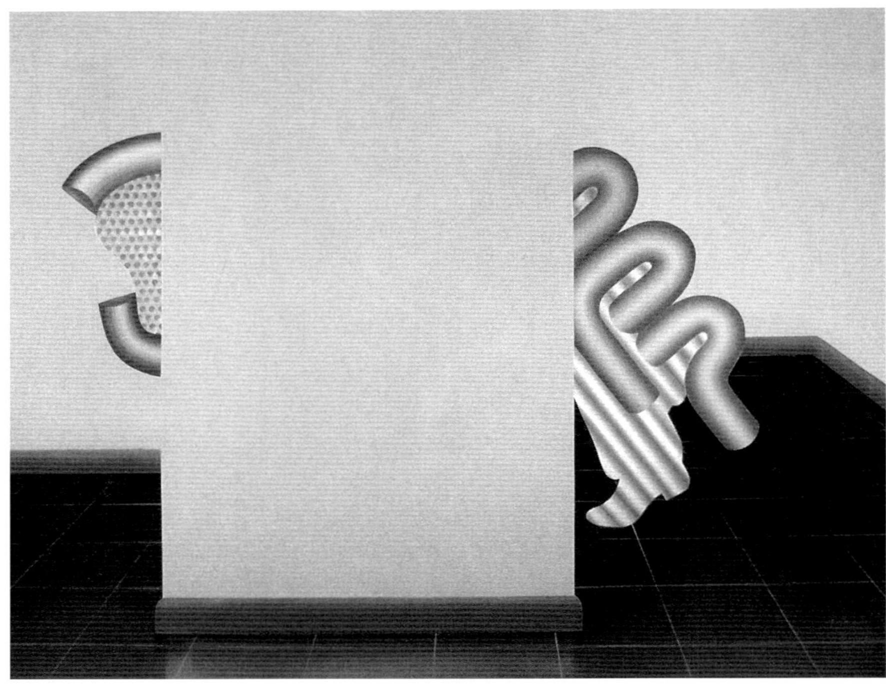

Lienhard von Monkiewitsch,
Raum – Fläche (Bild mit Figuren),
1968 | *Space-Surface (Picture with
Figures),* Acryl auf Leinwand,
163 × 200 cm | Acrylic on canvas

zones, is disillusioned by the surface zone – this surface zone, however, is understandable through the illusionism of the floor zone as a complex illusory space. In other words: One can conceive of it as a spatial system. What is produced is what Walter Vitt fittingly described as a "seeing-thinking process."[2] It is a spatial system that seems to open up between wall projections and behind walls, and to close at the same time. It goes unsaid that what can be shaped here are the fantasies one would like to think into it. The "seeing-thinking process" evokes the viewer's creative fantasy, makes him or her into a co-creator or temporary completer of the respective paintings. That which could fill Monkiewitsch's interiors with fantasies becomes the interior world of the interior spaces; it is a concept, remains unsaid, and yet it is a part of the painting.

The colored-pencil drawing *Flur* from 1972 may serve as an example to illustrate the process described (p. 51). The viewer is invited to enter a suggested room in a traditional way via the illusionistically drawn floor area, and then redirected into indefinite adjoining rooms. He loses himself, so to speak, along with his expectations and fantasies, unrecognized in the middle of the painting; he has been seduced by the artist to set himself up there in his own imagination. The viewer should – or can – encounter himself in what is unsaid in the images. This distinguishes these paintings from earlier examples of the work phase. The spaces filled with bizarre figurations from 1968 as well as *Raum – Fläche* are artificial, nonetheless conventional image confrontations; the figuratively emptied stripe paintings such as *Streifenraum,* which was produced in 1969, focus the idea on the irritation between illusion and disillusion (p. 37). Both stages of development confront the eyes with images or, as is the case with the stripe paintings, the mind. The large-format *Abknickender Gang* from 1969 shows the decisive continuation. The passageway emphatically reveals to the

ger Bilder. Das, was von Monkiewitschs Interieurs an Vorstellungen füllen könnte, wird zur Innenwelt der Innenräume, ist gedacht, bleibt ungesagt und ist dennoch Teil des Bildes.

Den beschriebenen Vorgang mag exemplarisch die Farbstiftzeichnung *Flur* aus dem Jahre 1972 verdeutlichen (S. 51). In traditioneller Weise wird der Betrachter über die illusionistisch gezeichnete Bodenfläche zum Eintritt in einen suggerierten Raum aufgefordert und dann in unbestimmte Nebenräume umgeleitet. Er verliert sich gleichsam mit seinen Erwartungen und Fantasien unerkannt inmitten des Bildes, ist vom Künstler verführt, sich in seinen je eigenen Vorstellungen dort einzurichten. Der Betrachter soll oder kann sich im Ungesagten der Bilder selbst begegnen. Dies macht die Differenz zu früheren Beispielen der Werkphase aus. Die mit skurrilen Figurationen besetzten Räume von 1968 wie die Darstellung *Raum – Fläche* sind artifizielle, gleichwohl konventionelle Bild-Konfrontationen; die figurativ entleerten Streifenbilder wie der 1969 entstandene *Streifenraum* konzentrieren den Einfall auf die Irritation zwischen Illusionierung und Desillusionierung (S. 37). Beide Entwicklungsstufen stellen Bilder vor Augen oder – wie in den Streifenbildern – vor Kopf. Die entscheidende Weiterführung zeigt die großformatige Darstellung *Abknickender Gang* aus dem Jahr 1969. Jener Gang erschließt dem Betrachter nachdrücklich einen Raum mit Mauerzungen und polygonal gewinkelten Wandfeldern und lässt ihn – folgt er der Einladung – hinter einer Ecke im Innern des Bildes verschwinden; das suggerierte Wandsystem ist monochrom angelegt. Diese Art der Gestaltung eröffnet dem Künstler zwei parallele Wege weiterer Bildfindungen: einmal den oben genannten der Zeichnung *Flur,* zum andern den großformatiger Bodenbilder, in denen jeweils die Illusionsform des Fußbodens ausgeschnitten als Cut-out-Painting in einem Realraum an der

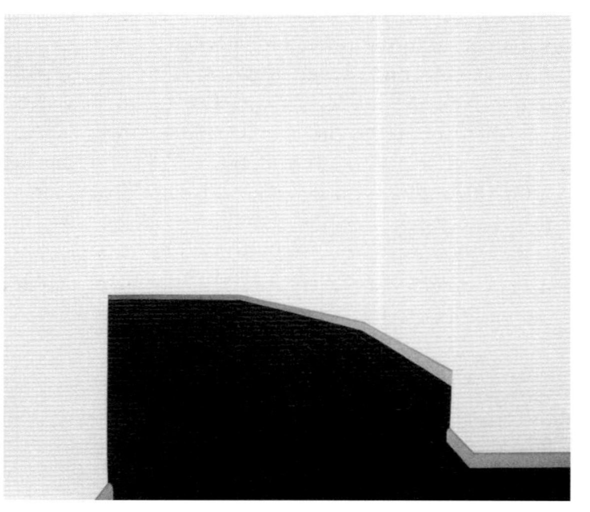

Lienhard von Monkiewitsch,
Abknickender Gang, 1969
Bending Space, Dispersion und
Acryl auf Leinwand, 179 × 210 cm,
Dispersion and acrylic on canvas

Fußzone einer Wand aufgestellt wird. Das Cut-out *Zwei Lichtquellen,* 1971 entstanden (S. 47), verwandelt eine ganze Wand und löst im Schein ihrer Umgestaltung die Raumgrenzen auf. Verblieben die ersten Entwicklungsschritte der Raum-Wand-Thematik in den spielerischen Reizen effektvoller Inszenierungen, so ist nun in den tatsächlichen oder den in Farbstiftzeichnungen vorgeblichen Cut-out-Paintings eine Überschreitung bisheriger Grenzen vollzogen: Ein künstlerischer Einfall wird essentiell.

Von Monkiewitschs Verführung ins Bild geschieht über Andeuten und Verschweigen zugleich. Dem Betrachter ist dies Anlass, auf sich selbst gestellt mit seinen Erwartungen und Phantasien im Bild autonom zu werden. Dem Künstler verschafft es Spielraum, sich verbrauchten Bildwelten zu verweigern und gleichwohl reflektiert in der Tradition der Bildgattung im Unvollständigen ein vollständiges Bild zu schaffen – ein ebenso innovativer wie eminent kritischer Vorgang.[3] Das, was der Künstler dem Betrachter vorenthält, befindet sich als mögliche Fülle der Fantasie, des Gedachten oder Empfundenen, hinter den denkbaren Wänden im Bild, genauer: hinter dem Sichtbaren und als ansichtig Suggerierten. Dies hat kunstgeschichtlich bedeutsame Vorbilder, die von Monkiewitsch – bewusst, unbewusst – weiterentwickelte. Üblicherweise versteht man Bilder als Fenster in eine irgendwie geartete, vom Künstler gestaltete Wirklichkeit. Von Monkiewitschs Bilder sind in der elaborierten Stufe der hier interessierenden Werkphase Türen in eine sich öffnende und gleichwohl verstellte Wirklichkeit; sie intendieren, den Betrachter in sich hineinzuziehen mit dem Versprechen, noch Interessanteres finden zu können als das, was zu sehen ist. Vergleichbare Darstellungen gibt es im Œuvre von Vilhelm Hammershøi, so sein 1905 entstandenes Gemälde *Weiße Türen/Offene Türen:*

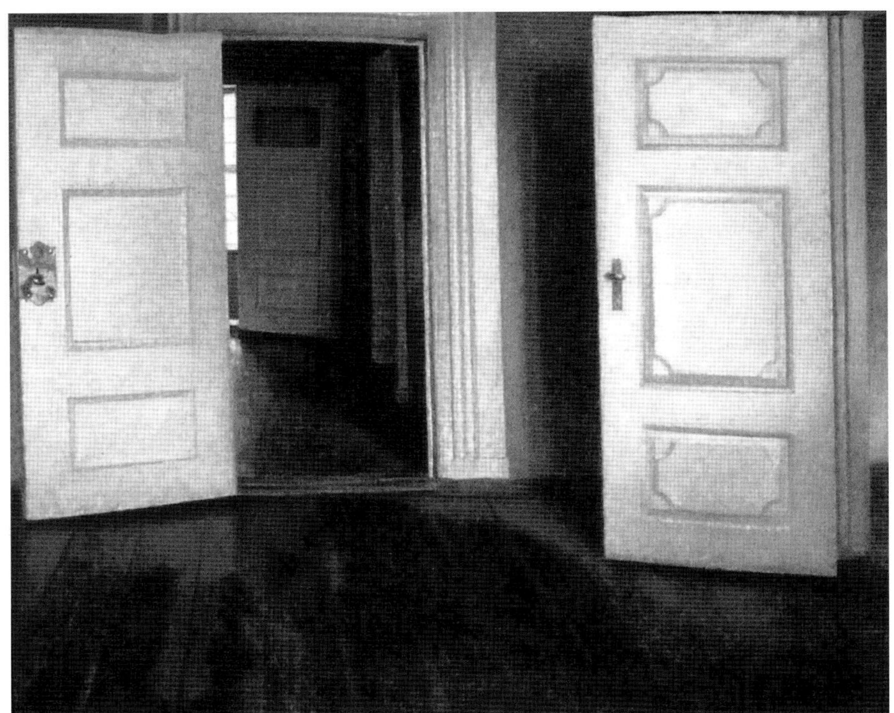

viewer a room with wall projections and polygonally angled wall areas and lets him – if he accepts the invitation – disappear behind a corner in the interior of the picture; the suggested wall system is monochrome. This kind of arrangement opens up two parallel paths of further pictorial composition to the artist: one is the path described above in the drawing *Flur,* and the other is that of the large-format floor pictures, in each of which the illusory form of the floor is stood up against the base zone of a wall as a cut-out painting in a real space. The cut-out *Zwei Lichtquellen,* which was done in 1971 (p. 47), transforms an entire wall and dissolves the room's boundaries in the appearance of its rearrangement. Whereas the first developmental phases of the room-wall theme remained in the playful stimuli of effective productions, in the actual cut-out paintings – or in the case of the colored-pencil drawings the alleged cut-outs – a transgression of previous boundaries occurs: An artistic idea becomes essential.

Von Monkiewitsch's seduction into the picture occurs through intimation and concealment at the same time. This prompts the viewer, fending for himself, to become autonomous within the picture with his expectations and fantasies. This gives the artist the leeway to refuse used worlds of images and nevertheless reflectively create in the unfinished a complete picture in the tradition of the pictorial genre – as much an innovative as an eminently critical process.[3] That which the artist denies the viewer can be found behind the conceivable walls in the picture as the possible abundance of fantasy, thoughts, or feelings. To be more precise: behind the visible and visually suggested. This has art-historically significant models, which von Monkiewitsch – consciously, unconsciously – further developed. One normally regards paintings as windows into a somehow constituted reality created by the artist. In the elaborated stage of the work phase in question, von Monkiewitsch's pictures are doors into a reality that is opening up and yet disguised; their intention is to draw the viewer inside with the promise of being able to find something even more interesting than what can already be seen. There are comparable depictions in Vilhelm Hammershøi's œuvre, for instance his painting *White Doors/Open Doors* from 1905: The depth suction of recognizable or intimated paths into indefinite, empty spaces behind the visible evokes effects corresponding to those in von Monkiewitsch's interior rooms. Moritz von Schwind also many times conceived paintings of this kind, for example *Farewell at Dawn* from 1859: A traveler leaves the courtyard, open towards the painting's viewer, through a gate in the back wall to step out into an intimated wooded area, i. e., to disappear into the depths of or behind the painting. Again, the space behind the visibly concrete and known is an unknown, at least an unsaid – the imaginary space behind the painting becomes the painting's real theme.

With his concept of concealment in the interior worlds of his interior spaces, von Monkiewitsch possibly – and possibly unconsciously – eludes the politico-social stand he also demanded in those years and which marks his artistic relevance, a stand he is willing to adhere to on the one hand, but which on the other hand remains foreign to him in the desired consequences.[4] Finally, he apparently feels directed by others in two ways: firstly, due to the intimated expectations, and secondly, due to his success on the art market combined with the pressure of being expected to continue to produce works of art of the same highly regarded kind. In 1973, von Monkiewitsch abruptly and self-ironically ended the path he had pursued with the colored-pencil drawing *Brüchiger Raum* (p. 59). He fills the room, at the center of which there is a drain, in the detailed formality of an additive diversity – the open spatial system has disappeared down the drain and consequently all fantasy, including the viewer's. Beginning in 1979, after an extended period of preparation von Monkiewitsch does away with staged 'self-destruction' with the series of brilliant images of architecture.

Der Tiefensog erkennbarer oder angedeuteter Wege hinein in unbestimmte, zudem leere Räume hinter dem Sichtbaren evoziert entsprechende Wirkungen wie die Innenräume von Monkiewitschs. Auch Moritz von Schwind konzipierte mehrfach Bilder in der beschriebenen Art, beispielhaft die 1859 datierte Darstellung *Abschied im Morgengrauen:* Ein Wanderer verlässt durch eine Pforte in der rückwärtigen Mauer den zum Betrachter hin offenen Hof, um in den angedeuteten Waldraum hinauszutreten, das heißt: in der Tiefe des Bildes oder hinter dem Bild zu verschwinden. Wiederum ist der Raum hinter dem sichtbar Konkreten und Bekannten ein Unbekanntes, zumindest aber Ungesagtes – der Phantasieraum hinter dem Bild wird zum eigentlichen Thema des Bildes.

Möglicherweise und möglicherweise unbewusst entzieht sich von Monkiewitsch mit seinem Konzept des Verschweigens in den Innenwelten seiner Innenräume einer in jenen Jahren auch von ihm eingeforderten, seine künstlerische Relevanz markierenden politisch-gesellschaftlichen Positionierung, der er einerseits zu folgen bereit ist, die ihm andererseits in den erwünschten Konsequenzen fremd bleibt.[4] Offenbar empfindet er sich schließlich in doppelter Weise fremdbestimmt: einmal durch die angedeuteten Erwartungen, dann aber durch die Erfolge am Kunstmarkt, verbunden mit dem Druck, auf Dauer in der geschätzten Art weiter produzieren zu sollen. 1973 beendet von Monkiewitsch abrupt und selbstironisch den eingeschlagenen Weg mit der Farbstiftzeichnung *Brüchiger Raum* (S. 59). In der detaillierten Äußerlichkeit einer additiven Vielfalt füllt er den Raum, im Zentrum ein Abfluss – das offene Raumsystem ist im Abfluss entschwunden und mithin alle Phantasie, auch die des Betrachters. Die inszenierte ‚Selbstvernichtung' wird von Monkiewitsch nach längerer Vorbereitung mit der Serie der fulminanten Architekturbilder ab 1979 aufheben.

1   Walter Vitt, *Lienhard von Monkiewitsch*, Kunst der Gegenwart aus Niedersachsen, vol. 43 (Hannover, 1994).
2   Vitt 1994 (see note 1), p. 29.
3   Heino R. Möller, *Innenräume/Außenwelten. Studien zur Darstellung bürgerlicher Privatheit in Kunst und Warenwerbung* (Gießen, 1981), pp. 8–10 and 208–211; Heino R. Möller, "Lienhard von Monkiewitsch: Räume und Architekturen," *Kunst im 20. Jahrhundert. Studien zur Malerei und Plastik im Sprengel Museum Hannover*, ed. Ingeborg Bloth and Heino R. Möller (Hameln, 1992), pp. 85–92.
4   Vitt 1994 (see note 1), p. 36.

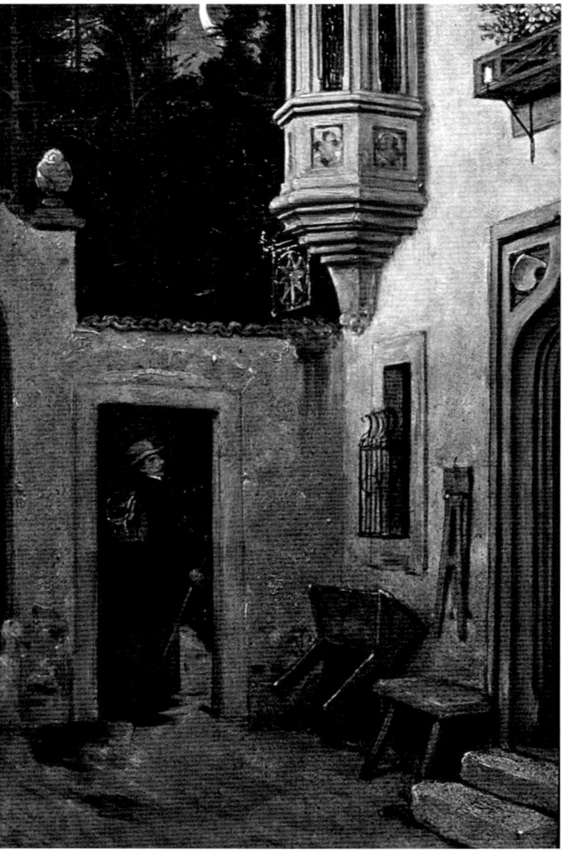

1   Walter Vitt, *Lienhard von Monkiewitsch*, Kunst der Gegenwart aus Niedersachsen, Bd. 43, Hannover 1994.
2   Vitt (wie Anm. 1), S. 29.
3   Heino R. Möller, *Innenräume/Außenwelten. Studien zur Darstellung bürgerlicher Privatheit in Kunst und Warenwerbung*, Gießen 1981, S. 8–10 und S. 208–211. Ders.: „Lienhard von Monkiewitsch: Räume und Architekturen", in: Ingeborg Bloth/Heino R. Möller, *Kunst im 20. Jahrhundert. Studien zur Malerei und Plastik im Sprengel Museum Hannover*, Hameln 1992, S. 85–92.
4   Vitt (wie Anm. 1), S. 36.

MORITZ VON SCHWIND,
Abschied im Morgengrauen, 1859 | *Farewell at Dawn*, Öl auf Pappe, 36 × 24 cm | Oil on cardboard, Alte Nationalgalerie, SMPK Berlin

Walter Vitt

Malewitsch und andere Väter. Zum Konstruktiv-Konkreten im Werk von Lienhard von Monkiewitsch

Malevich and Other Fathers. On the Constructive and Concrete in Lienhard von Monkiewitsch's Work

Das Jahr 1983 markiert einen deutlichen Wandel im Werk von Lienhard von Monkiewitsch, der bis heute nachwirkt. Seit diesem Jahr bestimmen Maß und Zahl seine Bilder, die ganz unterschiedlichen Ordnungsprogrammen unterworfen sind. Da der Maler seine verschiedenen Systemvorgaben nebeneinander zur Bildproduktion nutzt, ist in seinem Werk seit 1983 die Gleichzeitigkeit unterschiedlichster Form-Gestaltung wirksam. Die Wende von 1983 vollzog sich im Juli/August im Sommerhaus des Malers in Lu Fraili auf Sardinien, und ich habe es als eine schöne Fügung empfunden, dass ich zur selben Zeit im Nachbarhaus mit meiner Familie Urlaub machte und diesen Werkwandel miterleben durfte. Von Monkiewitsch zeigte mir in Abständen von jeweils einigen Tagen seine Ergebnisse, und wir diskutierten über ihre Tragfähigkeit sowie über die Möglichkeit von Varianten (S. 78/79). Ich glaube noch heute, dass ihm meine Anwesenheit in Lu Fraili wichtig und problematisch zugleich gewesen ist: ich war dem Maler ja damals – wie heute – nicht nur freundschaftlich verbunden, ich hatte mich auch als kunstkritischer Experte im Bereich der konstruktiv-konkreten Kunst erwiesen. So war ihm, denke ich, der Freund in der Nähe wichtig, der mögliche Kritiker seines neuen Kunstansatzes aber eher störend, denn er hatte noch keine gereifte Position im Konkreten erreicht. Während der gemeinsamen Wochen auf Sardinien fiel darüber kein Wort. Erst viel später sagte mir der Maler einmal, möglicherweise habe ihm meine Anwesenheit damals in Lu Fraili sogar Mut gemacht, so zu handeln, wie er gehandelt habe, nämlich sich das konkrete Bild, das nach System gebaute Bild zu erobern.

Niemals hatte Lienhard von Monkiewitsch bis dahin in seinem Haus auf Sardinien gemalt. Es war sein Arkadien. Es war die Zeit des Müßiggangs, wenn er dort war. Es war Loslösung von persönlichen und künstlerischen Sorgen des Braunschweiger Alltags. Er ignorierte auch die politische und gesellschaftliche Realität auf Sardinien, um sein Arkadien nicht zu gefährden. Das alles galt ihm nun im Jahre 1983 nicht mehr. Die vorangegangenen vielen Monate seines Stipendiums in der römischen Villa Massimo hatten ihn auch das politische Italien nicht länger unter Verschluss halten lassen, und der innere Druck zum Werkwandel war offenbar so stark, dass er erstmals auf Sardinien nicht nur sein Arkadien suchte, sondern seine Kunst nach neuen Wegen ausforschte. Diesmal ist es ein Abschied von den intuitiv gefundenen Bildformen. An die Stelle des Form-Erfinders tritt die Arbeit mit vorhandenen Modulen, mit flächig angelegten Bildbau-Einheiten wie Rechteck, Quadrat, Parallelogramm, Gerade, Dreieck, die aber dennoch in ein Raumgefüge verwoben werden. Zugleich bringt der neue Weg die Hinwendung zu einer Ästhetik, die den Künstler nicht als Schöpfer einzelner endgültiger Bilder in Anspruch nimmt, sondern an diese Stelle die Serienproduktion setzt. 1983 auf Sardinien war natürlich überhaupt nicht absehbar, dass von Monkiewitsch hier die Fundamente

The year 1983 marks a significant transition in Lienhard von Monkiewitsch's work, the influence of which continues to this day. Since then, dimension and number define his paintings, which are subject to very different programs of order. Because the painter uses his various system specifications side by side to produce paintings, the simultaneity of the most varied organization of form has been effective in his work ever since. The change occurred in July/August in the artist's summer house in Lu Fraili on Sardinia. I considered it to be a wonderful stroke of good fortune that my family and I were vacationing in the house next-door and that I was allowed to experience this transition. Von Monkiewitsch showed me his results at intervals of several days each, and we discussed their sustainability as well as the possibility of variation (pp. 78/79). I still believe that my presence in Lu Fraili was both important and problematic for him: at the time, we were not only friends – as we continue to be – but I had proved myself to be an expert art critic in the area of constructive/concrete art. Thus while I think having a friend nearby was important to him, in my role as a possible critic of his new approach to art I was more of a disturbance, as he had not yet attained a matured position in the concrete. There were no words lost in this respect during the weeks we spent together on Sardinia. It was not until much later that the artist told me that my presence in Lu Fraili had possibly even encouraged him to act the way he did, that is, to conquer the concrete painting, the painting constructed according to a system.

Until that time, Lienhard von Monkiewitsch had never painted in his house on Sardinia. It was his Arcadia. The time spent there was one of idleness. It was time to free himself from the personal and artistic worries associated with his everyday life in Braunschweig. He also ignored the political and social reality on Sardinia so as not to jeopardize his Arcadia. Beginning in 1983, all of this no longer applied. The previous, many months of his sojourn in the Roman Villa Massimo also no longer allowed him to keep a political Italy under lock and key, and the inner pressure to alter his artistic approach was clearly so profound, that for the first time, he not only sought his Arcadia on Sardinia, but also examined his art for new paths. This time it is a farewell from the intuitively found

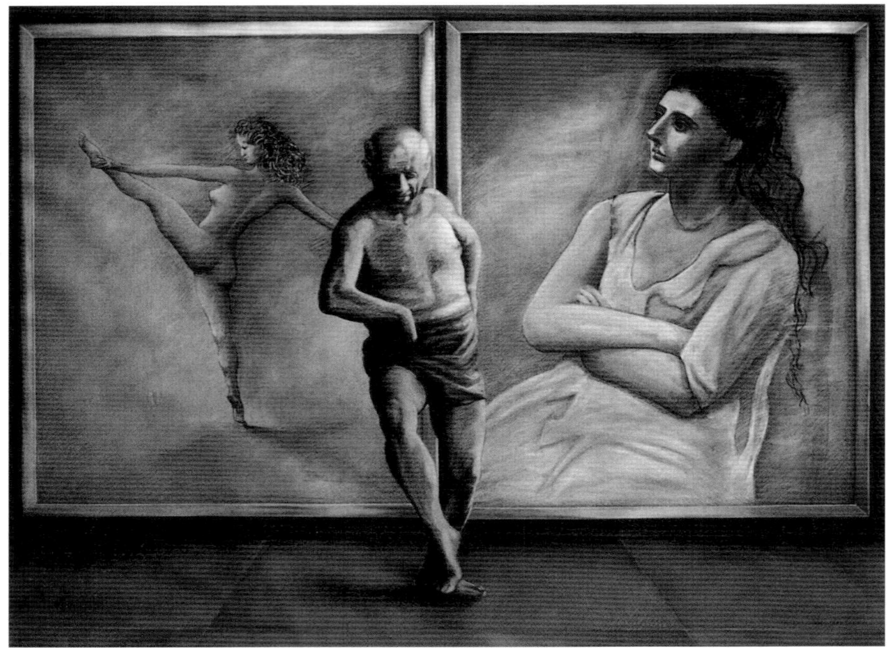

forms. Work with available modules, with flatly applied
image construction units such as the rectangle, the
square, the parallelogram, the straight line, the triangle,
which are nevertheless woven into a spatial structure,
takes the place of the invention of form. At the same time,
this new path brings with it a turn towards an aesthetics
which the artist does not enlist as the creator of individual final images, but instead applies to serial production.

In 1983 on Sardinia, there was, of course, absolutely
no telling that von Monkiewitsch would lay the foundation
here for a building which he in the meantime has been
working on for a quarter of a century. After abandoning
his early invention – the uninhabited interior spaces lim-
ited to floors and baseboards – in 1973, the painter had
often enough sought innovative paths in ever new approaches. Initially, he found support in art history by plac-
ing modern artists into his own paintings: Pablo Picasso,
Paul Klee, Kurt Schwitters, Cy Twombly. Then works
emerged which one could assign to Critical Realism and
into which he also put human figures. Finally, beginning
in 1979/80 in Rome, he began painting the large architectural rudiments as Shaped Canvases (pp. 63–75).

In 1992, in a statement regarding his art the painter
pointed out that since 1968, his theme has been space:
in his current work the suggestion of space, "using only
surface and color," and in his early interior space pictures
and the architecture cut-outs produced in Rome, using
perspective.[1] I see this permanent interest in space in
von Monkiewitsch's work; however, I would like to point
out that his method of structuring a painting has always
been constructive, combined with a constant eye for
detail. Von Monkiewitsch is not a painter of large-scale
pictorial panoramas, rather he is interested in the arrangement of detail problems, which then – elaborated
and expressed in series – develop into a whole. This has

für ein Gebäude legen würde, an dem er inzwischen fast ein Vierteljahrhundert
baut. Zu oft hatte der Maler nach dem 1973 vollzogenen Verzicht auf seine frühe Erfindung – auf die Bilder mit den menschenleeren, auf Böden und Wand-
leisten begrenzten Innenräumen – in immer wieder neuen Ansätzen nach
Wegen der Innovation gesucht. Zunächst hatte er sich Halt verschafft in der
Kunstgeschichte, indem er Künstler der Moderne in einigen seiner Bilder auf-
treten ließ: Pablo Picasso, Paul Klee, Kurt Schwitters, Cy Twombly. Dann entstanden Werke, die man einem *Kritischen Realismus* zuordnen könnte und in
denen er ebenfalls Menschen ins Bild einbrachte. In Rom schließlich malte er
von 1979/80 an die großen Architektur-Rudimente als *Shaped Canvas* (S.63–75).

1992 hat der Maler in einem Statement zu seiner Kunst darauf hingewiesen,
dass sein Thema seit 1968 der Raum ist: im aktuellen Werk als Raumsugges-
tion „allein mit den Mitteln der Fläche und der Farbe", in den frühen Innen-
raum-Bildern und bei den in Rom entstandenen Architektur-*Cut-outs* mittels
der Perspektive.[1] Ich sehe dieses permanente Interesse am Raum bei von
Monkiewitsch, möchte aber auch darauf hinweisen, dass seine Methode, ein
Bild zu gestalten, immer schon der konstruktive Bild-Bau gewesen ist, verbunden mit einem anhaltenden Detail-Blick. Von Monkiewitsch ist nicht ein Maler
großer bildnerischer Panoramen, sondern interessiert an der Gestaltung von
Detail-Problemen, die sich dann – in Bilder-Serien erarbeitet und vorgetragen –
zum großen Ganzen auffüllen. Dieses Verfahren ist seit dem Eintritt von Ma-
lern wie Kasimir Malewitsch, Piet Mondrian oder Theo van Doesburg in die
Kunstgeschichte eine Arbeitsweise konstruktiver und konkreter Künstler. Und
so erscheint es mir plausibel, dass jemand mit exakt diesem mondrianschen
Detail-Blick und diesem an Dexel oder van Doesburg erinnernden strengen
Bildbau-Willen jetzt zu jenen Gegenwartskünstlern gehört, die der *Konkreten
Kunst* so etwas wie eine Frischzellenkur haben verordnen können.

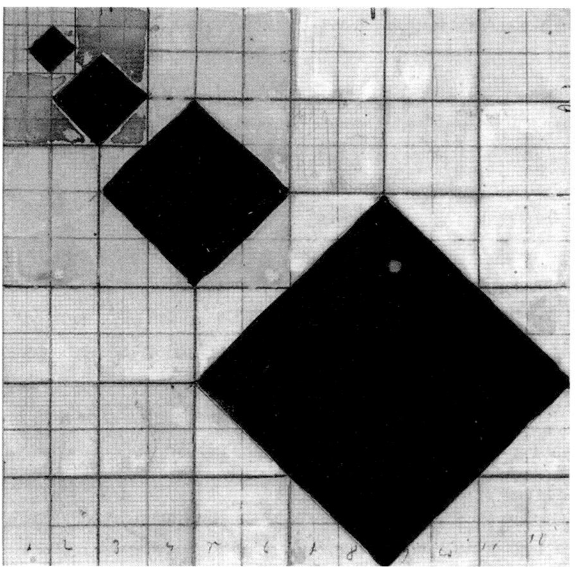

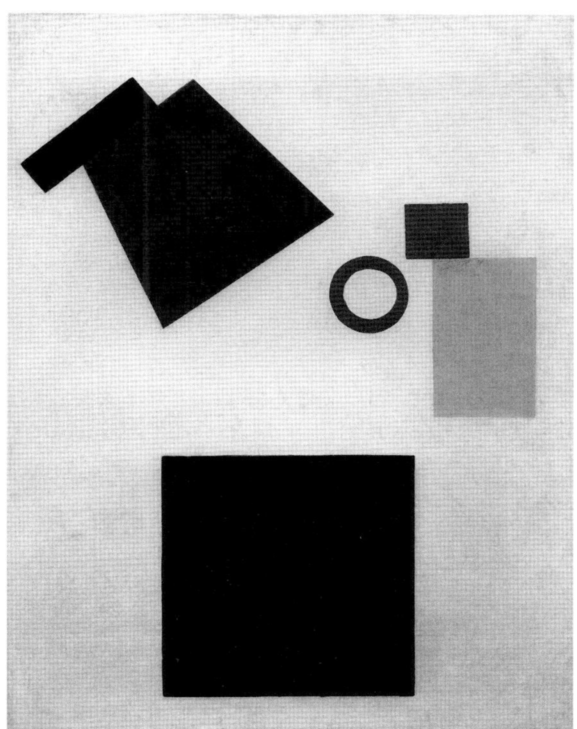

Walter Dexel beeindruckte ihn erstmals 1962, als der damals gerade 21-Jährige im Städtischen Museum in Braunschweig die erste Retrospektive des konstruktivistischen Malers nach dem Krieg sah, die dessen Wiederentdeckung einleitete.[2] Und seit 1971 hängt Dexels druckgrafisches Blatt *Weißes Kreuz – Silberner Grund*, entworfen 1926 in einer Collage-Fassung[3], in den Wohnräumen von Monkiewitsch, der Dexel auch noch persönlich gekannt hat. Denn Walter Dexel lebte zuletzt in Braunschweig, wo sein Spätwerk entstanden ist – zur selben Zeit, als von Monkiewitsch in dieser Stadt seine ersten Bilder malte. 1979 in Rom entsteht eine *Hommage à Dexel* für die Festschrift zum 90. Geburtstag des Malers.[4] Die Arbeit *Weißes Kreuz – Silberner Grund* ist von Monkiewitsch einmal mit dem Satz kommentiert worden, sie habe ihn damals mit ihrer konstruktiven Klarheit mehr und mehr fasziniert und mit dazu beigetragen, dass es ihm schließlich leicht gefallen sei, von Realismus und Figurenmalerei Abschied zu nehmen.[5]

Der wichtigste seiner künstlerischen Ahnherren ist Malewitsch. Man kann dies an vielen Bildtiteln ablesen, die etwa lauten *Zwei Schnitte in das suprematistische Rechteck* oder auch *Zwei Schnitte in das suprematistische Quadrat* (S. 84–103). Das Werk des Pioniers der nicht-abbildenden Malerei war ihm „seit der Geburt seiner Karriere als Maler" ein „Säulenheiliger". Der Ukrainer habe ihm wohl, sagt von Monkiewitsch in dem ihm eigenen Humor, beim Planen und Herumspielen mit dem Quadrat über die Schulter geschaut.[6] Eines Tages geht von Monkiewitsch das Wagnis ein, seinem Vorbild zu zeigen, wie schwarz ein Schwarz wirklich sein kann. Mehr noch: mit den Schnitten in die suprematistischen Formen wie Quadrat und Rechteck „beging ich sozusagen einen spielerischen ‚Vatermord' an Malewitsch", schreibt er in einem Statement von 2001, in dem es weiter heißt: „Die intensive Beschäftigung mit seinem Werk und vor allem mit seinem Denken hat mir aber auch die Grenzen meiner Bewunderung für seine religiös-dogmatische, suprematistisch-

1 Zit. nach: Michael Stoeber, „Lienhard von Monkiewitsch", in: *Künstler. Kritisches Lexikon der Gegenwartskunst*, Ausgabe 68, Heft 27, 4. Quartal 2004, S. 2.
2 Die Ausstellung *Walter Dexel – Gemälde, Hinterglasbilder, Aquarelle, Collagen 1912 bis 1932* war in Braunschweig vom 25.2. bis 25.3.1962 zu sehen und wurde von einem Katalog begleitet. Sie ging anschließend mit identischem Katalog nach München, Wiesbaden und Oldenburg.
3 Walter Dexel, *Werkverzeichnis der Druckgrafik 1915–1973*, Köln ²1998, WVZ Nr. 45.
4 Walter Vitt (Hrsg.), *Hommage à Dexel (1890–1963) – Beiträge zum 90. Geburtstag des Künstlers*, Starnberg 1980, S. 61.
5 Im Gespräch mit dem Verfasser.

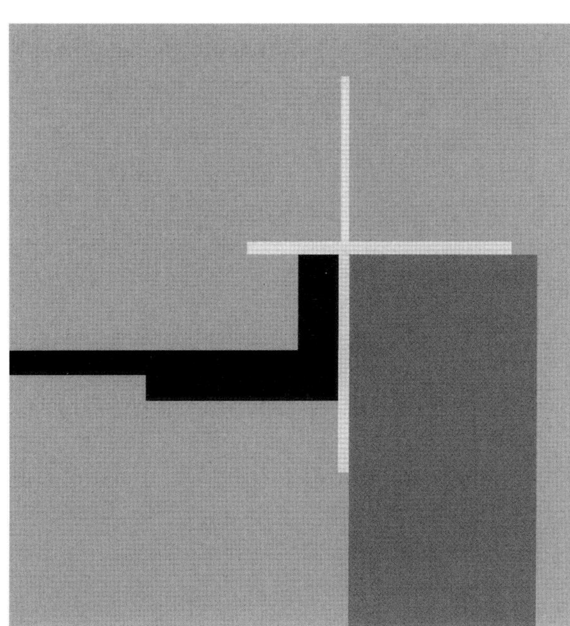

been a working method of constructive and concrete artists since the entry into art history of painters such as Kasimir Malevich, Piet Mondrian, or Theo van Doesburg. And thus it seems plausible to me that someone with precisely this Mondrianian eye for detail and this strong, constructive will reminiscent of Dexel or van Doesburg now belongs to those contemporary artists who can prescribe Concrete Art something like a live cell cure.

Walter Dexel made an impression on him for the first time in 1962 when von Monkiewitsch, who was twenty-one at the time, saw the constructivist painter's first retrospective since the war, which initiated his rediscovery, at the Städtisches Museum in Braunschweig.[2] And Dexel's print *Weißes Kreuz – Silberner Grund*, drafted in 1926 in a collage version,[3] has hung in von Monkiewitsch's living room since 1971. Von Monkiewitsch was personally acquainted with Dexel, who last lived in Braunschweig, where he produced his late work – and where at the same time von Monkiewitsch produced his first paintings. In Rome in 1979, the artist painted an *Hommage à Dexel* to commemorate the painter's ninetieth birthday.[4] Von Monkiewitsch once commented on the work *Weißes Kreuz – Silberner Grund* by saying that at the time, its constructive clarity fascinated him more and more, and that it contributed to his finally being able to easily break with Realism and figurative painting.[5]

The most important of his artistic ancestors is Malevich. One can see this in many of his paintings' titles, such as *Zwei Schnitte in das suprematistische Rechteck* or

Zwei Schnitte in das suprematistische Quadrat (pp. 84–103). "[S]ince the birth of his career as a painter," the work by the pioneer of non-representational painting was a "stylite" to him. With his unique sense of humor, von Monkiewitsch says that during his planning of and playing about with the square, the Ukrainian was looking over his shoulder.[6] One day, von Monkiewitsch took the risk of showing his model how black black can really be. Even more: In a statement from 2001 he writes that he "committed playful 'patricide,' so to speak, on Malevich" with the cuts he made in the suprematist forms such as square and rectangle. He goes on to write: "The intense preoccupation with his work, and above all with his thinking, also showed me the boundaries of my admiration for his religious-dogmatic, suprematist-abstract world. Thus my relationship to him is characterized by both admiration and distance, which makes possible what seems to be my irreverent treatment of him."[7]

Von Monkiewitsch saw himself particularly challenged in attaining a painter's black from the transcendentally conceived black of his model; achieving a black that, so to speak, seems blacker than black and that above all does not reflect light, but has to be made with "deep, matte, absorbing colors" so that it can swallow it, soak it in. Von Monkiewitsch achieves this – as he calls it – "magic black"[8] by adding black coloring pigment to the not quite dry oil paint until it is saturated and dry bits remain on the surface. He then brushes what remains of the pigment off of the black form so that black traces of it are left, which lend the form three-dimensionality beyond all four boundaries. For him, black is the most important color of all. For him, black is not a linear framework of forms, is not background, is not the shadow of something colored – here, black is color. In fact, it is a unique product of painterly craftsmanship that becomes immediately noticeable when one stands in front of these paintings, and it can seduce the viewer into touching the velvety surface of the black with his or her hands. In the meantime, von Monkiewitsch has headed three of his exhibitions *Noli me tangere:* Don't touch me.

In the broad stream of constructive and concrete composition, Lienhard von Monkiewitsch is an amiable loner. On another occasion, I placed him in a position on the periphery of Concrete Art.[9] I now see him pressing more and more towards the center. With his consistent appropriation of the variety of material required for constructive composition and his simultaneous – or constant – irreverent reinterpretation, cutting up, and finally destruction, in his own way he has initiated a fresh start for thinking in terms of constructive-concrete form.

gegenstandslose Welt aufgezeigt. So ist mein Verhältnis zu ihm gekennzeichnet durch Bewunderung und Distanz zugleich, was mir diesen scheinbar respektlosen Umgang mit ihm ermöglicht".[7]

Besonders herausgefordert sah sich von Monkiewitsch in der Frage, von dem transzendental gedachten Schwarz seines Vorbildes zu einem *Maler-Schwarz* zu gelangen, ein Schwarz zu erreichen, das sozusagen noch schwärzer als schwarz wirkt und das vor allem nicht reflektiert, sondern mit „tiefen, matten, saugenden Farben" hergestellt werden muss, damit es das Licht schlucken, aufsaugen kann. Von Monkiewitsch erreicht dieses – wie er sagt – „magische Schwarz"[8], indem er der noch feuchten Ölfarbe schwarzes Farbpigment hinzugibt, bis die Farbe gesättigt ist und schließlich trockene Reste an der Oberfläche bleiben. Diese Pigmentreste bürstet er von der schwarzen Form herunter, so dass jenseits aller vier Begrenzungen schwarze Spuren zurückbleiben, die der Form Räumlichkeit geben. Schwarz ist ihm die wichtigste Farbe überhaupt. Schwarz ist ihm nicht lineares Gerüst von Formen, ist nicht Hintergrund, ist nicht Schatten von etwas Farbigem – Schwarz ist hier Farbe, und zwar von einer malerisch-handwerklichen Einzigartigkeit, die sofort auffällt, wenn man vor diesen Bildern steht, und die den Betrachter dazu verführen kann, die samtene Oberfläche des Schwarz mit den Händen zu erfühlen. *Noli me tangere* hat von Monkiewitsch inzwischen drei seiner Ausstellungen überschrieben: *Rühr mich nicht an.*

Im breiten Strom konstruktiv-konkreter Gestaltung ist Lienhard von Monkiewitsch ein sympathischer Einzelgänger. Ich habe ihn bei anderer Gelegenheit in eine Randposition konkreter Kunst gestellt.[9] Ich sehe ihn jetzt mehr und mehr in die Mitte drängen. Mit der konsequenten Aneignung der Vielfalt des konstruktiven Gestaltungsmaterials und dessen gelegentlicher oder auch ständiger respektloser Umdeutung, Zerschneidung, letztlich Zerstörung hat er auf seine Weise einen Neuanfang konstruktiv-konkreten Formdenkens eingeleitet.

1   Cited in Michael Stoeber, "Lienhard von Monkiewitsch," *Künstler: Kritisches Lexikon der Gegenwartskunst* 68, no. 27 (4th Quarter 2004), p. 2.

2   The exhibition *Walter Dexel – Gemälde, Hinterglasbilder, Aquarelle, Collagen 1912 bis 1932* ran from February 25 – March 25, 1963, in Braunschweig and included a catalogue. It subsequently traveled with the same catalogue to Munich, Wiesbaden and Oldenburg.

3   Walter Dexel, *Werkverzeichnis der Druckgrafik 1915–1973* (Cologne, 1998), WVZ no. 45.

4   Walter Vitt (ed.), *Hommage à Dexel (1890–1963): Beiträge zum 90. Geburtstag des Künstlers* (Starnberg, 1980), p. 61.

5   In a conversation with the author.

6   Compare Walter Vitt, opening address on January 29, 1997, on the occasion of the Monkiewitsch exhibition in the Hirschwirtscheuer in Künzelsau, reproduced on the homepage of the Galerie Spielvogel, Munich, www.spielvogel-galerie.de.

7   Cited in Stoeber 2004 (see note 1), p. 14.

8   Compare the accordion-fold invitation to the Monkiewitsch exhibition *Noli me tangere III – Malerei seit 1991*, in the St. Maternus Church in Cologne, September 29 – November 3, 2005.

9   Walter Vitt, *Lienhard v. Monkiewitsch,* Kunst der Gegenwart aus Niedersachsen, vol. 43 (Hannover, 1994), p. 91.

6   Vgl. Walter Vitt, Eröffnungsrede am 29. 1. 1997 zur Monkiewitsch-Ausstellung in der Hirschwirtscheuer in Künzelsau, wiedergegeben auf der Homepage der Galerie Spielvogel, München, www.spielvogel-galerie.de.

7   Zit. nach Stoeber (wie Anm. 1), S. 14.

8   Vgl. Einladungs-Leporello zur Monkiewitsch-Ausstellung *Noli me tangere III – Malerei seit 1991,* Kirche St. Maternus zu Köln, 29. 9. bis 3. 11. 2005.

9   Walter Vitt, *Lienhard von Monkiewitsch,* Kunst der Gegenwart aus Niedersachsen, Bd. 43 , Hannover 1994, S. 91.

Ulrike Lehmann

Vom Cut-out zum Shaped Canvas
From the Cut-Out to the Shaped Canvas

In einem Text von 1992 stellte der Künstler Lienhard von Monkiewitsch fest: „Ein Thema bestimmt seit 1968 meine Arbeit: Raum. Waren es früher Innenräume oder Architekturen, bei denen ich mit Hilfe der Perspektive Raumsuggestionen anstrebte, so versuche ich Letzteres seit 1985 allein mit den Mitteln der Fläche und der Farbe".[1]

Zunächst wollte von Monkiewitsch wie sein Vater Architektur studieren, doch festigte sich mehr und mehr der Wunsch, Künstler zu werden. Es ist daher nicht verwunderlich, dass sich seine ersten bildkünstlerischen Arbeiten auf den Raum beziehen und ihn das Thema bis heute nicht loslässt – rückblickend ist es eine wunderbare und spannende Symbiose zwischen den beiden Bereichen Kunst und Architektur geworden, die sich in von Monkiewitschs Bildern manifestiert.

Nach einigen frühen gebauten Bildern in der Gymnasialzeit entstand 1969 als erstes Bild mit der Darstellung eines leeren Raums der *Streifenraum* (S. 37). Auf ein braun-rot-gestreiftes Geschenkpapier (er verwendete später auch Markisenstoff, wie er aus den zeitgleichen Arbeiten von Daniel Buren bekannt ist) malte er mit einem Farbstift einen gekachelten grauen Boden mit Fußleisten und perspektivischer Verjüngung der quadratischen Bodenkacheln nach hinten hinein. Dabei ließ er das Streifenmuster stehen und als Tapete der Wände erscheinen.

Diese zwei Darstellungsebenen verhalten sich wie zwei zusammencollagierte Puzzleteile zueinander, die nur auf den ersten Blick scheinbar zusammengehören. In dieser Arbeit manifestiert sich durch die Anschauungsebene in der Fläche bereits die erste Form des *Cut-outs,* ein Verfahren, das in späteren Arbeiten von Lienhard von Monkiewitsch relevant wird. Die zwei Flächen – die gezeichnete Fläche des Fußbodens und die industriell gedruckten Streifenmuster – könnten vom Betrachter gedanklich als zwei unabhängige disparate Teile voneinander abgeschnitten werden, zumal die Trennung zwischen beiden Ebenen an exakten Linien verläuft.

1979/80 greift der Künstler auf seine erste Werkgruppe zurück und realisiert in überdimensional großen Bildern, die während seines Stipendiums in der Villa Massimo in Rom entstehen, tatsächliche *Cut-outs.* Seine überdimensional großen Architekturbilder suggerieren auch hier eine gewaltige Räumlichkeit, doch nun erscheinen die Räume wie Fragmente von Schächten, Betonvorsprüngen oder zusammengestellten Eisenplatten und erhalten auch Titel wie *Torso III* (S. 70), *Fragment II* (S. 71) oder *Gebäude-Torso II* (S. 66). Von Monkiewitsch malte diese Räume, sparte aber die weißen Negativräume durch Wandvorsprünge oder Raumverjüngungen im Bild aus und schnitt nun diese verbleibenden Ne-gativformen aus dem Bildformat aus. Oder anders gesagt: Das Bildformat – die äußere Bildform – richtete sich nach der Darstellung. Das Bildformat und die Darstellung wurden nun deckungsgleich,

In a text appearing in 1992, the artist Lienhard von Monkiewitsch made the following remark: "Since 1968, a single theme has characterized my work: space. Whereas I used to use interior spaces or structures to suggest space with the aid of perspective, since 1985 I have attempted to do so using surface and color."[1] Like his father, von Monkiewitsch initially wanted to study architecture; however, his desire to become an artist grew stronger and stronger. Thus it is not surprising that his first creative works make reference to space and that this theme has not let go of him to this day – in retrospect, what manifests itself in von Monkiewitsch's images is a wonderful and exciting symbiosis between the areas of art and architecture.

After several early, constructed pictures made during high-school, in 1969 von Monkiewitsch created his first representation of an empty space: *Streifenraum* (p. 37). Using a colored pencil, on brown-red striped gift wrapping paper (he later also used sunblind fabric, which we are familiar with from Daniel Buren's works from the same period) he drew a gray, tiled floor with baseboards and a tapering in perspective towards the back of the square floor tiles. In doing so, he maintains the stripes, which appear to be wallpaper.

These two levels of representation are to one another like two collaged-together parts of a puzzle, which only seem to belong together at first glance. In this work, the first form of the cut-out, a method that becomes relevant in later works by Lienhard von Monkiewitsch, already manifests itself through the visual level in the surface. Since the separation between both levels runs along precise lines, in the mind of the viewer, the two surfaces – the drawn surface of the floor and the industrially printed striped pattern – could be cut away from one other as two independent, disparate parts.

In 1979/80, the artist falls back upon his first group of works and actually realizes huge cut-outs, which he produces during his sojourn in the Villa Massimo in Rome. His oversized architectural paintings also suggest tremendous spaciousness, but now the spaces seem to be fragments of shafts, cement projections, or iron plates that have been assembled together and also bear titles such as *Torso III* (p. 70), *Fragment II* (p. 71) or

Gebäude-Torso II (p. 66). Von Monkiewitsch painted these spaces, leaving the white, negative spaces blank using wall projections or the tapering of space in the picture, and then cut these remaining negative forms out of the picture format. In other words: The picture format – the outer form of the picture – follows the representation. The picture format and the representation now became congruent and indispensably related to one another. Consequently, the white wall on which the picture hung was pulled into the picture and played an active part. Whereas in the first series of floor pictures, the imaginary white walls were still contained within the rectangular surface of the picture, they now became a real part of it. Whereas previously, it was a question of the interplay between painted and imagined space, it is now shifted outside the picture into real space. Painted, illusionary three-dimensionality within a picture connects to the real wall and thus with reality. By means of this artistic strategy and illusionistic painting, these pictures actually fake being a three-dimensional architectural fragment.

Those monumental paintings painted with earth colors from Tuscany resist the tradition of the classic square painting format. Their cuts and the intended interrelation to the real wall cause them to become objects, *Shaped Canvases.* In contrast to traditional pictorial composition, in which the various elements of the painting make reference to one another, in this case there are no details or subordination. Paradoxically, the painted architectural fragment has to be perceived in its totality because it is not part of a composition, but the painting itself, which at the same time determines the form of the painting. And the painted architecture now logically connects with the real space.

All of the images of architecture produced during his sojourn in Rome have a further similarity: the lower edge of the picture is the only horizontal line, thus the only one to run parallel to the baseboard of the real space. With regard to the visual representation, it optically cuts off the painted space, allowing it to again appear to be a fragment. Yet it is precisely this straight, lower edge of the picture that lends the format its stabilizing weight on the wall, anchoring itself in the real space, where the viewer is, through the parallel line to the floor.

Von Monkiewitsch's beginnings as a painter occurred at a time during which important new approaches were

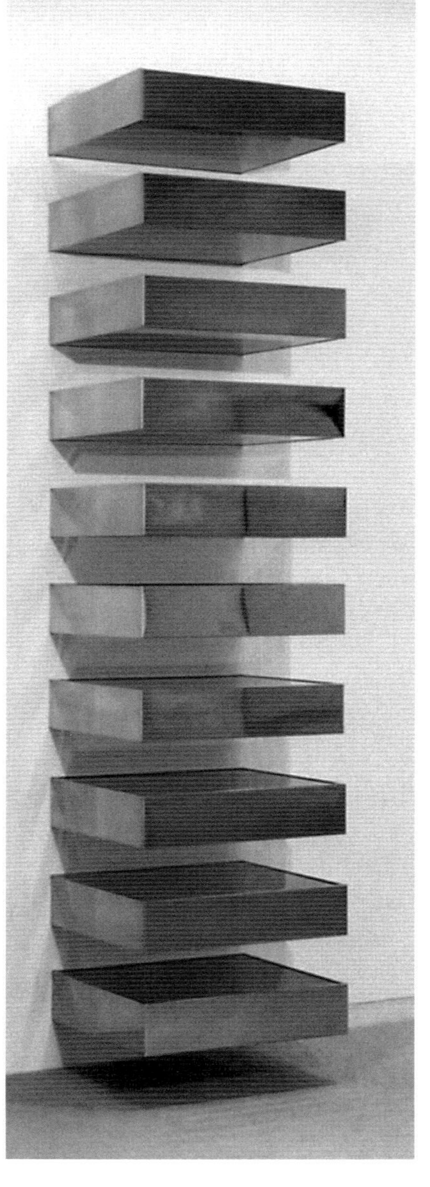

DONALD JUDD, *Untitled*, 1969 Messing und rot fluoreszierendes Plexiglas, zehn Einheiten, je 15,2 × 68,6 × 62 cm | Brass and red fluorescent Plexiglas, ten units, Hirshhorn Museum and Sculpture Garden, Smithsonian Institute, Washington, DC

konkruent und unabdingbar aufeinander bezogen. Infolgedessen wurde die weiße Wand, auf der das Bild hing, als aktiver Part ins Bild hineingezogen. Waren in der ersten Serie der Bodenarbeiten die imaginären weißen Wände noch innerhalb der rechteckigen Bildfläche, so wurden sie nun realer Bestandteil des Bildes. Galt zuvor das Wechselspiel zwischen gemaltem und imaginiertem Raum, so wird es nun außerhalb des Bildes in den realen Raum verlagert: Gemalte, illusionäre Dreidimensionalität verbindet sich innerhalb eines Bildes mit der realen Wand und damit mit der Wirklichkeit. Jene Bilder täuschen durch diese künstlerische Strategie und eine illusionistische Malerei vor, tatsächlich ein dreidimensionales Architekturfragment zu sein.

Jene monumentalen Gemälde, die mit Erdfarben aus der Toskana bemalt sind, widersetzen sich der Tradition des klassischen rechteckigen Bildformats. Durch ihre Einschnitte und den damit intendierten Wechselbezug zur realen Wand werden die Bilder zu Bildobjekten, zu geformten Leinwänden, zu *Shaped Canvases*. Im Gegensatz zur traditionellen Bildkomposition, in der die verschiedenen Bildelemente aufeinander bezogen sind, gibt es hier keine Details oder Subordinationen. Das gemalte Architekturfragment muss paradoxerweise als Ganzes, in seiner Totalität wahrgenommen werden, weil es nicht Teil einer Komposition ist, sondern das Bild selbst, das zugleich die Bildform bestimmt. Und die gemalte Architektur verbindet sich nun konsequenterweise mit dem realen Raum.

Alle römischen Architekturbilder aus der Zeit weisen eine weitere Gemeinsamkeit auf: die untere Bildkante verläuft als einzige horizontal und damit parallel zur Bodenleiste des realen Raumes. Im Hinblick auf die bildnerische Darstellung schneidet sie optisch den gemalten Raum ab und lässt ihn einmal mehr als Fragment erscheinen. Doch durch diese gerade Bildunterkante erhält das Bildformat sein stabilisierendes Gewicht auf der Wand und verankert sich durch die Bodenparallele mit dem realen Raum, in dem sich auch der Betrachter befindet.

Von Monkiewitschs bildkünstlerische Anfänge liegen in einer Zeit, in der es vor allem in Amerika bedeutende neue Ansätze gab, die auch von Monkiewitsch in Deutschland beeinflusst haben. Während in Deutschland zu der Zeit Ende der 1960er Jahre der Realismus Einzug hielt, formierten sich in Amerika neben der Pop-Art neue ungegenständliche Richtungen, die von Jackson Pollocks *Drippings* und deren *Allover*-Struktur sowie Barnett Newman beeinflusst wurden, doch zugleich neue Wege gingen. Gemeint sind die Künstler Frank Stella und Ellsworth Kelly sowie Künstler der Minimal Art wie Donald Judd, Sol LeWitt, Carl Andre, Robert Mangold.

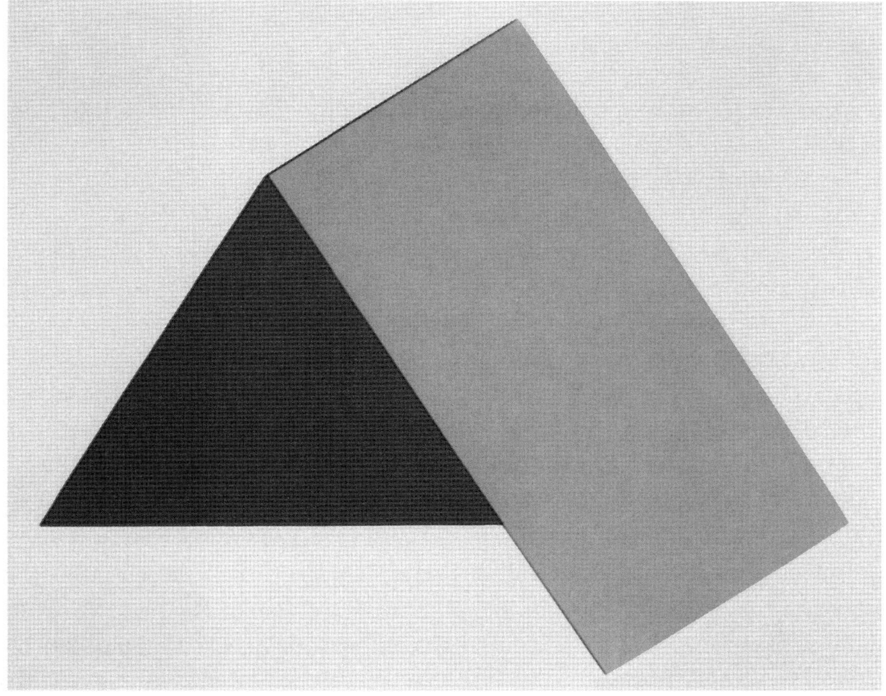

emerging, in particular in America, which also influenced von Monkiewitsch in Germany. While at the end of the 1960s, Realism was beginning to make itself felt in Germany, in America, besides Pop Art, new abstract movements, which were influenced by Jackson Pollock's *Drippings* and their *Allover* structure as well as by Barnett Newman, began to align themselves and at the same time tread new paths. What I am referring to are the artists Frank Stella and Ellsworth Kelly as well as representatives of Minimal Art such as Donald Judd, Sol LeWitt, Carl Andre and Robert Mangold.

At the end of the 1950s, influenced by Henry Matisse's scissor-cuts, the so-called *Cut-outs*, Ellsworth Kelly was the first to develop irregularly distorted paintings, the composition of the color surfaces bearing a non-relational relation to one another and to the painting's format. At the beginning of the 1960s, Frank Stella also parted with the traditional square picture format. While in the *Black Paintings,* he still painted black stripes parallel to the edge of the canvas, thus lending the painting a distinct symmetry and flatness, in the ensuing *Aluminum Series* from 1960 he cut the elements that did not conform with the striped patterns out of the square surface of the painting and discovered the *Shaped Canvas,* in which the outer form of the painting corresponds with the abstract forms on the painting's surface, and there is no longer a figure-ground relation. The L, T and U shapes in the subsequent *Copper Series* from 1960/61, which "appear to be giant scissor-cuts," [2] no longer make reference to the traditional square painting.

For Kelly and Stella, the abstractness, the anti-illusionism, and thus the emphasis of the flatness of the visual representation were of primary importance. The *Shaped Canvas* was not intended to be the portrayal of a real representationalism, but to assert itself as the object

Ellsworth Kelly entwickelte als Erster Ende der 1950er Jahre (beeinflußt von Henry Matisses Scherenschnitten, den sogenannten *Cut-outs*) irregulär verzerrte Bilder, deren Farbflächen in einem non-relationalen Kompositionsverhältnis zueinander und zum Bildformat stehen. Auch Frank Stella verabschiedete sich Anfang der 1960er Jahre vom traditionellen rechteckigen Bildformat. Während er noch in den *Black Paintings* schwarze Streifen parallel zum Bildrand malte und dem Bild damit eine ausgesprochene Symmetrie und Flächigkeit verlieh, schnitt er in der nachfolgenden *Aluminum Series* von 1960 die mit den Streifenmustern nicht konformen Elemente aus der rechteckigen Bildfläche aus und entdeckte das *Shaped Canvas,* in dem die Außenform des Bildes mit den ungegenständlichen Formen auf der Bildfläche übereinstimmt und kein Figur-Grund-Verhältnis mehr existiert. Seine L-, T- und U- Formen der anschließenden *Copper Series* von 1960/61, die „wie riesige Scherenschnitte wirken" [2], weisen keinen Bezug mehr zum traditionellen Bildrechteck auf.

Für Kelly und Stella waren die Ungegenständlichkeit, der Anti-Illusionismus und damit die Betonung der Flächigkeit der bildnerischen Darstellung von großer Bedeutung. Das *Shaped Canvas* sollte nicht Abbild einer realen Gegenständlichkeit sein, sondern sich selbst als Gegenstand, als Bildobjekt behaupten. Der Betrachter ist dabei nachgerade gefordert, weil das Bildobjekt mit seiner offenen und überschaubaren Struktur die Hermetik des traditionellen Bildrechtecks aufbricht und eine Verbindung zwischen Werk und Betrachter, der sich im gleichen Raum wie das Werk befindet, forciert. Donald Judd nannte diese neuartige Verbindung von Bild und Objekt, Skulptur und Malerei *Specific Objects.* Vergleichbar zu von Monkiewitschs Architekturbildern sind auch Mangolds *Walls* von 1964/65, deren Bildformen durch das Erlebnis der

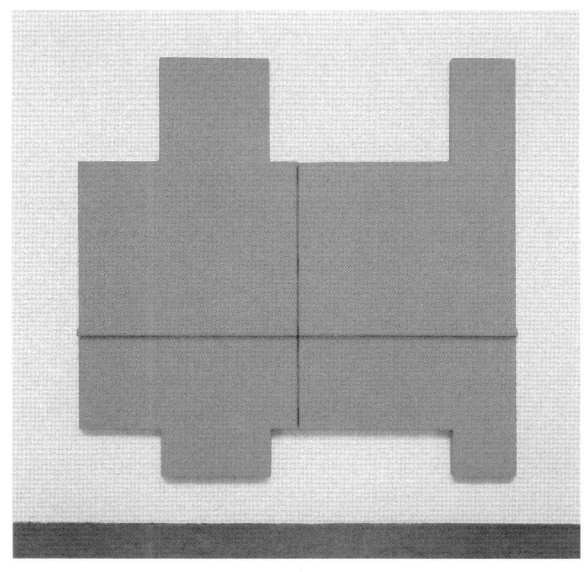

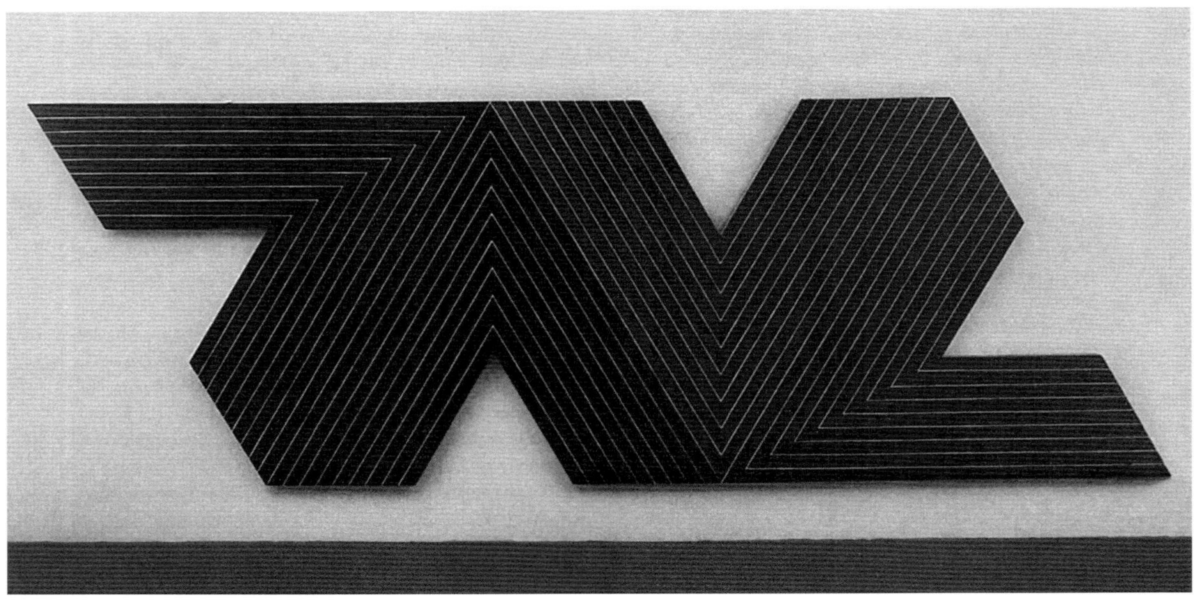

Frank Stella, *Empress of India*, 1965, Metallpuder auf Leinwand, 189,0 × 549,0 cm | Metal powder on canvas, Museum of Modern Art, New York

itself. The viewer is practically challenged, because with its open and clear structure, the painting breaks open the hermetics of the traditional square painting and forces a connection between the work and the viewer, who is in the same room with the work. Donald Judd referred to this new connection between image and object, sculpture and sculpture as *Specific Objects*. Mangold's *Walls* from 1964/65, whose forms emerged from the experience of viewing the sky between skyscrapers, can also be compared to Monkiewitsch's pictures. Von Monkiewitsch was fascinated by the materiality of the walls: iron hinges, nails, wood, and hard fiber as well as wide side walls made of wooden slats lend the anti-illusionistic, monochrome painting the added status of being a three-dimensional object. The *Walls* appear to be real walls with horizontal and vertical incisions.

Lienhard von Monkiewitsch used the *Shaped Canvas;* however, in doing so he did not comply with the associated American demand for abstract painting. His architecture paintings are illusionistic and make reference to an object outside the picture. Yet because they also contain a connection between the figure and the body of the painting, von Monkiewitsch moves into the tradition of the American view of the picture as object. However, by combining an illusionistic representation, von Monkiewitsch creates a completely new form of painting, a *Shaped Canvas* with a picture-like representation that connects the painted space with the real space and in doing so, connects European with American art in a unique way.

Sicht des Himmels zwischen den Wolkenkratzern entstanden sind. Von Monkiewitsch war fasziniert von der Materialität, durch die die Walls gemacht sind: Eisenscharniere, Nägel, Holz und Hartfaser sowie breite Seitenwände aus Holzlatten verleihen dem anti-illusionistischen, monochromen Bildobjekt zusätzlich den Status eines dreidimensionalen Bild-Dings. Die *Walls* erscheinen wie reale Wände mit horizontalen und vertikalen Einschnitten.

Lienhard von Monkiewitsch verwendete das *Shaped Canvas*, jedoch folgte er nicht der damit verbundenen amerikanischen Forderung einer ungegenständlichen Malerei. Seine Achitekturbilder sind illusionistisch und verweisen auf einen Gegenstand außerhalb des Bildes. Doch da auch bei ihnen ein Zusammenhang zwischen Bildfigur und Bildleib besteht, rückt von Monkiewitsch in die Tradition der amerikanischen Auffassung vom Bild als Objekt. Mit der Kombination einer illusionistischen Darstellung kreiert von Monkiewitsch jedoch eine gänzlich neue Bildform, ein *Shaped Canvas* mit abbildhafter Darstellung, die den gemalten Raum mit dem realen Raum verbindet und damit die europäische mit der amerikanischen Kunst auf einzigartige Weise verbindet.

1   Lienhard von Monkiewitsch, in *Kritisches Lexikon der Gegenwartskunst*, vol. 68 (Munich, 2004), p. 2.
2   Hans Strelow, "Über Frank Stella," *Kritisches Lexikon der Gegenwartskunst*, vol. 7 (Munich, 1989), p. 3.

1   Lienhard von Monkiewitsch, in: *Kritisches Lexikon der Gegenwartskunst*, Ausgabe 68, München 2004, S. 2.
2   Hans Strelow, „Über Frank Stella", in: *Kritisches Lexikon der Gegenwartskunst*, Ausgabe 7, München 1989, S. 3.

MICHAEL SCHWARZ

Innovationen des Zufalls. Anmerkungen zur Rolle des Betrachters im Werk von Lienhard von Monkiewitsch

Innovations of Coincidence: Remarks on the Role of the Viewer in Lienhard von Monkiewitsch's Work

Seit Anfang der 1980er Jahre findet Lienhard von Monkiewitsch die Kompositionen seiner Bilder immer häufiger nach dem Zufallsprinzip. Zu diesem Zeitpunkt entwickelte der Künstler Bildsysteme, die eine große Zahl von Variationen zulassen. So enthält die 1983 konzipierte Serie *6-teiliges Rechteck* eine Vielzahl von Möglichkeiten, die auszuführen sehr viel Zeit in Anspruch genommen hätte (S. 78/79). Wenn aber eine Auswahl getroffen werden musste, welche Bilder aus dem Programm ausgeführt werden sollten, dann musste sich der Künstler entscheiden – oder die Entscheidung dem Zufall überlassen. Um Bilder zu erhalten, die offen genug sind, das gewählte System zu repräsentieren, legte Lienhard von Monkiewitsch die Komposition fest, indem er Teile des Bildsystems auf den Bildgrund warf oder werfen ließ. Dieses Verfahren ist dem dadaistischen Würfeln von Hans Arp und Sophie Täuber-Arp in den Rasterbildern von 1918 nicht unähnlich und auch Marcel Duchamps *Trois stoppages étalon* von 1913/14 gehören zur Vorgeschichte derartiger Zufallskompositionen. Der Kontext, in dem dieser Bildfindungsprozess bei Lienhard von Monkiewitsch gesehen werden muss, ist gleichwohl ein anderer. Er speist sich aus der Logik der Serie, der Rolle des Betrachters und dem Selbstverständnis des Künstlers. Von diesem Kontext als Bedingung für die Partizipation des Betrachters wird im Folgenden die Rede sein.

Since the beginning of the 1980s, Lienhard von Monkiewitsch has more and more frequently discovered the compositions of his paintings according to the principle of coincidence. At the time, the artist developed systems of images which allow a large number of variations. Thus the series *6-teiliges Rechteck*, conceived in 1983, contains a variety of possibilities which would have taken a lot of time to execute (pp. 78/79). However, when a selection had to be made of which of the program's paintings were to be executed, then the artist had to make a decision – or leave the decision to coincidence. In order to obtain images that are open enough to represent the system selected, Lienhard von Monkiewitsch determined the composition by throwing parts of the system of images – or having them thrown – onto the picture's ground. This method is not unlike the Dadaist cubes by Hans Arp and Sophie Taeuber-Arp in the raster images from 1918, and Marcel Duchamp's *Trois stoppages étalon* from 1913/14 are also part of the past history of these types of coincidental compositions. The context within which this compositional process has to be regarded is nevertheless a different one for Lienhard von Monkiewitsch. It sustains itself on the logic of the series, the role of the viewer, and the artist's self-image. The following will deal with this context as a condition for the viewer's participation.

In mathematics, the logic of the series requires complete representation or its condensing in a formula. In art, the representation of extensive series often leads to a lack of clarity and an apparent redundancy. For the viewer, those series that remain easily comprehensible in size and number are ideal. Lienhard von Monkiewitsch has compiled the series *Zwei Schnitte in das suprematistische Rechteck* and *Zwei Schnitte in das suprematistische Quadrat*, produced in 1985/86, for the exhibition in the Städtische Galerie Wolfsburg. Both series are clearly arranged, and the viewing conditions are optimal. Other systems of images result in far more extensive numbers of sequences. *Zwei Schnitte in das suprematistische Quadrat*, produced in 1985, has 1,500 variations, all of which could have been executed – after all, a lack of clarity and apparent repetition are not sufficient reasons to refrain from realizing them. But do they have to be executed like

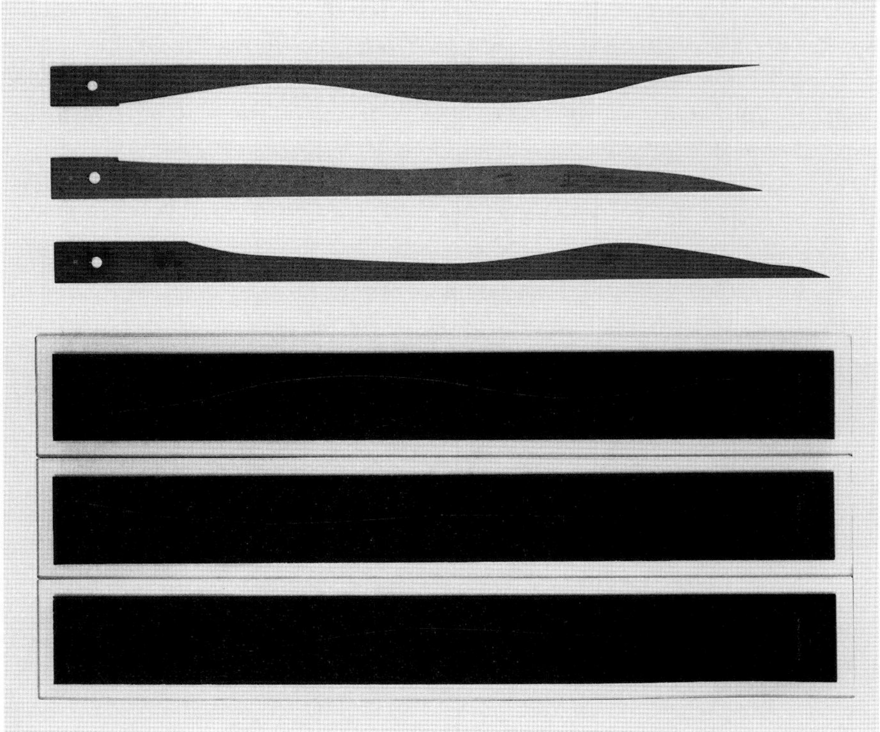

MARCEL DUCHAMP, *Trois stoppages étalon*, 1913/14, Assemblage, je 13,3 × 120 cm, Museum of Modern Art, New York

Hanne Darboven's number systems, because one day is followed by another? Or is it possible to make a selection? A selection is possible because the individual works in a series are autonomous. Their formal structure does not result from the relentless continuation of a number system, rather it results from the possible constellations of partial surfaces. It is (almost) like dice: Three six-sided dice produce x^n possible number combinations, whereby individual combinations count more than others. Can one also say the same for certain pictorial solutions? Are individual compositions more convincing, more exciting, more beautiful than others? And if so, what influence would this have on a possible selection? The following applies for the image systems used by Lienhard von Monkiewitsch: The individual pictures in the series remain autonomous. It is no different than for the group of floor/space works, that series of canvas paintings, drawings, and silkscreen prints produced between 1969 and 1973. In this case, the individual image even has to be viewed independent of the others if that process of seeing and thinking is to set in that the artist wants to trigger off in the viewer: He asks: "How much of a space do I have to represent? ... The floor is the initial form for a process of seeing and thinking. Space emerges and dissolves again in surface. What is there is cropped by what is not there, obtains its form from it. The more information what is there provides about itself, the more detailed what is not there is conceived of. The more detailed the

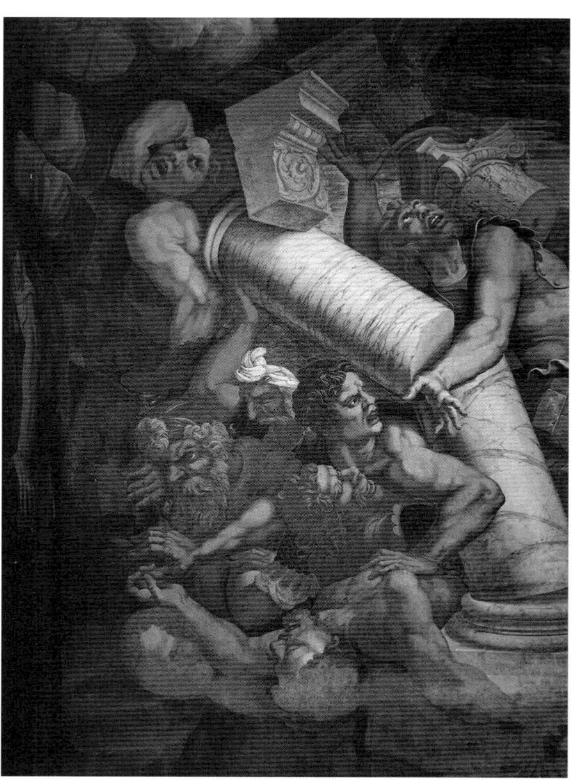

In der Mathematik erfordert die Logik der Serie die vollständige Darstellung oder ihre Verdichtung in einer Formel. In der Kunst führt die Darstellung umfangreicher Serien oft zu Unübersichtlichkeit und einer scheinbaren Redundanz. Für den Betrachter sind Serien ideal, die in Größe und Anzahl der Arbeiten überschaubar bleiben. Für die Ausstellung in der Städtischen Galerie Wolfsburg hat Lienhard von Monkiewitsch die 1985/86 entstandenen Serien *Zwei Schnitte in das suprematistische Rechteck* und *Zwei Schnitte in das suprematistische Quadrat* vorbereitet. Sie sind dort übersichtlich und unter optimalen Bedingungen zu betrachten. Bei anderen Bildsystemen ergeben sich zahlenmäßig weit umfangreichere Folgen. Bei *Zwei Schnitte in das suprematistische Quadrat* von 1985 sind es über 1500 Variationen. Doch auch diese hätten ausgeführt werden können, schließlich sind Unübersichtlichkeit und scheinbare Wiederholung keine hinreichenden Gründe, die Ausführung zu unterlassen. Aber müssen sie ausgeführt werden wie die Zahlensysteme von Hanne Darboven, weil ein Tag auf den anderen folgt? Oder ist eine Auswahl möglich? Eine Auswahl ist möglich, weil die einzelnen Arbeiten einer Serie autonom sind. Ihre formale Anlage ergibt sich nicht aus dem unerbittlichen Fortschreiben eines Zahlensystems, sondern aus den möglichen Konstellationen von Teilflächen. Es ist (fast) wie beim Würfelspiel: Mit drei sechsseitigen Würfeln ergeben sich x mögliche Zahlenkombinationen. Dabei zählen einzelne Kombinationen mehr als andere. Lässt sich das auch von bestimmten Bildlösungen sagen? Sind einzelne Kompositionen überzeugender, spannungsreicher, schöner als andere; und wenn ja, welchen Einfluss hätte dies auf eine mögliche Auswahl? Für die von Lienhard von Monkiewitsch verwendeten Bildssysteme gilt: Die einzelnen Bilder der Serie bleiben autonom. Es ist nicht anders als bei der Werkgruppe der Boden-Raum-Arbeiten, jener Serie von Leinwandbildern, Zeichnungen und Siebdrucken, die zwischen 1969 und 1973 entstanden ist. Hier muss das einzelne Bild sogar unabhängig von den anderen betrachtet werden können, soll sich jener Seh-Denk-Vorgang einstellen, den der Künstler beim Betrachter auslösen will: „Wie viel muss ich von einem Raum darstellen [...]" , so fragt er. „Der Boden ist die Ausgangsform für einen Seh-Denk-Vorgang. Raum entsteht und löst sich wieder in Fläche auf. Das Vorhandene wird von dem Nichtvorhandenen beschnitten, erhält von ihm seine Form. Je mehr Informationen das Vorhandene über sich gibt, desto detaillierter wird das Nichtvorhandene gedacht. Je detaillierter der Boden, desto größer die Möglichkeit, den Raum aufzubauen, um ihn zu begehen. Dann füllt sich der Raum wieder mit Gegenständen".[1]

Nun ist die Wirkung von Kunstwerken auf den Betrachter seit langem Gegenstand umfangreicher wissenschaftlicher Untersuchungen. Schon im 16. Jahrhundert empfiehlt Gabriele Paleotti dem Maler, durch Genauigkeit, gefällige Farben und andere Überraschungen „auch die Augen des Unerfahrenen zur Bewunderung zu zwingen"[2] Die Ausmalung des Palazzo del Te in Mantua durch Giulio Romano ist ein frühes Beispiel für eine Malerei, die den Bildraum in den Raum des Betrachters öffnet. Erreicht wird dies durch eine Aufhebung des Bildrahmens und einen totalen Illusionismus, der die architektonische Begrenzung der Innenräume überwindet. Lienhard von Monkie-

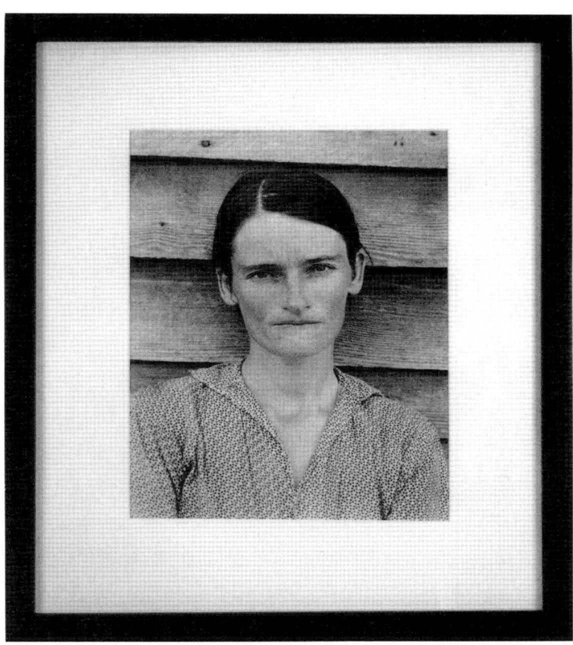

witsch setzt weniger auf die Bewunderung als auf die Vorstellungskraft des Betrachters, der durch die genau gezeichneten Bodenflächen und Fußleisten den nicht gezeichneten oder gemalten Raum darüber imaginiert. Der Betrachter all dieser Bilder bleibt jedoch ein betrachtender Betrachter.

In den Serien mit den Bildsystemen Quadrat, Parallelogramm und Rechteck und in den Konstruktionen mit aufeinander folgenden Fibonacci-Zahlen beteiligt der Künstler immer häufiger den Betrachter am Produktionsprozess der Bilder selbst. Der Betrachter wird Co-Autor. Er verantwortet die entscheidende Phase der Bildfindung. Auf den Künstler hingegen gehen das Bildsystem, für das die Komposition gefunden wurde, und die Ausführung zurück, die schon aufgrund der technisch-handwerklichen Erfahrung, die sie erfordert, nicht delegiert werden kann.

Zeitgleich mit der Appropriation Art, mit den Arbeiten von Sherrie Levine, Richard Prince, von Allan McCollum und Louis Lawler verlässt Lienhard von Monkiewitsch mit diesem Konzept das humanistische Modell des Künstlersubjekts und übergibt den Bildentwurf an den Betrachter. „Der Sinn eines Bildes liegt nicht in seinem Ursprung, sondern in seiner Bestimmung. Die Geburt des Betrachters geschieht auf Kosten des Malers", sagt Sherrie Levine. Schon 1968 hatte Roland Barthes nicht nur den Tod des Autors, sondern zugleich die Geburt des Betrachters vorausgesehen – eine Prophezeiung, die sich weder im Pariser Mai von 1968 noch in der Behauptung von Joseph Beuys, „jeder ist ein Künstler" nachhaltig erfüllte.[3] Erst als die Autoren selbst bereit waren, ihre Autorität, Originalität und Kreativität rhetorisch und faktisch in Frage zu stellen, konnte der Betrachter als Autor geboren werden. Aber ihre Namen und Signaturen haben die Künstlerinnen und Künstler nicht abgegeben. Hier bestehen sie vorerst noch auf Singularität und eignen sich die Werke ihrer Kollegen, Bildikonen der Werbung oder eben Kompositionsentwürfe von Atelierbesuchern an. Selbst in den Serien nach Fibonacci-Zahlen, in denen einem zentralen schwarzen Rechteck zwei buntfarbige, von zufälligen Passanten oder seiner Frau Regine angemischte Farben zugeordnet werden, bleibt das Werk eine Arbeit von Lienhard von Monkiewitsch. Die AutorInnen bleiben anonym.[4]

floor, the greater the possibility of structuring the space in order to walk into it. The space then fills itself with objects again."[1]

Now, the effect of works of art on the viewer has long been the subject of extensive scientific research. As early as the sixteenth century, Gabriele Paleotti recommended painters "to also force the eyes of the inexperienced into admiration" by implementing accuracy, pleasant colors, and other surprises.[2] Giulio Romano's painting of the Palazzo del Te in Mantua is an early example for painting which opens the space of the image into the viewer's space. This is achieved by abolishing the picture frame and through total illusionism, which overcomes the architectural limitation of the interior spaces. Lienhard von Monkiewitsch relies less on admiration than on the power of imagination of the viewer, who by way of the precisely drawn floor surfaces and baseboards imagines the space, which has been neither drawn or painted, above them. The viewer of all of these images, however, remains a viewing viewer.

In the series with the image systems square, parallelogram, and rectangle, and in the constructions with successive Fibonacci numbers, the artist more and more frequently involves the viewer in the production process. The viewer becomes the co-author. He/She is responsible for the decisive phase of pictorial composition. On the other hand, the image system, for which the composition was found, and the execution, which due to the skilled experience it requires cannot be delegated, go back to the artist.

Contemporaneous to Appropriation Art and works by Sherrie Levine, Richard Prince, by Allan McCollum, and Louis Lawler, with this concept, Lienhard von Monkiewitsch abandons the humanistic model of the artist subject and hands the concept of the image over to the viewer. Sherrie Levine once said: "A painting's meaning lies not in its origin, but in its destination. The birth of the viewer must be at the cost of the painter." As early as 1968, Roland Barthes predicted not only the death of the author, but at the same time the birth of the viewer – a prophecy that was neither lastingly fulfilled in May of 1968 in Paris, nor in Joseph Beuys' claim that "everyone is an artist."[3] It was not until the authors themselves were willing to rhetorically and factually question their authority, originality, and creativity that the viewer could be born as an author. However, the artists have not relinquished their names and signatures. For the time being, they still continue to insist on singularity and appropriate the works by their colleagues, image icons from advertising, or even concepts for compositions from visitors to their studios. Even in the series based on Fibonacci numbers, in which two brightly colored paints, mixed by chance passers-by or by his wife, Regine, are assigned to a central black rectangle, the work remains one by Lienhard von Monkiewitsch. The co-authors remain anonymous.[4]

What role, then, does the unnamed co-author have? In contrast to Appropriation Art, Lienhard von Monkiewitsch does not relativize the originality and authenticity of his pictures through appropriation, rather he attempts to augment them. Especially in his series on the Black Square, because the artist and the co-author, like with the *Cadavre exquis,* are not familiar with each other's paint mixtures, combinations emerge which are deeply alien to the artist and which he would have not necessarily accepted had he been responsible for the color field painting – but has to accept according to his rules of image production. The same applies to the thrown image compositions. The completed series on the suprematist square already contains highly unusual mutations of the black surface. However, these can be derived from the discernible system of the series and justified based on this system. The purely *Zufallswürfe,* such as the forty drawings from 1987/88 which were no longer produced in series and in which nearly each throw results in a composition that ignores all of the traditions of the occidental organization of images, are innovations of coincidence. The author would have hardly decided on any of these forms. For Lienhard von Monkiewitsch, the active participation of the viewer and accepting coincidence present opportunities for departing from traditional rules of composition and color contrasts and expanding our notion of the organized, equilibrated, object-free painting. This removal of the limitations of convention is supported by painting that has no signature and thus makes no reference to an author. And yet it is the artist and the deep, immaterial, mysterious black of his paintings which force the eyes not only of the inexperienced into admiration.

Welche Rolle hat dann aber der ungenannte Co-Autor? Im Gegensatz zur amerikanischen Appropriation Art relativiert Lienhard von Monkiewitsch durch Aneignung nicht die Originalität und Authentizität seiner Bilder, sondern versucht sie zu erweitern. Gerade in den Serien über das Schwarze Quadrat entstehen durch die Tatsache, dass Künstler und Co-Autor wie beim *Cadavre exquis* die Farbmischung des anderen nicht kennen, Kombinationen, die dem Maler zutiefst fremd sind und die er als selbst verantwortetes Farbfeldbild nicht in jedem Falle akzeptiert hätte – innerhalb seiner Regeln der Bildproduktion aber akzeptieren muss. Bei den gewürfelten Bildkompositionen ist es nicht anders. Schon die vollständig ausgeführten Serien über das suprematistische Quadrat enthalten höchst ungewöhnliche Mutationen der schwarzen Fläche. Diese lassen sich jedoch aus der erkennbaren Systematik der Serie ableiten und mit dieser begründen. Die reinen *Zufallswürfe,* wie jene 40 Zeichnungen von 1987/88, die nicht mehr durch das Programm der Serie getragen werden und bei denen nahezu jeder Wurf eine Komposition ergibt, die sämtliche Traditionen abendländischer Bildgestaltung ignoriert, haben wir es mit Innovationen des Zufalls zu tun. Der Autor hätte sich kaum für eine dieser Formen entschieden. Für Lienhard von Monkiewitsch liegen in der aktiven Beteiligung des Betrachters und im Akzeptieren des Zufalls Möglichkeiten, die tradierten Kompositionsregeln und Farbkontraste zu verlassen und unsere Vorstellung vom gestalteten, ausponderierten gegenstandsfreien Bild zu erweitern. Diese Entgrenzung der Konventionen wird unterstützt durch eine Malerei, die keine Handschrift hat und also auch auf keinen Autor verweist. Und doch ist es der Künstler, der mit dem tiefen, immateriellen, rätselhaften Schwarz seiner Bilder nicht nur die „Unerfahrenen zur Bewunderung zwingt".

1 Lienhard von Monkiewitsch in a text from 1970, cited in Walter Vitt, *Lienhard v. Monkiewitsch,* Kunst der Gegenwart aus Niedersachsen, vol. 43 (Hannover, 1994), p. 30.
2 Wolfgang Kemp, "Kunstwissenschaft und Rezeptionsästhetik," *Der Betrachter ist im Bild: Kunstwissenschaft und Rezeptionsästhetik,* ed. Wolfgang Kemp, (Cologne, 1985), p. 9.
3 Compare David Deitcher, "Die Geburt des Betrachters," Wolfgang Kemp, *Zeitgenössische Kunst und ihre Betrachter,* Jahresring 43 (Cologne, 1996), pp. 53–63.

4 They are often mentioned on the back of the paintings. This is also where the artist signs his works. However, it is decisive that those who have collaborated on the works are not mentioned in the captions or anywhere else within the distribution process. Thus an important reference to the production process is dropped – which is not the case for Sherrie Levine or Elaine Sturtevant, who disclose the names of their co-authors.

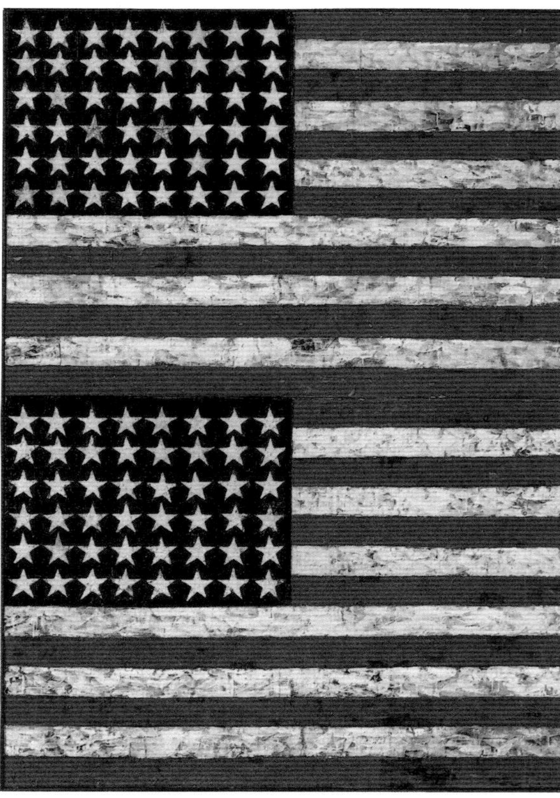

ELAINE STURTEVANT, *Johns Double Flag,* 1966, Enkaustik, Collage auf Leinwand,
180,0 × 120,0 cm | Encaustic, collage on canvas

1 Lienhard von Monkiewitsch in einem Text von 1970, zit. nach Walter Vitt, *Lienhard von Monkiewitsch,* Kunst der Gegenwart aus Niedersachsen Bd. 43, Hannover 1994, S. 30.
2 Wolfgang Kemp, „Kunstwissenschaft und Rezeptionsästhetik", in: Wolfgang Kemp (Hrsg.), *Der Betrachter ist im Bild. Kunstwissenschaft und Rezeptionsästhetik,* Köln 1985, S. 9.
3 Vgl. David Deitcher, „Die Geburt des Betrachters", in: Wolfgang Kemp, *Zeitgenössische Kunst und ihre Betrachter.* Jahresring 43, Köln 1996, S. 53–63.
4 Auf der Rückseite der Bilder werden sie häufig genannt. Hier signiert der Künstler auch seine Werke. Entscheidend jedoch ist, dass die Mitwirkenden in der Beschriftung und bei der weiteren Verbreitung der Werke nicht genannt werden. Damit entfällt ein wichtiger Hinweis auf den Produktionsprozess – anders als bei Sherrie Levine oder Elaine Sturtevant, die ihre Vorbilder offen legen.

Michael Stoeber

Alles eine unendliche Wiederkehr. Sehen und Verstehen im Werk von Lienhard von Monkiewitsch

All an Eternal Recurrence: Seeing and Understanding in Lienhard von Monkiewitsch's Work

Frank Stella, *Jill*, 1959, Emaille auf Leinwand, 229,6 × 200 cm | Enamel on canvas, Allbright-Knox Art Gallery, Buffalo, NY

In den Jahren 1959 und 1960 malt der amerikanische Künstler Frank Stella seine berühmt gewordene Serie der *Black Paintings*. Sie umfasst 21 Gemälde, bei denen Stella handelsübliche schwarze Emaille verwendet. Schicht um Schicht schafft er damit auf hell grundierten Leinwänden Oberflächen aus symmetrischen Streifen. Seine Malerei treibt den Bildern jede persönliche Handschrift aus und jeden räumlichen Illusionismus. Allem Anschein nach gibt es keine Symbole und keine Botschaften, nichts als flache, wenn auch energetisch pulsierende Oberflächen. Die Bilder widersetzen sich der Interpretation. Man kann sie offenbar nicht verstehend lesen, sondern nur sehen. In einem viel zitierten Interview im Jahre 1964 hat Stella daher über sie gesagt: „Das einzige, was bei meinen Bildern unbedingt zum Vorschein kommen soll und das einzige, was für mich bei ihnen auch jemals zum Vorschein gekommen ist, ist, dass man die Idee völlig unverstellt vor sich hat. Was man sieht ist, was man sieht".[1] Aber – was ist die Idee der Bilder, die sich nach Stellas Auffassung völlig unverstellt präsentiert? Nicht mehr als eine auf Symmetrie, Opposition und Wiederholung gründende Konstellation von Form und Farbe? Sehen wir wirklich, was wir sehen?

Schauen wir auf die abstrakten Werkserien von Lienhard von Monkiewitsch, die generisch Ähnlichkeit mit Stellas *Black Paintings* haben – wie diese stehen sie in der bildnerischen Tradition der konkreten Kunst –, stellen wir fest, dass wir entschieden mehr sehen, als wir sehen, wenn wir die konstruktive Manier dieser Werke verstehen. 1983 wendet sich der damals 42-jährige Künstler nach vielen artistischen Häutungen und Transformationen, nach gestischer Malerei und Pop Art, nach der Produktion augentäuschender Innenräume und realistischer Porträts, nach politischen Interventionen und Architekturbildern, ganz und gar einem konstruktiven Vokabular zu. Mit dieser Festlegung liquidiert von Monkiewitsch auch die narrativen Tendenzen, die es bis dahin in seinen Bildern gegeben hat. Die Konzentration auf eine von Maß und Zahl, von Symmetrie und Proportion bestimmte Form folgt einer Tradition, die vom russischen Suprematismus über die niederländische De Stijl-Bewegung bis hin zum deutschen Bauhaus reicht. Im Mittelpunkt seiner Werke steht dabei das durch Kasimir Malewitsch berühmt gewordene *Schwarze Quadrat*. Auch wenn es in von Monkiewitschs Bildern nicht da ist, ist es doch da. Es ist da in den aus ihm sich ableitenden Formen wie Rechteck, Dreieck und Parallelogramm, die zu Agenten der Werke werden.

Ist für Malewitsch das *Schwarze Quadrat* hochgradig bedeutungsvoll als abstrakte Ikone voll spiritueller Kraft und als Symbol einer neu heraufdämmernden Zeit und Gesellschaft, hat das Quadrat für von Monkiewitsch keine spezifische symbolische Bedeutung. In seinem Konstruktivismus träumen keine Erlösungsfantasien. Es geht ihm nicht um ultimative ästhetische Formen und Formeln, um die Errettung der Welt *de more geometrico*. Sondern die

In 1959 and 1960, the American artist Frank Stella painted his now famous series *Black Paintings*. It includes twenty-one paintings in which Stella implements commercial black enamel, with which he layer for layer creates surfaces of symmetrical stripes on light-grounded canvas. His method of painting drives any personal signature and any spatial illusionism out of the pictures. Evidently there are no symbols and no messages, nothing other than flat, if energetically pulsating surfaces. The images resist interpretation. One apparently cannot understand them by reading them; one can only see them. In a frequently quoted interview from 1966, Stella said: "All I want anyone to get out of my paintings, and all I ever get out of them, is the fact that you can see the whole idea without any confusion. ... What you see is what you see."[1] But – what is the idea of the paintings that, according to Stella, presents itself without any confusion? No longer a constellation of form and color based on symmetry, opposition, and repetition? Do we really see what we see?

If we look at the series of abstract works by Lienhard von Monkiewitsch, which have a generic similarity to Stella's *Black Paintings* – like these, they stand in the artistic tradition of Concrete Art – we can establish that we see decisively more than we see if we understand the constructive manner of these works. After many artistic sloughings and transformations, after gestural painting and Pop Art, after the production of illusionistic interior spaces and realistic portraits, after political interventions and architectural images, in 1983, the artist, who was forty-two at the time, devoted himself exclusively to a constructive vocabulary. By committing himself in this way, von Monkiewitsch also liquidated the narrative tendencies that had been present in his pictures until that time. The concentration on a form determined by dimension and number, symmetry and proportion, adheres to a tradition that ranges from Russian Suprematism and the Dutch De Stijl movement to the German Bauhaus. The focal point of his works is the *Schwarzes Quadrat* (Black Square) made famous by Kasimir Malevich. Even if it is not included in von Monkiewitsch's paintings, it is still there. It is there in the forms derived from it such as the rectangle, triangle, and parallelogram, which become the works' agents.

If the *Black Square* is meaningful for Malevich as an abstract icon full of spiritual strength and as a symbol of a newly dawning age and society, for von Monkiewitsch the square has no specific symbolic meaning. There are no fantasies of deliverance being dreamt in his constructivism. He is not concerned with ultimate aesthetic forms and formulae, with the salvation of the world *de more geometrico*. Rather the elevation of constructive modules to the motifs of his paintings relieves von Monkiewitsch of the problem of having to decide time and again what he should paint, a problem every artist has been confronted with since art became autonomous. It is not quite unimportant for the viewer to know this in order to do justice to von Monkiewitsch's pictures. We humans are beings who seek meaning and endure nothing with more difficulty than the unexplained. In this sense, it is just as important to know in which way von Monkiewitsch, besides the "What to paint?", solves the second essential production question: "How to paint?" According to which mode do his constructive motifs move into the painting? How does the artist deal with structure and composition? Here, too, von Monkiewitsch does without exposition and the cult of a subjective ingenuity and lets himself be guided by the vicissitudes of coincidence on the one hand, and by the law of systems on the other.

Making coincidence a friend and an ally when creating art has tradition in art history. It was above all the Dadaists and the Surrealists who relied time and again on the creative and formative power of coincidence. Marcel Duchamp painted paintings whose lines followed the pattern of strings he let fall from his hand onto the floor.

Erhebung konstruktiver Module zu Bildmotiven enthebt von Monkiewitsch des Problems, immer wieder aufs Neue entscheiden zu müssen, was er denn malen soll, ein Problem mit dem seit der Autonomie der Kunst jeder Künstler konfrontiert ist. Das zu wissen, ist für den Betrachter nicht ganz unwichtig, um von Monkiewitschs Bildern gerecht zu werden. Wir Menschen sind ja Sinn suchende Wesen und halten nichts so schwer aus wie das Unerklärte. In diesem Sinne ist es ebenso wichtig zu wissen, in welcher Weise von Monkiewitsch die zweite essentielle Produktionsfrage neben dem „Was malen?" löst: das „Wie malen?" Nach welchem Modus ziehen seine konstruktiven Motive ins Bild? Wie bewältigt der Künstler Aufbau und Komposition? Auch hier verzichtet von Monkiewitsch auf Entfaltung und Kult eines subjektiven Ingeniums und lässt sich zum einen von den Wechselfällen des Zufalls bestimmen, zum anderen von der Gesetzmäßigkeit von Systemen.

Sich bei der Erzeugung von Kunst den Zufall zum Freund und Verbündeten zu machen, hat Tradition in der Kunstgeschichte. Vor allem die Dadaisten und Surrealisten haben immer wieder auf die kreative und formgebende Kraft des Zufalls gesetzt. Marcel Duchamp hat Bilder gemalt, deren Lineaturen dem Verlauf von Bindfäden folgten, die er aus der Hand auf den Fußboden gleiten ließ. Ganz ähnlich kommt auch von Monkiewitsch zu Bildfindungen, wenn er bei der Arbeit *6-teiliges Rechteck* (1983, S.78/79) sein Bildfeld in zwanzig gleich große Quadrate gliedert, das er mit sechs Motiven bespielt. Sie bestehen aus drei Quadraten im Format der Rasterquadrate, aus einem Rechteck, das der Größe zweier Rasterquadrate entspricht, und aus zwei Dreiecken, die sich dem Diagonalschnitt durch ein Rasterquadrat verdanken. Von Monkiewitsch hat die sechs Formen aus Pappe geschnitten und wirft sie mit geschlossenen Augen über seine Schulter auf das Bild, um sie anschließend exakt so zu malen, wie sie gefallen sind. Nicht anders verfährt er zehn Jahre später, als er nun auch Freunde und Bekannte bittet, die von ihm vorgegebenen Formelemente, Quadrat, Rechteck, Parallelogramm, nach derselben Strategie auf den Bildgrund zu werfen. Das tut er bis heute so. Danach notiert er den Fall und malt die *Rekonstruktion eines Zufalls* (S. 120/121).

Eine andere Manier, zu Bildfindungen zu kommen, liegt in der Erzeugung planvoller Strukturen und Schnitte und in der Anlehnung an die Fibonacci-Zahlenreihe. Bei den Schnitten bezieht sich von Monkiewitsch einmal mehr auf Malewitsch: das machen seine Bildtitel deutlich, in denen das Quadrat als suprematistisches auftaucht. Mit diesem Attribut pflegte der russische Künstler die Einzigartigkeit seines Motivs zu betonen. Was Malewitsch als gloriosen Endpunkt der Malerei gedacht hat, wird für von Monkiewitsch zum Neuanfang. Für die Werkserie *Zwei Schnitte in das Suprematistische Quadrat* (Beginn 1985, S. 95–103) sind ihm bis heute etwa 1500 Bildrealisierungen eingefallen. Die abgeschnittenen Teile fügt er bei dieser Strategie stets aufs Neue an die Rumpfform an, wobei er die Umsetzung auf ganz unterschiedlichen Bildträgern wie Leinwand, Holz, Beton oder Karton vornimmt. Auch die Fibonacci-Zahlenreihe erlaubt es dem Künstler, sein Bild nach streng systematischen Kriterien zu konstruieren. Die Zahlen, gefunden im 13. Jahrhundert von dem italienischen Mathematiker Leonardo da Pisa, bilden sich durch Addition der zwei jeweils vorangegangenen Zahlen. Es handelt sich dabei um Relationen,

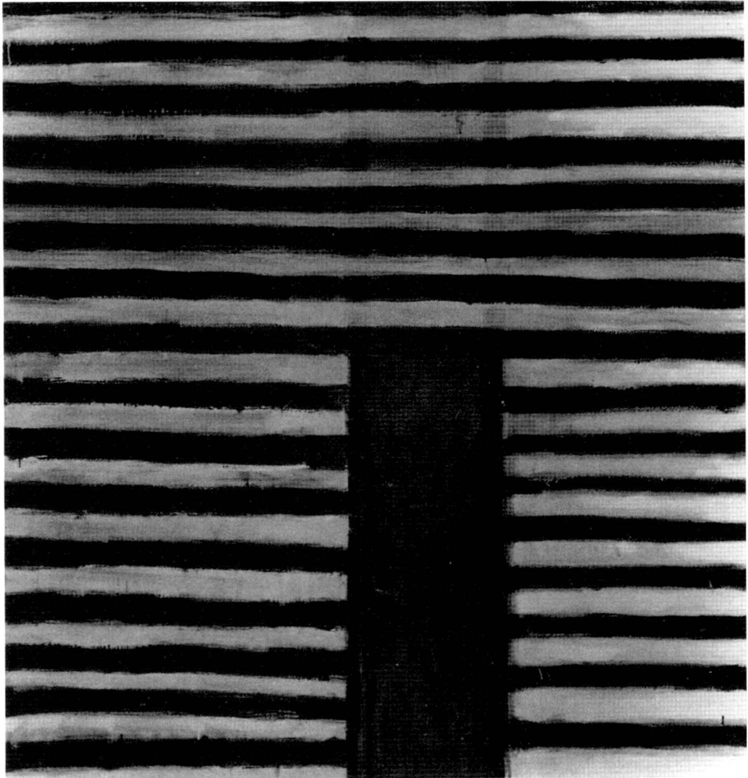

Von Monkiewitsch arrives at his pictorial compositions in a similar way when in his work *6-teiliges Rechteck* (1983, pp. 78/79), he divides the painting field up into twenty squares of equal size, onto which he then records six motifs. They consist of three squares in a grid-square format, of a rectangle that corresponds to the size of two grid squares, and of two triangles created by a diagonal cut to one grid square. Von Monkiewitsch cuts the six forms out of cardboard and throws them with eyes closed over his shoulder onto the canvas, after which he paints them exactly as they fell. He proceeds the same way ten years later when he asks friends and acquaintances to throw the prescribed elements – square, rectangle, and parallelogram – onto a canvas according to the same strategy. He continues to do so to this day. Afterwards he notes the way the forms have fallen and paints the *Rekonstruktion eines Zufalls* – the reconstruction of a coincidence (pp. 120/121).

Another manner of arriving at pictorial compositions lies in the production of planned structures and cuts and in following the Fibonacci number series. In his cuts, von Monkiewitsch once again makes reference to Malevich: This is made clear by the titles of his paintings, in which the square appears as a suprematist one. The Ukrainian artist used this attribute to emphasize the uniqueness of his motif. What Malevich regarded as the glorious end of painting is a new beginning for von Monkiewitsch. To this day, he has thought of circa 1,500 paintings for the series *Zwei Schnitte in das Suprematistische Quadrat*, which he began in 1985 (pp. 95–103). His strategy is to continue to apply the parts he has cut off to the form which remains, carrying out the implementation on a variety of carrier materials, such as canvas, wood, concrete, or cardboard. The Fibonacci series also allows the artist to construct his painting according to strictly systematic criteria. The numbers, discovered in the thirteenth century by the Italian mathematician Leonardo da Pisa, are formed through the addition of the two preceding numbers. They are relations such as those produced by the Golden Cut. Von Monkiewitsch applies the principle so that the two greatest numbers of his selection determine the painting's format, the others its surfaces in space. For certain number combinations, a square results in the center of the painting.

Von Monkiewitsch frequently relies on the law of coincidence in the attribution and determination of color. A friend or acquaintance selects one color, and the artist, without knowing which one has been chosen, selects another. Coincidence and law blend. As proven by the paintings, this results time and again in strong and beautiful color contrasts, though there is also a constant – a color effect that continues to reappear in von Monkiewitsch's work and represents something like the signature of this œuvre. It is the utterly unusual black in his pictures, as velvety and radiant as it is fragile and robust. The artist achieves this effect by scattering black pigment onto the not yet dry layer of black oil paint. This pigment ensures that the black absorbs all the light and opens an intense effect of depth in the painting. The impression is heightened even more when the artist smudges the pigment, thus producing a dark halo around the color surface, which intensifies the corporeality of the black even further. This produces a paradoxical alternation between surface and space. The color fields take up mass and broaden the painting into an unspecific depth. An architectural component unexpectedly enters the painting, which connects the works to earlier works, and at the same time one feels reminded of the *trompe l'œil* with which von Monkiewitsch's most recent furniture sculptures operate.

The artist's strategies of pictorial composition by means of system and coincidence – a coincidence he consistently places into the work in a planned manner, which, as paradoxical as it may sound, is thus ultimately a systematically operating coincidence – is reminiscent of the thought patterns of the Structuralists. Similar to the way in which they derive the variety of manifestations in the world and in society, in language and in culture, from the structures they are based on, von Monkiewitsch creates a variety of compositions by selecting only a few elements, which he combines in a variety of ways. It is only the direction of movement which distinguishes an artist from the thinker. The one explains the world as it exists, the other constructs a new one. Whereas the structuralist thinker attributes the complexity of being to the effect of only several parameters with the aid of his analytical model, the structuralist artist operates as a kind of demiurge – without, however, any pathetic or romantic excessiveness – who creates his own artistic world with the aid of parameters that he selects himself and consistently rearranges. For this reason, the French cultural philosopher Roland Barthes placed – and rightly so – the thinkers and interpreters under the headword "structuralist activity" in the ranks of artists and producers.[2]

"What you see is what you see." No, we do not see things because they are visible, rather they become visible because we see them. Goethe's words still apply: "One only sees what one knows." The laconism of form and color in Stella's *Black Paintings* did not prevent him from giving them titles laden with meaning, which make reference to William Blake, Charles Baudelaire and Duke Ellington, to the slums in big American cities and the National Socialist reign of terror. The exegetes – and rightly so – did not allow the paradox between semantically

wie sie auch der Goldene Schnitt kennt. Von Monkiewitsch nutzt das Prinzip so, dass die beiden größten Zahlen seiner Auswahl das Bildformat bestimmen, die anderen seine Flächen im Raum. Bei bestimmten Zahlenkombinationen entsteht dabei in der Bildmitte ein Quadrat.

Auch bei der Zuschreibung und Bestimmung der Farbe verlässt sich von Monkiewitsch häufig auf das Gesetz des Zufalls. Ein Freund oder Bekannter wählt eine Farbe, und der Künstler, ohne sie zu kennen, eine andere. Hier mischen sich Zufall und Gesetzmäßigkeit. Und dabei kommt es, wie die Bilder zeigen, immer wieder zu starken und schönen Farbkontrasten. Allerdings gibt es im Werk von Lienhard von Monkiewitsch auch eine Konstante, einen farblichen Effekt, der stets aufs Neue auftritt und so etwas wie die Signatur dieses Œuvres darstellt. Es ist das ganz und gar außergewöhnliche Schwarz in seinen Bildern, ebenso samten wie strahlend, ebenso fragil wie robust. Die Wirkung erreicht der Maler, indem er in die noch feuchte schwarze Ölschicht zusätzliche schwarze Pigmente streut. Sie sorgen dafür, dass dieses Schwarz wirklich alles Licht absorbiert und im Bild einen intensiven Tiefenraum öffnet. Der Eindruck steigert sich noch, wenn der Maler das Pigment verwischt und so um die Farbfläche herum einen Hof erzeugt, eine dunkle Gloriole, welche die Körperlichkeit des Schwarz weiter intensiviert. Dadurch kommt es zu einem paradoxen Changieren zwischen Fläche und Raum. Die Farbfelder nehmen Masse auf und weiten das Bild hin in eine unbestimmte Tiefe. Unvermittelt tritt eine architekturale Komponente ins Bild, welche die Werke mit dem Frühwerk verbindet, und zugleich fühlt man sich an das Trompe l'œil erinnert, mit dem von Monkiewitschs allerneueste Möbelskulpturen operieren.

Des Künstlers Strategien der Bildfindung mit den Mitteln von System und Zufall – einem stets planvoll ins Werk gesetzten und damit, so paradox es auch klingen mag, letztlich systematisch operierenden Zufall – erinnern an die Denkmodelle der Strukturalisten. Wie diese die Vielfalt der Erscheinungen in Welt und Gesellschaft, Sprache und Kultur aus den ihnen zu Grunde liegenden Strukturen ableiten, so schafft von Monkiewitsch eine Vielzahl von Kompositionen durch Wahl weniger Bildelemente, die er vielfältig kombiniert. Den Künstler und den Denker unterscheidet nur die Bewegungsrichtung. Der eine erklärt die vorhandene Welt, der andere baut eine neue auf. Während der strukturalistische Denker die Komplexität des Seienden mit Hilfe seines analytischen Modells zurückführt auf das Wirken einiger weniger Parameter, operiert der strukturalistische Künstler als eine Art Demiurg – indes ohne jede pathetische und romantische Überhöhung der mit Hilfe der von ihm gewählten und stets neu arrangierten Parameter eine eigene künstlerische Welt schafft. Daher hat der französische Kulturphilosoph Roland Barthes unter dem Stichwort der „strukturalistischen Tätigkeit" die Denker und Interpreten zu Recht in eine Reihe gestellt mit den Künstlern und Produzenten.[2]

„Was man sieht ist, was man sieht?" Nein, wir sehen die Dinge nicht, weil sie sichtbar sind, sondern sie werden sichtbar, weil wir sie sehen. Nach wie vor gilt das Goethe-Wort: „Man sieht nur, was man weiß." Der Lakonismus von Form und Farbe seiner *Black Paintings* hat Stella nicht daran gehindert, ihnen bedeutungsschwere Titel zu geben. Sie beziehen sich auf William Blake, Charles Baudelaire und Duke Ellington, auf die Elendsviertel amerikanischer Großstädte und die Terror-Herrschaft der Nationalsozialisten. Das Paradox zwischen semantisch aufgeladenem Titel und semantisch leerer Form hat die Exegeten zu Recht nicht ruhen lassen. Die Farbe Schwarz im symbolischen Sinne mit der Düsternis der Werktitel kurzzuschließen und daraus eine Botschaft von Trauer, Bedrückung und Depression zu destillieren, war ein Leichtes. Sehr viel schwerer war es, in den auf Wiederholung, Symmetrie und Opposition gründenden Formschemata der Stella-Bilder die Formprinzipien der Beckettschen Stücke zu erkennen und in den Bildern wie den Texten einen identischen *élan vital* des Absurden auszumachen. Aber den detektivisch vorgehenden Exegeten war nicht verborgen geblieben, dass Stella sich bereits in einer seiner Vorzeichnungen zu der *Pre-Black Series* identifikatorisch auf Beckett bezogen hatte: „I am long and thin, I have one eye, and I don't cry"[3] Oder in der Terminologie des großen Iren: „Alles eine unendliche Wiederkehr"[4].

charged title and semantically empty form to rest. To short-circuit the color black in a symbolic sense with the gloom of the title of the work and to distill from it a message of sadness, dejection, and depression did not present a problem. It was much more difficult to recognize the principles of form of Beckett's plays in the formal schemes of Stella's paintings, which are based on repetition, symmetry, and opposition, and to discern an identical *élan vital* of the absurd in the paintings as well as the texts. But it did not remain hidden to the exegetes, who proceeded in a detective-like fashion, that Stella had already made identificatory reference to Beckett in the preliminary drawings to his *Pre-Black Series:* "I am long and thin, I have one eye, and I don't cry."[3] Or in the terminology of the Great Irishman: "All an eternal recurrence."[4]

1   Aus einem Interview mit dem Titel „New Nihilism or New Art?", geführt von Bruce Glaser mit Frank Stella und Donald Judd. Ausgestrahlt von WBAI-FM, New York, im Februar 1964. Veröffentlicht unter dem Titel „Questions to Stella and Judd", in: *Artnews*, September 1966, S.55–61.

2   Roland Barthes, „Die strukturalistische Tätigkeit", in: *Kursbuch 5*, Frankfurt am Main 1966, S.190.

3   Hubertus Gaßner, „Der Raum bewohnbarer Illusionen", *Frank Stella*, Ausstellungskatalog, Haus der Kunst München, München 1996, S.80.

4   Samuel Beckett, „Aus einem aufgegebenen Werk", in: *Stücke. Kleine Prosa, Auswahl in einem Band*, Frankfurt am Main 1969, S.241.

1   Taken from an interview entitled "New Nihilism or New Art?" conducted by Bruce Glaser with Frank Stella and Donald Judd. It was broadcast on WBAI-FM, New York, in February 1964. Published under the title "Questions to Stella and Judd," *Artnews*, September 1966, pp.55–61.

2   Roland Barthes, "Die strukturalistische Tätigkeit," *Kursbuch* 5 (Frankfurt am Main, 1966), p.190.

3   Hubertus Gaßner, "Der Raum bewohnbarer Illusionen," *Frank Stella*, exh. cat., Haus der Kunst München (Munich, 1996), p.80.

4   Samuel Beckett, "Aus einem aufgegebenen Werk," *Stücke: Kleine Prosa, Auswahl in einem Band* (Frankfurt am Main, 1969), p.241.

Elke Bippus

Serielle Taten: Kunstgeschichtliche Dekonstruktionen.
Zu den seriellen Zeichnungen von Lienhard von Monkiewitsch

Serial Deeds: Art-Historical Deconstructions. On the Serial Drawings by Lienhard von Monkiewitsch

In 2004, the *Fibonacci Drawings* by Lienhard von Monkiewitsch were shown at the exhibition "Infinite Possibilities: Serial Imagery in 20th-Century Drawings."[1] The exhibition presented serial images primarily from the 1960s and 1990s which contained aspects of infinity and intermediality with regard to artistic, linguistic and mathematic working methods.

Seriality as a methodical process based on rules is a phenomenon of modern art. Regularity as a characteristic of the series emerged with Claude Monet's series.[2] The law of a series of images or serial painting is produced with the repetition of a motif, a specific perspective, a dimension, or a stylistic design. The series distinguishes itself from subject, variation, or group of works in its regularity.[3] The serial principle is necessarily linked with self-reflectivity. Thus Claude Monet's paintings may be based on real motifs; they were, however, no longer of interest solely in a depictive sense. Rather they became an opportunity to fathom out the possibilities of creative processes. Serial painting of the twentieth century, for example that by Piet Mondrian or Josef Albers, underscores self-reflectivity by expressing the serial principles with the aid of concrete geometric forms.

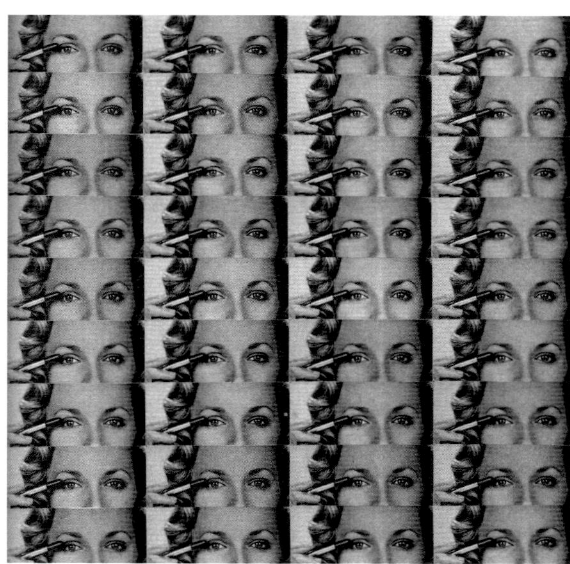

Peter Roehr, *o. T.* (FO-29), 1965
Untitled (FO-29), Papier auf Karton, 22,4 × 23,4 cm | Paper on cardboard

Im Jahr 2004 wurden die *Fibonacci Zeichnungen* Lienhard von Monkiewitschs in der Ausstellung *Infinite Possibilities: Serial Imagery in 20th-Century Drawings*[1] gezeigt. Die Ausstellung präsentierte serielle Zeichnungen vornehmlich aus den 1960er und 90er Jahren, die Aspekte der Unendlichkeit und Intermedialität zu musischen, sprachlichen und mathematischen Arbeitsweisen aufweisen.

Serialität als ein auf Regeln basierendes methodisches Verfahren ist ein Phänomen moderner Kunst. Mit den Serien von Claude Monet trat die Regelhaftigkeit als Charakteristikum der Serie hervor.[2] Das Gesetz einer Bildserie oder seriellen Malerei bildet sich mit der Wiederholung eines Motivs, einer bestimmten Perspektive, eines Maßes oder einer stilistischen Gestaltung. In ihrer Gesetzmäßigkeit unterscheidet sich die Serie von Thema, Variation oder Werkgruppe.[3] Das serielle Prinzip ist notwendigerweise mit Selbstreflexivität verknüpft. So liegen Claude Monets Bildern zwar reale Motive zugrunde, diese waren jedoch nicht mehr allein im abbildlichen Sinne von Interesse, sie wurden vielmehr zum Anlass, bildkünstlerische Verfahren in ihren Möglichkeiten auszuloten. Die serielle Malerei des 20. Jahrhunderts, etwa die von Piet Mondrian oder Josef Albers, unterstreicht die Selbstreflexivität, indem die seriellen Prinzipien mit Hilfe konkreter geometrischer Formen zum Ausdruck gebracht werden.

Lienhard von Monkiewitschs Arbeiten wurden in *Infinite Possibilities* im Kontext von Arbeiten aus den 1960er Jahren gezeigt. In dieser Zeit gewann Serialität in den USA und in Europa durch das Prinzip der technischen Reproduzierbarkeit und der Selbstreflexivität des seriellen Konzeptes innerhalb einer Arbeit an neuer Qualität. Beispielhaft hierfür sind etwa die Siebdrucke Andy Warhols oder die Collagen Peter Roehrs, welche auf massenmedialen Motiven basieren, aber auch eher systemorientierte Arbeiten wie die *Serial Projects* von Sol LeWitt oder serielle Arbeiten von Charlotte Posenenske. Die Produktion in Serie war in kunsttheoretischer, konzeptueller und gesellschaftspolitischer Hinsicht bedeutsam. Mit ihr richteten sich Künstler zugunsten von permutativen, progressiven, rationalen wie irrationalen Verfahrensweisen gegen den Ausdrucksgehalt von Kunst und die Bindung von Kunst an die Tätigkeit eines Künstlersubjekts. Oder sie verfolgten gesellschaftskritische Anliegen, die mit den Stichworten Demokratisierung von Kunst, Ars Multiplicata und Interaktivität angespielt sind.[4] Vor allem ist Serialität aber mit Prozessualität verknüpft und damit mit Zeit. Nicht allein das Machen, sondern auch die Betrachtung serieller Arbeiten im zwei- wie dreidimensionalen Medium, wird als ein Prozess erfahren. Dieses Charakteristikum ist auch kunsttheoretisch von zentraler Bedeutung, da hier die Kunst strukturell dem Medium der Schrift analog wird: Serialität gehorcht nicht mehr der Vorstellung der Augenblicklichkeit, des unmittelbaren Sehens, der Präsenz, sondern ist dem Lesen vergleichbar. Die Produktion wie die Rezeption serieller Kunst wird als Handlung erfahren.

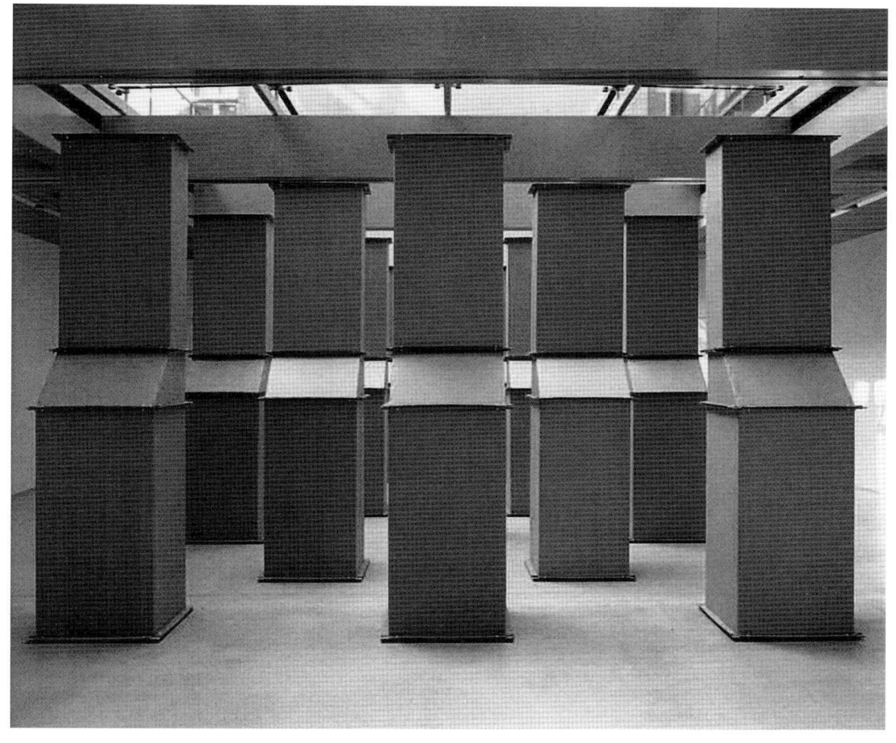

Von verschiedenen Seiten wurde festgestellt, dass der konkrete wie imagi-
nierte Raum im Zentrum der Werke von Lienhard von Monkiewitsch steht.[5]
Der Künstler veranschaulicht meines Erachtens mit seiner Technik, Pigment
in die Ölfarbe einzureiben, das imaginative Moment der konkreten Malerei
selbst und widerspricht damit dem Glauben, alles Erzählerische zugunsten
des vermeintlich rein Faktischen austreiben zu können. Über seine Arbeit sagt
Lienhard von Monkiewitsch: „Das Schwarz, die Spuren der Arbeitsprozesse
und die Sprache der Materialien sind emotional genug".[6] Für die ästhetische
Artikulation dieses Interesses an ephemeren und materiellen Aspekten ist die
serielle Struktur von großer Bedeutung. Sie sensibilisiert die Betrachter für
eben diese Modi. Das einfache System entwickelt in der Anschauung einen
ästhetischen Reiz und verbindet so das kognitive Erkennen mit einem perzep-
tiven Genuss. Diesem Ansatz und der von Lienhard von Monkiewitsch humor-
und lustvoll betriebenen Dekonstruktion kunstgeschichtlicher Mythen kommt
das Arbeiten in Serie entgegen, da es ein Sehen und Lesen mobilisiert.

Lienhard von Monkiewitsch arbeitet bereits seit 1969 in Serie. Zunächst
waren es allerdings thematische Bildserien wie die *Fußböden* (1969–1973) und
ab 1977 die Werkserie *Architekturen*.[7] Die Arbeiten ab 1983 möchte ich im en-
geren Sinne als serielle Malerei bezeichnen. In ihnen sind serielle Verfahren
zur Bildgenerierung eingesetzt, Serialität ist hier eher methodisches Prinzip.
Den Darstellungsweisen der seriellen Kunst in den 1960er Jahren vergleichbar,
nutzt der Künstler mathematische Gesetze und ein geometrisch modulares
Bildinventar, das ihn frei von gemeinhin erwarteten Bilderfindungen macht.
Mit *6-teiliges Rechteck* (1983, S.78/79) hat sich Lienhard von Monkiewitsch von

In "Infinite Possibilities," Lienhard von Monkiewitsch's
works were shown within the context of works from
the 1960s. At the time, seriality achieved new quality in
the United States and Europe through the principle of
mechanical reproduction and the self-reflection of the
serial concept within a work. Andy Warhol's silk-screens
and Peter Roehr's collages, which are based on mass
medial motifs, are exemplary of this, as are more system-
oriented works such as Sol LeWitt's *Serial Projects* or
the serial works by Charlotte Posenenske. Producing in
series was significant from an art-theoretical, conceptual,
and sociopolitical point of view. Artists leveled against
the expressive content of art and the commitment of art
to the activity of an artist subject in favor of permuta-
tive, progressive, rational, as well as irrational methods.
Or they pursued matters critical of society, alluded to
with keywords such as the democratization of art, Ars
Multiplicata, and interactivity.[4] However, seriality is
primarily linked with processuality and thus with time.
Not only the production of, but also the viewing of serial
works in a two- as well as a three-dimensional medium
is experienced as a process. This characteristic is also of
central importance from an art-theoretical perspective,
as here, art is structurally analogue to the medium of
writing: Seriality no longer obeys the idea of immediacy,
direct seeing, presence, but is comparable to reading.
The production as well as the reception of serial art is
experienced as an act.

Lienhard von Monkiewitsch's work focuses on concrete as well as imaginary space.[5] In my opinion, the artist's technique of rubbing pigment into the oil paint illus-
trates the imaginative element of concrete painting and
thus contradicts the belief in being able to drive out
everything narrative in favor of what is supposedly purely
factual. Lienhard von Monkiewitsch once made the following comment about his work: "The black, the traces of
the working process, and the language of the materials
are emotional enough."[6] The serial structure is of primary
importance for the aesthetic articulation of this interest
in ephemeral and material aspects. It makes the viewer
aware of precisely these modes. The simple system develops an aesthetic appeal and in this way connects cog-
nitive recognition with perceptive pleasure. Because it
mobilizes seeing and reading, working in series accom-
modates this approach and the deconstruction of art-
historical myths pursued by Lienhard von Monkiewitsch
with both humor and joy.

Lienhard von Monkiewitsch has been working in series since 1969. Initially, however, they were thematic series of images such as *Fußböden* (1969–73), and beginning in 1977 the sequence *Architekturen*.[7] I would like to
refer to the works after 1983, in which the artist implements serial methods to generate images, as serial painting in a stricter sense; seriality is more of a methodical
principle. Comparable to the representation of serial art

in the 1960s, the artist uses laws of mathematics and a geometrically modular stock of images, which makes him independent of generally expected pictorial inventions. With *6-teiliges Rechteck* (1983, pp. 78/79), Lienhard von Monkiewitsch parted with intuitive pictorial composition. From this time on he uses modules such as rectangle, square, parallelogram, straight line, and triangle and develops systems for these modules that generate images.[8] Six partial forms are to be arbitrarily arranged on a rectangular grid divided up into twenty squares of the same size and emphasized according to color. Lienhard von Monkiewitsch bases this on various modules: six squares of the same size which correspond to the division of the grid; a rectangle the size of two squares and two isosceles triangles produced from the diagonal cut of one of the grid's squares. Von Monkiewitsch carries out the distribution of these modules on the one hand, while on the other hand using a technique that allows coincidence to intervene: He throws sample shapes out of cardboard which correspond to the modules onto a format he has laid out on the floor. If a module lands outside the grid, the throw has to be repeated. Throws with overlapping shapes are transferred onto 20 × 16 cm paper.[9] The artist extends this methodical process and allows a systematic method and the play of coincidence mesh with one another, such as, for example, in the group of works *Konstruktion mit den aufeinander folgenden Fibonacci-Zahlen* using several bright colors. The construction of the painting is not carried out according to compositional points of view or imaginative-intuitive ideas, rather it is exactly determined in accordance with the Fibonacci numbers,[10] in which here, too, different variations are possible, for instance in the constructions with the numbers 13−21−34−55−89 (pp. 146/147). Lienhard von Monkiewitsch again leaves the distribution of color in this series to coincidence: One color is mixed by the artist, the other color is mixed by another person without knowing which color von Monkiewitsch has chosen. In this way, composition and color are removed from compositional restrictions as well as the artist's feeling for aesthetics or taste. The pleasure lies in the doing.

With his working method, on the one hand Lienhard von Monkiewitsch adopts the model of the artist that began in the 1960s with the dethronization of the artist as creator and which Sol LeWitt's formulation on the serial artist gets to the heart of: "The serial artist does not attempt to produce a beautiful or mysterious object but functions merely as a clerk cataloging the results of his premise."[11] On the other hand, he shifts the serial concept developed at the time by attaching great importance to doing things manually. Von Monkiewitsch is not concerned with the aesthetic surprise as demanded by modern art theory; rather he wants to be surprised himself. He uses processes which are open for the unexpected, not leaning on traditional and conventionalized patterns

der intuitiven Bildfindung verabschiedet. Fortan nutzt er Module wie Rechteck, Quadrat, Parallelogramm, Gerade und Dreieck und entwickelt für diese Module Systeme, die in bildgenerierender Weise wirksam werden.[8] Auf ein rechteckiges, in zwanzig gleich große Quadrate unterteiltes Rasterfeld sollen sechs Teilformen beliebig angeordnet und farblich hervorgehoben werden können. Lienhard von Monkiewitsch legt verschiedene Module zugrunde: sechs gleich große Quadrate, die der Rastereinteilung entsprechen; ein Rechteck in der Größe von zwei Quadraten und zwei gleichschenklige Dreiecke, die aus dem Diagonalschnitt eines der Rasterquadrate gewonnen wurden. Die Verteilung dieser Module wird einerseits von Lienhard von Monkiewitsch vorgenommen, andererseits nutzt er eine Technik, die den Zufall eingreifen lässt: Er wirft Musterformen aus Pappe, die den Modulen entsprechen, auf ein Format, das er auf den Boden gelegt hat. Liegt ein Modul außerhalb des Rasters, muss der Wurf wiederholt werden. Dagegen werden Würfe mit sich überlagernden Formen auf das Papierformat von 20 × 16 cm übertragen.[9] Dieses methodische Verfahren baut der Künstler aus und lässt ein systematisches Vorgehen und das Spiel des Zufalls ineinander greifen. So beispielsweise in der Werkgruppe *Konstruktion mit den aufeinander folgenden Fibonacci-Zahlen* mit mehreren Buntfarben. Die Bildkonstruktion erfolgt nicht nach kompositorischen Gesichtspunkten oder imaginativ-intuitiven Vorstellungen, sondern wird den Fibonacci-Zahlen[10] gemäß exakt bestimmt, wobei auch hier unterschiedliche Varianten möglich sind, wie beispielsweise in den Konstruktionen mit den Zahlen 13−21−34−55−89 (S. 146/147). Die Farbverteilung dieser Serie überlässt Lienhard von Monkiewitsch erneut dem Zufall: Eine Farbe mischt der Künstler, die andere Farbe wird von einer anderen Person gemischt, ohne Kenntnis der von Lienhard von Monkiewitsch gewählten Farbe. Komposition

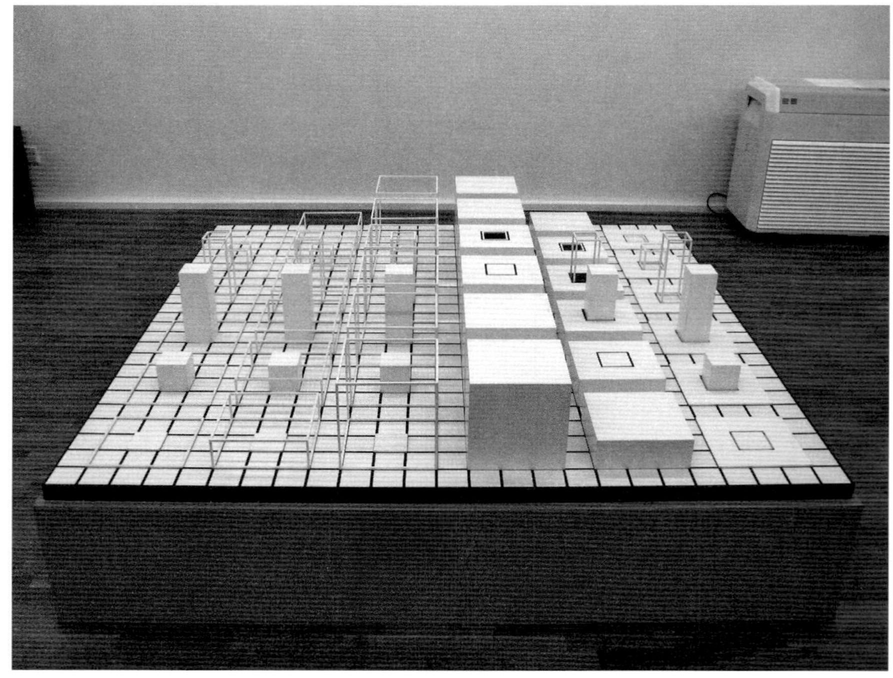

Sol LeWitt, *Serial Project No. 1 (ABCD)*, 1966, Eisen, einbrennlackiert, 22,5 × 175,0 × 175,0 cm | Galvanized iron, Installationsansicht | Exhibition view, Museum für Gegenwartskunst, Siegen 2005, Foto | Photograph: Elke Bippus

und Farbigkeit werden hierdurch dem kompositionellen Zugriff wie dem ästhetischen oder geschmacklichen Empfinden des Künstlers weitestgehend entzogen. Der Genuss liegt im Machen selbst.

Lienhard von Monkiewitsch übernimmt mit seiner Arbeitsweise einerseits das Modell vom Künstler, das in den sechziger Jahren mit der Entthronung des Künstlerschöpfers einsetzte und in Sol LeWitts Formulierung zum seriellen Künstler auf den Punkt gebracht ist: „Der serielle Künstler versucht nicht, ein schönes und geheimnisvolles Objekt herzustellen, sondern fungiert lediglich wie ein Angestellter, der die Resultate seiner Prämisse katalogisiert".[11] Andererseits verschiebt er die zu dieser Zeit entwickelte Serienkonzeption, indem er dem Machen, dem manuellen Tun großes Gewicht verleiht. Es geht Lienhard von Monkiewitsch nicht um die ästhetische Überraschung, wie sie von der Kunsttheorie der Moderne eingefordert wurde, vielmehr möchte er sich selbst überraschen lassen. Er nutzt Verfahren, die für Unvorhersehbares offen sind, und stützt sich gerade nicht auf tradierte und konventionalisierte Darstellungsmuster. Er beugt aber auch explizit dem Missverständnis einer Überhöhung der geistigen Konzeption vor. Diese Kritik wurde wiederholt für die Conceptual Art formuliert, war allerdings schon in der Minimal Art angelegt, insofern in ihr durch die Setzung eines seriellen Systems und die Serienfertigung die Tätigkeit des Künstlers auf die Herstellung eines Konzepts reduziert ist. Lienhard von Monkiewitsch stellt im Unterschied dazu die Prozessualität und die manuelle Realisierung eines Konzepts zur Schau und kennzeichnet dieses so als ein Denken mit der Hand. Das serielle Gesetz ist ohne seine Realisierung Makulatur – erst im Vollzug kommt es in seinen Möglichkeiten zur Wirkung. Transparent wird zudem die Abhängigkeit des Künstlers vom gesetzten System, insofern „jede Arbeit, die innerhalb der Serie nach den ‚Gesetzen' des Konzeptes entstanden ist, [...] ‚angenommen' werden [muss] auch wenn das Ergebnis dem Künstler anfänglich oder auf Dauer befremdlich erscheint".[12]

Die Serie *Zwei Schnitte in das suprematistische Quadrat* (S. 95, 97) basiert auf einem 1985 entwickelten Bildprogramm mit einer Fülle von Möglichkeiten. Lienhard von Monkiewitsch schneidet zwei Schnitte in das suprematistische Quadrat, das für Kasimir Malewitsch Modell und System einer neuen Gesellschaft war, Beginn einer neuen klassischen Form, eines neuen Geistes. Die Schnitte in das Quadrat bleiben auf dem zweiten Blatt nahezu unbemerkt, sie geraten dann durch die Ausbildung von Ecken und Kanten in den Blick und in Bewegung. Lienhard von Monkiewitsch entwickelt diese Bildformen, indem er von einem Pappquadrat zwei Dreiecksformen abschneidet, und sie in systematischer Weise – etwa spiegelverkehrt oder um 180° gedreht – an die Restform anlegt und um sie herumwandern lässt. Die jeweilige Umrissform liefert die Bildformen der Serie in Öl und Pigment auf Karton. In *Zwei Schnitte in das suprematistische Quadrat* hat Kunst nicht mehr die Funktion, ein Bild oder eine Idee zu setzen, sondern sie entfaltet ein Feld von Möglichkeiten. Die Ikone, das suprematistische Quadrat, wird nicht als untaugliches Modell verworfen, aber den veränderten gesellschaftlich-politischen Kontexten und Kunsttheorien entsprechend verschoben. Kunst kann und sollte nicht an die Stelle

of representation. But he also explicitly prevents the misunderstanding of a superelevation of the mental concept. This criticism was repeatedly formulated for Conceptual Art; however, it was already laid out in Minimal Art to the extent that the activity of the artist is reduced to the production of a concept through the posit of a serial system and through serial manufacture. In contrast to this, Lienhard von Monkiewitsch puts the processuality and the manual realization of a concept on display and characterizes this as thinking with one's hands. Without its realization, the serial law is rubbish – its possibilities do not take effect until it has been enforced. In addition, the dependence of the artist on the posited system becomes transparent to the extent that "each work created within the series according to the 'laws' of the concept must be 'accepted,' even if the result – initially or permanently – seems disconcerting to the artist."[12]

The series *Zwei Schnitte in das suprematistische Quadrat* (pp. 95, 97) is based on a program of images with an abundance of possibilities. Lienhard von Monkiewitsch makes two cuts in the suprematist square, which for Kasimir Malevich was the model and system of a new society; the beginning of a new, classic form, of a new spirit. On the second sheet, the cuts in the square remain nearly unnoticed; they become visible and begin to move through the formation of corners and edges. Von Monkiewitsch develops these forms by cutting two triangles off a cardboard square and systematically – either as a mirror image or rotated 180 degrees – applying them to the remaining form and allowing them to wander around it. The shape of the respective outline supplies the forms for the series of paintings in oil paint and pigment on cardboard. In *Zwei Schnitte in das suprematistische Quadrat,* art no longer has the function of positing an image or an idea, rather it opens out an array of possibilities. The icon, the suprematist square, is not condemned as an unsuitable model, but shifted to correspond to altered sociopolitical contexts and art theories. Art cannot – and should not – take the place of religious or political structures. Rather, like the black square in Lienhard von Monkiewitsch's series, these should begin to rotate. In his serial works, the artist parts with the myths still being reproduced by art history, such as that of the artist genius and artistic creation, by making the working processes visible in his series. While doing so, von Monkiewitsch's paintings and his attitude are anything but sustained by thoughts of loss. The room for maneuver of art is made the most of in a joyful and humorous way.

religiöser oder politischer Strukturen treten, diese sollten vielmehr wie das schwarze Quadrat in Lienhard von Monkiewitschs Serien in Rotation geraten. Der Künstler verabschiedet sich in seinen seriellen Arbeiten von immer noch reproduzierten Mythen der Kunstgeschichte, wie die vom Künstlergenie und der künstlerischen Schöpfung, indem er in seinen Serien seine Arbeitsprozesse ablesbar macht. Die Bilder und die Haltung Lienhard von Monkiewitschs sind dabei alles andere als von einem Verlustdenken getragen. In lust- und humorvoller Weise wird der Handlungsspielraum von Kunst ausgekostet.

1 *Infinite Possibilities: Serial Imagery in 20th-Century Drawings,* exh. cat. Davis Museum and Cultural Center (Wellesley, MA, 2004).
2 In the arts, the notion of the series was wide open until way into the nineteenth century. It was sufficient for pictures to be by one artist and have similar themes to refer to them as a series. On Claude Monet's series, compare Grace Seiberling, *Monet's Series* (New York, 1981).
3 Compare Gottfried Boehm, "Die Logik der Verwandlung: Zur Bildgeschichte der klassischen Moderne," *Die Metamorphosen der Bilder,* exh. cat. Sprengel Museum Hannover (Hannover, 1992), pp. 16–29.

4 The participation objects of Ars Multiplicata connected the democratization of art with an activation of the viewer, the consumer, a term that at the time had a positive connotation. Many of the objects were committed to the principle of "Do it yourself."
5 Compare Walter Vitt, *Lienhard v. Monkiewitsch,* Kunst der Gegenwart aus Niedersachsen, vol. 43 (Hannover, 1994); Michael Stoeber, "Über Lienhard von Monkiewitsch. Metamorphosen der Bildstruktur," *Künstler: Kritisches Lexikon der Gegenwartskunst* 68, no. 27 (4th Quarter 2004), pp. 3–11.
6 Lienhard von Monkiewitsch, cited in *Künstler: Kritisches Lexikon der Gegenwartskunst* 2004 (see note 5), p. 2.
7 Illustrations in Vitt 1994 (see note 5), nos. 2, 11, and 16.

8 Between 1983 and 1993, Lienhard von Monkiewitsch developed a total of fourteen image systems. He still uses eight of these for his current productions. Cf. Vitt 1994 (see note 5), pp. 81 f.
9 The pictorial solutions of *6-teiliges Rechteck* then became the point of departure for three-dimensional works. See the detailed interpretation by Vitt 1994 (see note 5), pp. 72 f.
10 The Fibonacci series results through the addition of two successive numbers: 0, 1, 1, 2, 3, 5, 8, etc.
11 Sol LeWitt, *Serial Project No. 1 (ABCD),* reproduced in *Minimal Art. Eine kritische Retrospektive,* ed. Gregor Stemmrich (Dresden, 1995), pp. 181–184, pp. 181 f.
12 Vitt 1994 (see note 5), p. 70.

1 *Infinite Possibilities: Serial Imagery in 20th-Century Drawings,* Ausst.-Kat. Davis Museum and Cultural Center Wellesley, Massachusetts 2004.
2 Bis ins 19. Jahrhundert hinein war der Serienbegriff in den Künsten sehr offen. Um von einer Serie zu sprechen, reichte es aus, dass die Bilder von einem Künstler waren und ähnliche Themen behandelten. Vgl. zu den Serien Claude Monets: Grace Seiberling: *Monet's Series,* New York 1981.
3 Vgl. hierzu Gottfried Boehm, „Die Logik der Verwandlung. Zur Bildgeschichte der klassischen Moderne", in: *Die Metamorphosen der Bilder.* Ausst.-Kat. Sprengel Museum, Hannover 1992, S. 16–29.
4 Die Partizipationsobjekte der Ars Multiplicata verbanden die Demokratisierung der Kunst mit einer Aktivierung der Betrachter, Konsumenten; ein zu dieser Zeit positiv konnotierter Begriff. Viele Objekte waren dem Prinzip des „Do it yourself" verpflichtet.
5 Vgl. Walter Vitt, *Lienhard v. Monkiewitsch,* Hannover 1994; Michael Stoeber, „Über Lienhard von Monkiewitsch. Metamorphosen der Bildstruktur", in: *Künstler. Kritisches Lexikon der Gegenwartskunst,* Ausgabe 68, Heft 27, 4. Quartal 2004, S. 3–11.
6 Lienhard von Monkiewitsch 1992, zitiert nach: *Künstler. Kritisches Lexikon der Gegenwartskunst* (wie Anm. 5), S. 2.

7 Abbildungen in: Vitt (wie Anm. 5), Abb. 2, 11, 16.
8 Lienhard von Monkiewitsch hat zwischen 1983 und 1993 insgesamt vierzehn unterschiedliche Bildsysteme entwickelt. Acht dieser Bildprogramme nutzt er noch für seine aktuellen Produktionen. Dazu: Vitt (wie Anm. 5), S. 81 f.
9 Die Bildlösungen von *6-teiliges Rechteck* wurden dann zum Ausgangspunkt dreidimensionaler Arbeiten. Siehe hierzu die ausführliche Darstellung von Vitt (wie Anm. 5), S. 72 f.
10 Die Fibonacci-Reihe entsteht durch die Addition zwei aufeinander folgender Zahlen: 0, 1, 1, 2, 3, 5, 8 usw.
11 Sol LeWitt, *Serial Project No. 1 (ABCD),* 1966, in: Gregor Stemmrich (Hrsg.), *Minimal Art. Eine kritische Retrospektive,* Dresden 1995, S. 181–184, hier S. 181 f.
12 Vitt (wie Anm. 5), S. 70.

Abbildungen | Illustrations

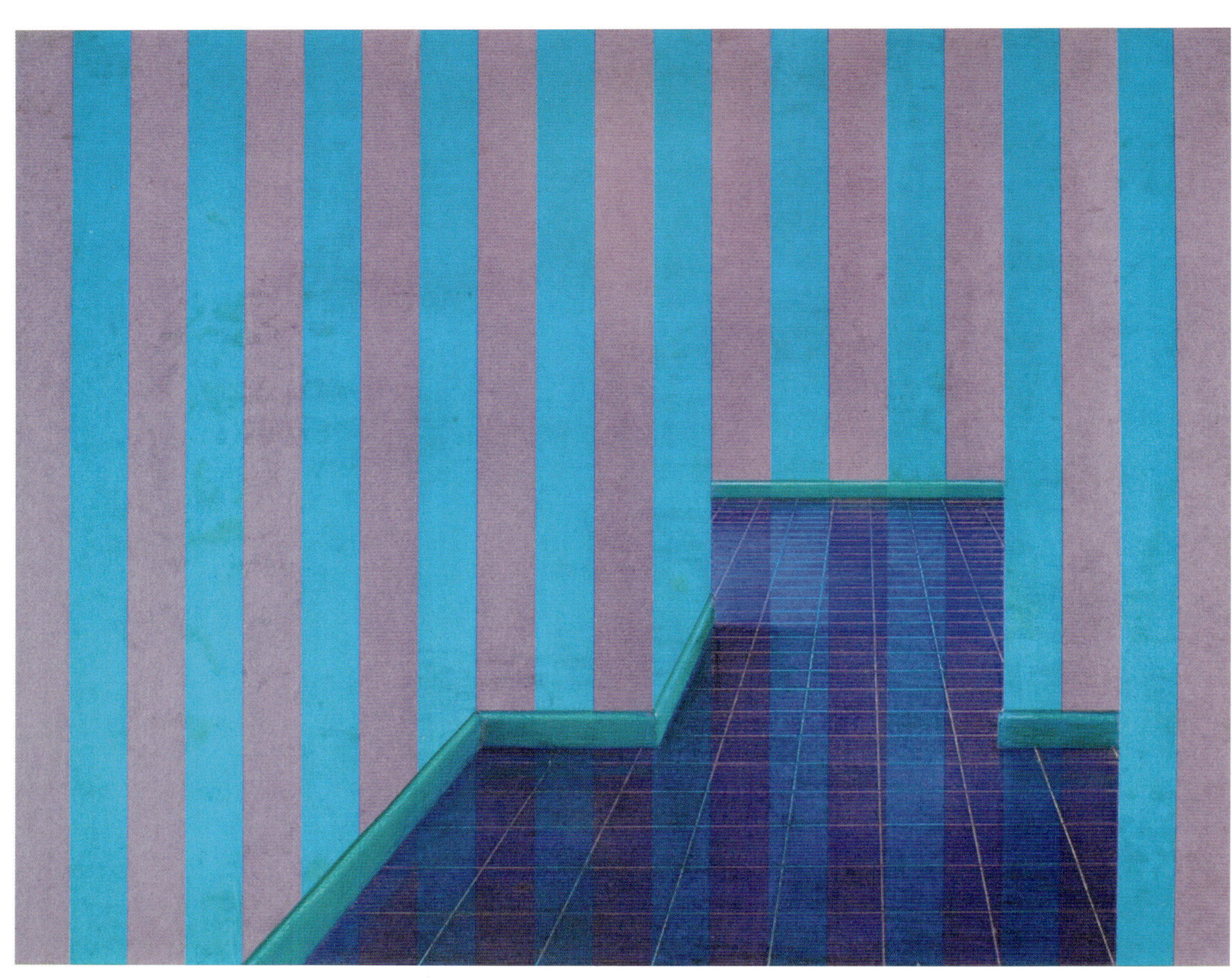

Streifenraum (Versuch), 1970
Striped Space (Attempt)
Farbstift auf Geschenkpapier, 34,5 × 43,5 cm
Colored pencil on gift-wrapping paper

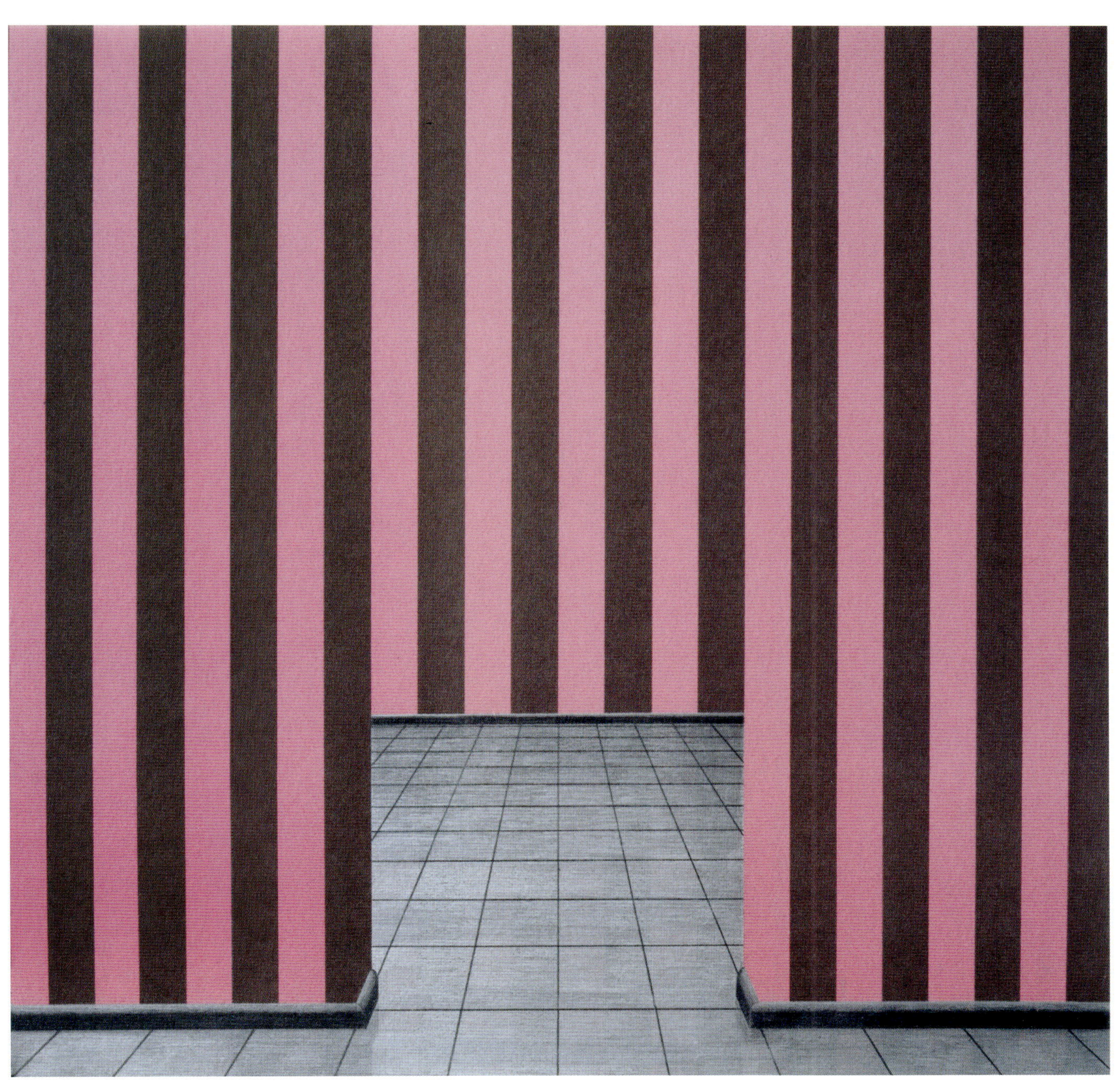

Streifenraum, 1969,
Striped Space
Farbstift auf Geschenkpapier, 47 × 50 cm
Colored pencil on gift-wrapping paper

Abknickender Gang, 1969
Bending Space
Dispersion und Kunstharz auf Jute, 180 × 210 cm
Dispersion and synthetic resin on jute

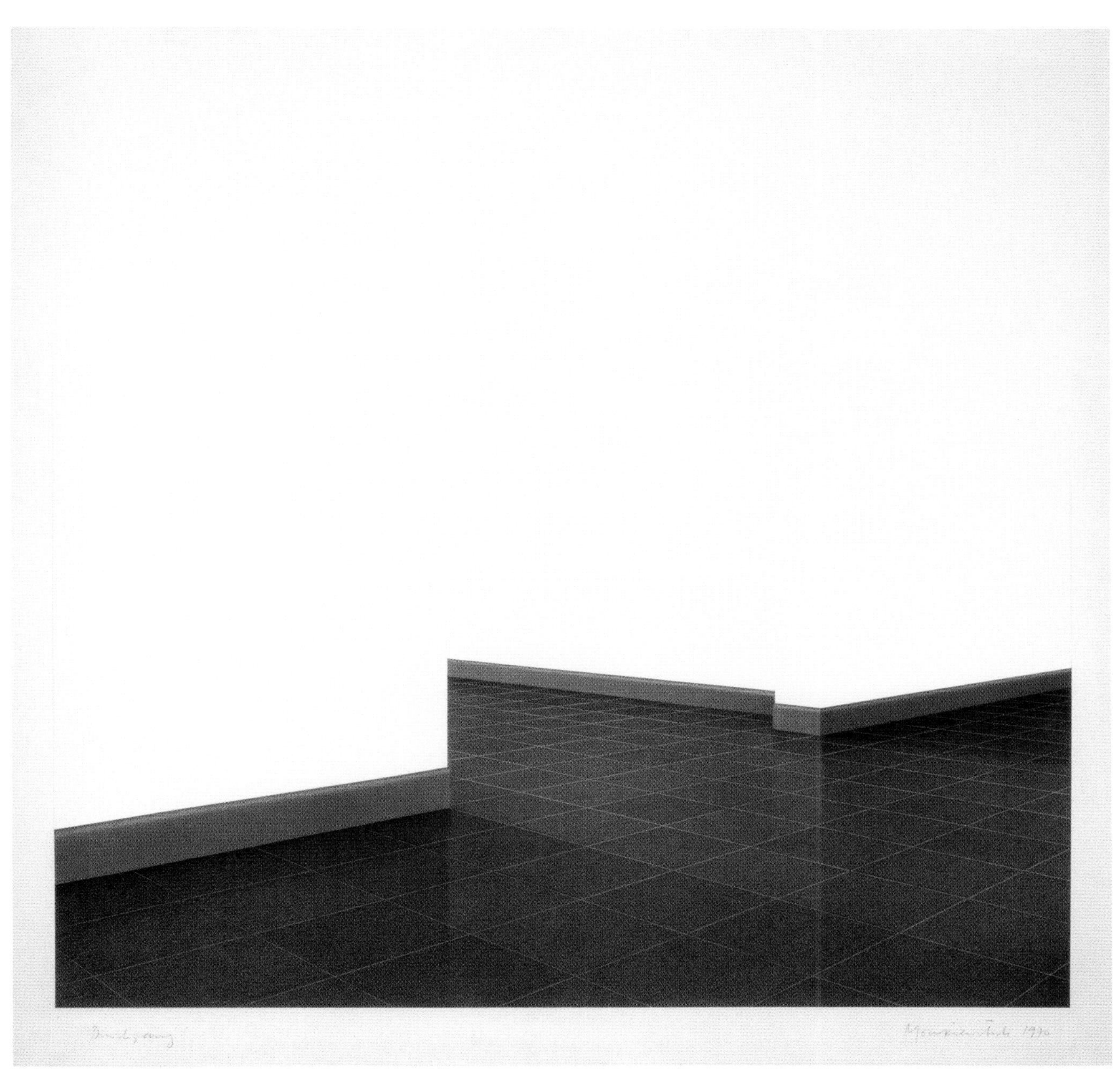

Durchgang, 1970
Corridor
Farbstift auf Karton, 60 × 60 cm
Colored pencil on cardboard

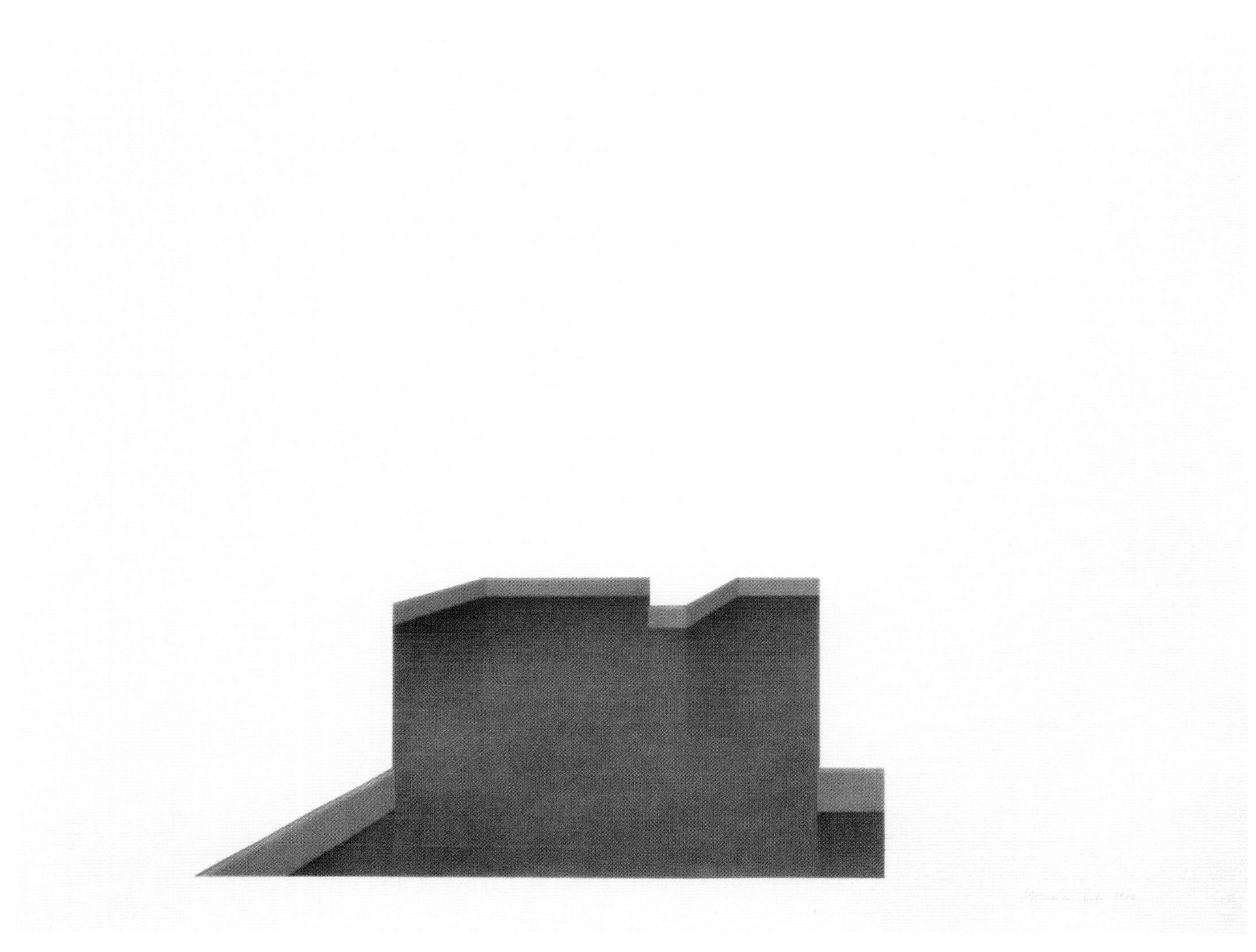

Raum xxv, 1970
Space xxv
Farbstift auf Karton, 62,5 × 81 cm
Colored pencil on cardboard

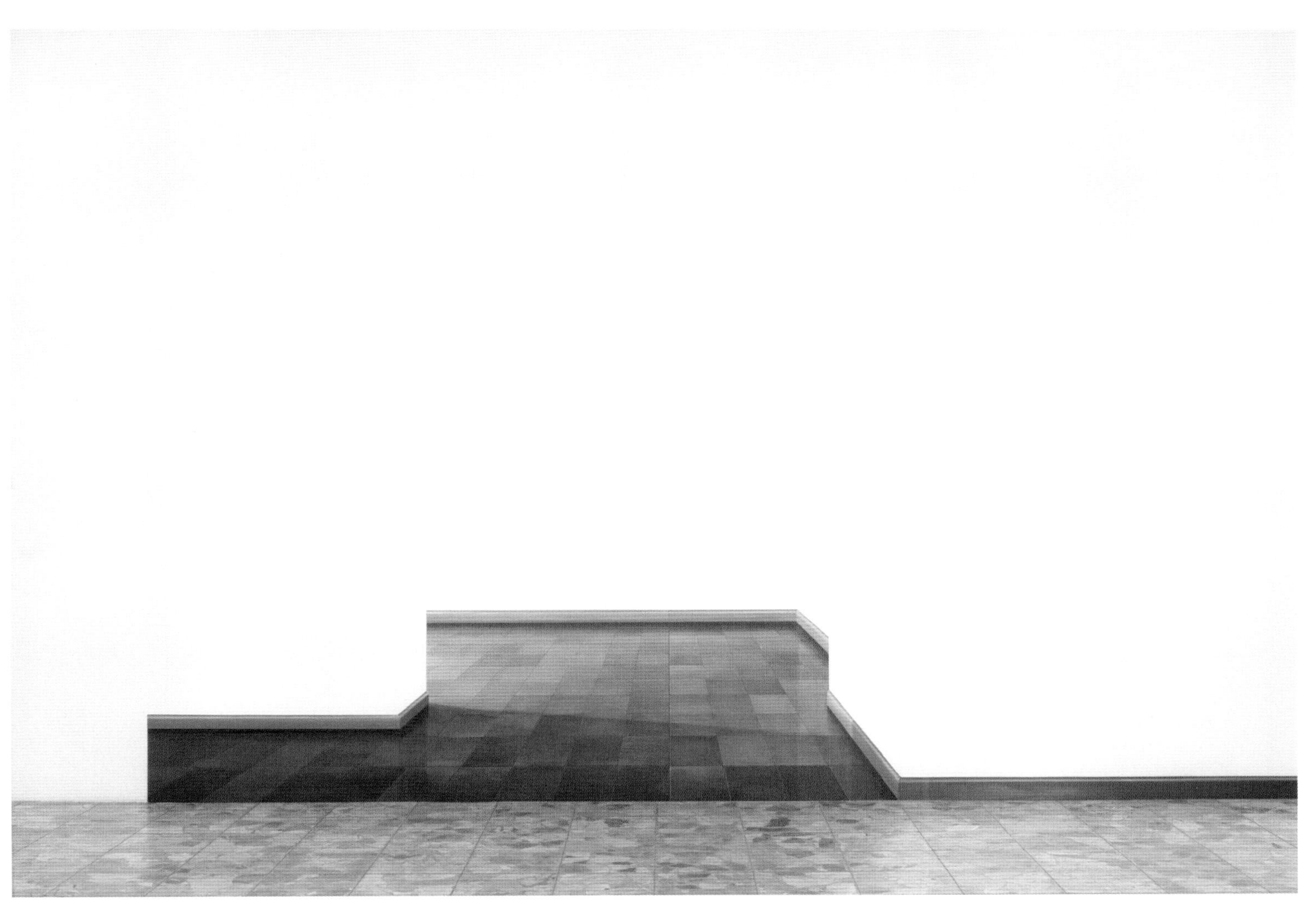

Zwei Räume, 1970/95
Two Spaces
Kunstharz und Öl auf Hartfaser, für eine
6 m lange Wand, 80 cm hoch
Synthetic resin and oil on hard fiberboard,
for a 6-m-long wall, 80 cm high

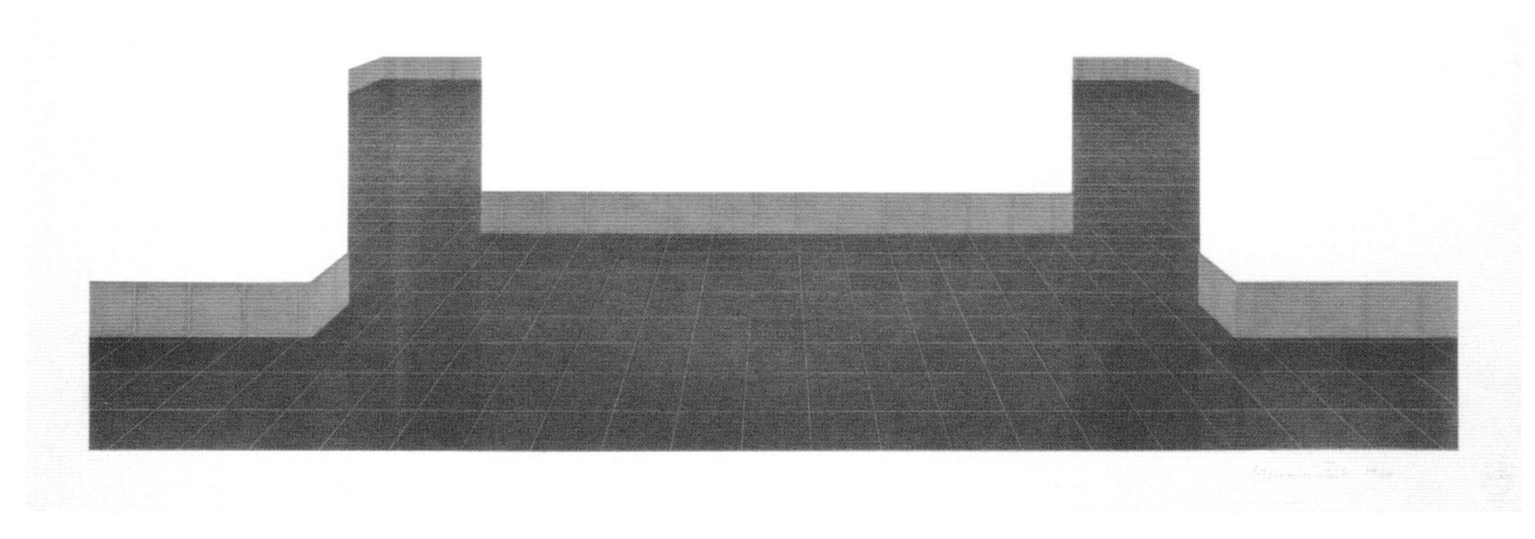

Raum XXIII, 1970
Space XXIII
Farbstift auf Karton, 62 × 82 cm
Colored pencil on cardboard

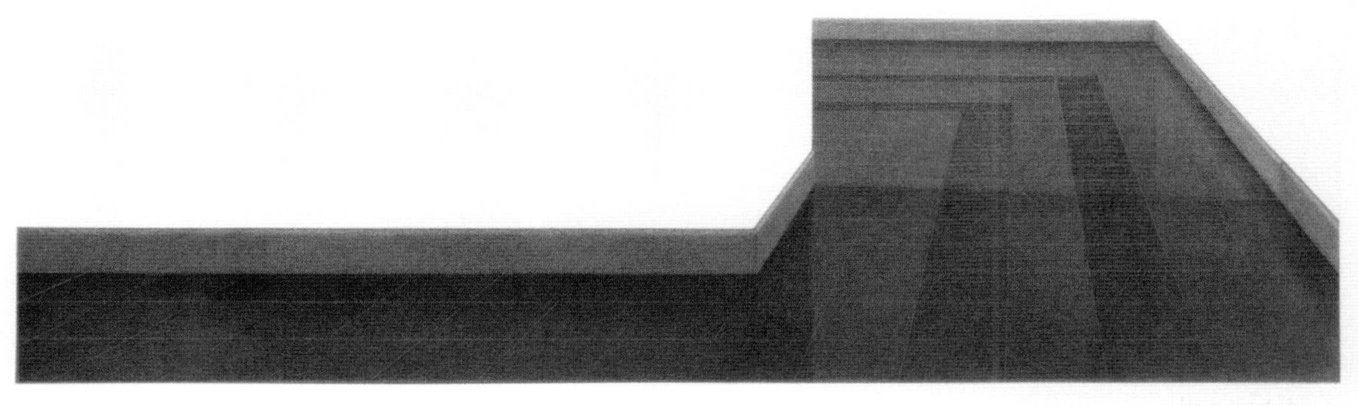

Raum xxvii, 1970
Space xxvii
Farbstift auf Karton, 63 × 81 cm
Colored pencil on cardboard

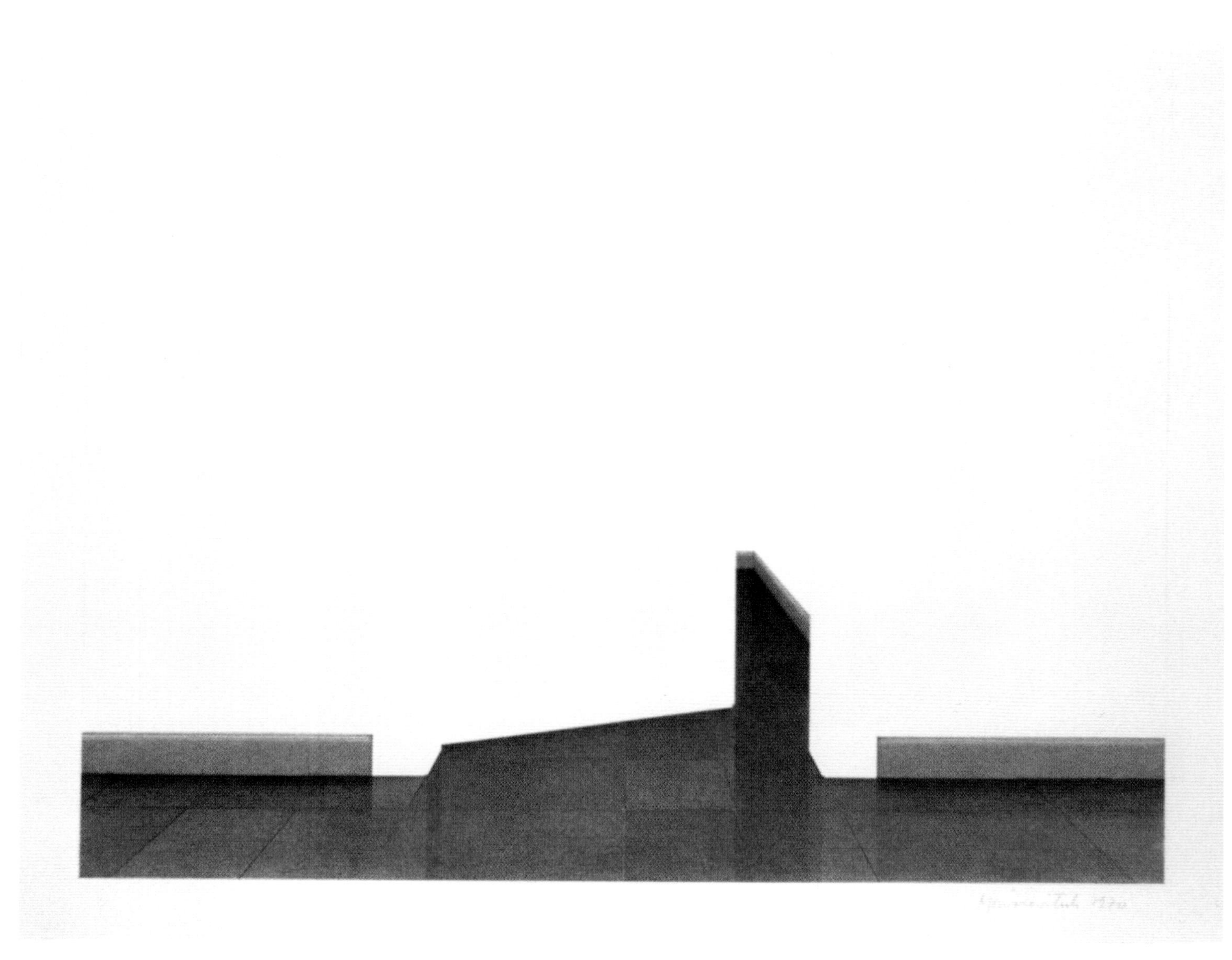

Tür II, 1970
Door II
Farbstift auf Karton, 50 × 65 cm
Colored pencil on cardboard

Heller Flur, 1971
Bright Corridor
Farbstift auf Karton, 73 × 95 cm
Colored pencil on cardboard

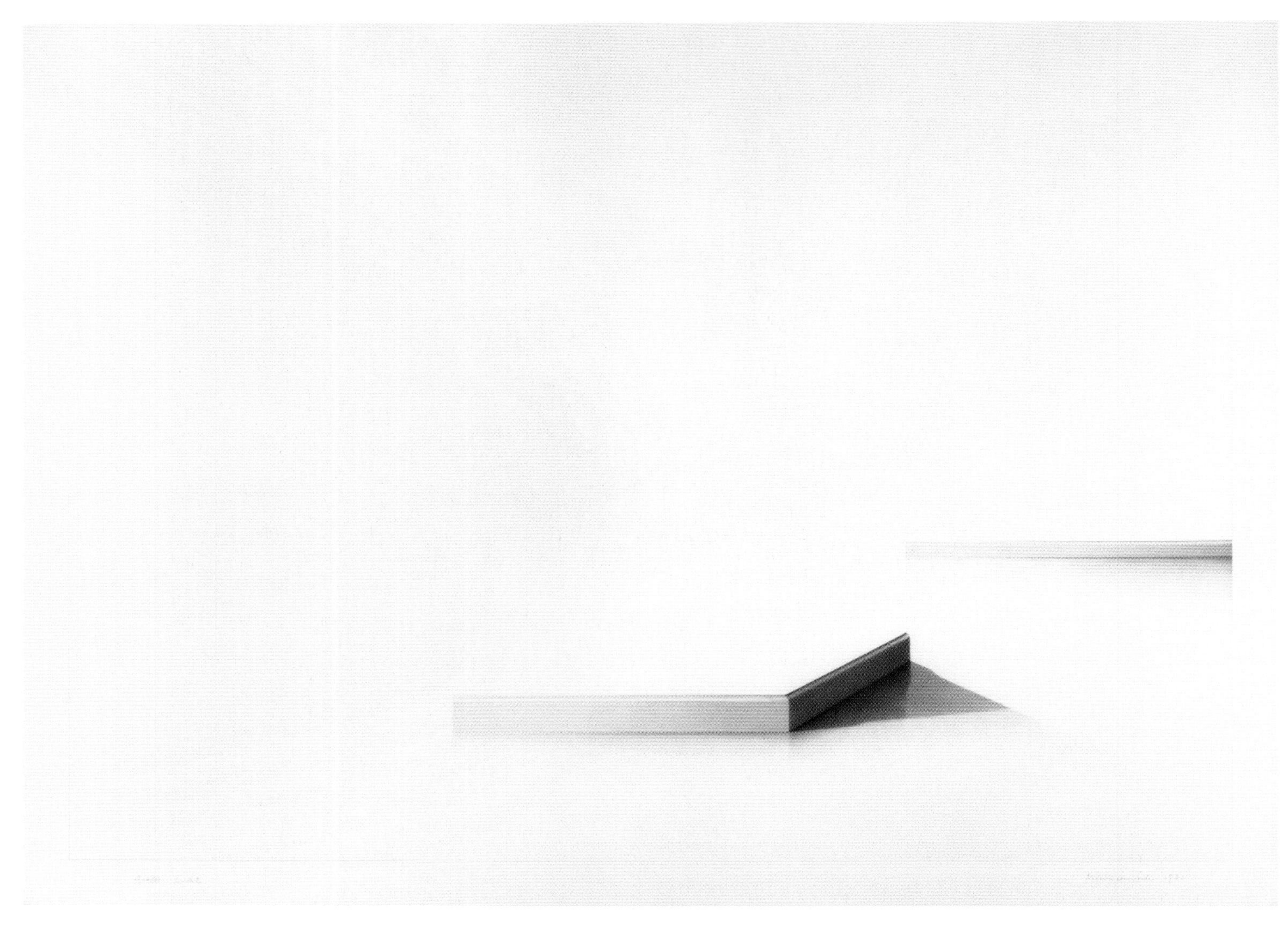

Grelles Licht, 1971
Glaring Light
Farbstift auf Karton, 73 × 100 cm
Colored pencil on cardboard

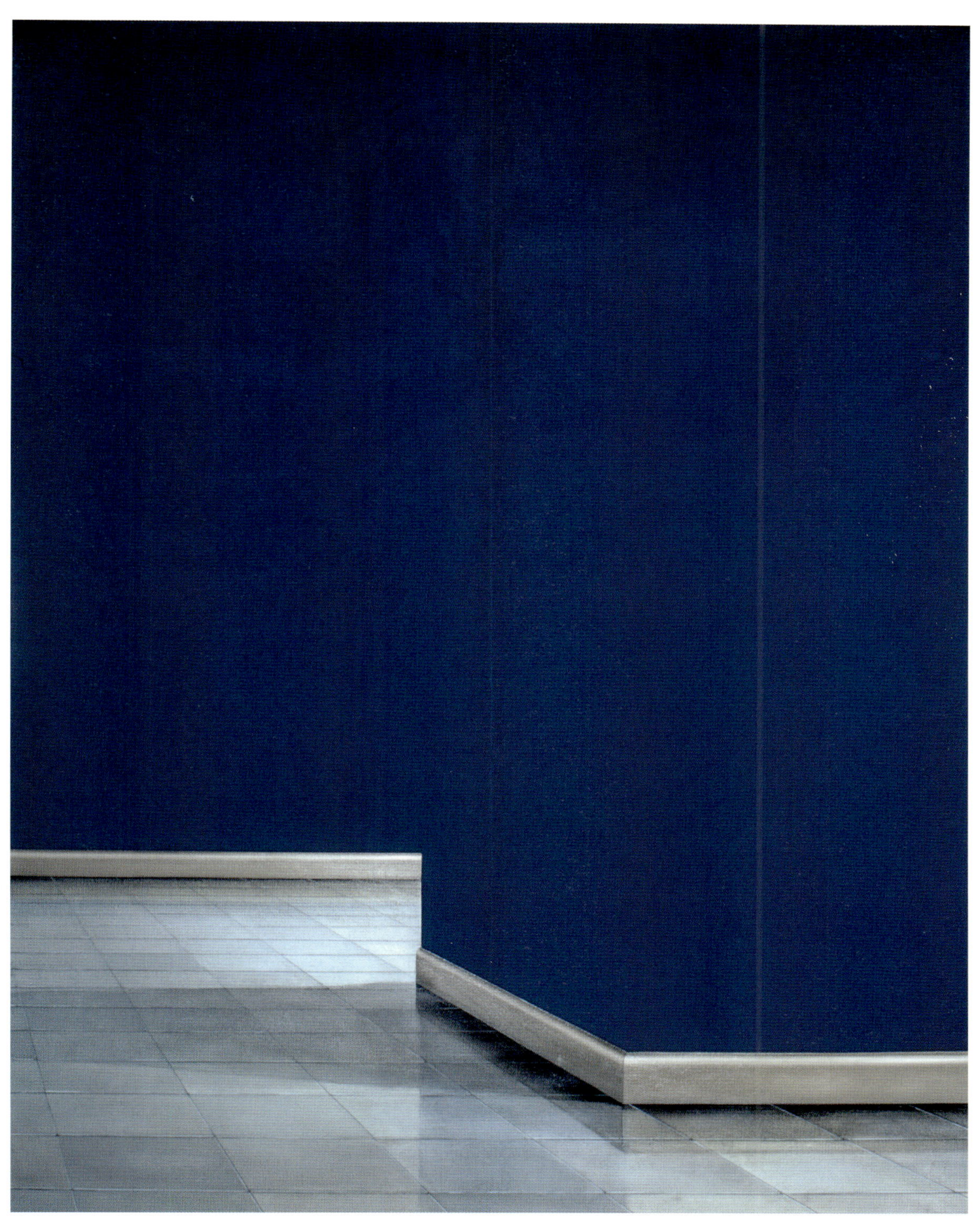

Zwei Lichtquellen, 1971
Two Sources of Light
Kunstharz und Öl auf Hartfaser, 75 × 155 cm
Synthetic resin and oil on hard fiberboard

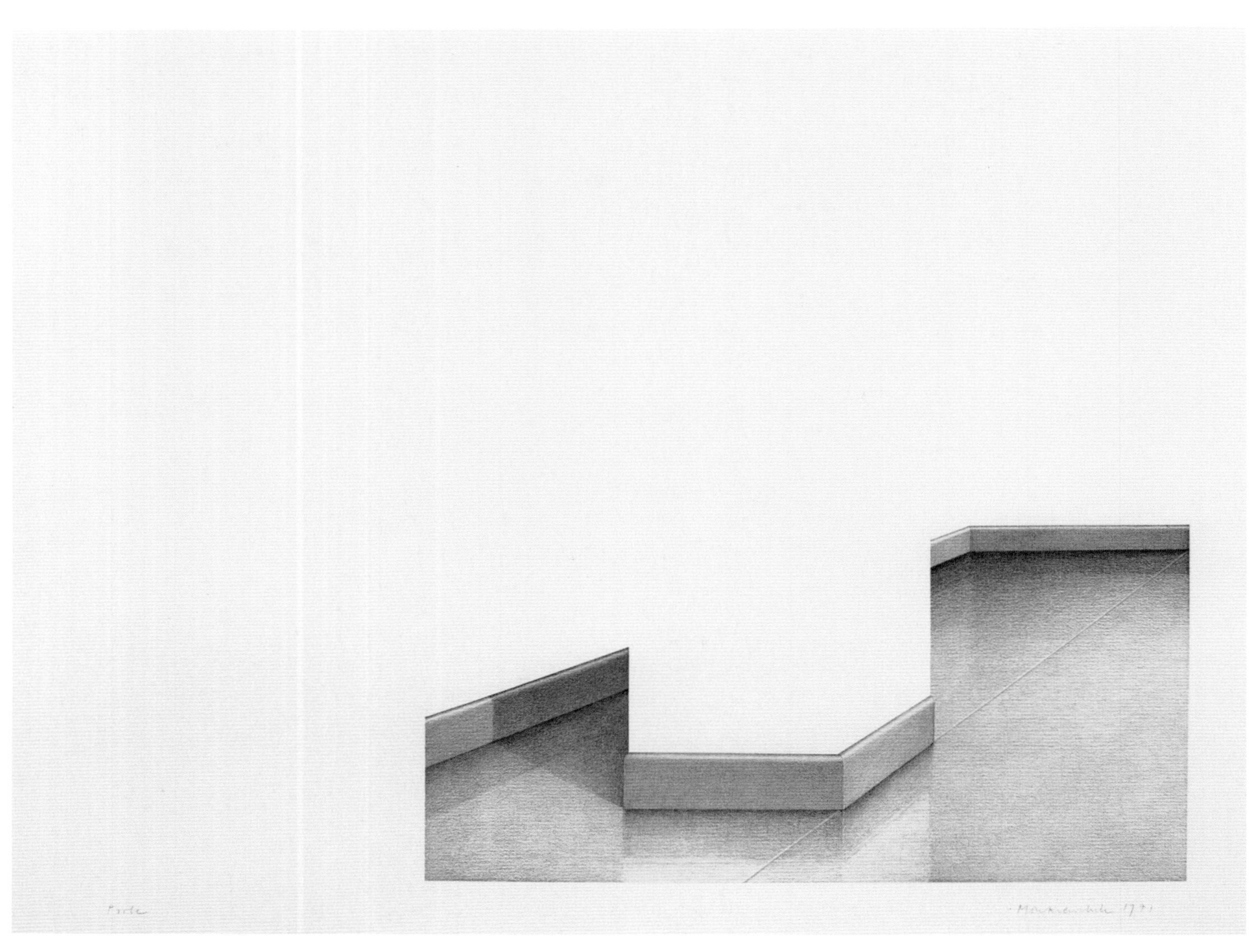

Stütze, 1971
Support
Siebdruck, 59 × 78 cm
Silkscreen print

Drei geöffnete Türen, 1971
Three Open Doors
Farbstift auf Karton, 73 × 102 cm
Colored pencil on cardboard

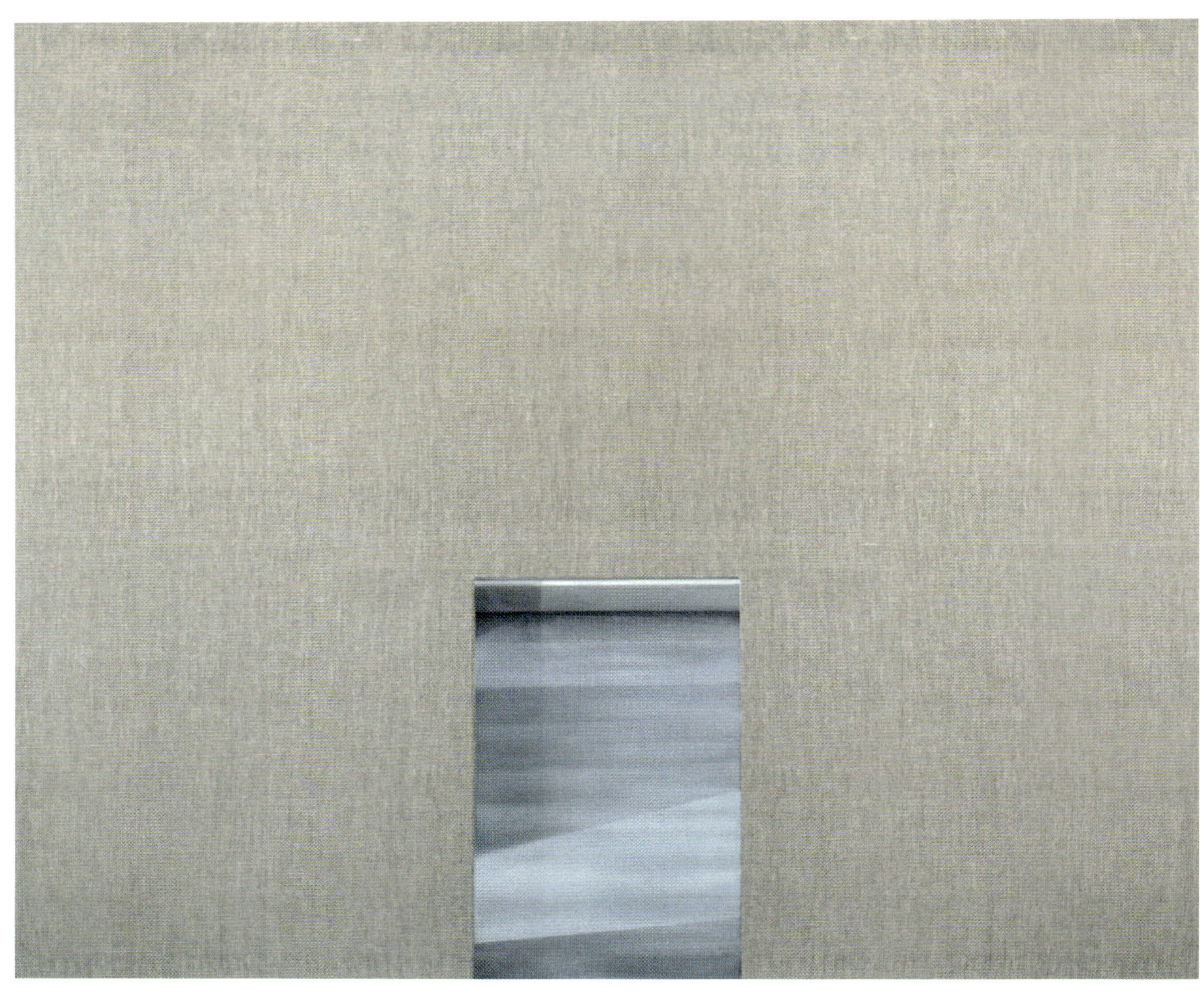

Drei geöffnete Türen, 1972
Three Open Doors
Kunstharz und Öl auf Leinwand, 150 × 180 cm
Synthetic resin and oil on canvas

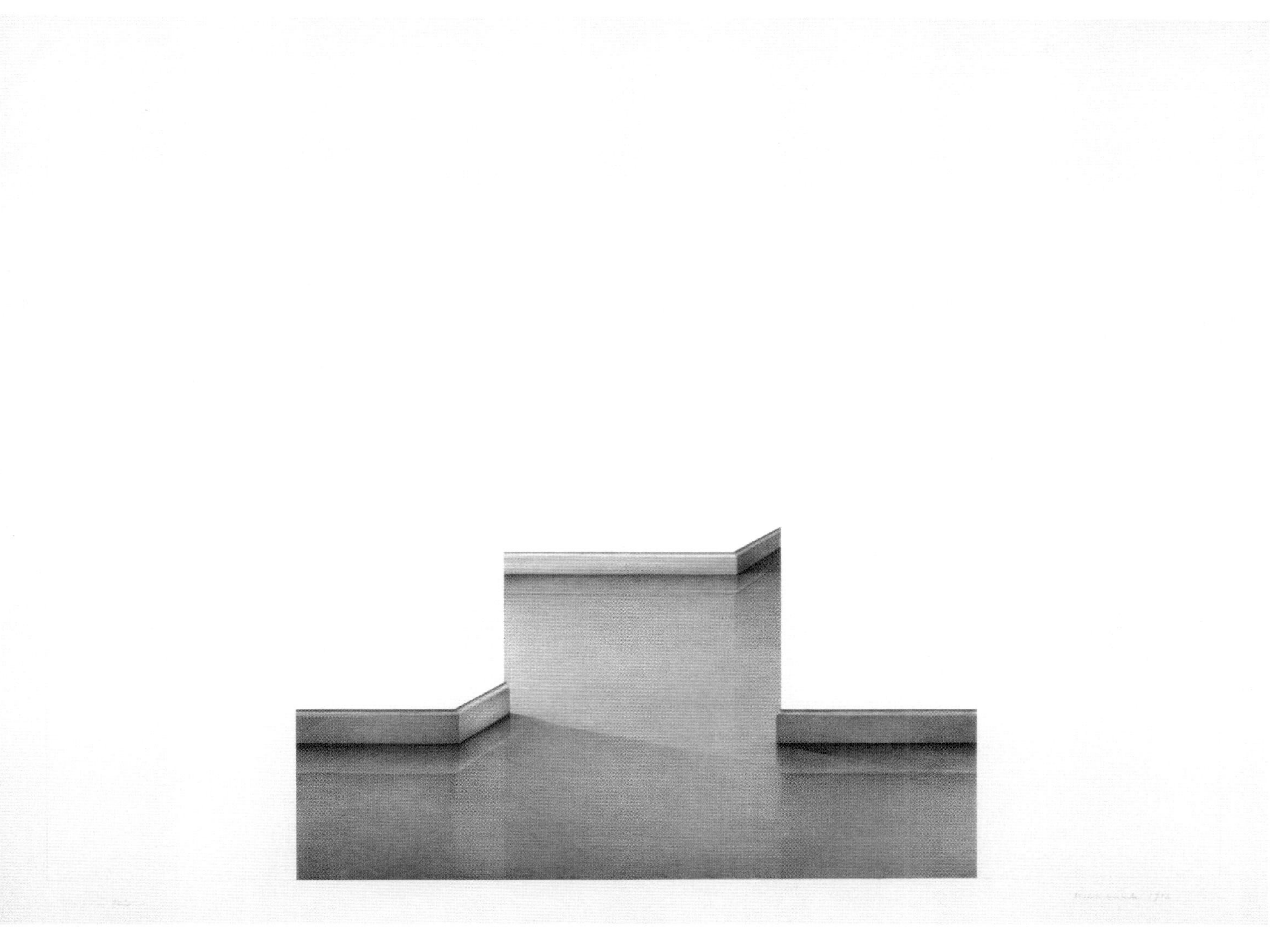

Flur, 1972
Corridor
Farbstift auf Karton, 73 × 98 cm
Colored pencil on cardboard

Glatter Boden, 1972
Smooth Floor
Kunstharz und Öl auf Leinwand, 130 × 160 cm
Synthetic resin and oil on canvas

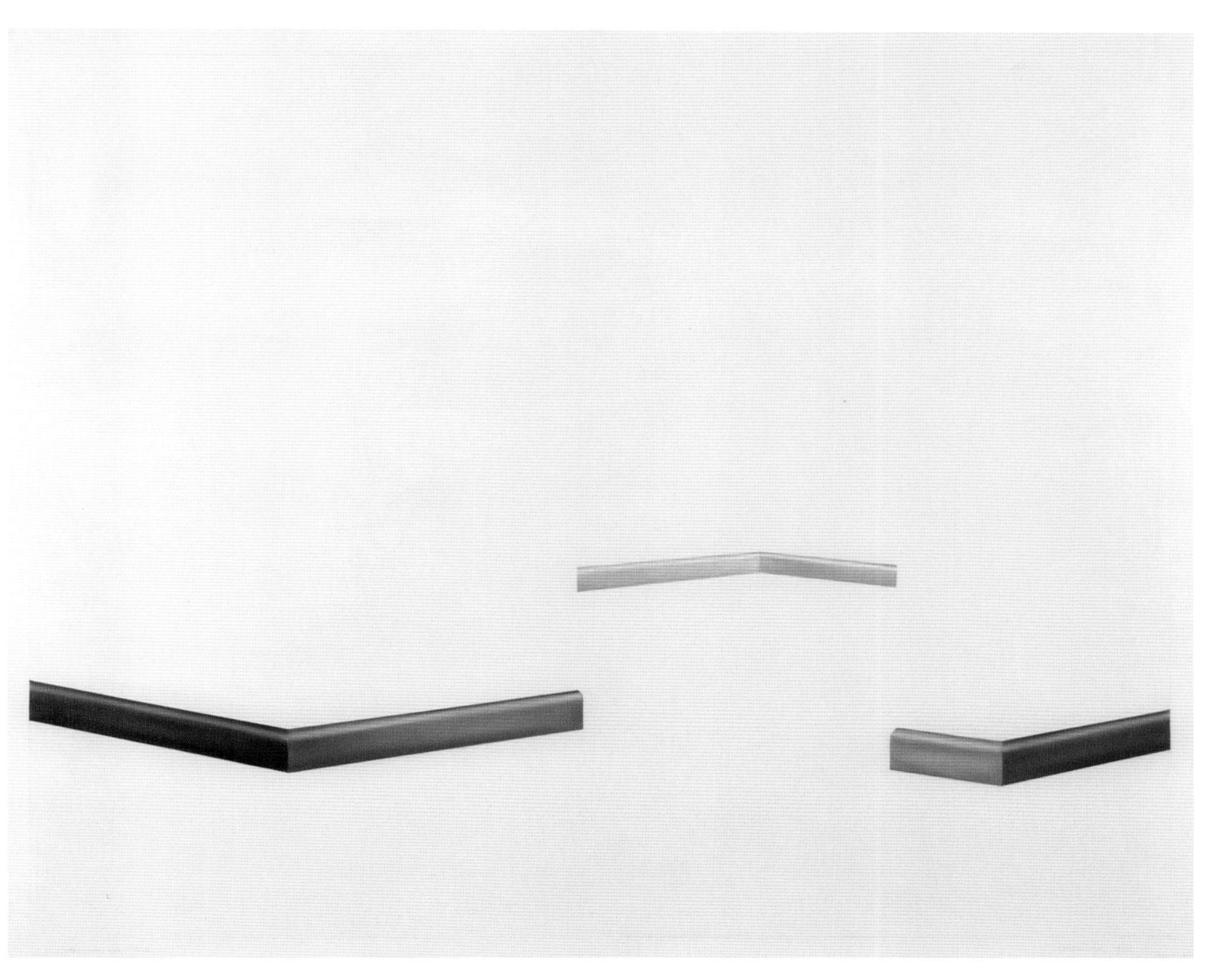

Boden und sechs Wände, 1972
Floor and Six Walls
Kunstharz und Öl auf Leinwand, 130 × 160 cm
Synthetic resin and oil on canvas

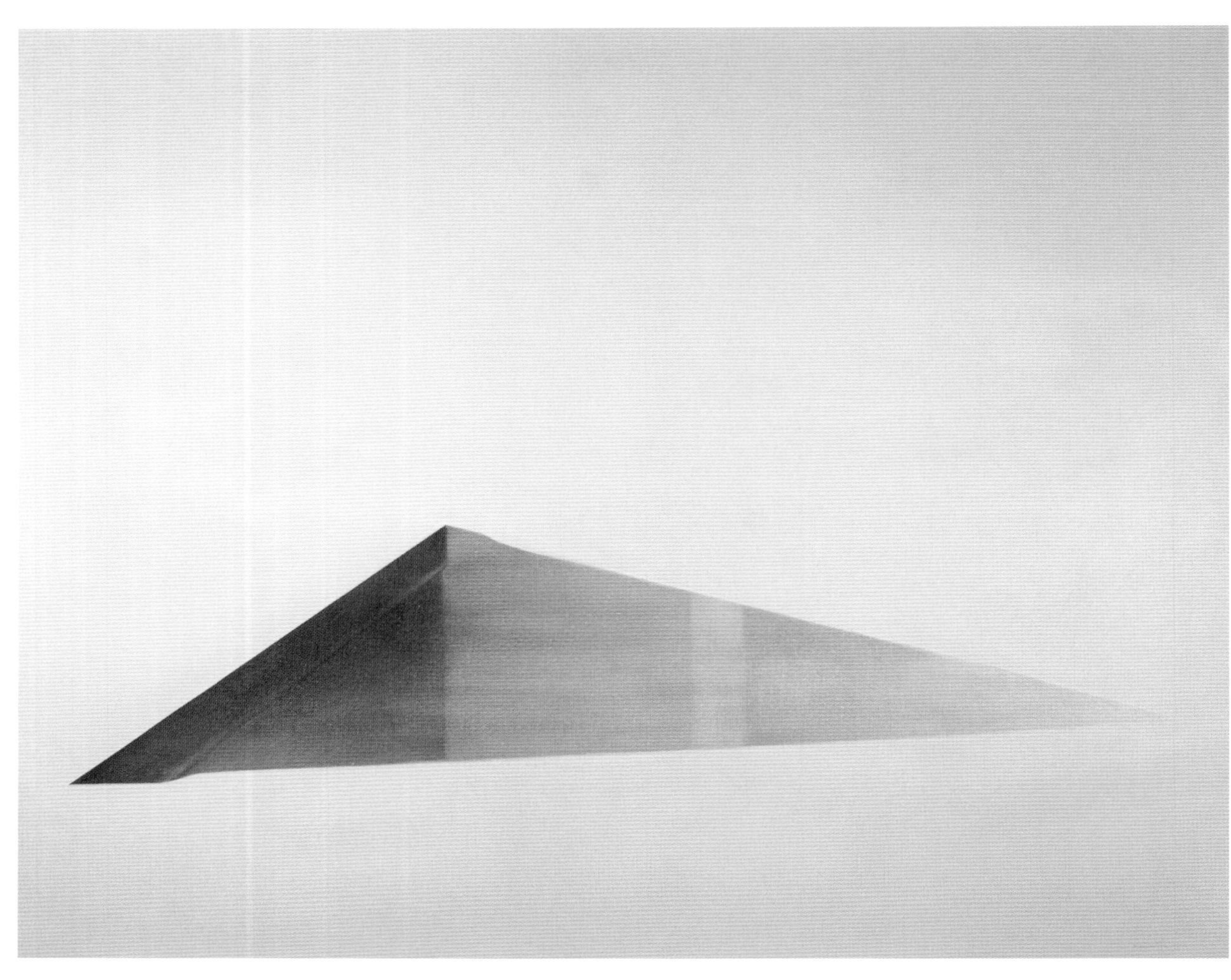

Schatten, 1972
Shadow
Kunstharz auf Leinwand, 160 × 200 cm
Synthetic resin on canvas

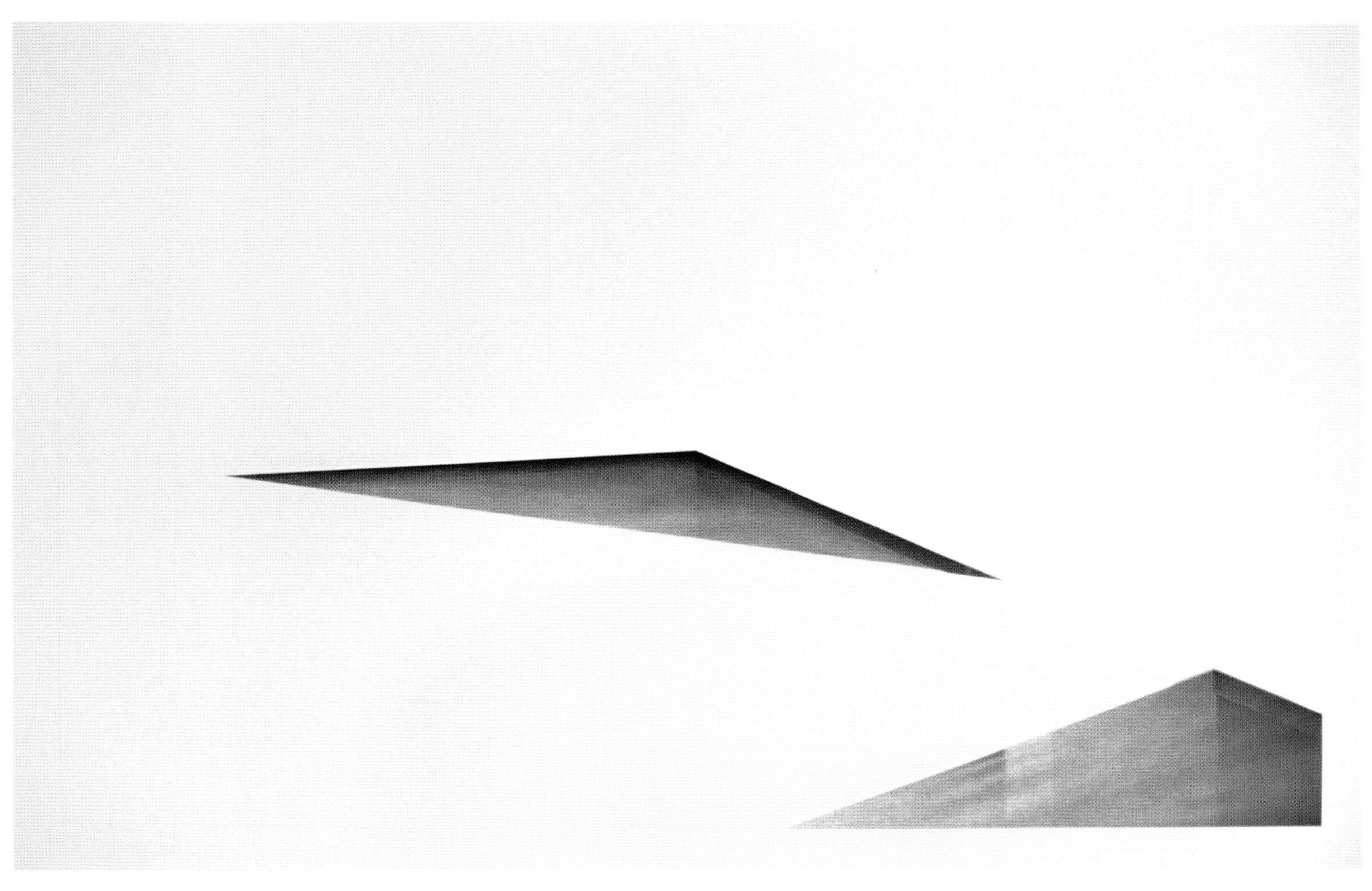

Tür, 1972
Door
Farbstift auf Karton, 73 × 98 cm
Colored pencil on cardboard

55

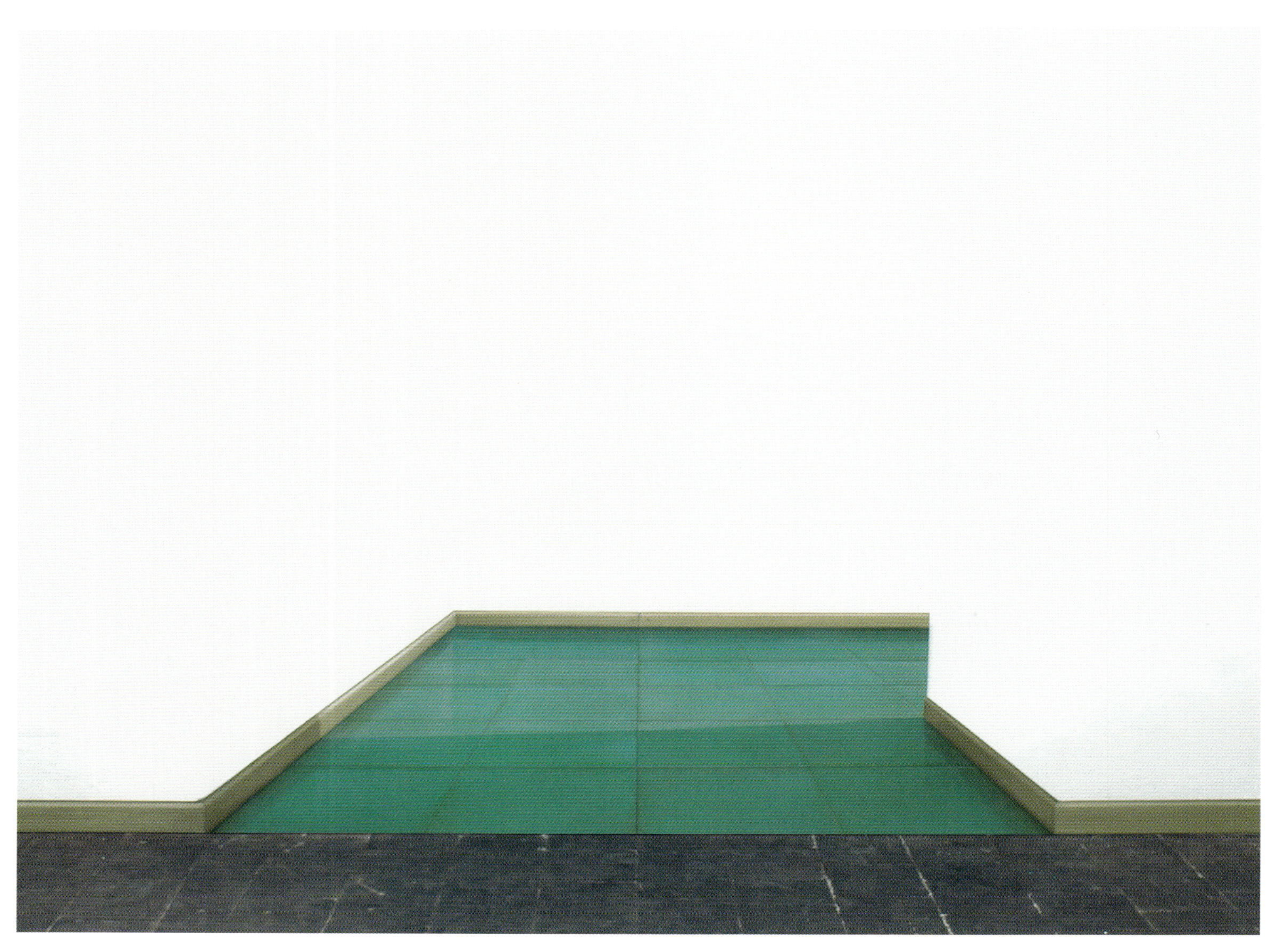

Licht in grünem Flur, 1972
Light in a Green Corridor
Kunstharz und Öl auf Hartfaser,
80 cm hoch für eine 6m lange Wand
Synthetic resin and oil on hard fiberboard,
80 cm high for a 6-m-long wall

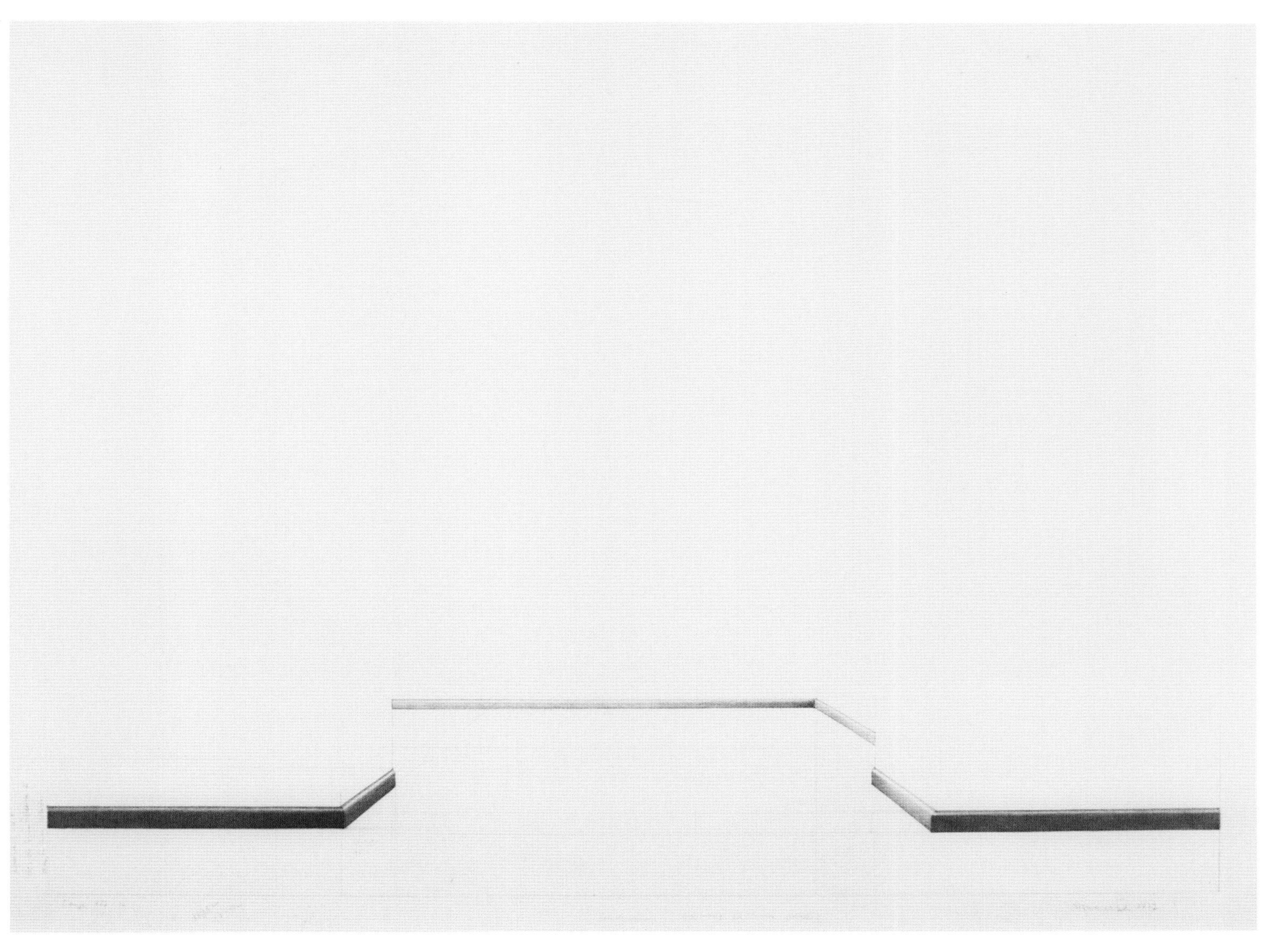

Leistenraum, 1972
Baseboard Space
Bleistift auf Karton, 79 × 104,5 cm
Pencil on cardboard

Licht für zwei Räume, 1973/81
Light for Two Spaces
Farbstift auf Karton, 82 × 108 cm
Colored pencil on cardboard

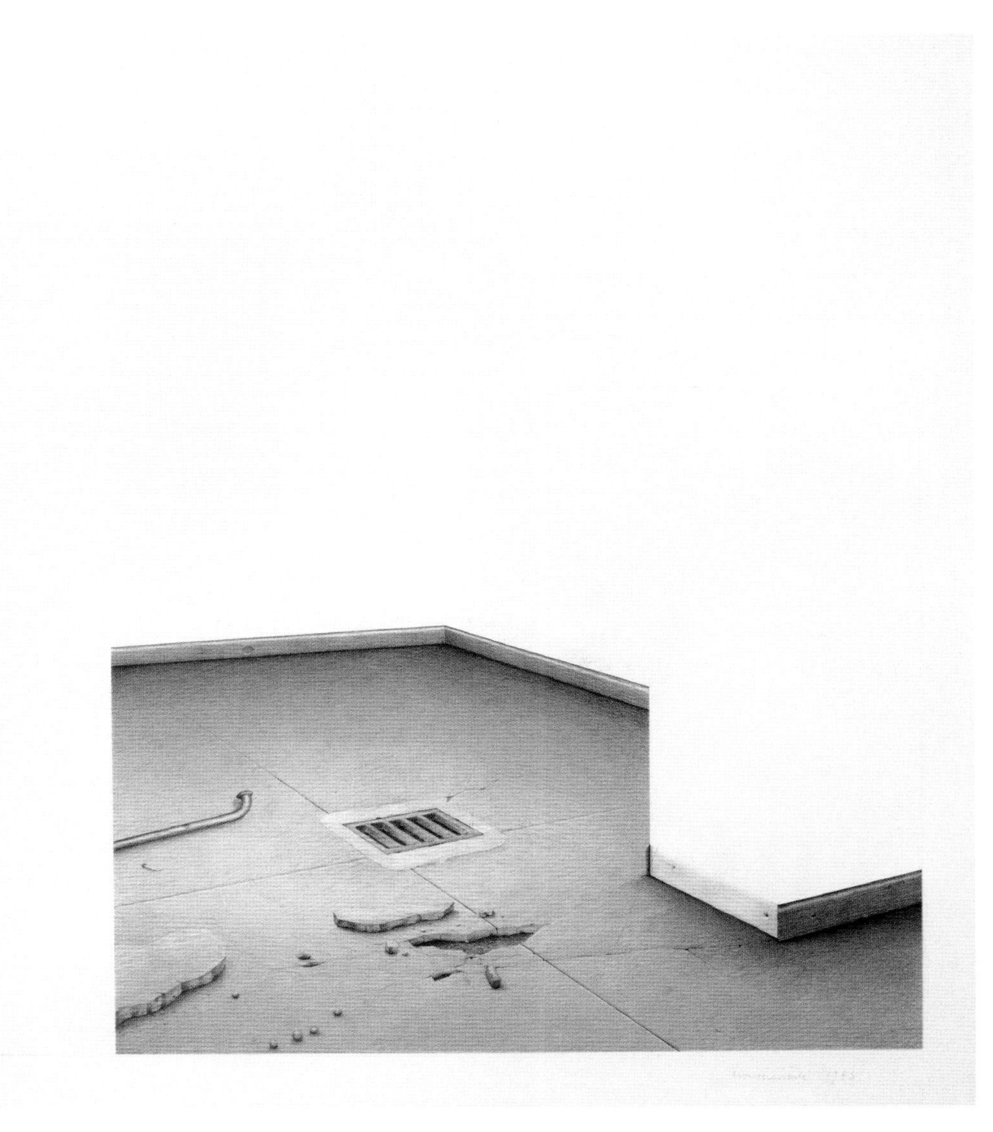

Brüchiger Raum, 1973
Crumbling Space
Farbstift auf Karton, 73 × 98 cm
Colored pencil on cardboard

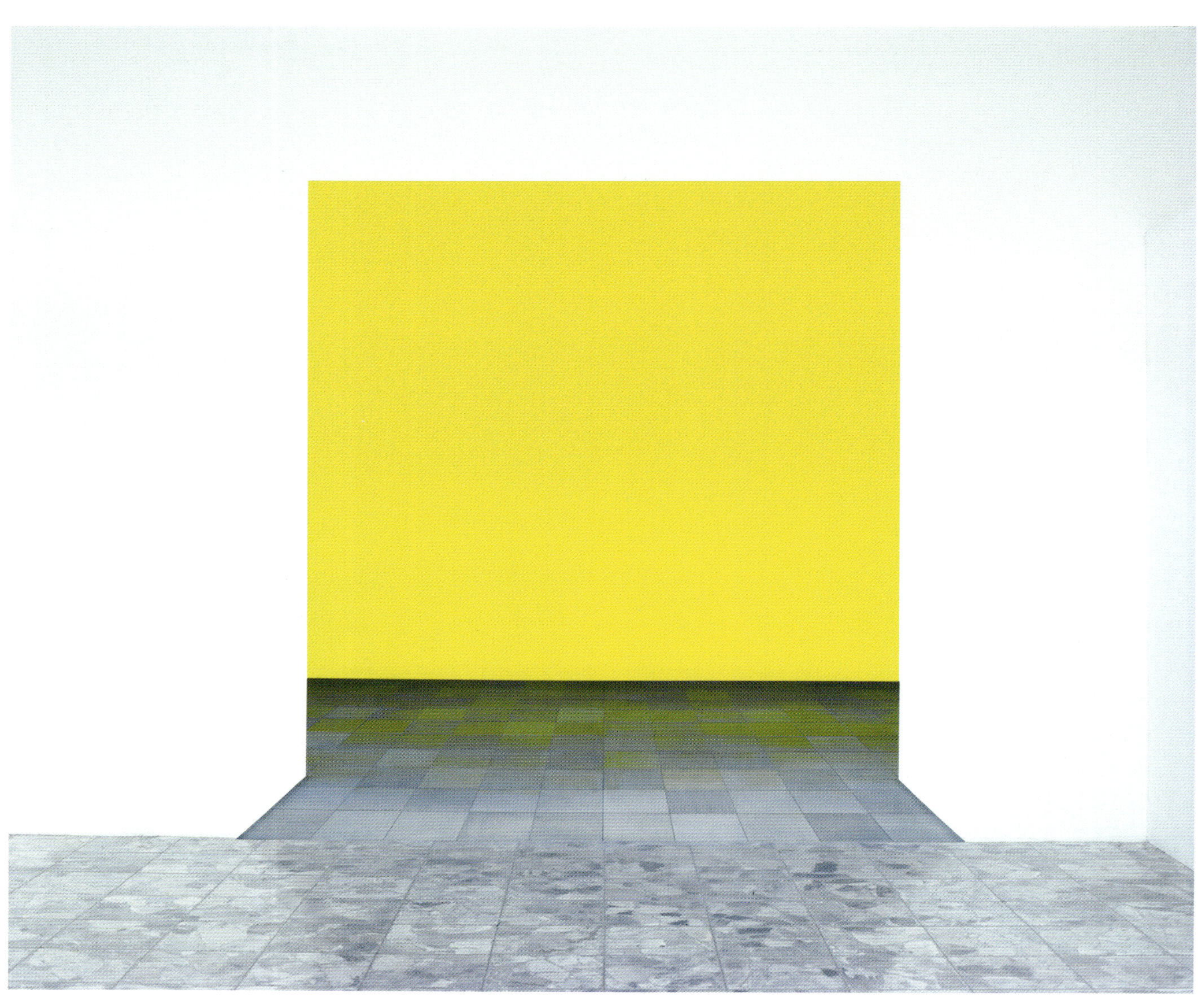

Farbraum Gelb, 2001
Colored Space Yellow
Acryl auf Sperrholz und Wand, 79 × 344 cm
Acrylic on plywood and wall

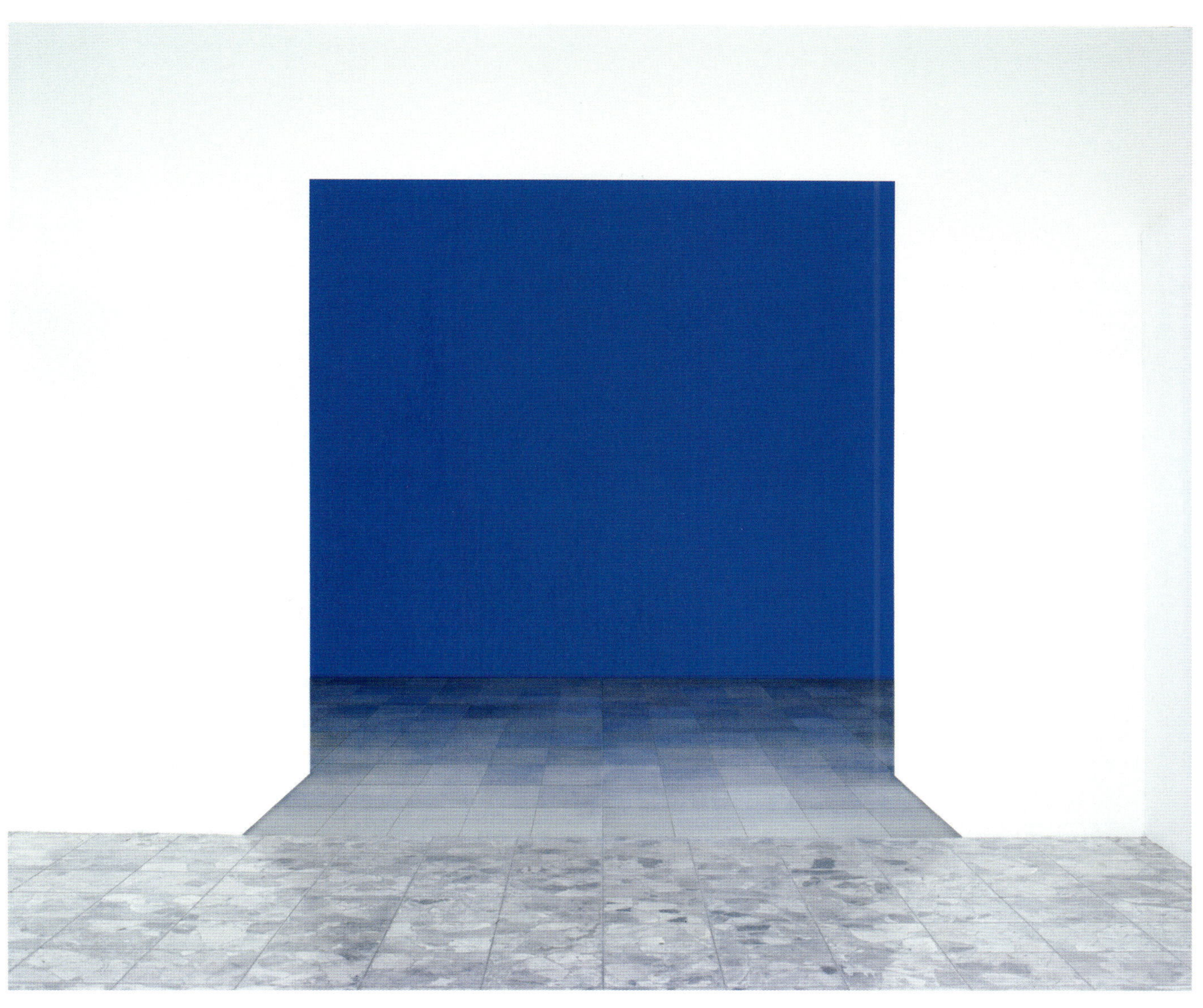

Farbraum Blau, 2001
Colored Space Blue
Acryl auf Sperrholz und Wand, 79 × 344 cm
Acrylic on plywood and wall

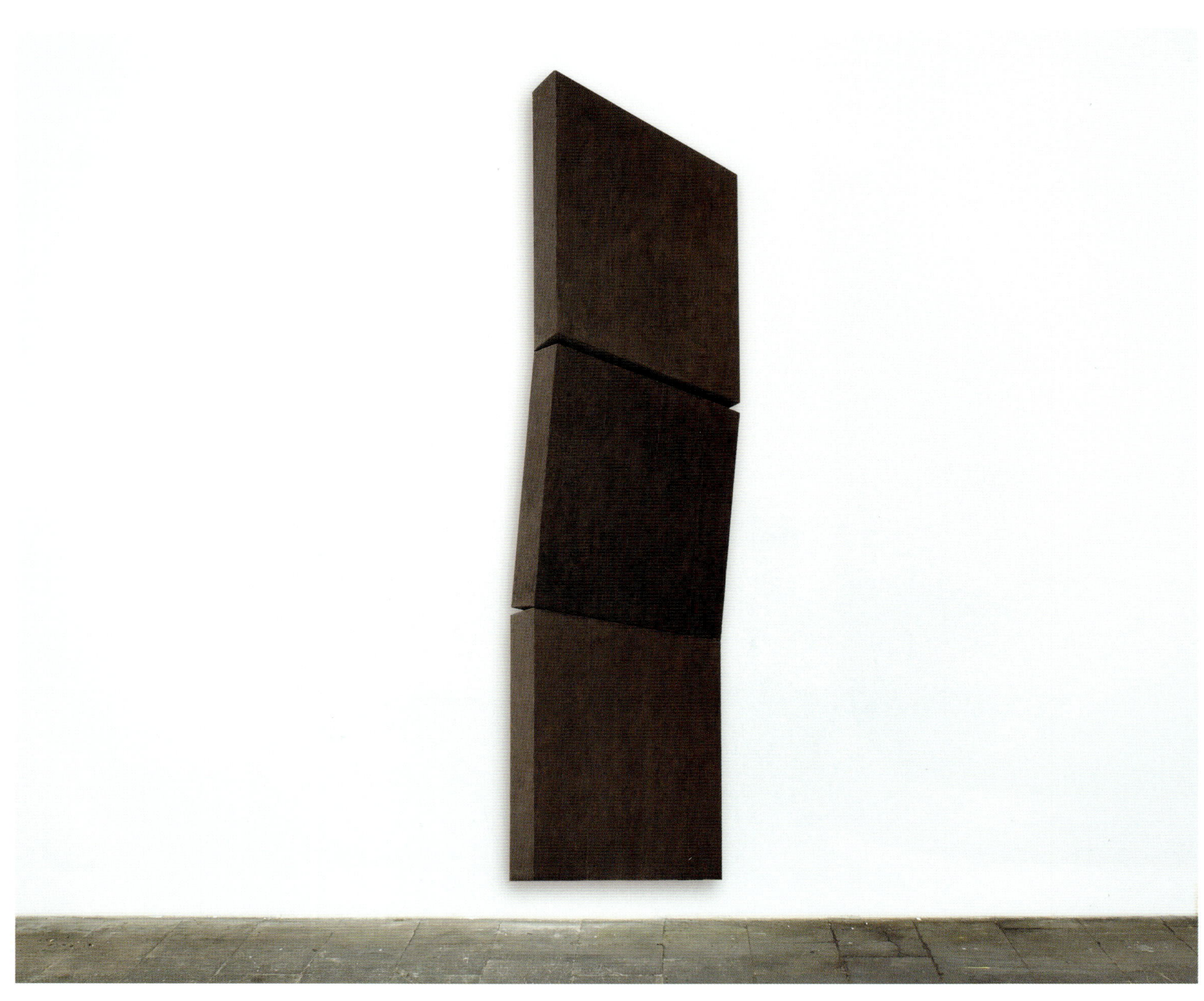

Zu Lessings Laokoon, 1979
On Lessing's Laokoon
Erde und Dispersion auf Leinwand, dreiteilig,
305 × 420 cm
Earth and dispersion on canvas, three-part

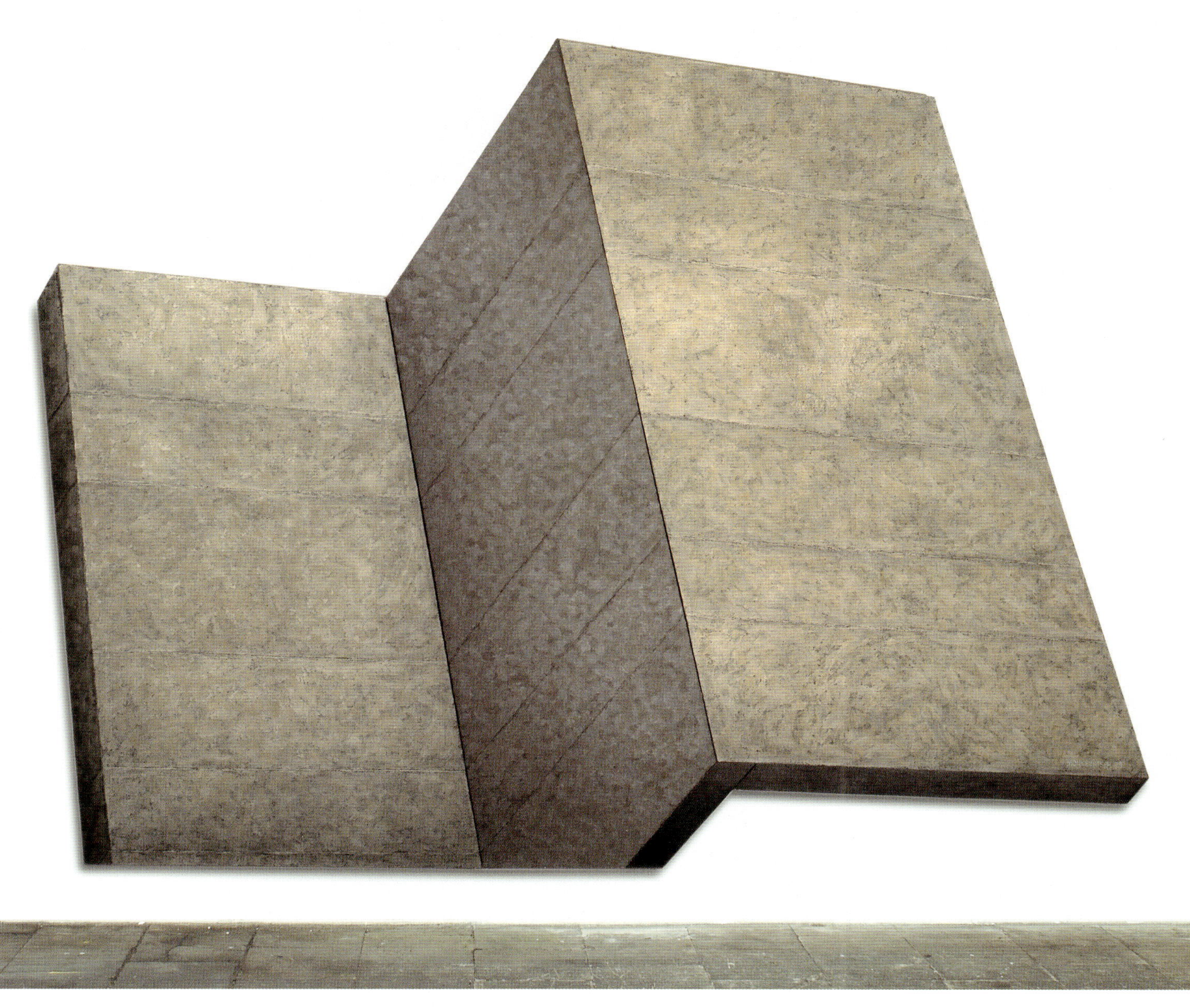

Drei Wände, 1979
Three Walls
Erde auf Leinwand, dreiteilig, 330 × 420 cm
Earth on canvas, three-part

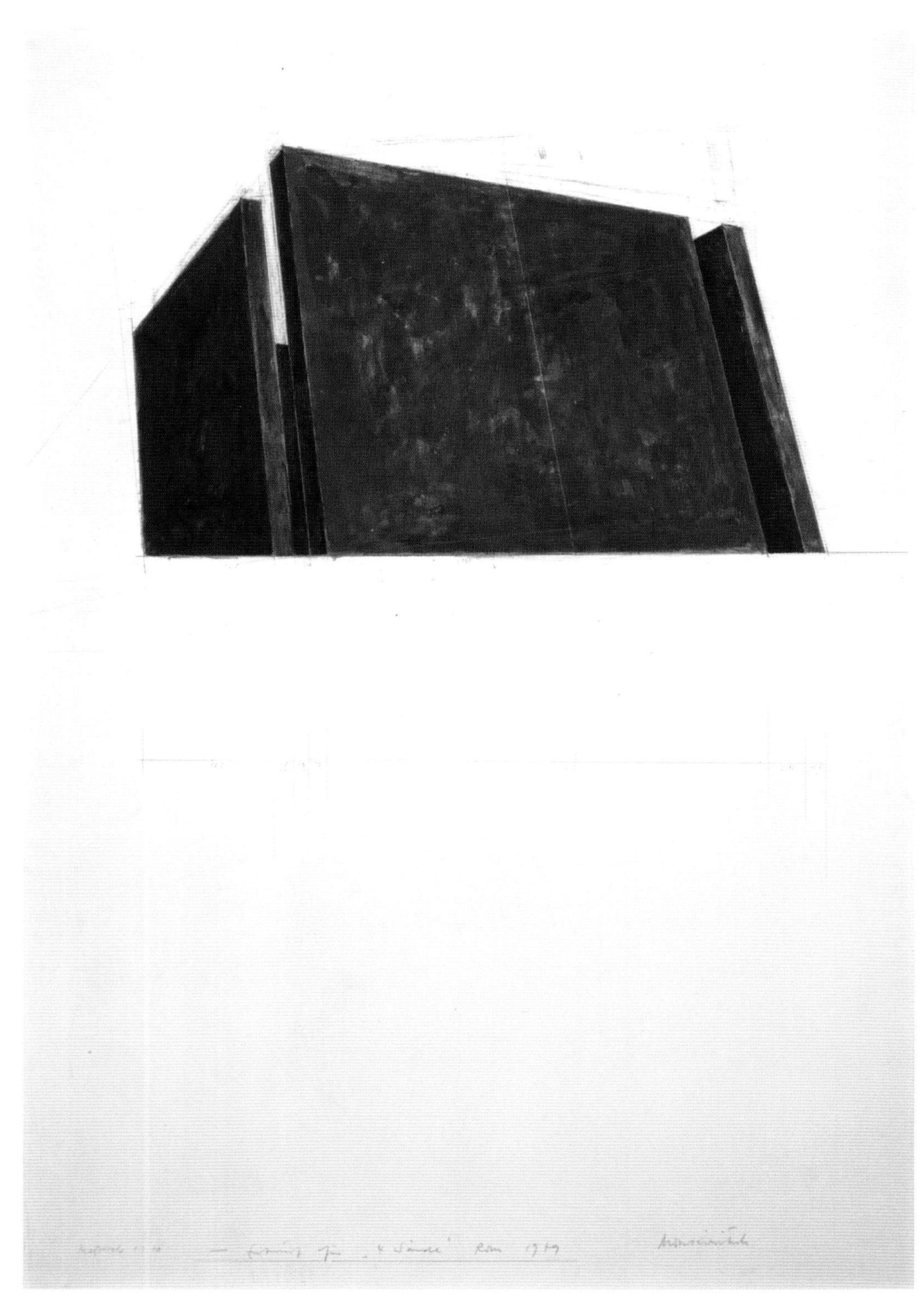

Vier Wände, 1979
Four Walls
Aquarell und Bleistift auf Fabriano, 100 × 70 cm
Watercolor and pencil on Fabriano

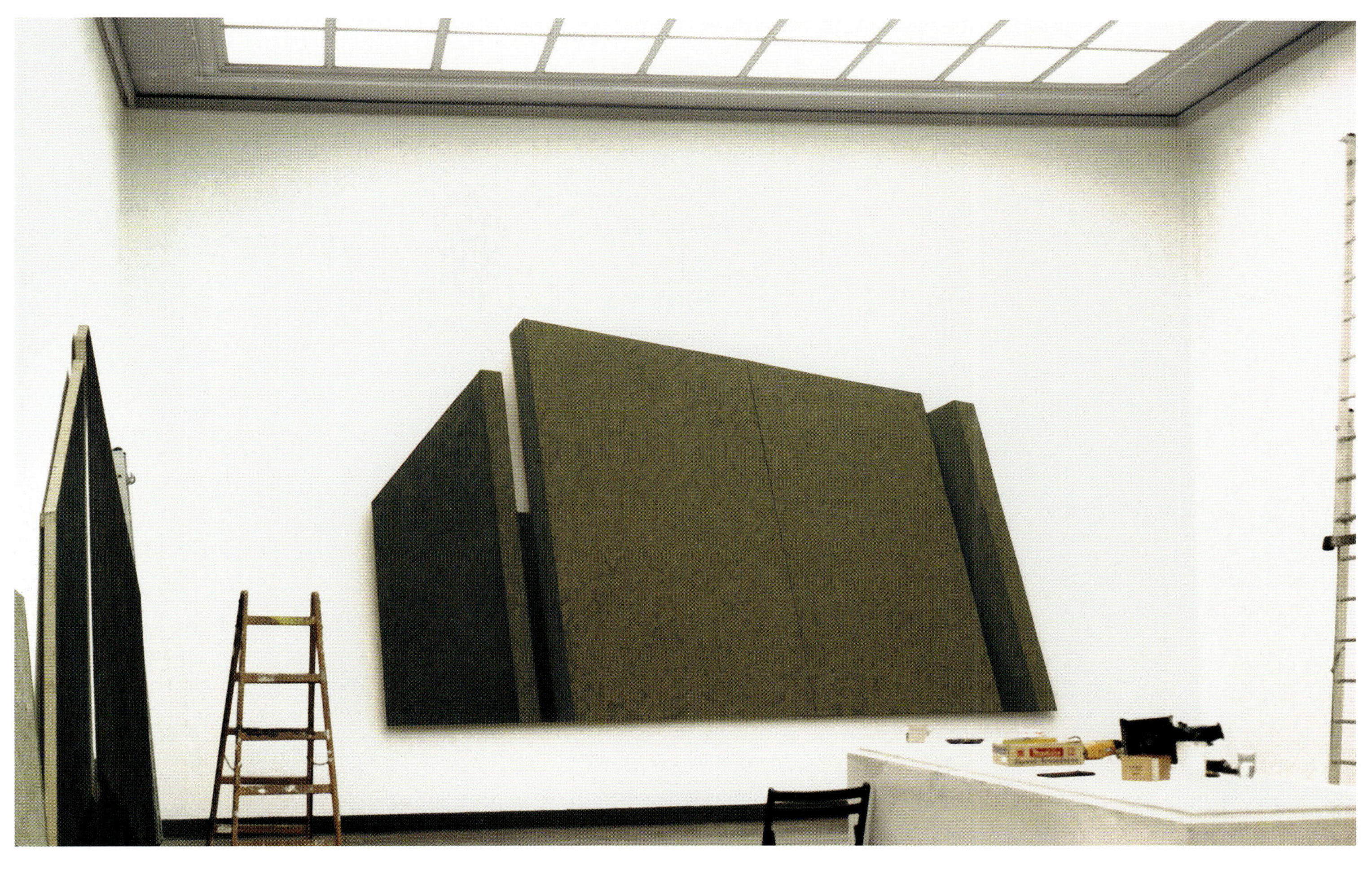

Vier Wände, 1979
Four Walls
Erde auf Leinwand, dreiteilig, 315 × 510 cm
Earth on canvas, three-part

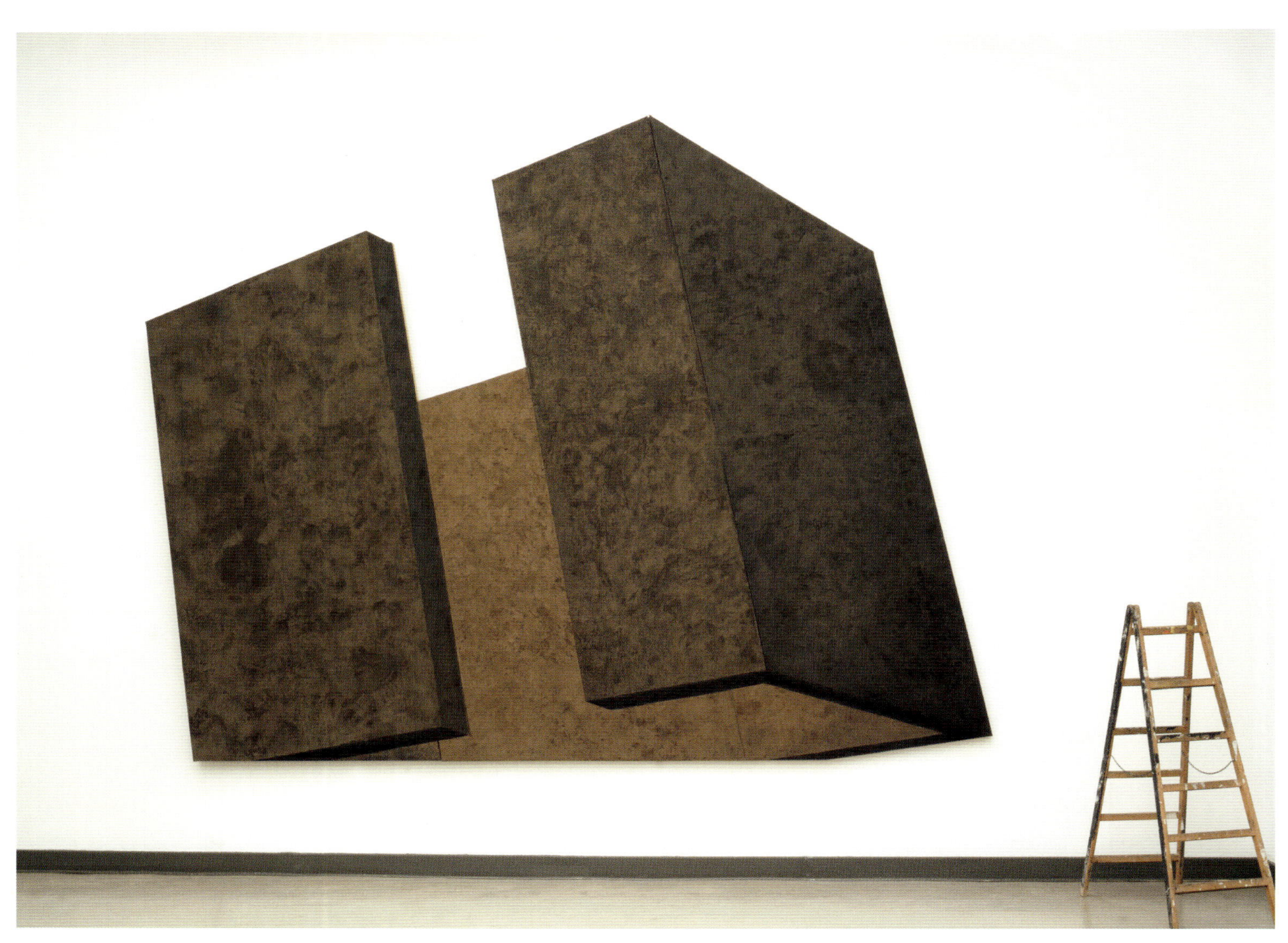

Gebäude-Torso II, 1979
Building Torso II
Erde auf Leinwand, dreiteilig, 400 × 520 cm
Earth on canvas, three-part

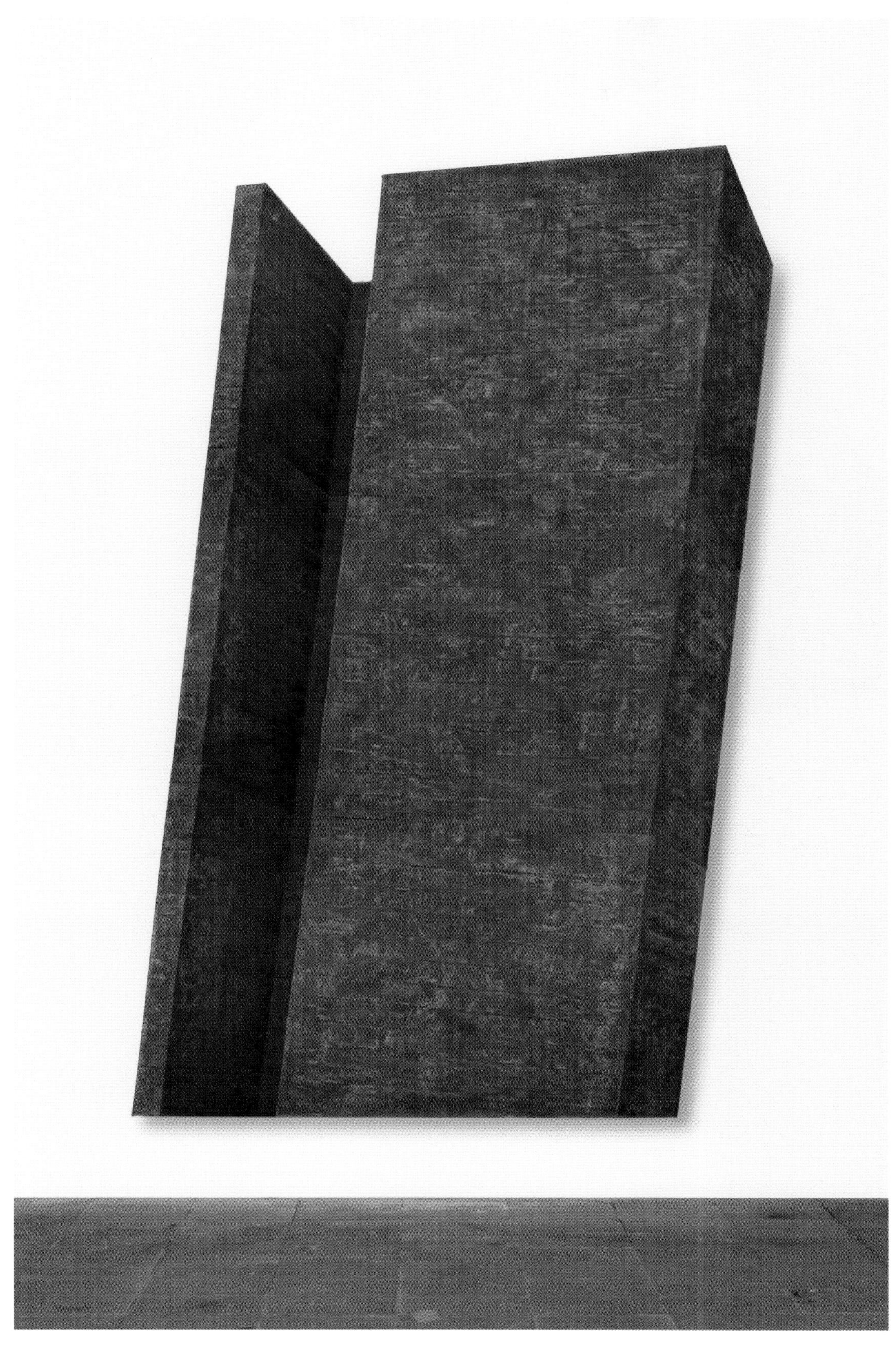

Torso I, 1979
Torso I
Erde auf Leinwand, dreiteilig, 440 × 250 cm
Earth on canvas, three-part

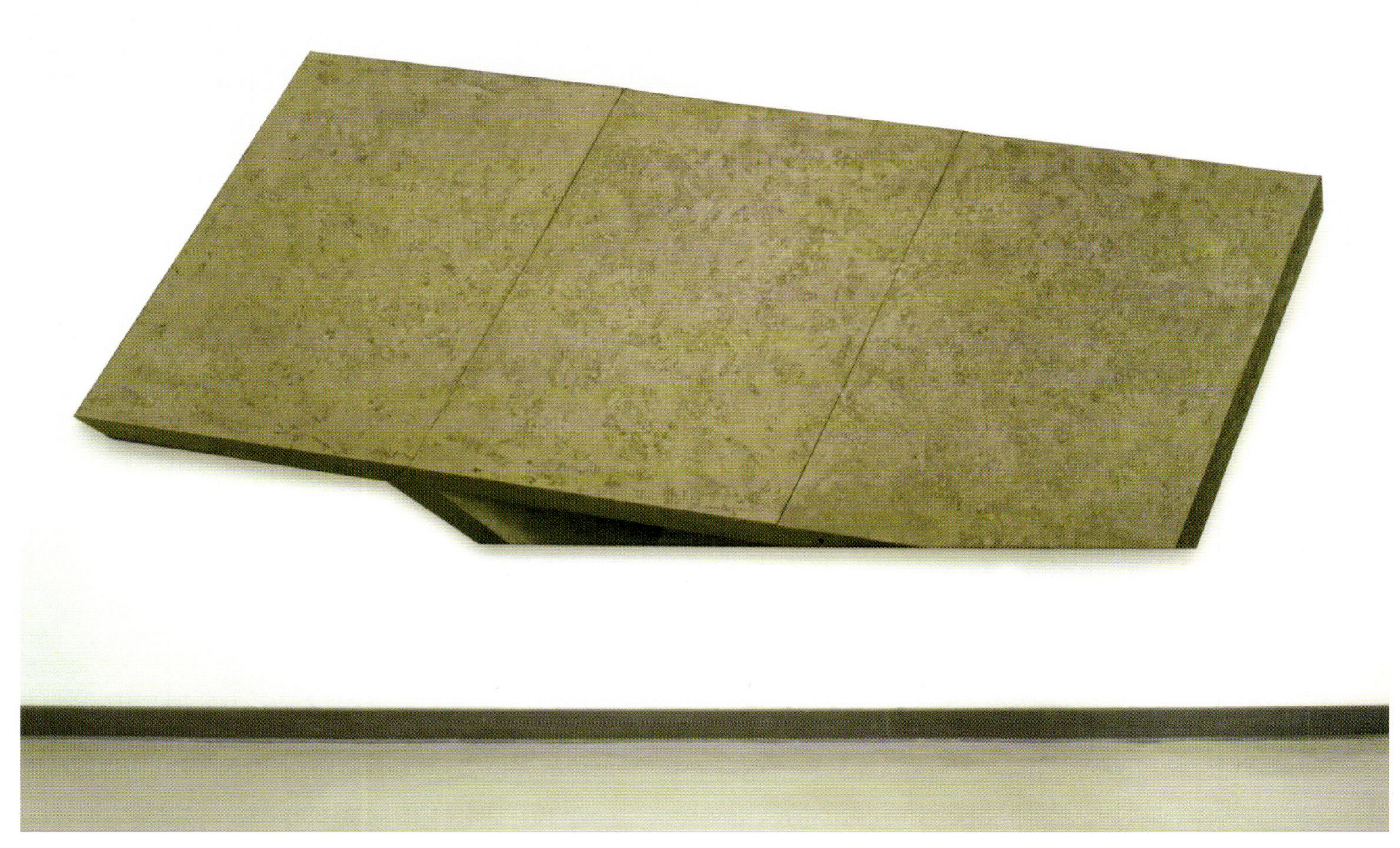

Schräge Wand, 1979
Slanted Wall
Sand auf Leinwand, dreiteilig, 220 × 530 cm
Sand on canvas, three-part

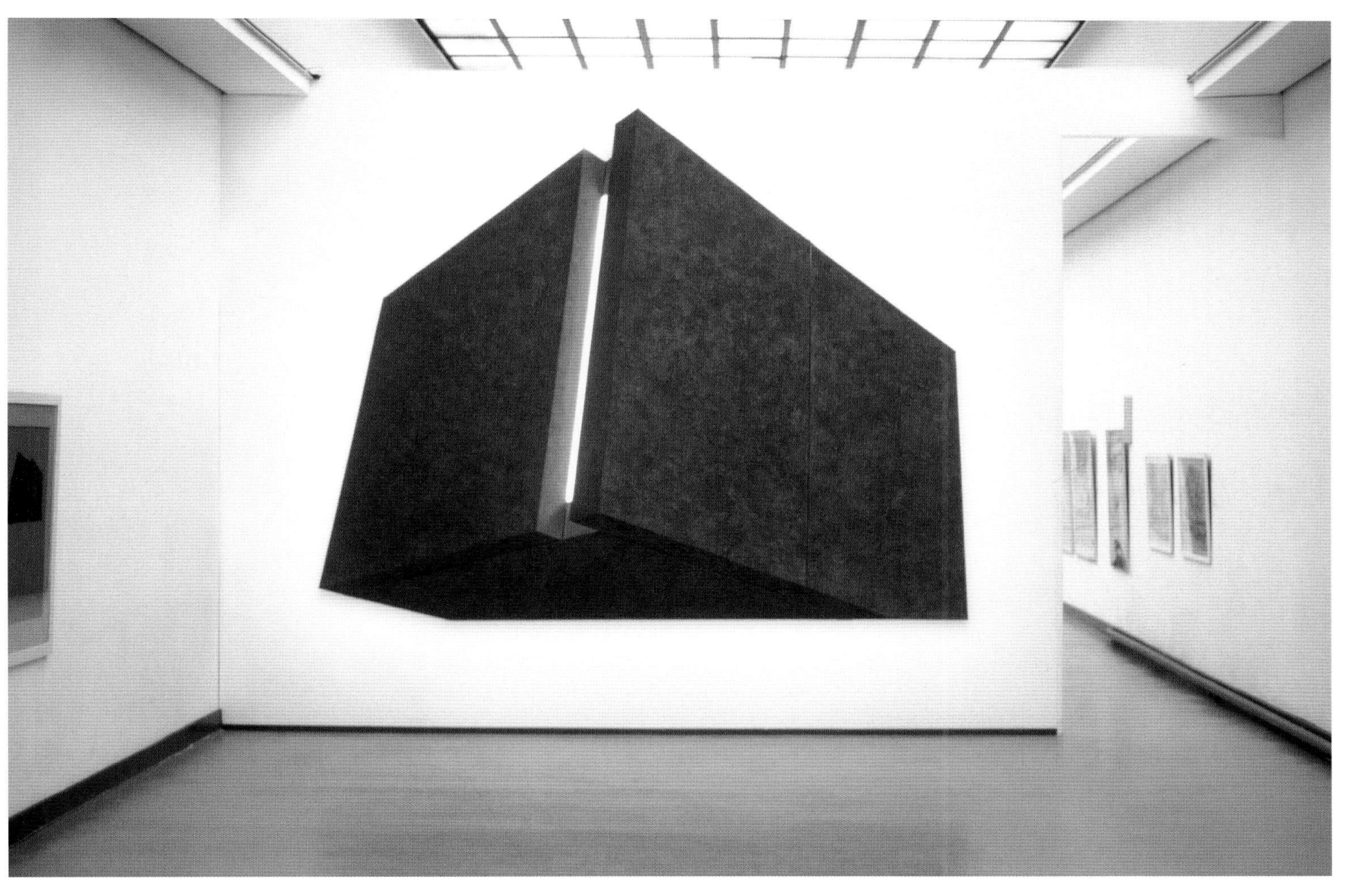

Raum-Energie, 1980
Space Energy
Erde auf Leinwand, Neonröhre, vierteilig, 350 × 430 cm
Earth on canvas, neon tube, four-part

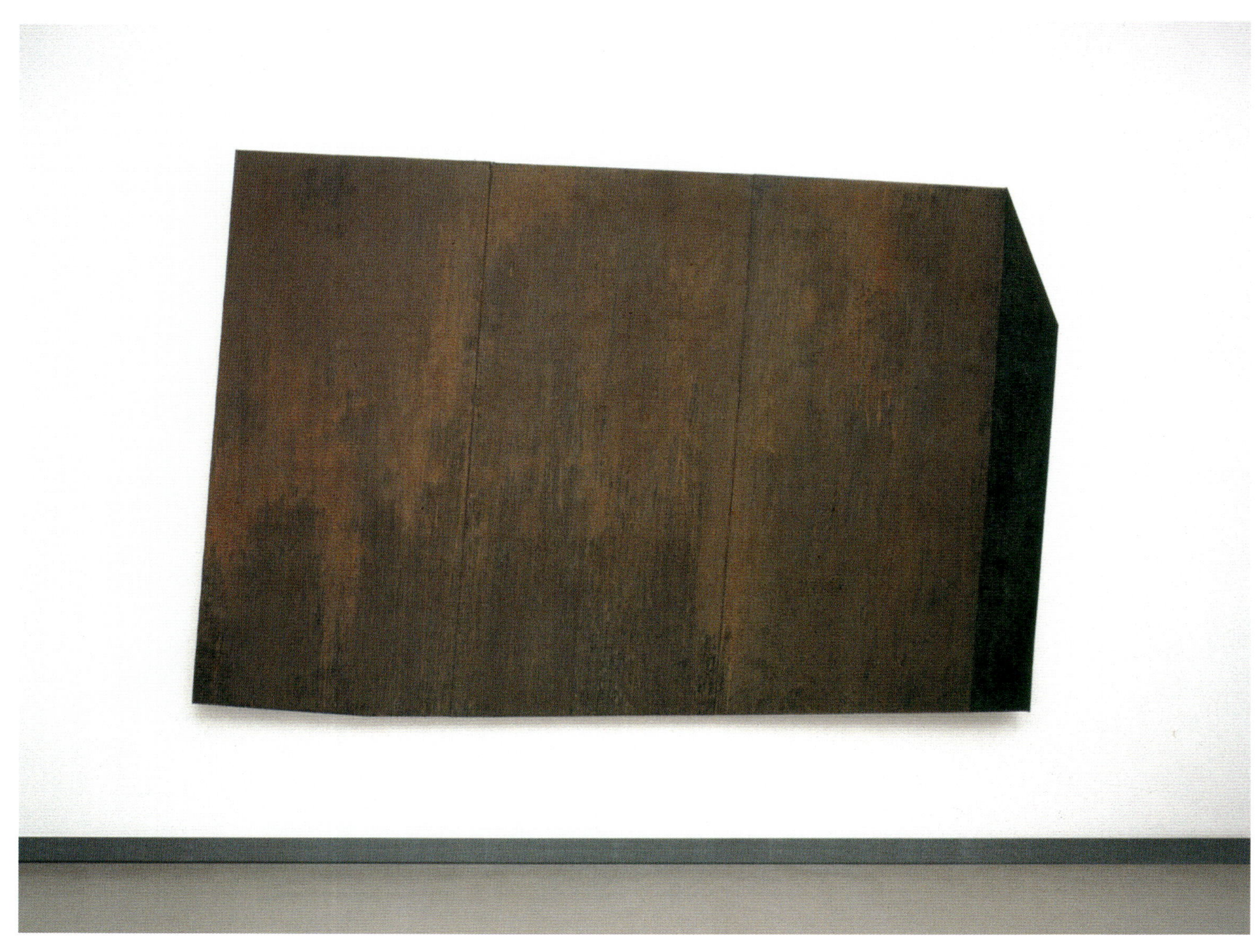

Torso III, 1980
Torso III
Erde auf Leinwand, dreiteilig, 325 × 470 cm
Earth on canvas, three-part

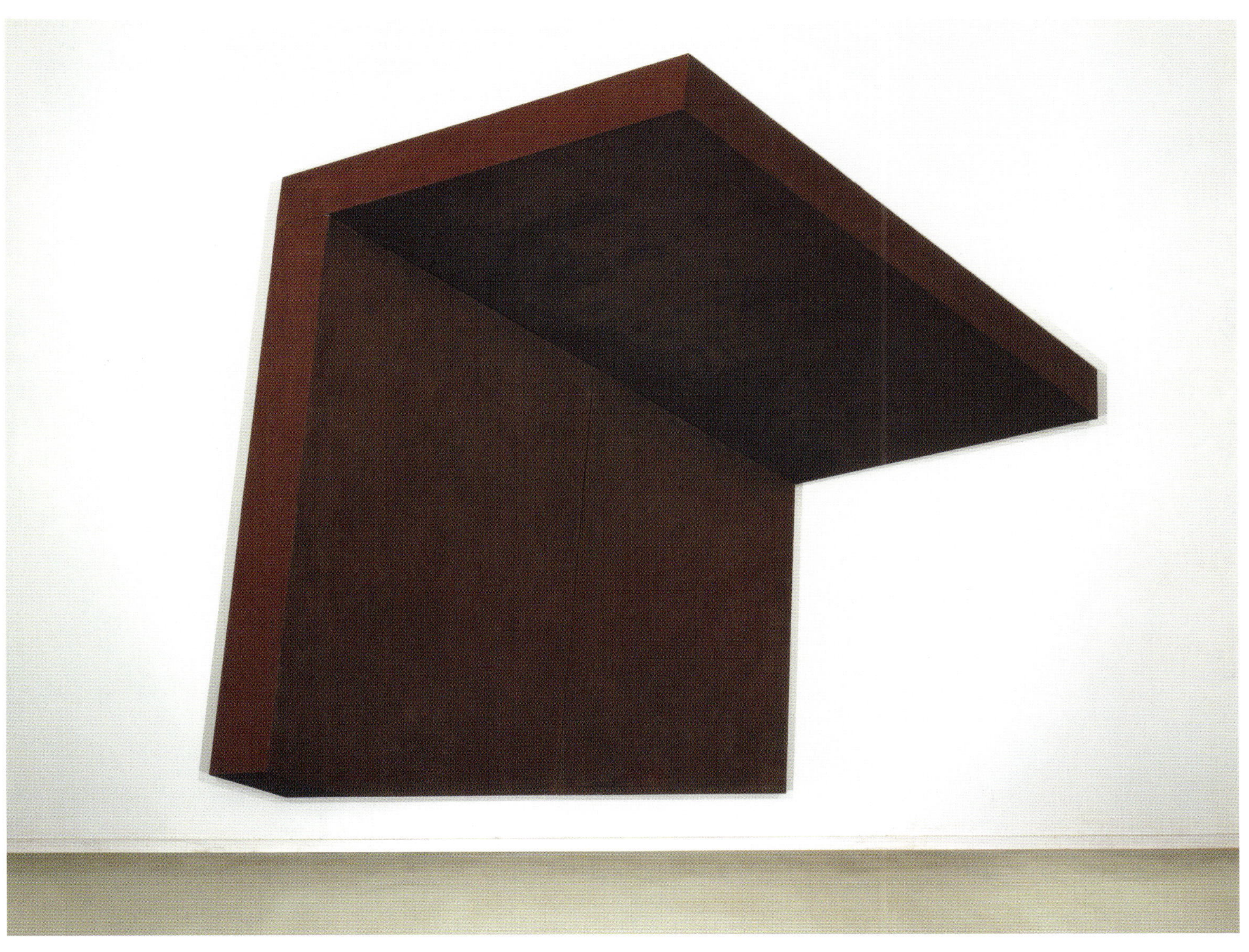

Fragment II, 1980
Fragment II
Erde und Pigment auf Leinwand, dreiteilig,
337 × 400 cm
Earth and pigment on canvas, three-part

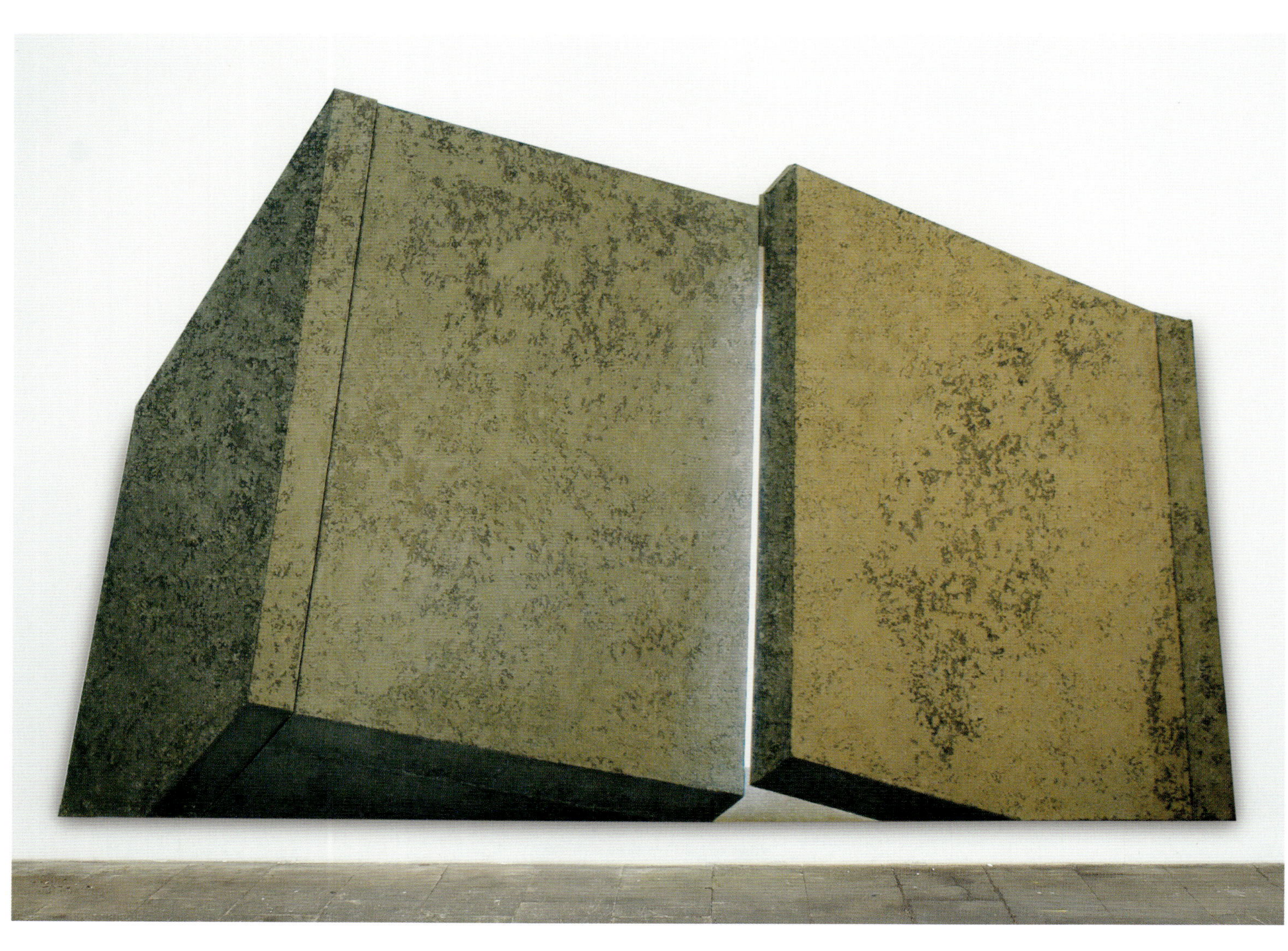

Neapel, 1980
Naples, 1980
Vulkanasche auf Leinwand, dreiteilig, 280 × 450 cm
Volcanic ash on canvas, three-part

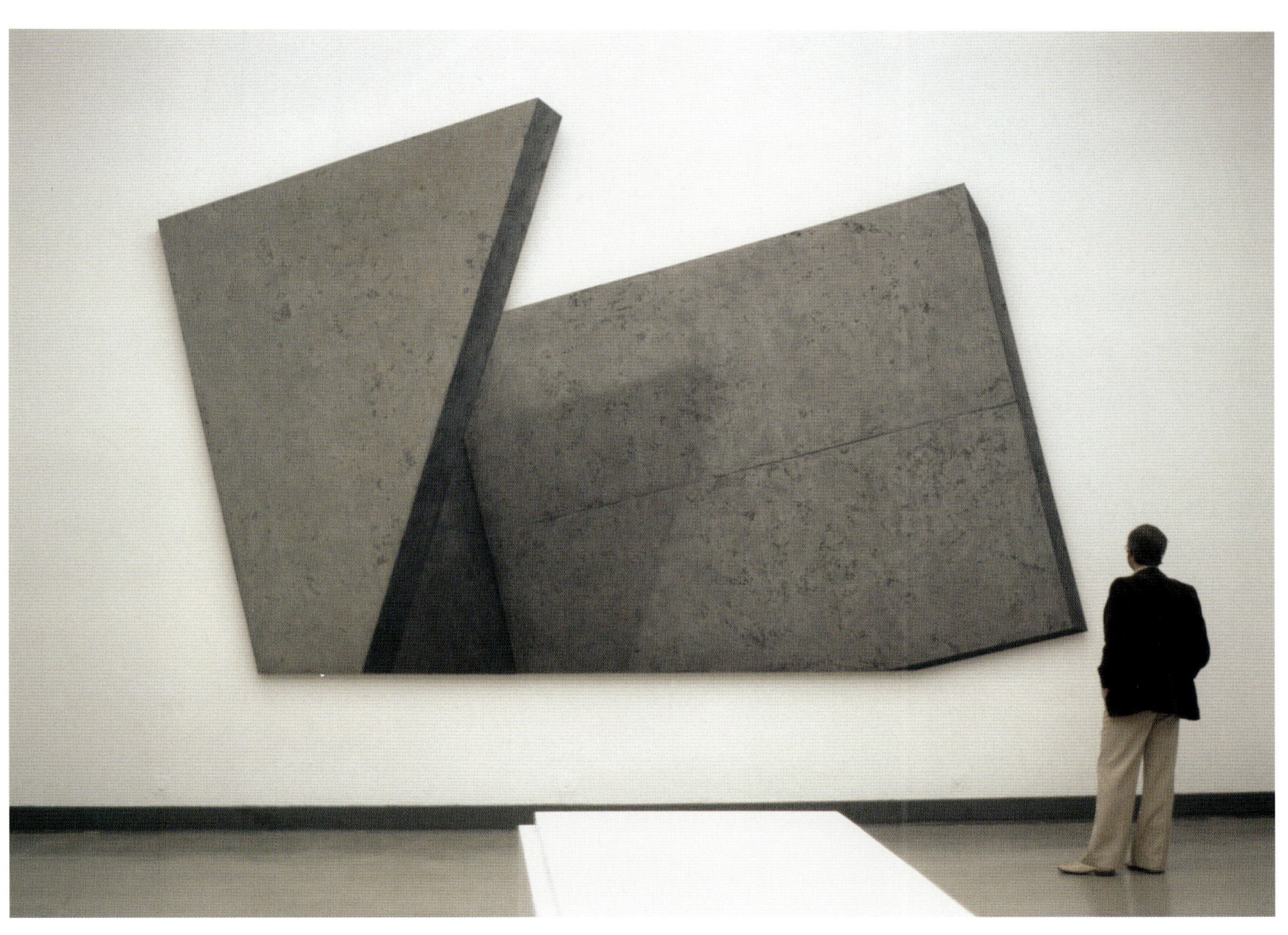

Torso II, 1980
Torso II
Sand auf Leinwand, dreiteilig, 320 × 500 cm
Sand on canvas, three-part

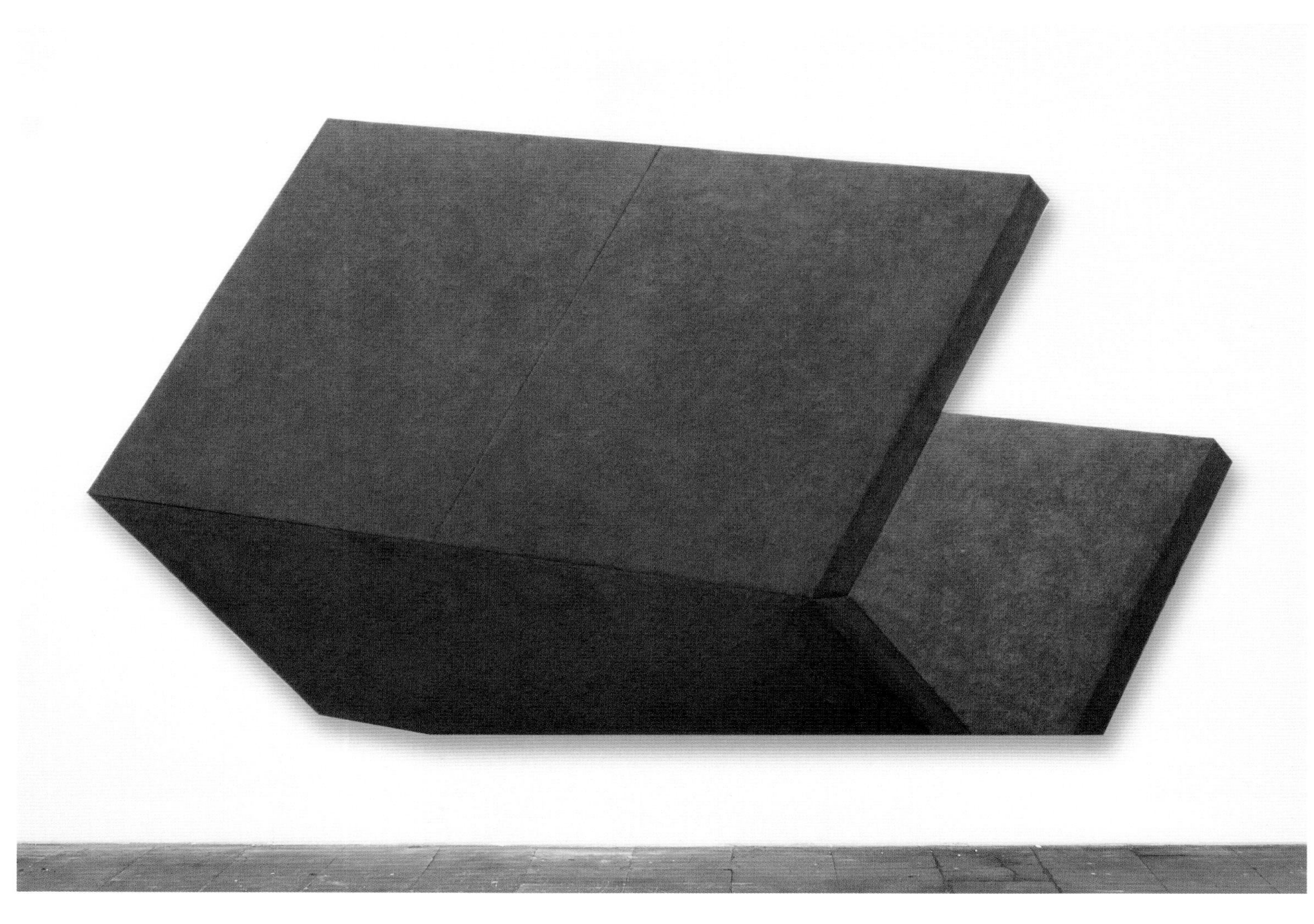

Gebäude-Fragment, 1981
Building Fragment
Erde und Pigment auf Leinwand, vierteilig,
250 × 460 cm
Earth and pigment on canvas, four-part

74

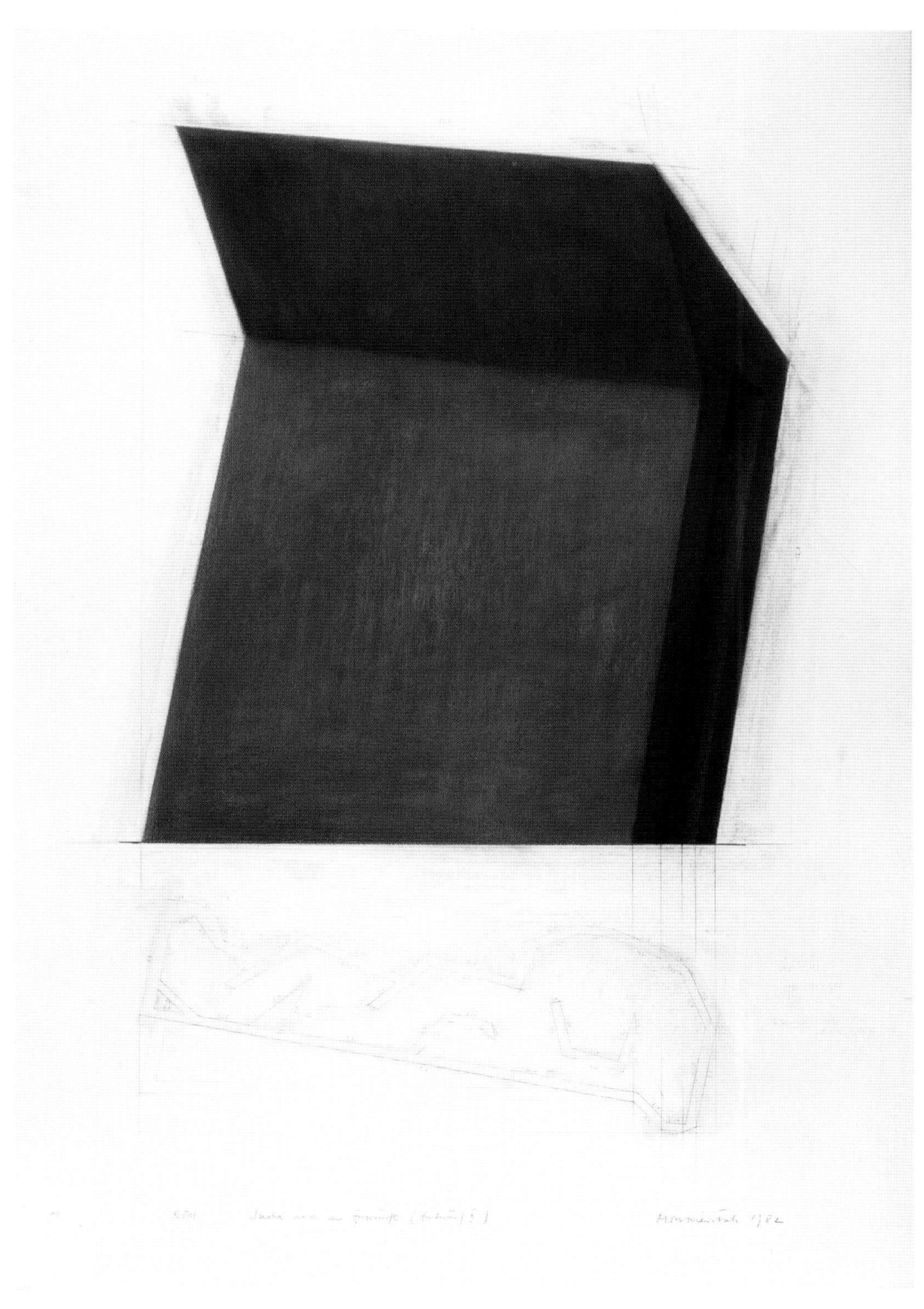

Suche nach der Zukunft, Entwurf II, 1982
Search for the Future, Draft II
Bleistift und Pastell auf Fabriano, 100 × 70 cm
Pencil and pastel on Fabriano

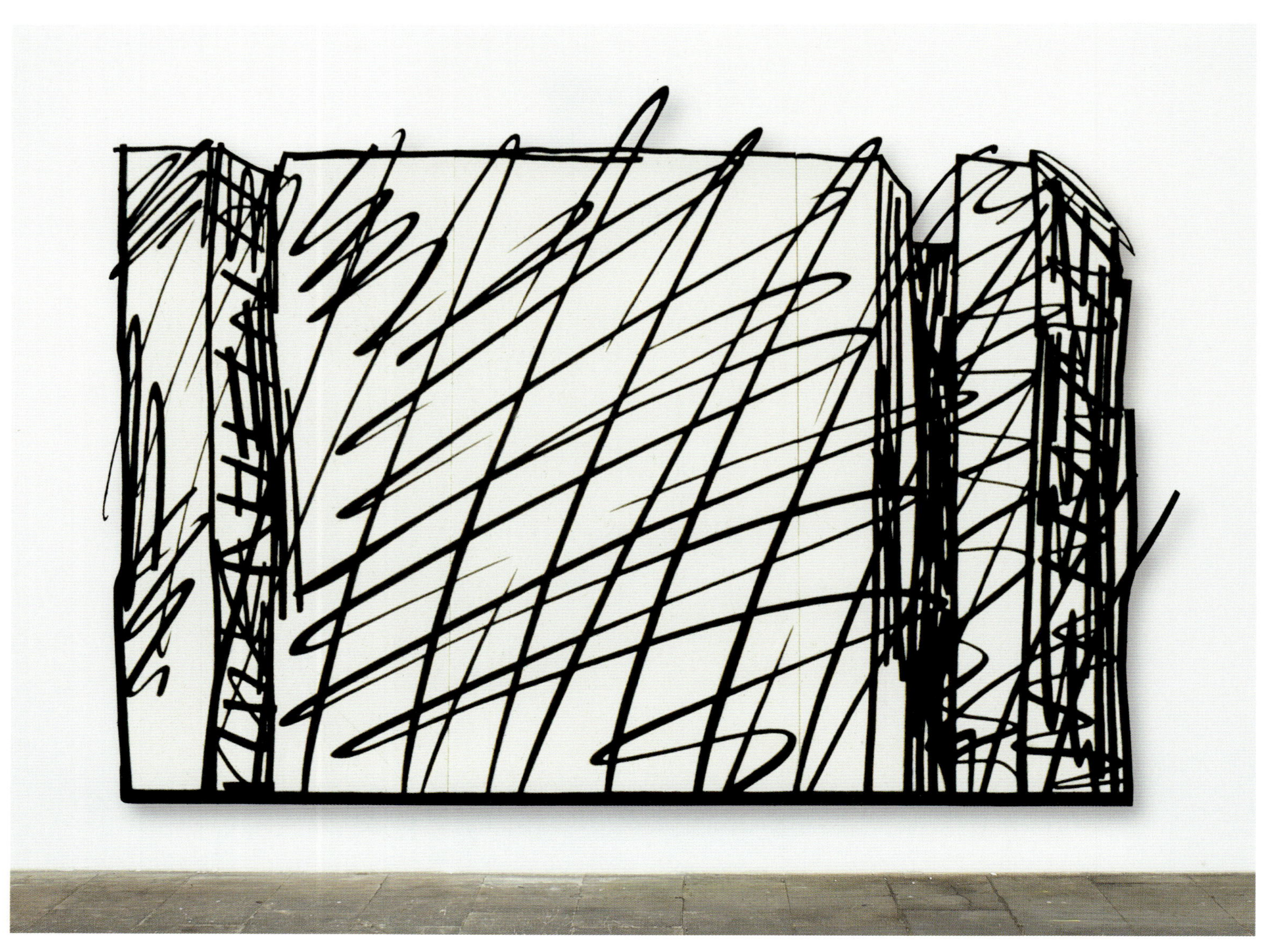

Macht der Skizze, 1981
The Power of the Sketch
Eitempera auf Leinwand, Stahlblech, dreiteilig,
308 × 450 cm
Egg tempera on canvas, sheet metal, three-part

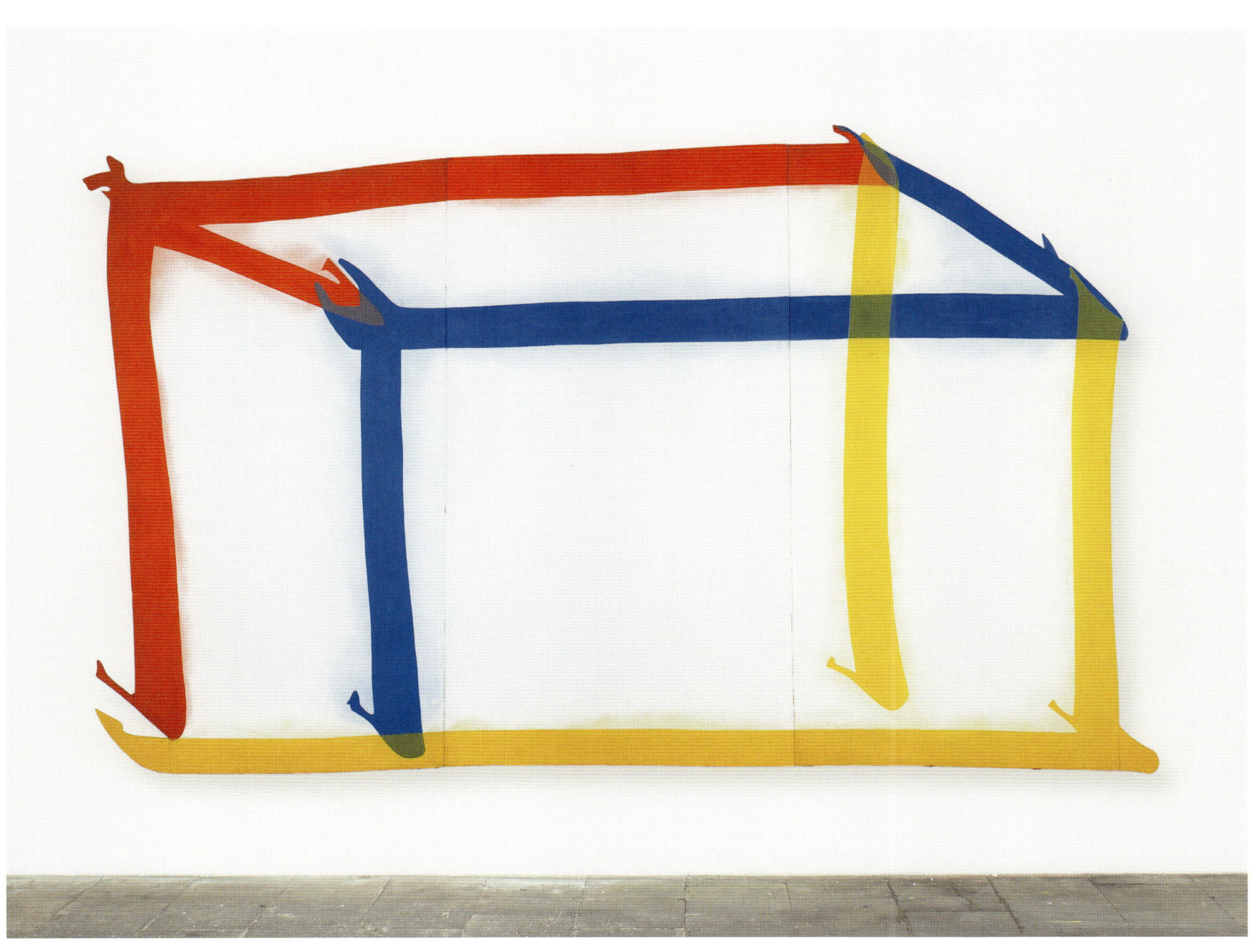

Raumskizze mit Pinselmarker, 1984
Sketch of a Space Using a Brush Marker
Dispersion, Leim und Pigment auf Leinwand, dreiteilig,
297 × 480 cm
Dispersion, glue and pigment on canvas, three-part

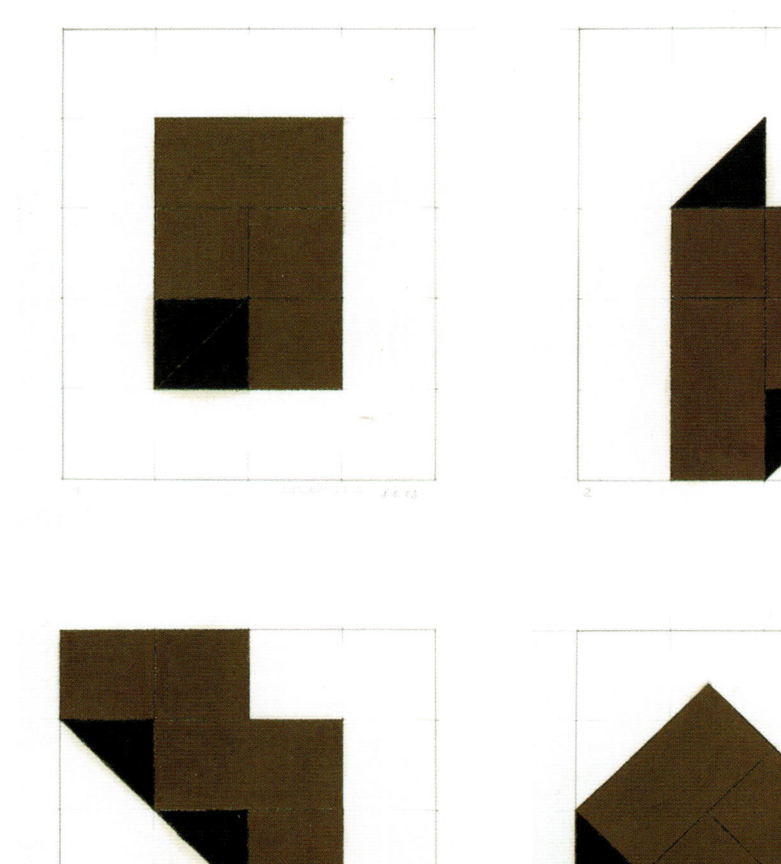

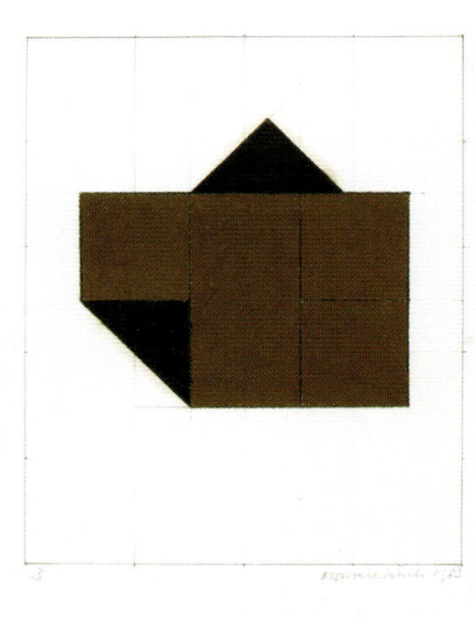

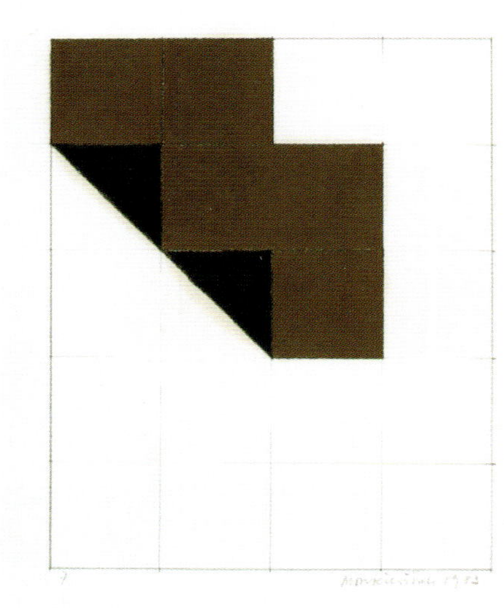

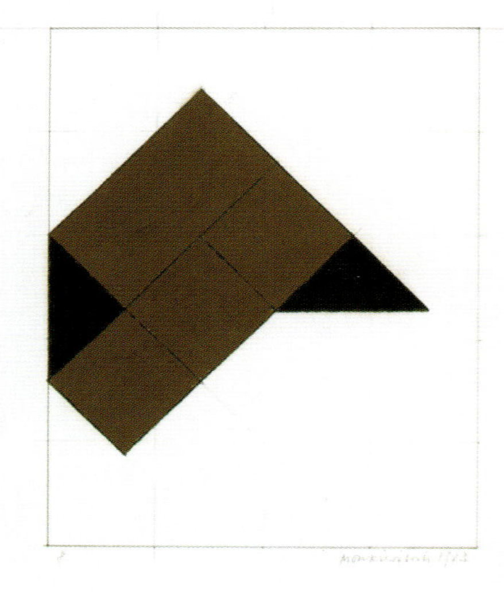

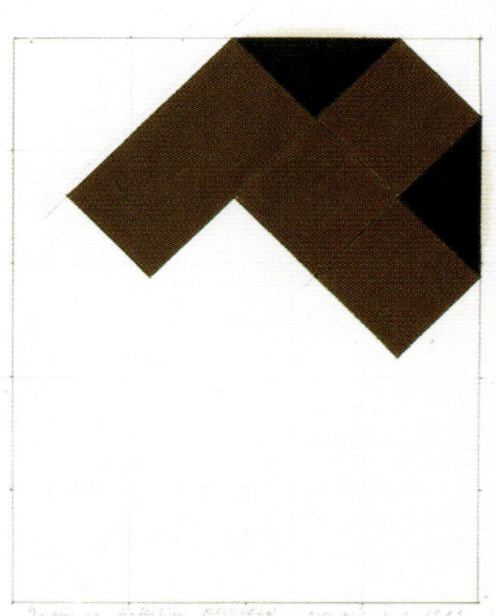

78

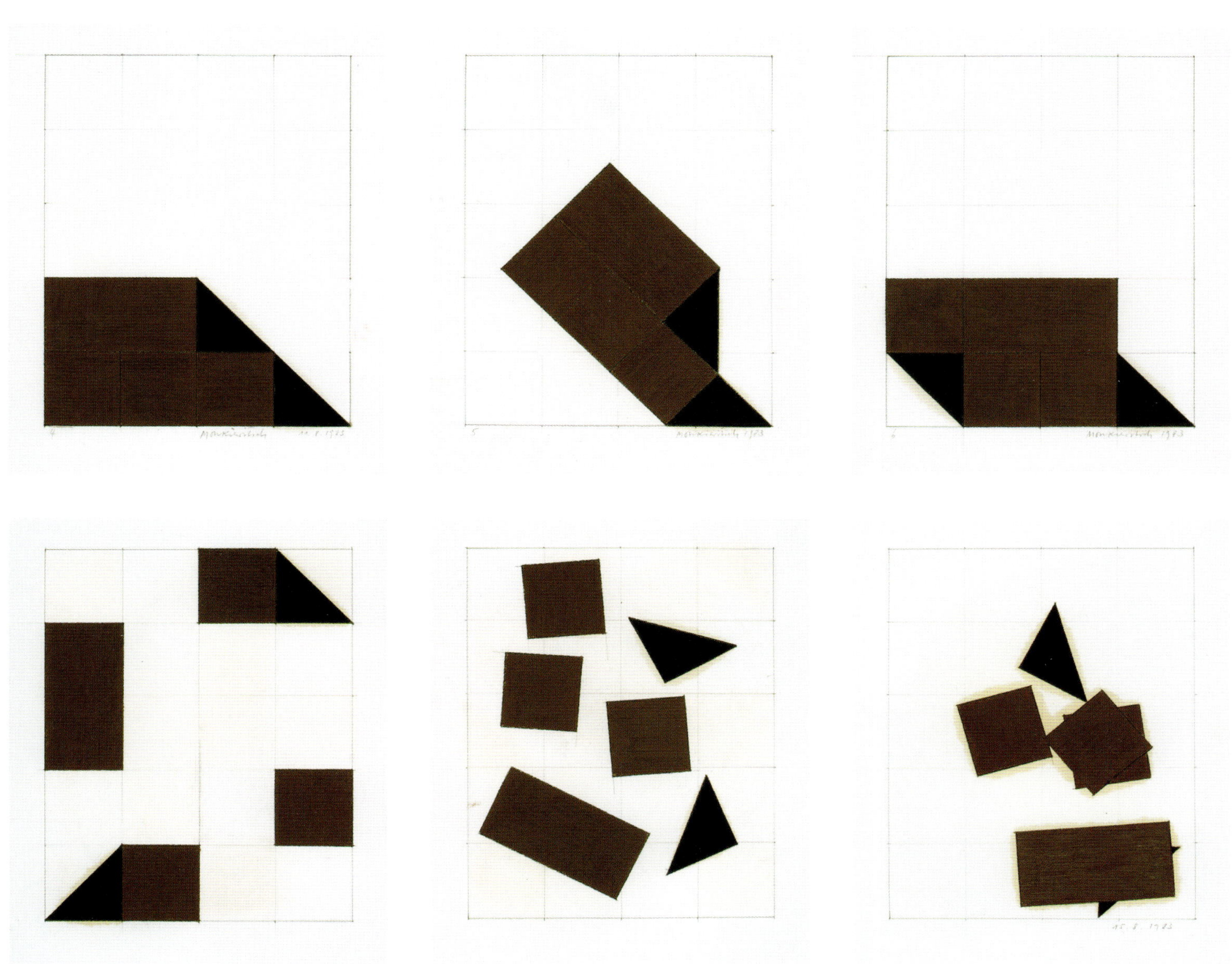

aus: **6-teiliges Rechteck,** 1983
From: Six-part Rectangle
Bleistift und Öl auf Karton, je 20 × 16 cm
Pencil and oil on cardboard

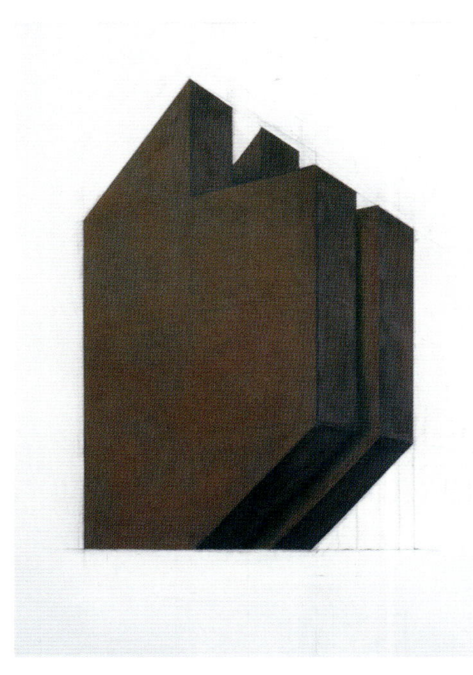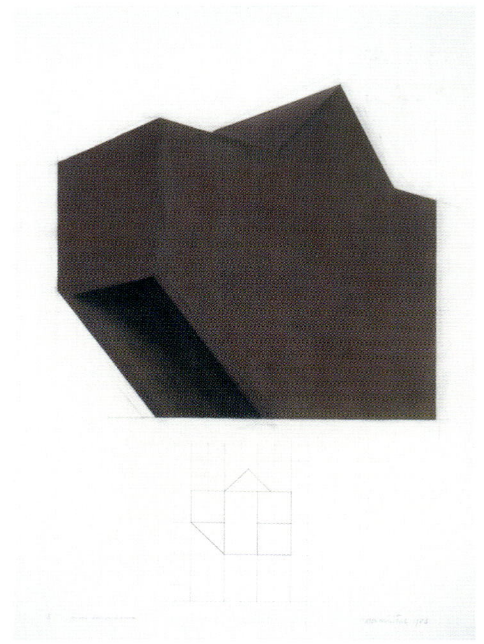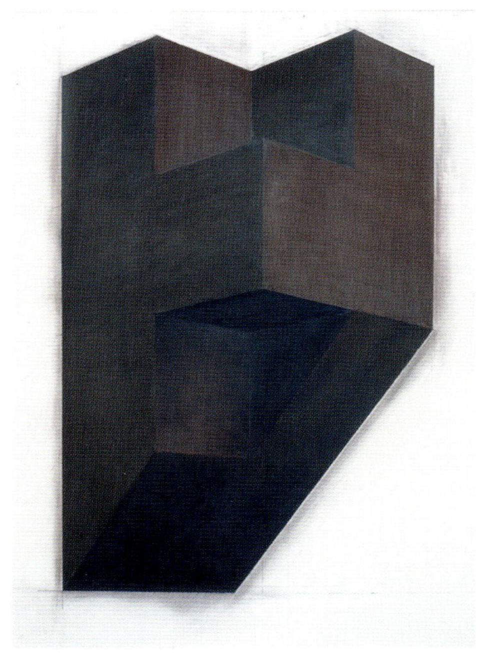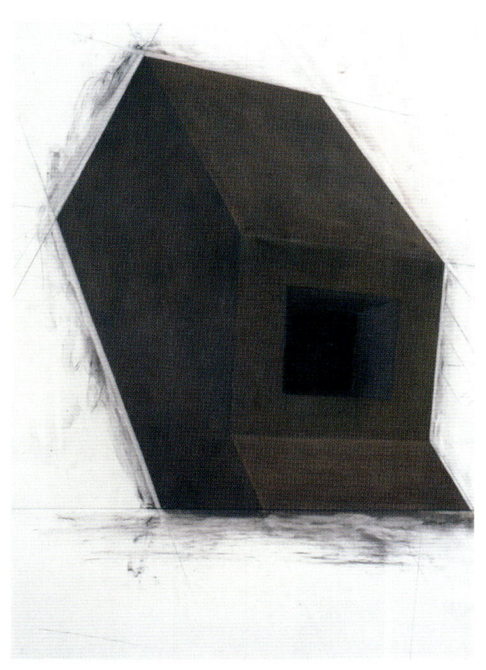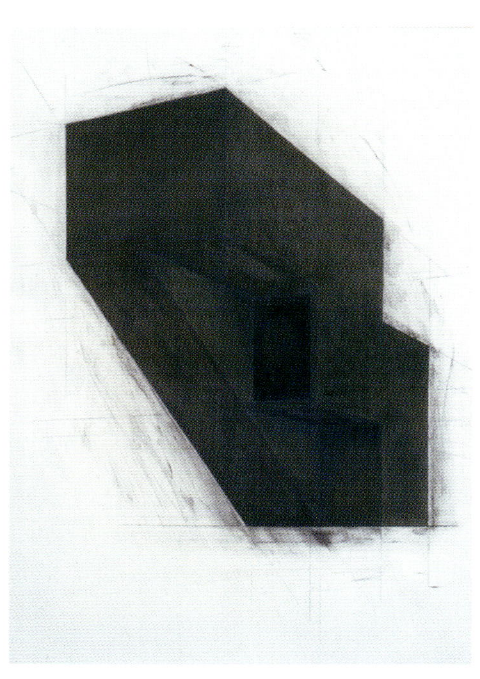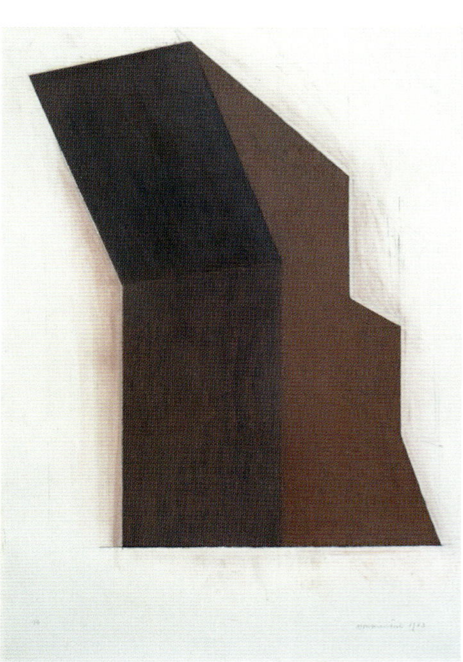

6 Raumveränderungen, 1983
Six Spatial Changes
Bleistift, Öl und Pigment auf Fabriano, 100 × 70 cm
Pencil, oil and pigment on Fabriano

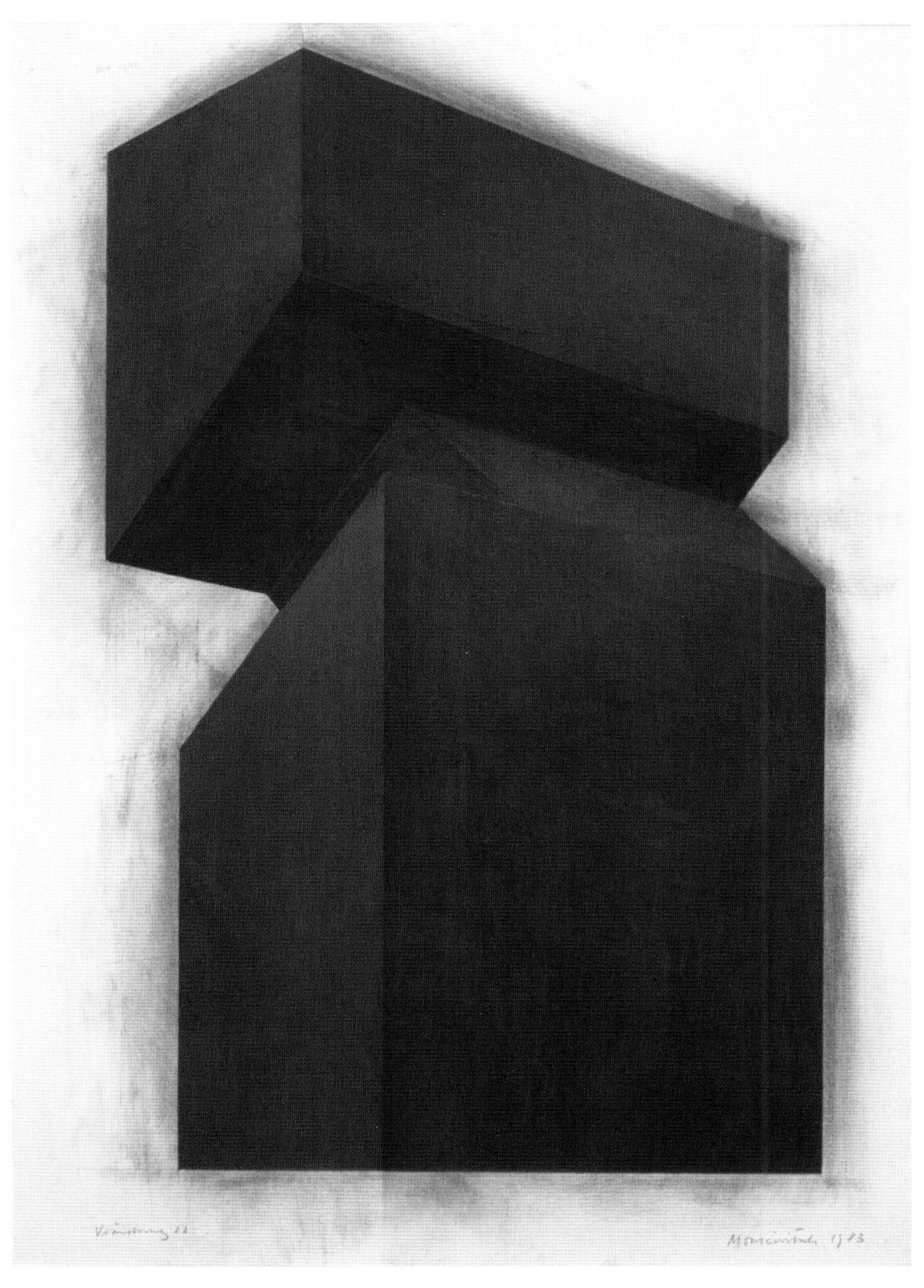

Raumveränderung XIII, 1983
Spatial Change XIII
Bleistift, Öl und Pigment auf Fabriano, 100 × 70 cm
Pencil, oil and pigment on Fabriano

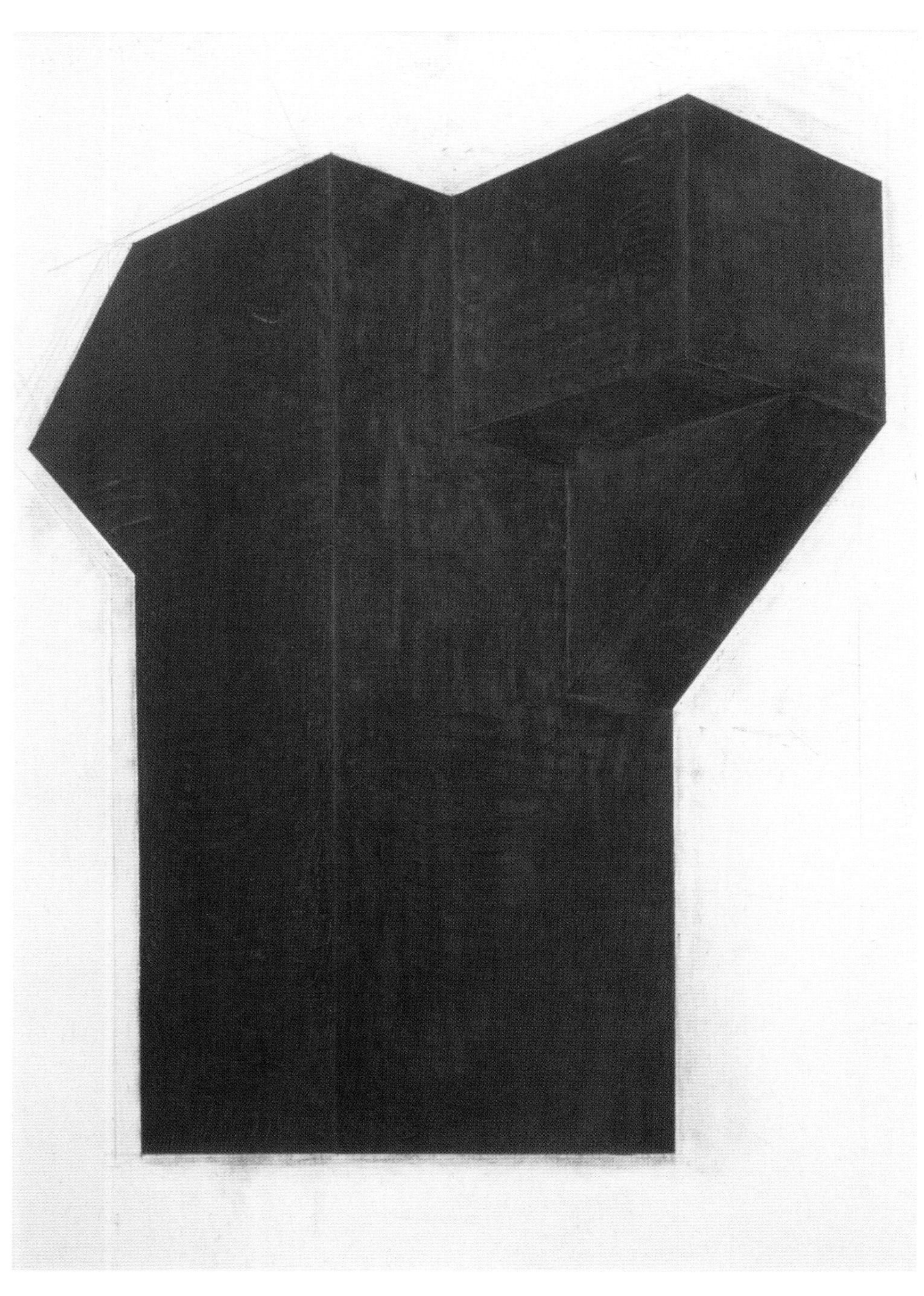

Raumveränderung VII, 1983
Spatial Change VII
Bleistift, Öl und Pigment auf Fabriano, 100 × 70 cm
Pencil, oil and pigment on Fabriano

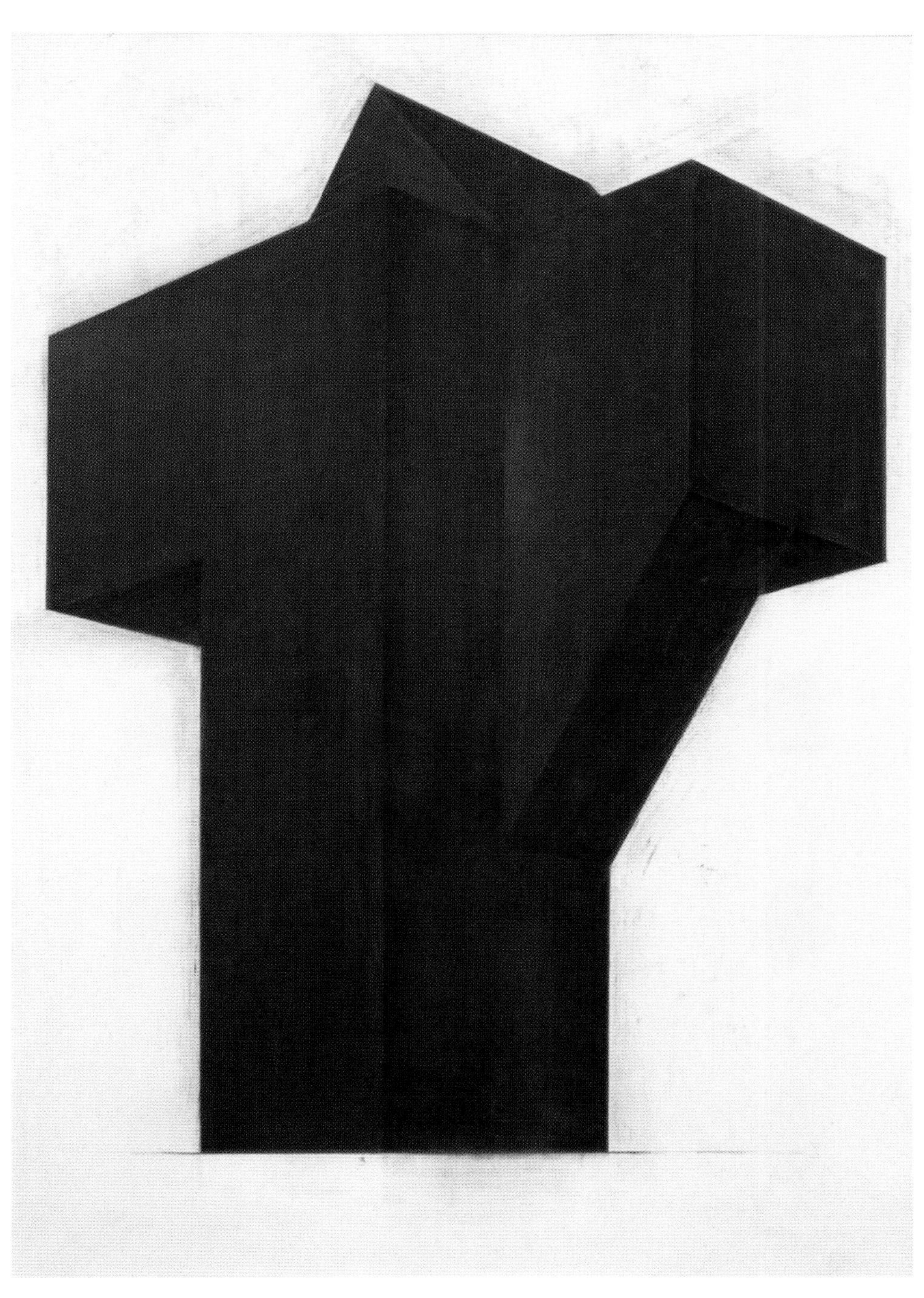

Raumveränderung XIV, 1983
Spatial Change XIV
Bleistift, Öl und Pigment auf Fabriano, 100 × 70 cm
Pencil, oil and pigment on Fabriano

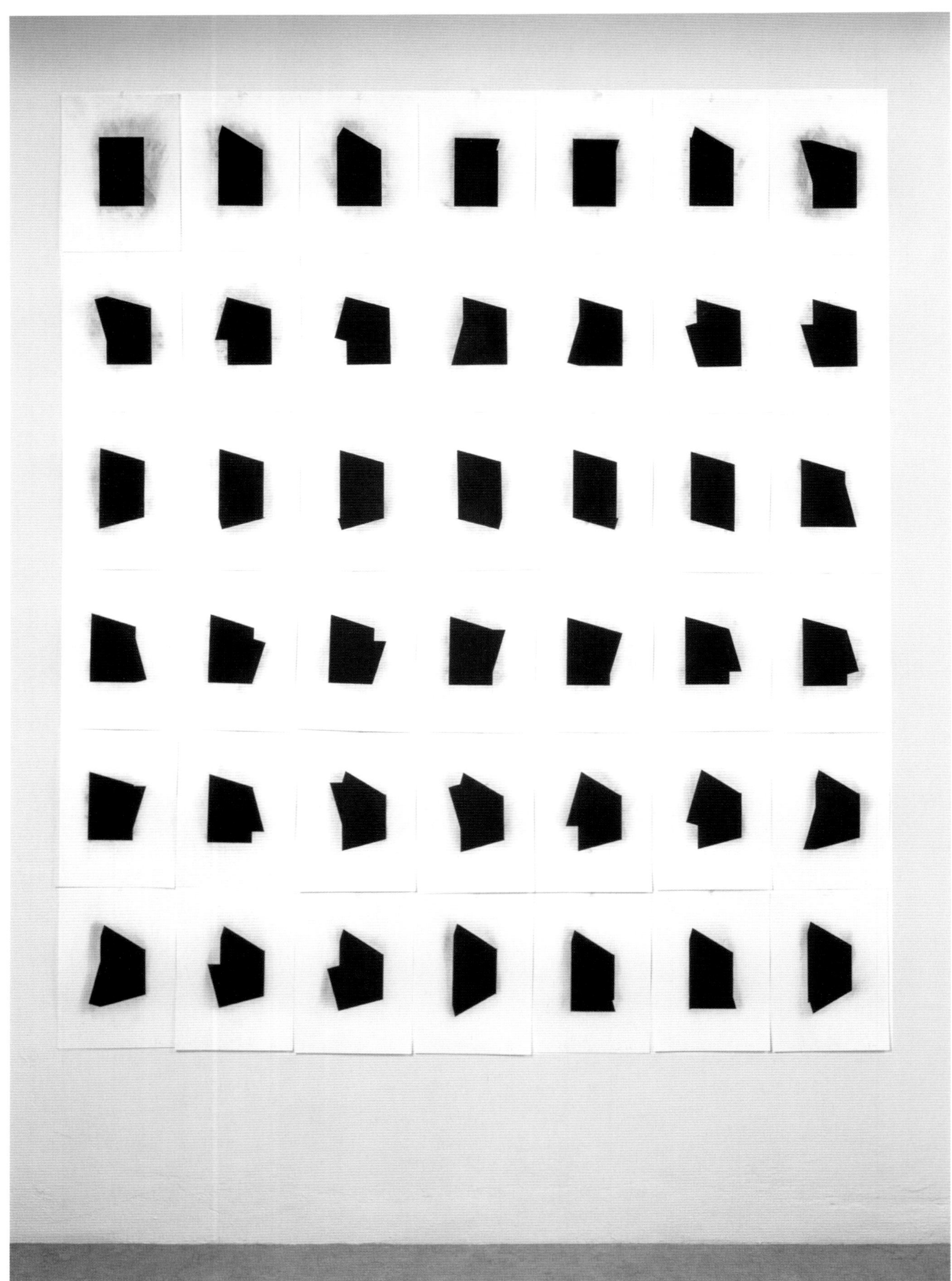

Zwei Schnitte in das suprematistische Rechteck, 1985
Two Cuts in the Suprematist Rectangle
42 Blätter von insgesamt 204, Öl und Pigment auf
Fabriano, je 33 × 24 cm
Forty-two of a total of 204 sheets, oil and pigment
on Fabriano

aus: **Zwei Schnitte in das suprematistische
Rechteck, 1/4,** 1985
From: *Two Cuts in the Suprematist Rectangle, 1/4*
Öl und Pigment auf Fabriano, 33 × 24 cm
Oil and pigment on Fabriano

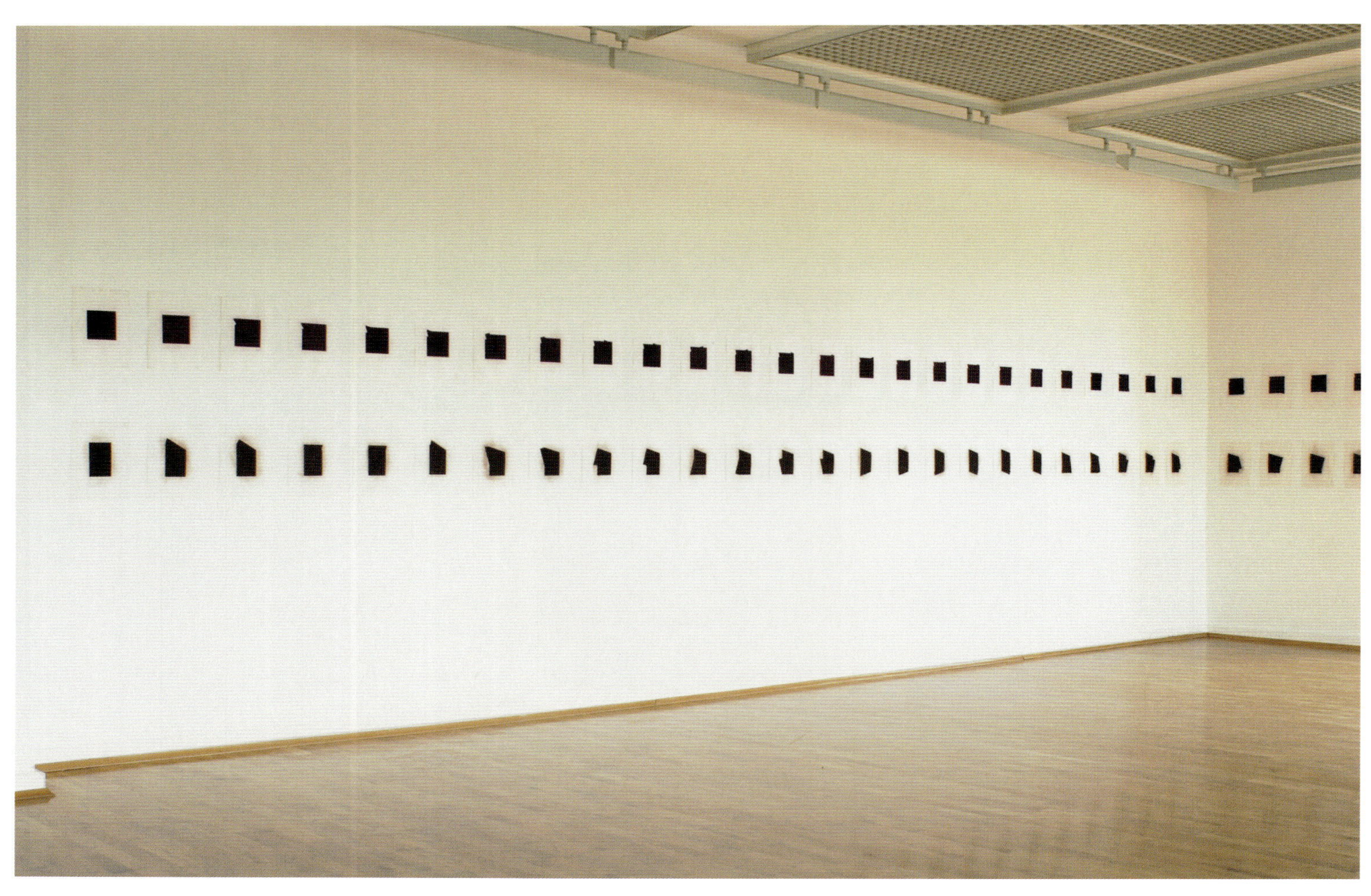

Installation des Beginns der beiden Serien:
Zwei Schnitte in das suprematistische Rechteck und
Zwei Schnitte in das Quadrat, 1985/86
Installation at the beginning of the two series:
Two Cuts in the Suprematist Rectangle and
Two Cuts in the Suprematist Square

Zwei Schnitte in das suprematistische Rechteck, IV/6,
1985
Two Cuts in the Suprematist Rectangle, IV/6
Öl und Pigment auf Holz, 36 × 29,5 × 12 cm
Oil and pigment on wood

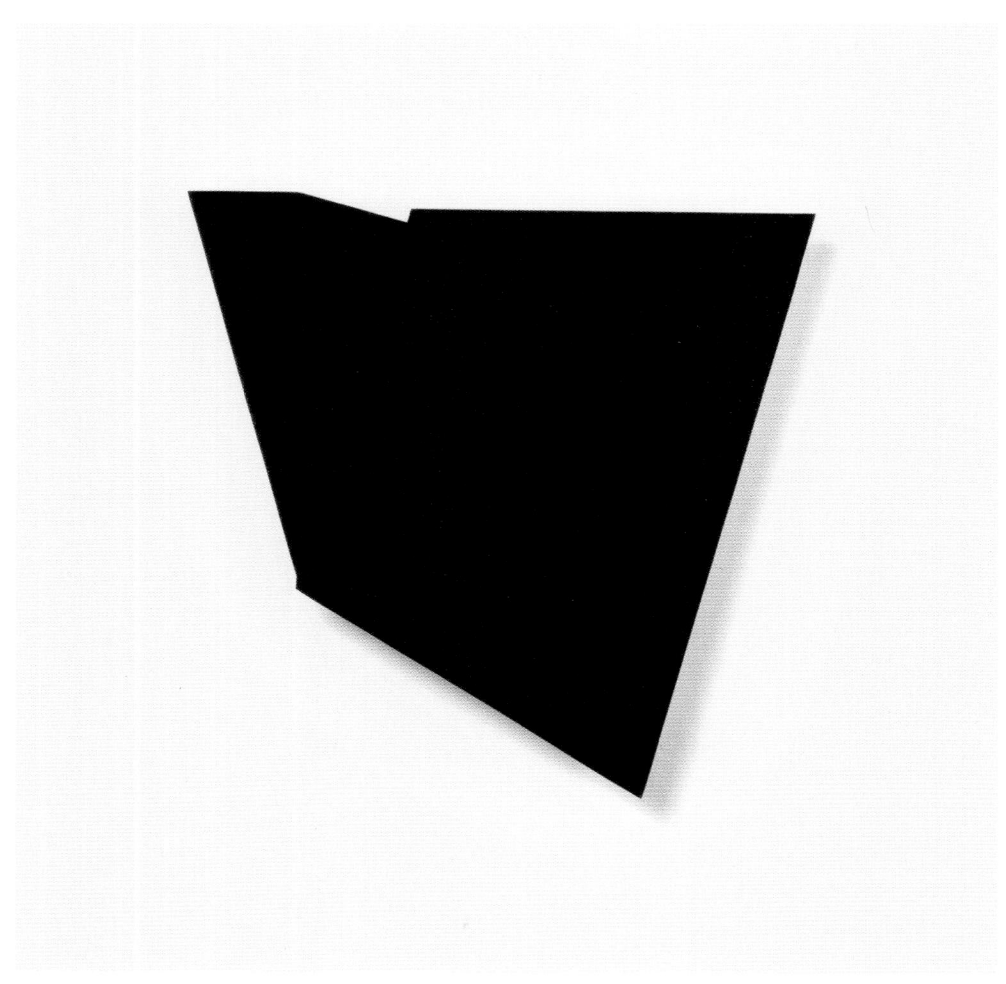

Zwei Schnitte in das suprematistische Rechteck, XIII/3,
1985
Two Cuts in the Suprematist Rectangle, XIII/3
Öl und Pigment auf Holz, 36 × 39 × 12 cm
Oil and pigment on wood

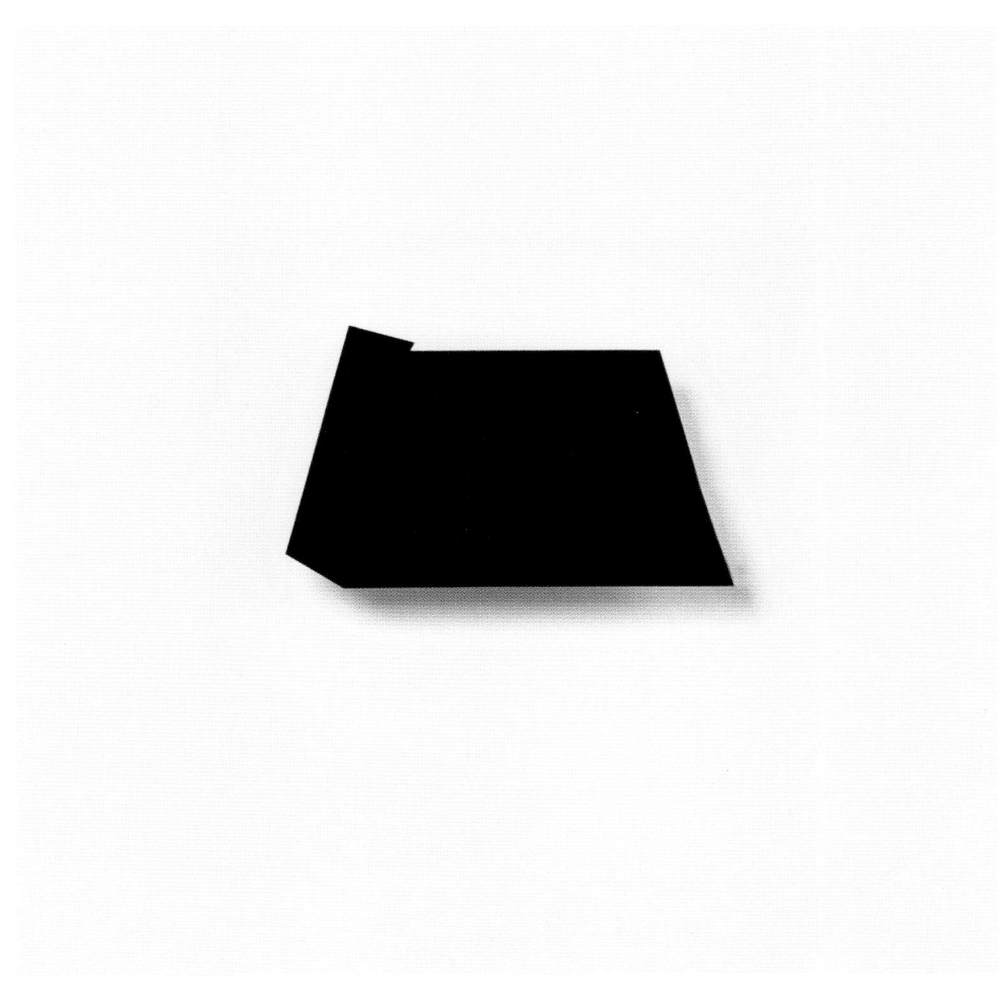

Zwei Schnitte in das suprematistische Rechteck, III/24,
1986
Two Cuts in the Suprematist Rectangle, III/24
Öl und Pigment auf Holz, 17 × 26 × 8 cm
Oil and pigment on wood

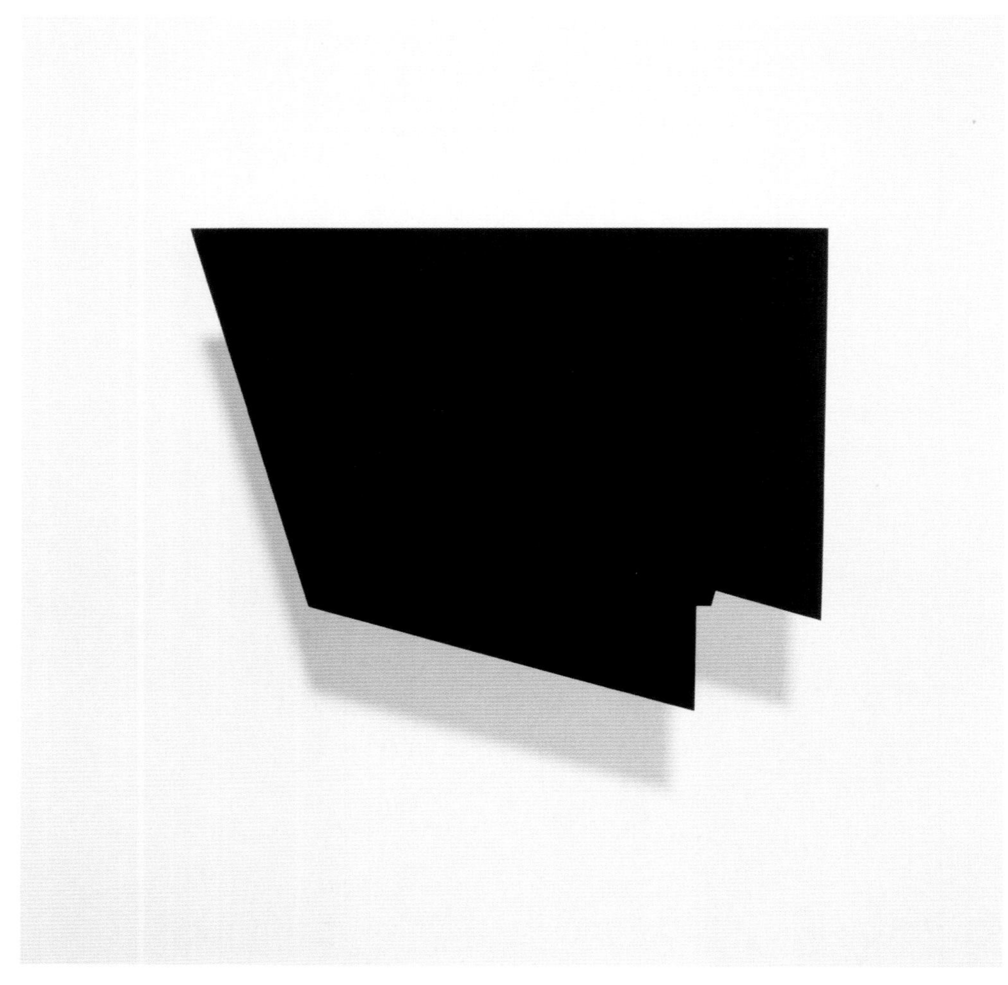

Zwei Schnitte in das suprematistische Rechteck, IV/11,
1986
Two Cuts in the Suprematist Rectangle, IV/11
Öl und Pigment auf Kirschholz, 36 × 29,5 × 14 cm
Oil and pigment on cherry

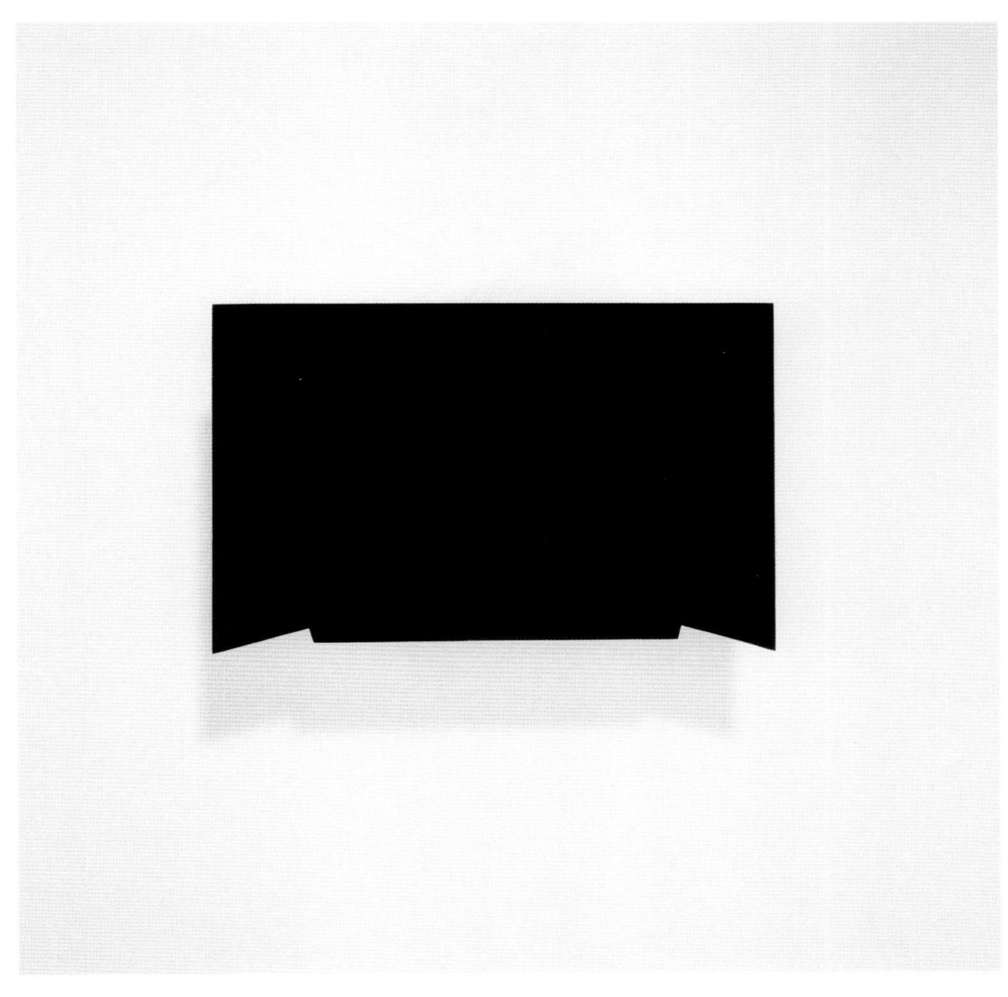

Zwei Schnitte in das suprematistische Rechteck, IV/7,
1986
Two Cuts in the Suprematist Rectangle, IV/7
Öl und Pigment auf Kirschholz, 36 × 25 × 14 cm
Oil and pigment on cherry

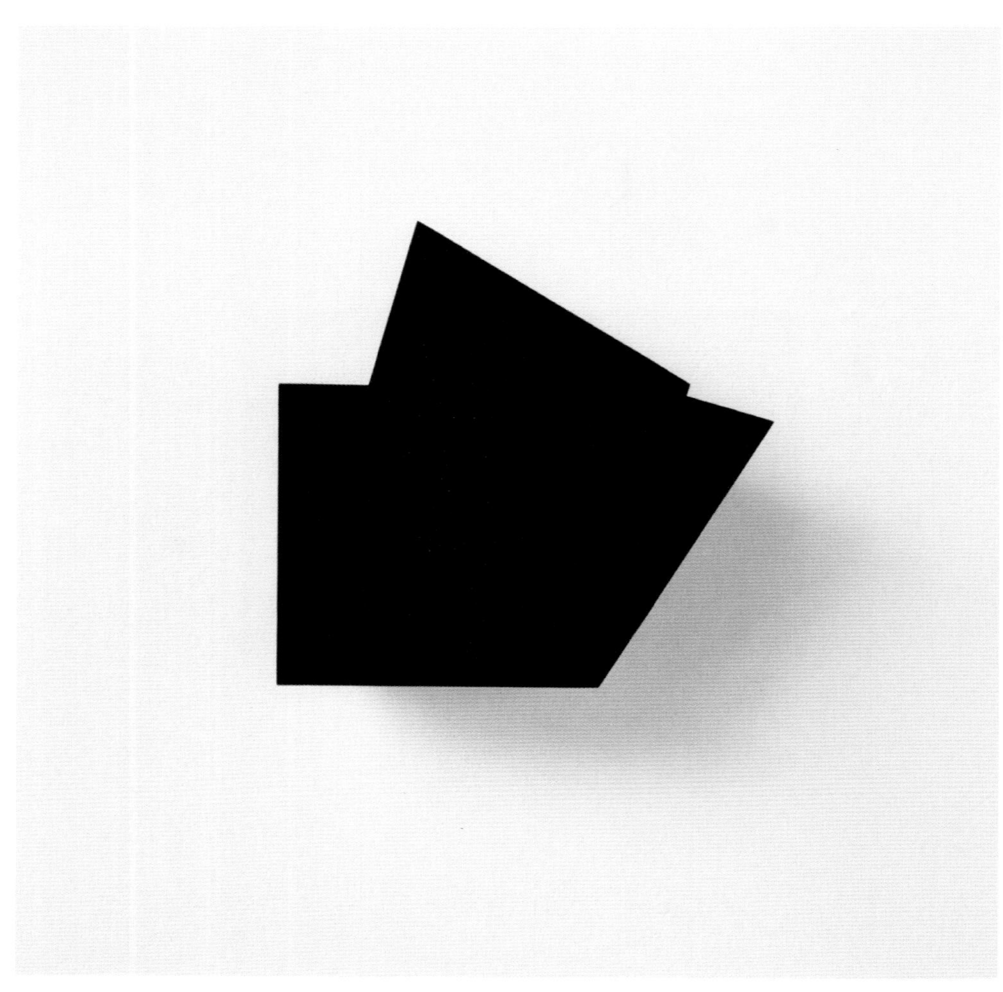

Zwei Schnitte in das suprematistische Rechteck, x/6,
1993
Two Cuts in the Suprematist Rectangle, x/6
Samt und Acryl auf Beton, 40,5 × 41 × 14 cm
Velvet and acrylic on concrete

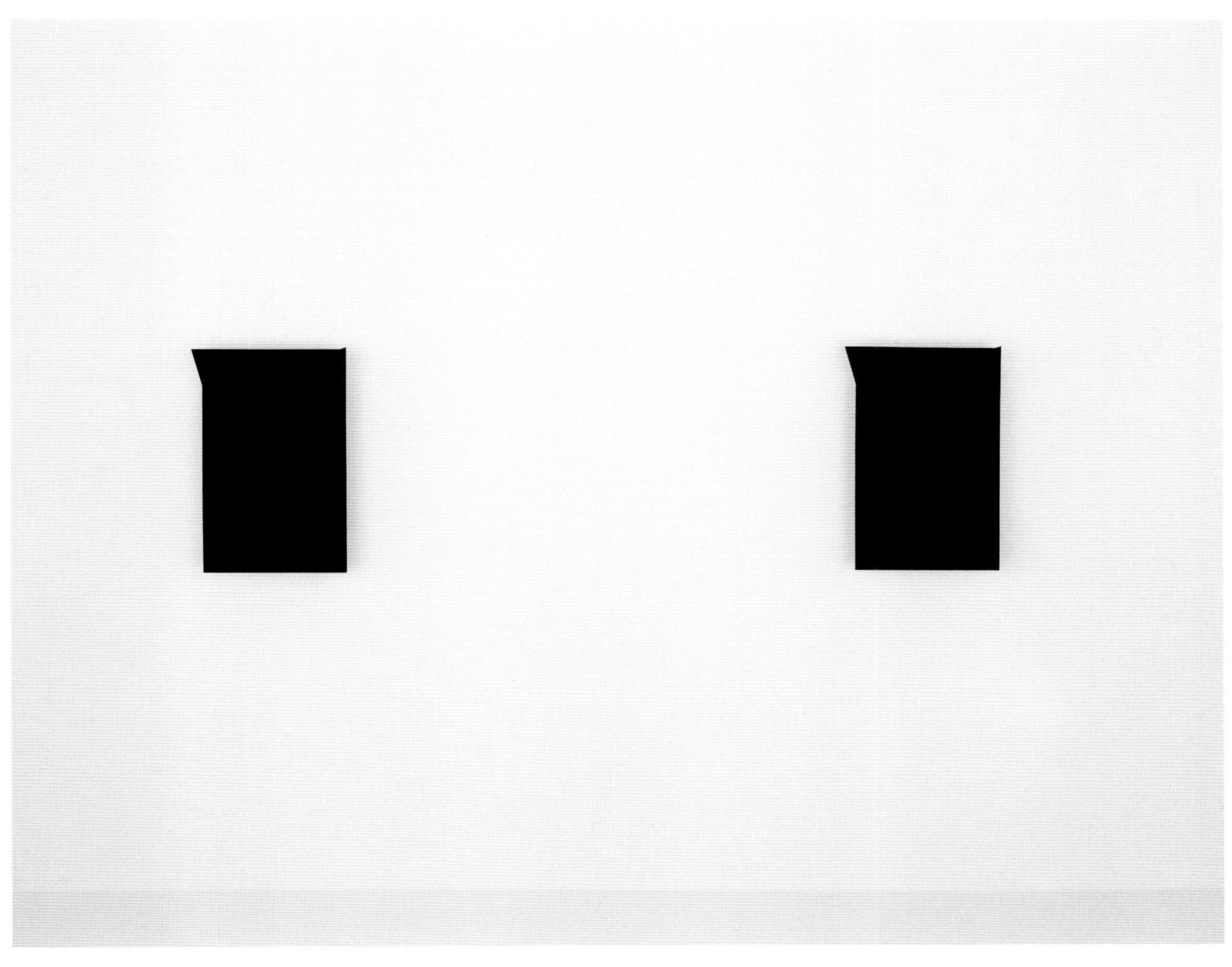

**Zwei Schnitte in das suprematistische Rechteck, 1/5
(Doppelstück),** 1991
Two Cuts in the Suprematist Rectangle, 1/5 (double work)
Samt und Öl auf Beton, 40 × 26 × 13 cm
Velvet and oil on concrete

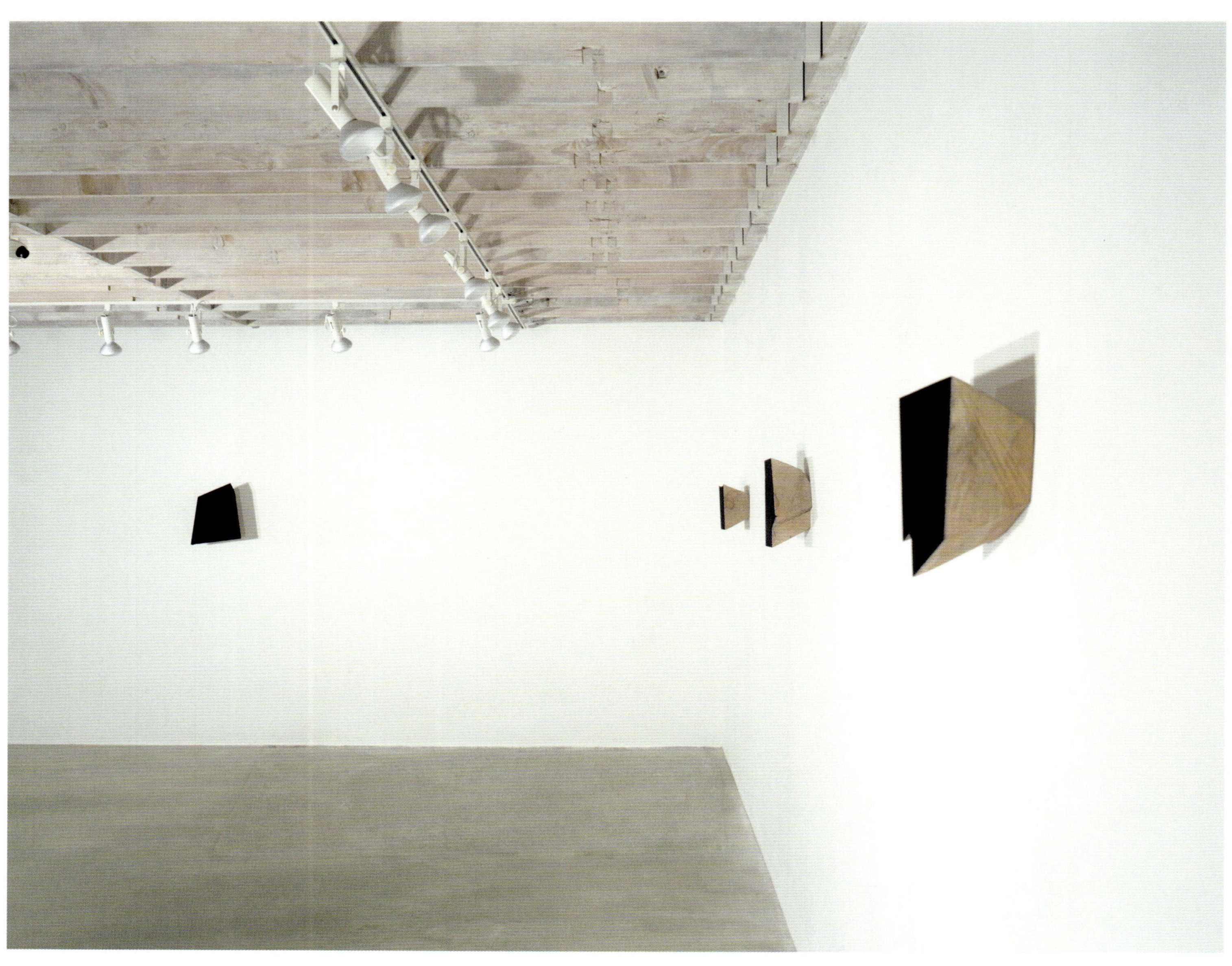

Zwei Schnitte in das suprematistische Rechteck und
Zwei Schnitte in das suprematistische Quadrat,
Installation 1987 Angles Gallery
Two Cuts in the Suprematist Rectangle and
Two Cuts in the Suprematist Square, installation at
the Angles Gallery, 1987

Zwei Schnitte in das suprematistische Quadrat, 1986
Two Cuts in the Suprematist Square
42 Blätter einer ca. 1 500 Blätter umfassenden Serie
(unvollendet)
Forty-two sheets of a series comprising circa 1,500
sheets (unfinished)
Öl und Pigment auf Fabriano, je 33 × 24 cm
Oil and pigment on Fabriano

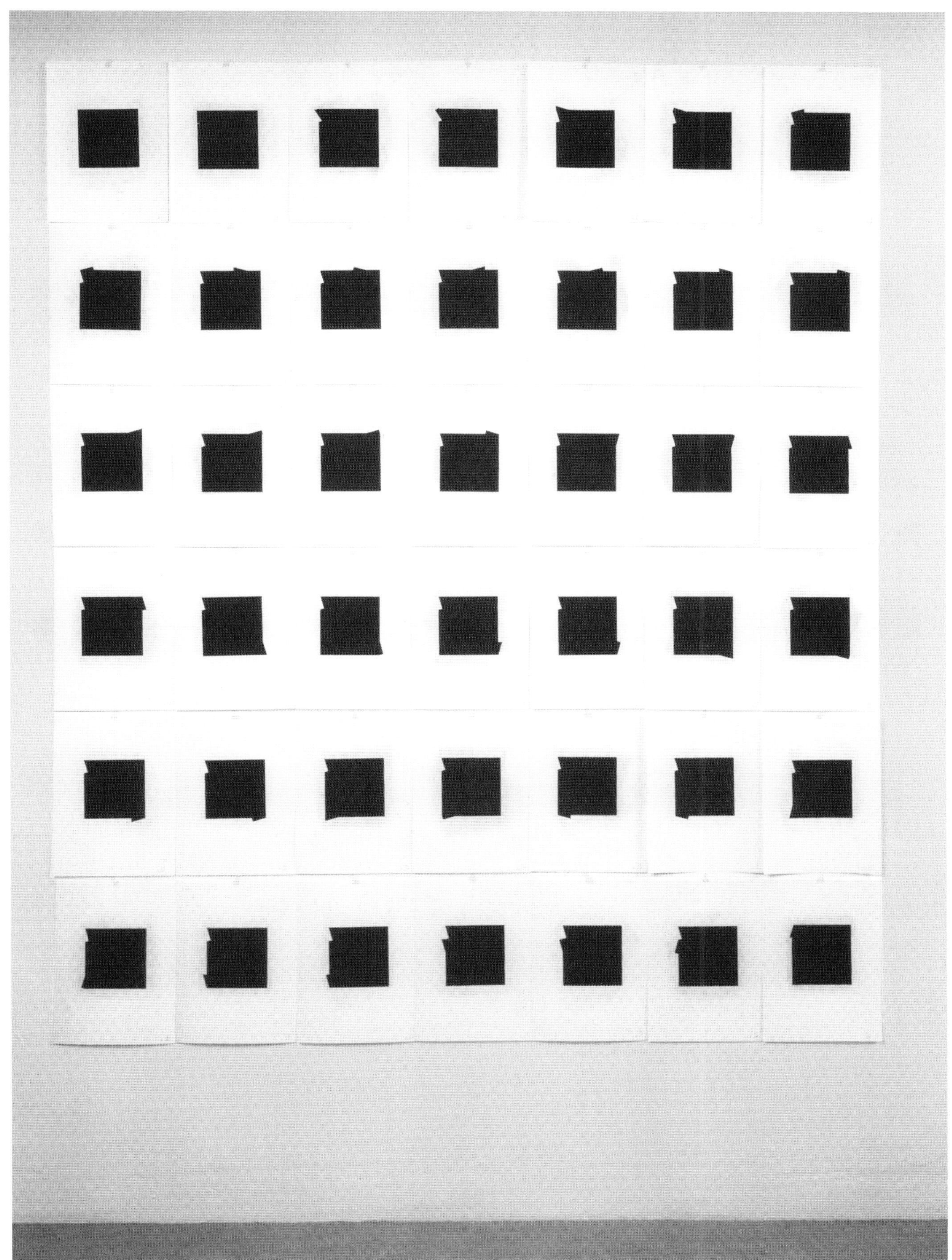

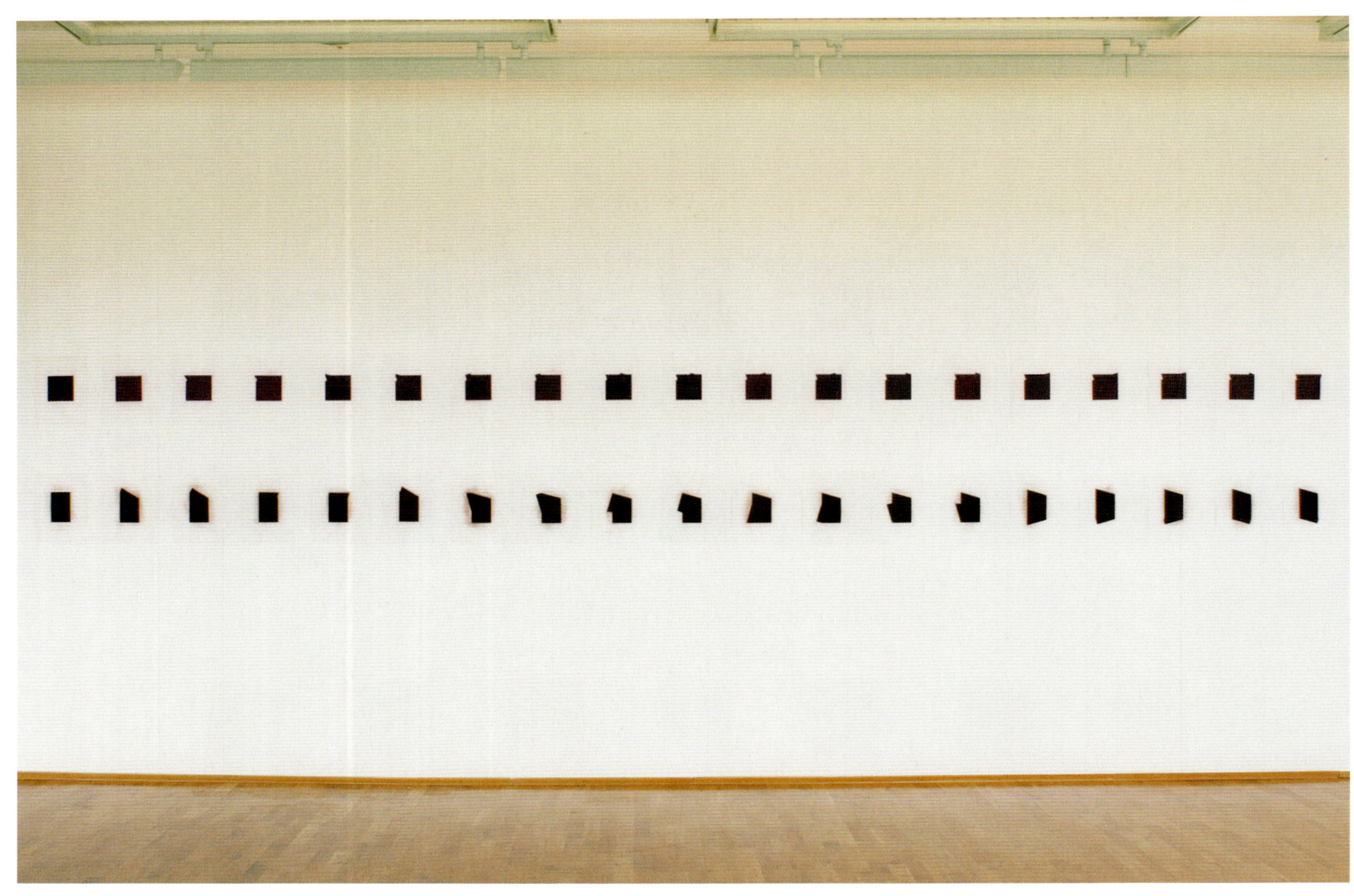

Installierte Serienanfänge: **Zwei Schnitte in das
suprematistische Rechteck** und **Zwei Schnitte in das
suprematistischein das Quadrat,** 1985/86
Installed beginnings of the series: *Two Cuts in the
Suprematist Rectangle* and *Two Cuts in the Suprematist
Square*
Öl und Pigment auf Fabriano, je 33 × 246 cm
Oil and pigment on Fabriano

Zwei Schnitte in das suprematistische Quadrat, 1/2,
1986
Two Cuts in the Suprematist Square, 1/2
Öl und Pigment auf Fabriano, 33 × 24 cm
Oil and pigment on Fabriano

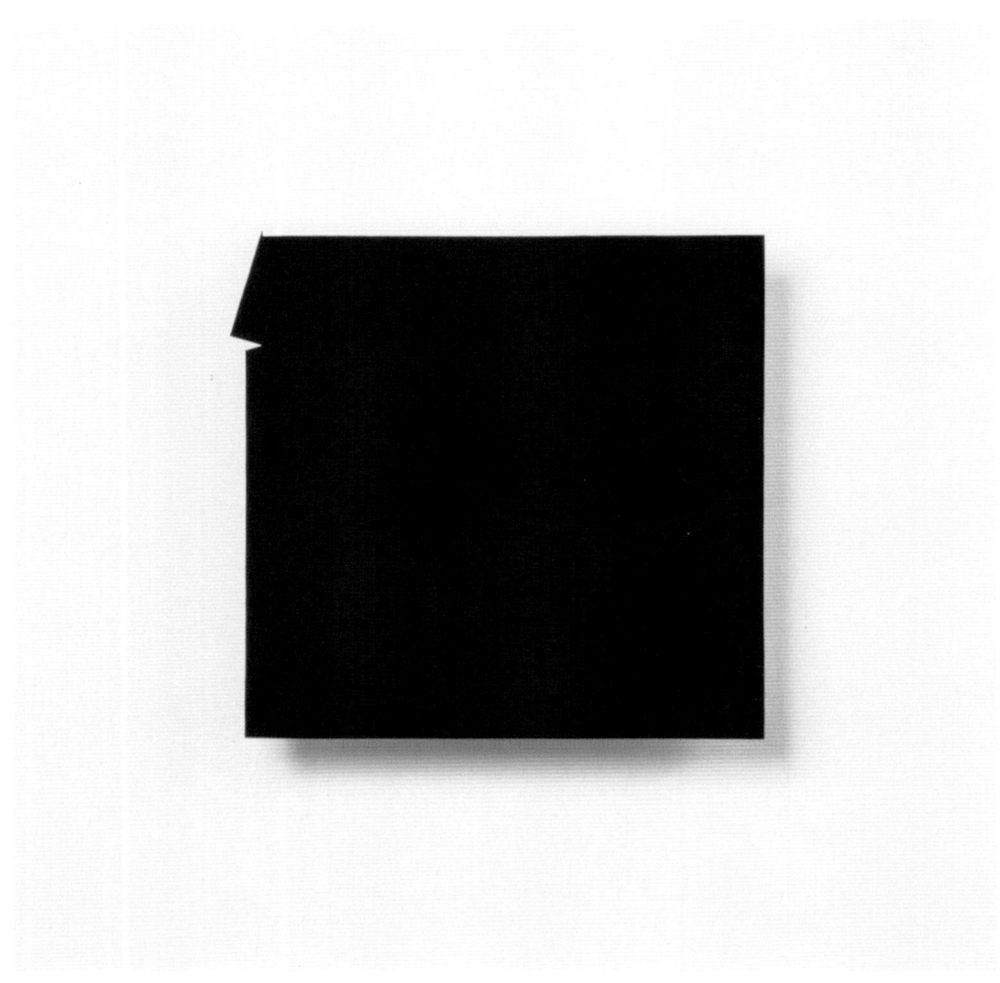

Zwei Schnitte in das suprematistische Quadrat, II/1,
1986
Two Cuts in the Suprematist Square, II/1
Öl und Pigment auf Holz, 36 × 37 × 4 cm
Oil and pigment on wood

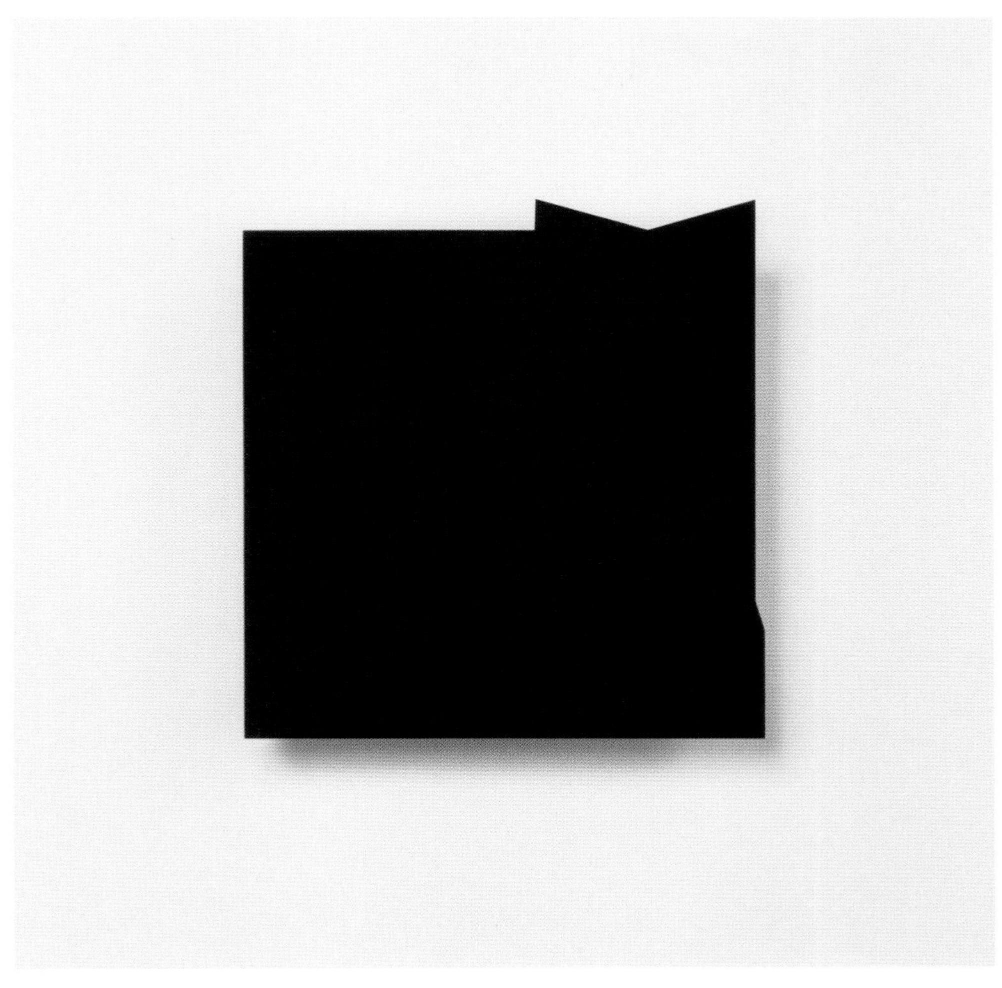

Zwei Schnitte in das suprematistische Quadrat, V/40,
1986
Two Cuts in the Suprematist Square, V/40
Öl und Pigment auf Holz, 36 × 38 × 4 cm
Oil and pigment on wood

Zwei Schnitte in das suprematistische Quadrat, 1/22,
1986
Two Cuts in the Suprematist Square, 1/22
Öl und Pigment auf Nussbaum, 30 × 31 × 14
Oil and pigment on walnut

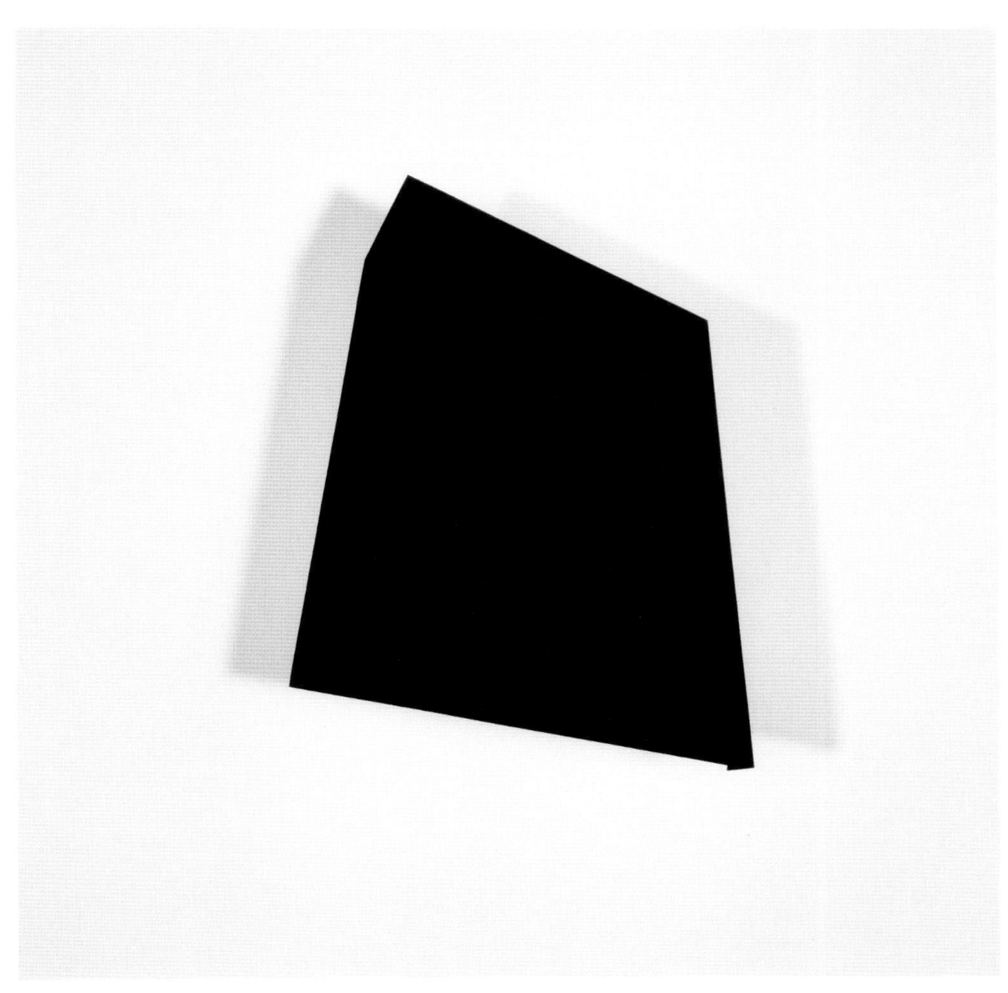

Zwei Schnitte in das suprematistische Quadrat, X/12,
1986
Two Cuts in the Suprematist Square, X/12
Öl und Pigment auf Apfelbaum, 39 × 34 × 14 cm
Oil and pigment on apple

Zwei Schnitte in das suprematistische Quadrat, xx/44,
1986
Two Cuts in the Suprematist Square, xx/44
Öl und Pigment auf Holz, 37 × 36 × 4 cm
Oil and pigment on wood

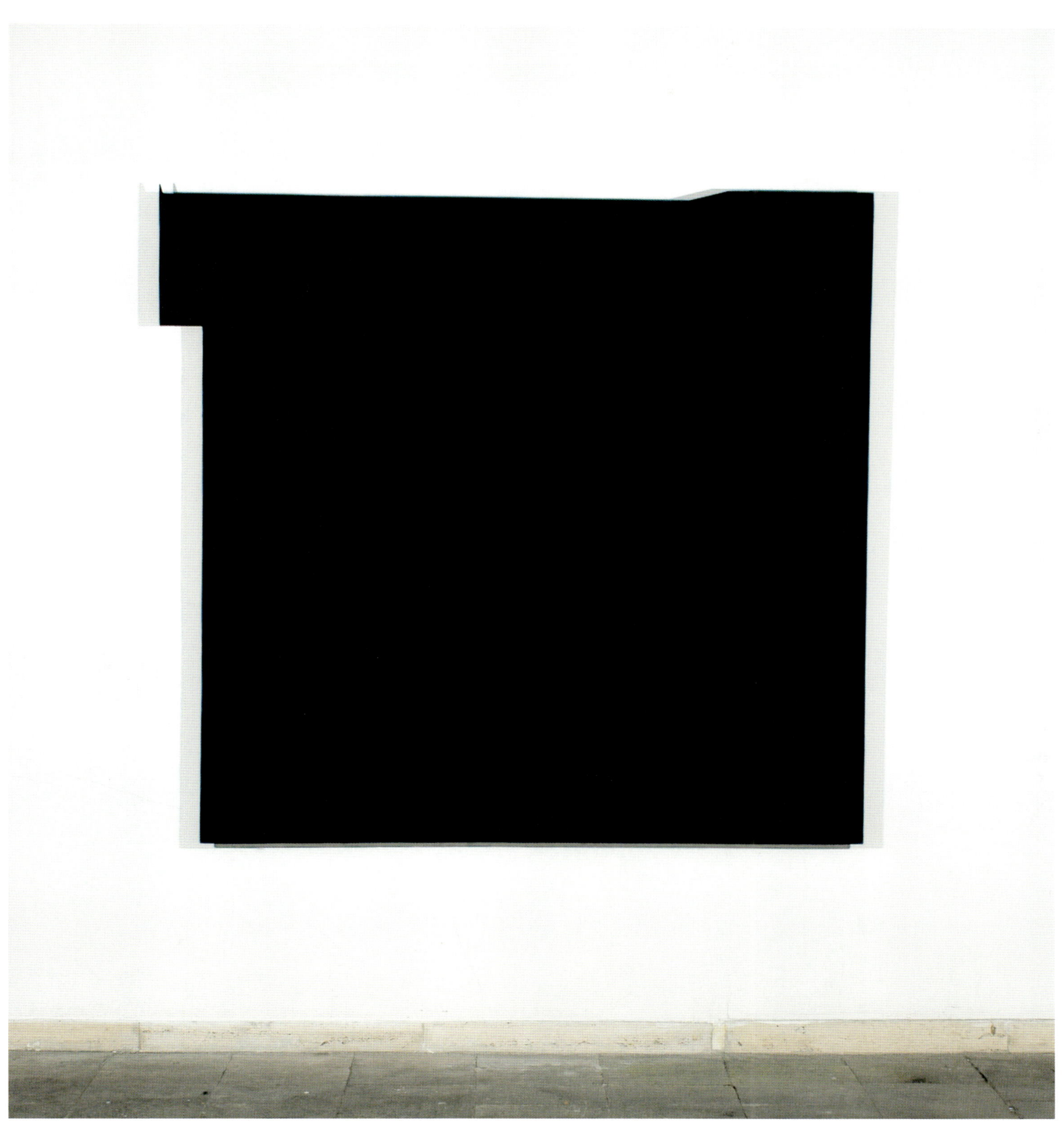

Zwei Schnitte in das suprematistische Quadrat, V/2,
1987
Two Cuts in the Suprematist Square, V/2
Öl und Pigment auf Leinwand, 149 × 154 cm
Oil and pigment on canvas

Vier Geraden, ein Quadrat, 1990
Four Straight Lines, One Square
Öl auf Köper, 195 × 130 cm
Oil on twill

Vier Geraden, ein Quadrat (14. 4. 90), 1990
Four Straight Lines, One Square (4/14/90)
Öl und Pigment auf Papier auf Leinwand, 200 × 135 cm
Oil and pigment on paper on canvas

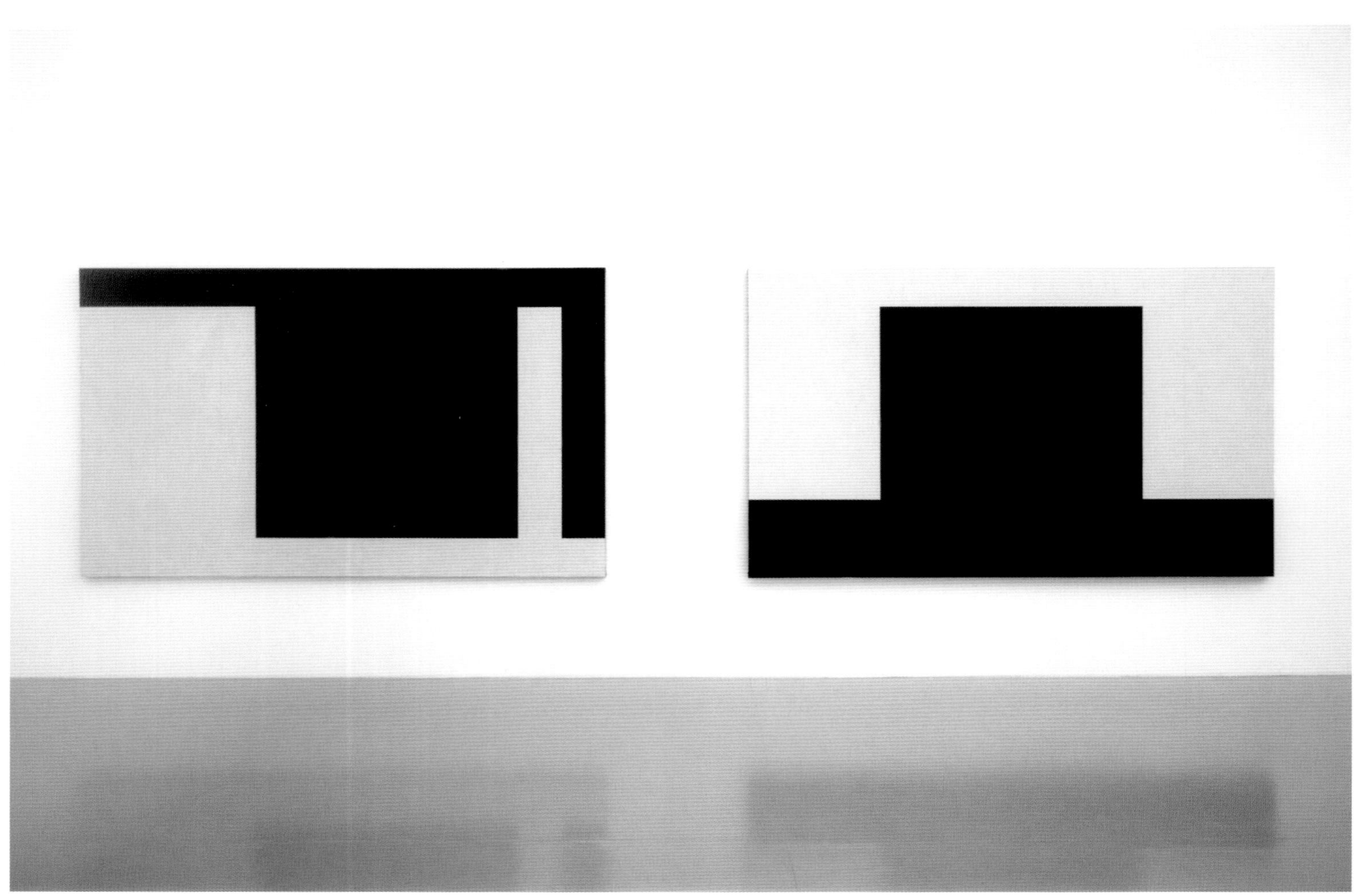

aus: **Vier Geraden, ein Quadrat,** 1990
From: *Four Straight Lines, One Square*
Makulatur, Öl und Pigment auf Leinwand,
je 180 × 270 cm
Wastepaper, oil and pigment on canvas

Der Architektur verpflichtet, 1990
Committed to Architecture
Makulatur, Öl und Pigment auf Leinwand, 181 × 271 cm
Wastepaper, oil and pigment on canvas

Jeder Ort hat sein Schicksal II, aus: Vier Geraden, ein Quadrat, 1990
Every Place Has its Destiny II, from: *Four Straight Lines, One Square*
Makulatur, Öl und Pigment auf Leinwand, 180 × 270 cm
Wastepaper, oil and pigment on canvas

Vier Geraden, ein Quadrat (Architektur bezogen 1),
1990
Four Straight Lines, One Square (architecture-related 1)
Öl und Pigment auf Karton, 20 × 30 cm
Oil and pigment on cardboard

Vier Geraden, ein Quadrat (Architektur bezogen), 1990
Four Straight Lines, One Square (architecture-related)
Öl und Pigment auf Karton, 20 × 30 cm
Oil and pigment on cardboard

Nacht am Tempel, 1989, aus: **Vier Geraden, ein
Quadrat**
Night at the Temple, 1989, from: *Four Straight Lines,
One Square*
Makulatur, Öl und Pigment auf Leinwand, 174 × 260 cm
Wastepaper, oil and pigment on canvas

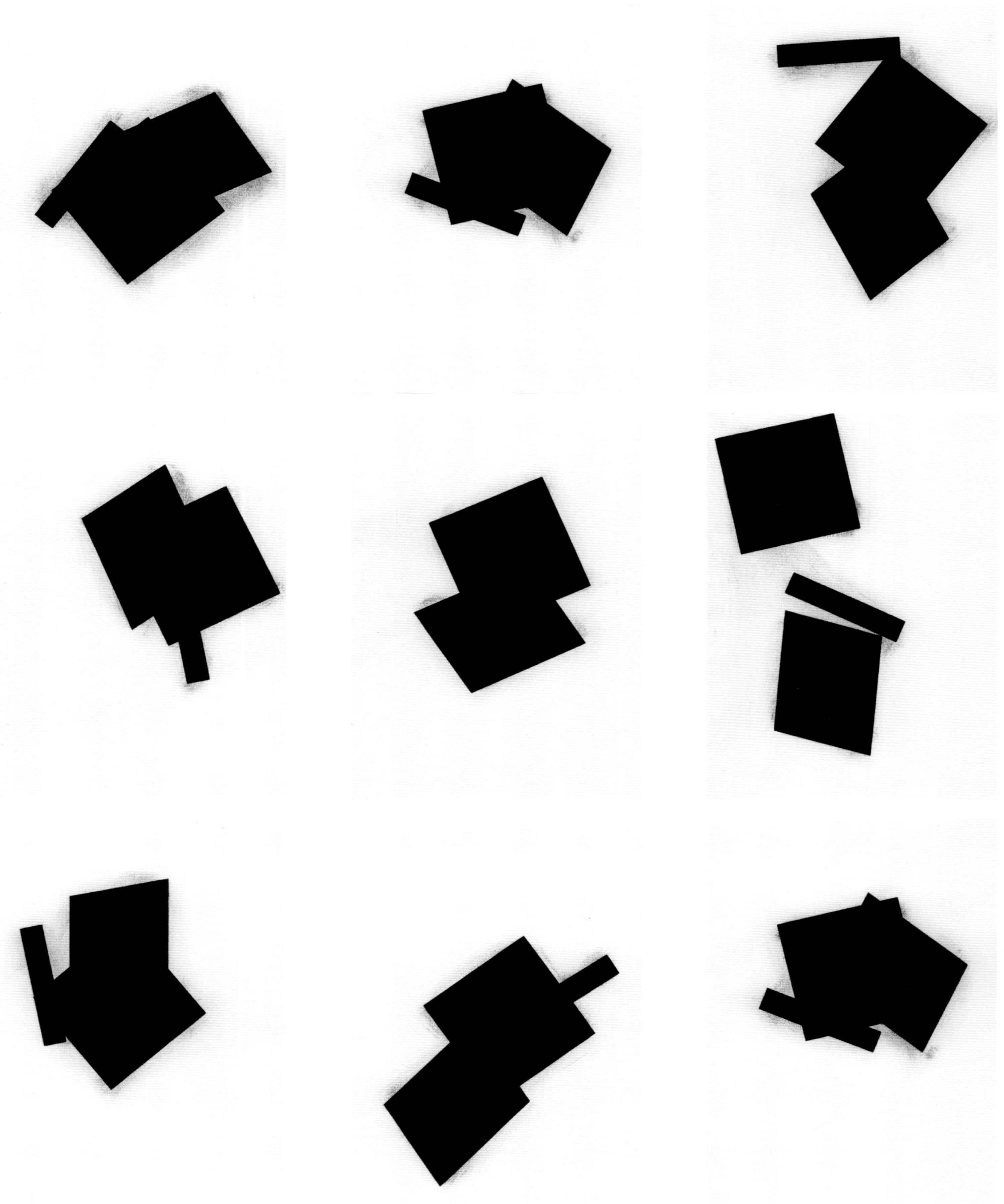

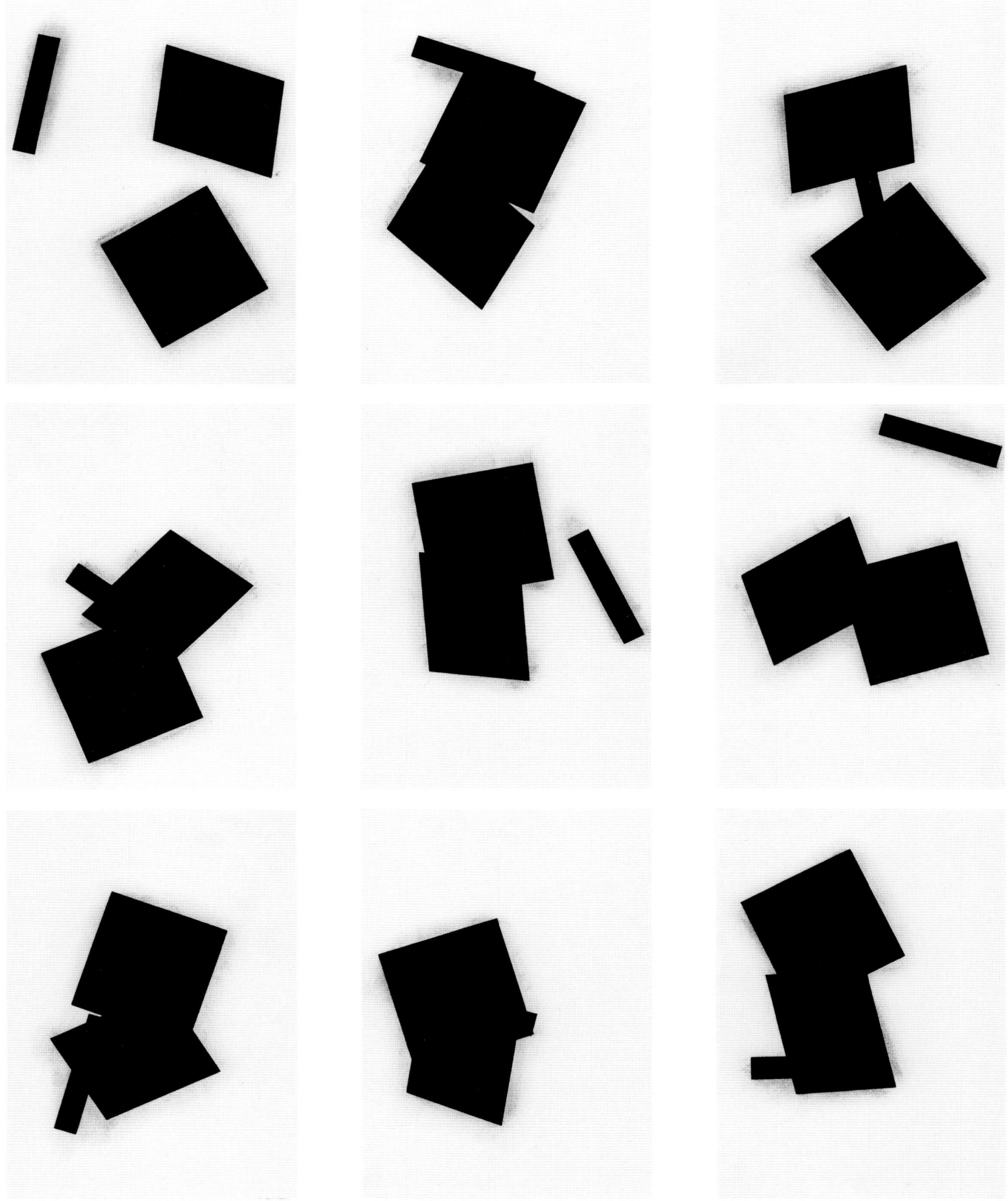

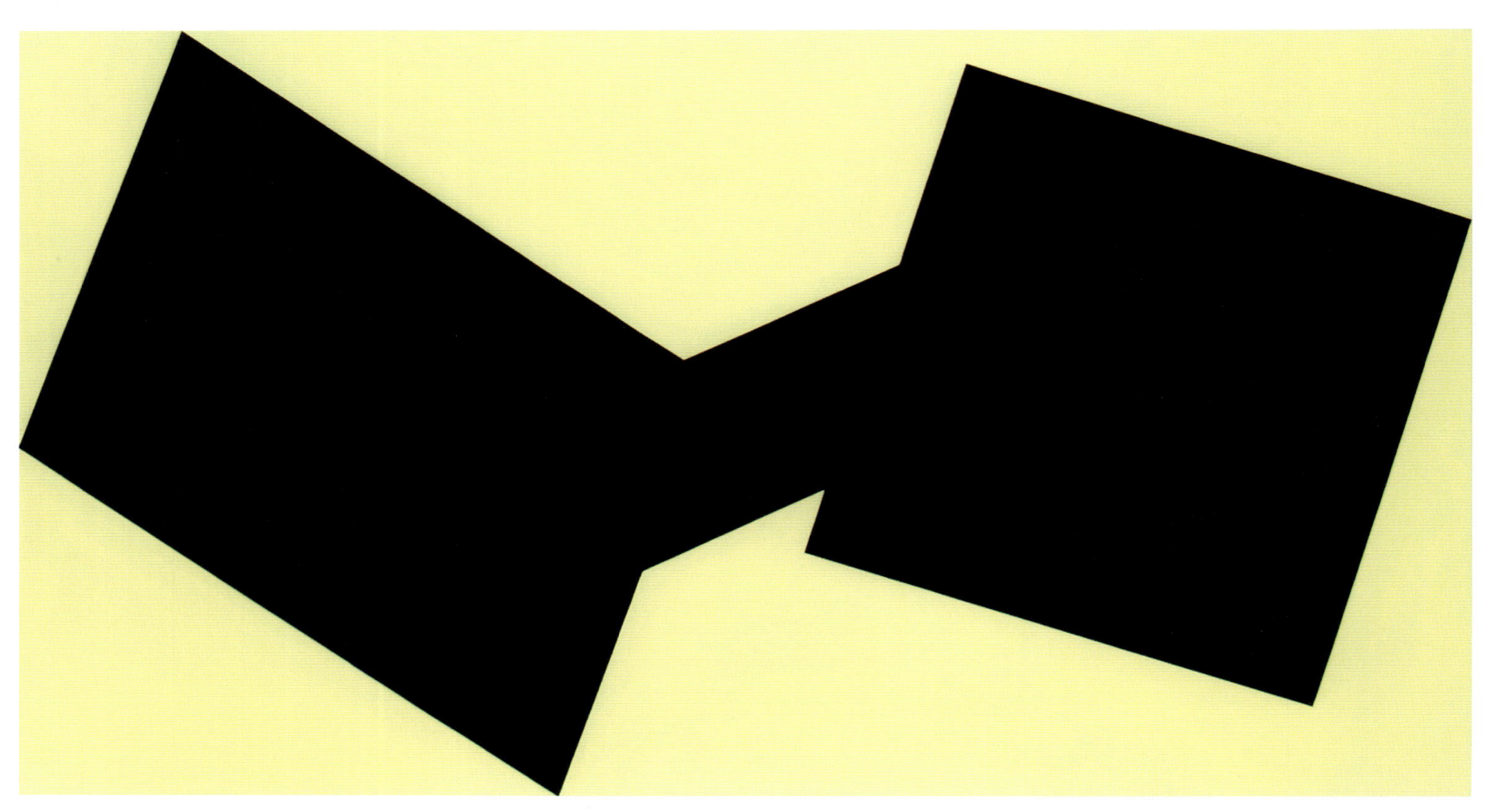

Kompositionen mit dem Zufall, 1988–2004
Compositions with Coincidence
Öl und Pigment auf Fabriano, je 33 × 24 cm
Oil and pigment on Fabriano

Komposition mit dem Zufall vom 28.7.94, 1994
Composition with Coincidence from 7/28/94
Dispersion, Öl und Pigment auf Leinwand, 149 × 273 cm
Dispersion, oil and pigment on canvas

Komposition mit dem Zufall vom 17. 5. 1988
Composition with Coincidence from 5/17/88
Öl und Pigment auf Köper, 150 × 274 cm
Oil and pigment on twill

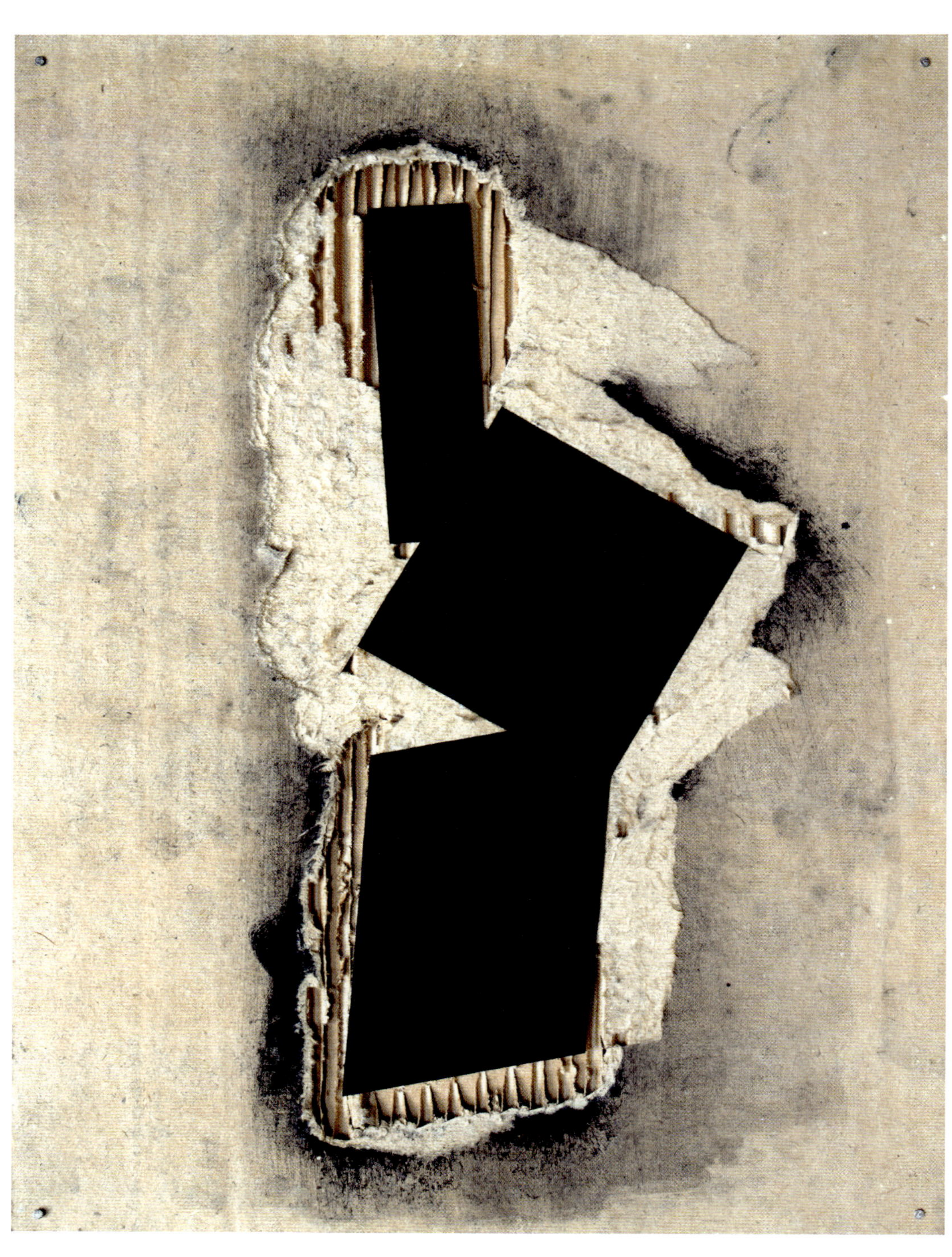

Komposition mit dem Zufall vom 11. 7. 88, 1988
Composition with Coincidence from 7/11/88
Öl und Pigment auf Wellpappe, 40 × 30 cm
Oil and pigment on corrugated cardboard

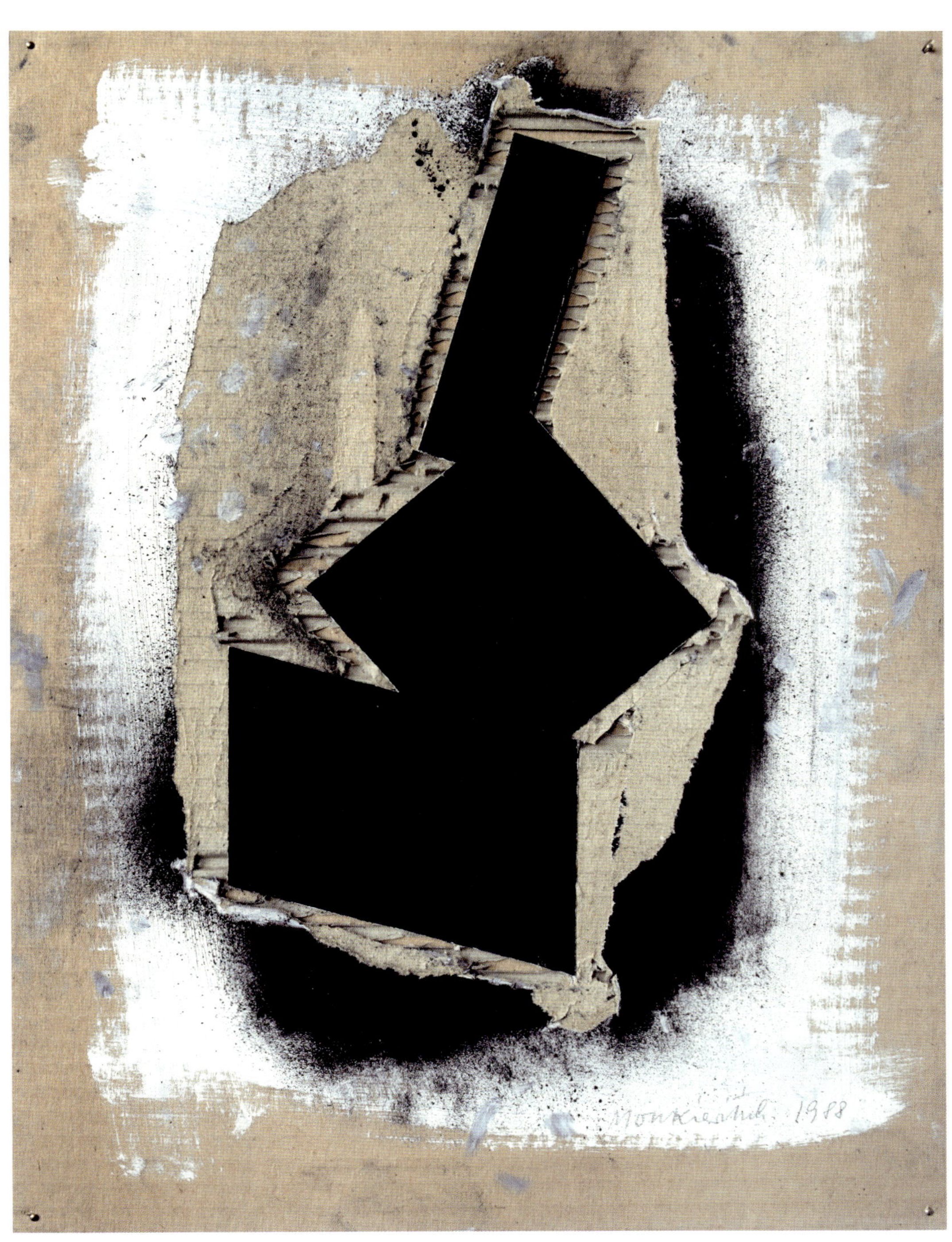

Komposition mit dem Zufall vom 13. 7. 88, 1988
Composition with Coincidence from 7/13/88
Öl und Pigment auf Wellpappe, 40 × 30 cm
Oil and pigment on corrugated cardboard

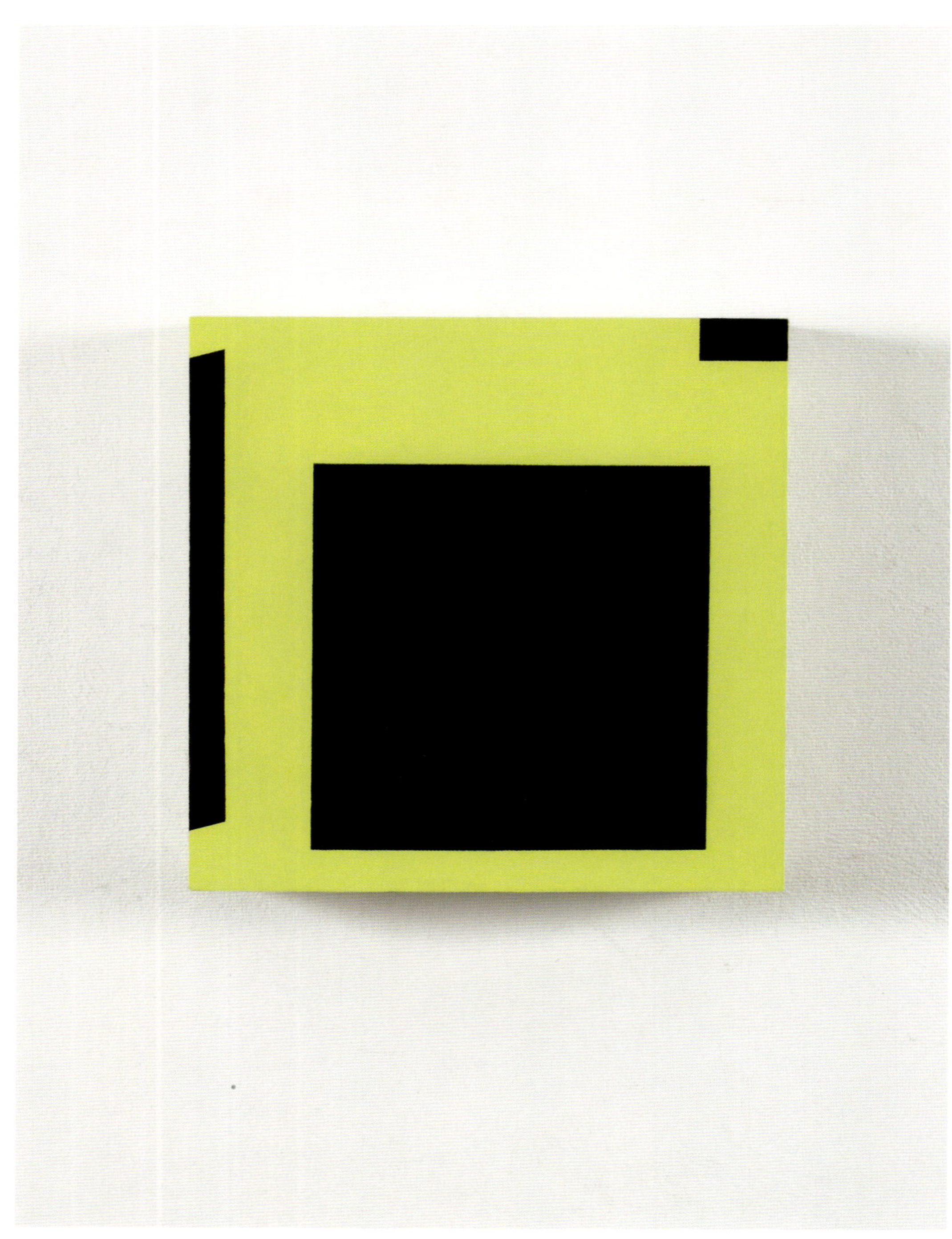

Komposition mit Quadrat, Rechteck, Parallelogramm
und Neongelb 1, 1990
*Composition with Square, Rectangle, Parallelogram
and Neon Yellow 1*
Dispersion, Öl und Pigment auf Holz und Leinwand,
40 × 40 × 12 cm
Dispersion, oil and pigment on wood and canvas

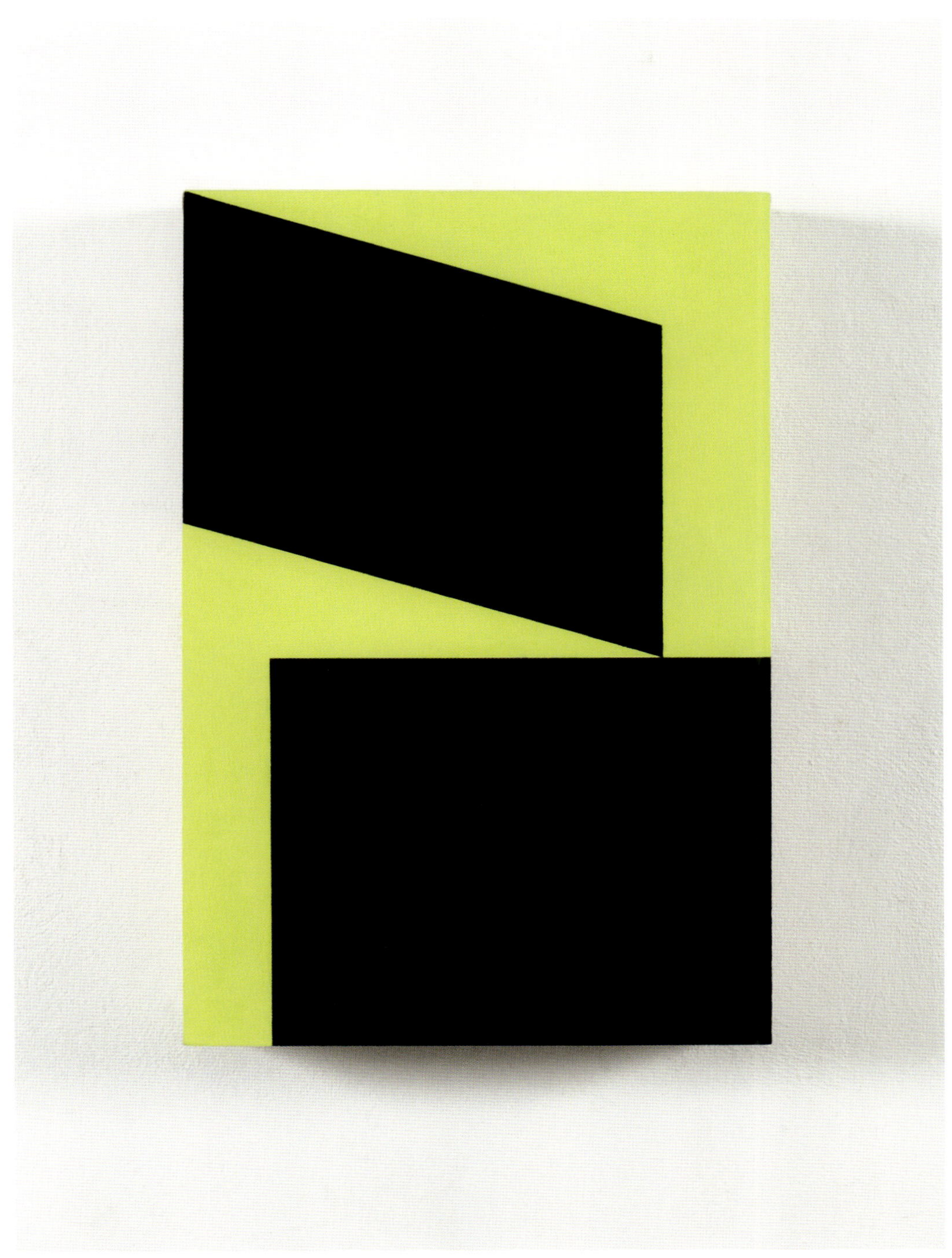

**Komposition mit Quadrat, Rechteck, Parallelogramm
und Neongelb II,** 1990
*Composition with Square, Rectangle, Parallelogram and
Neon Yellow II*
Dispersion, Öl und Pigment auf Holz und Leinwand,
40 × 60 × 12 cm
Dispersion, oil and pigment on wood and canvas

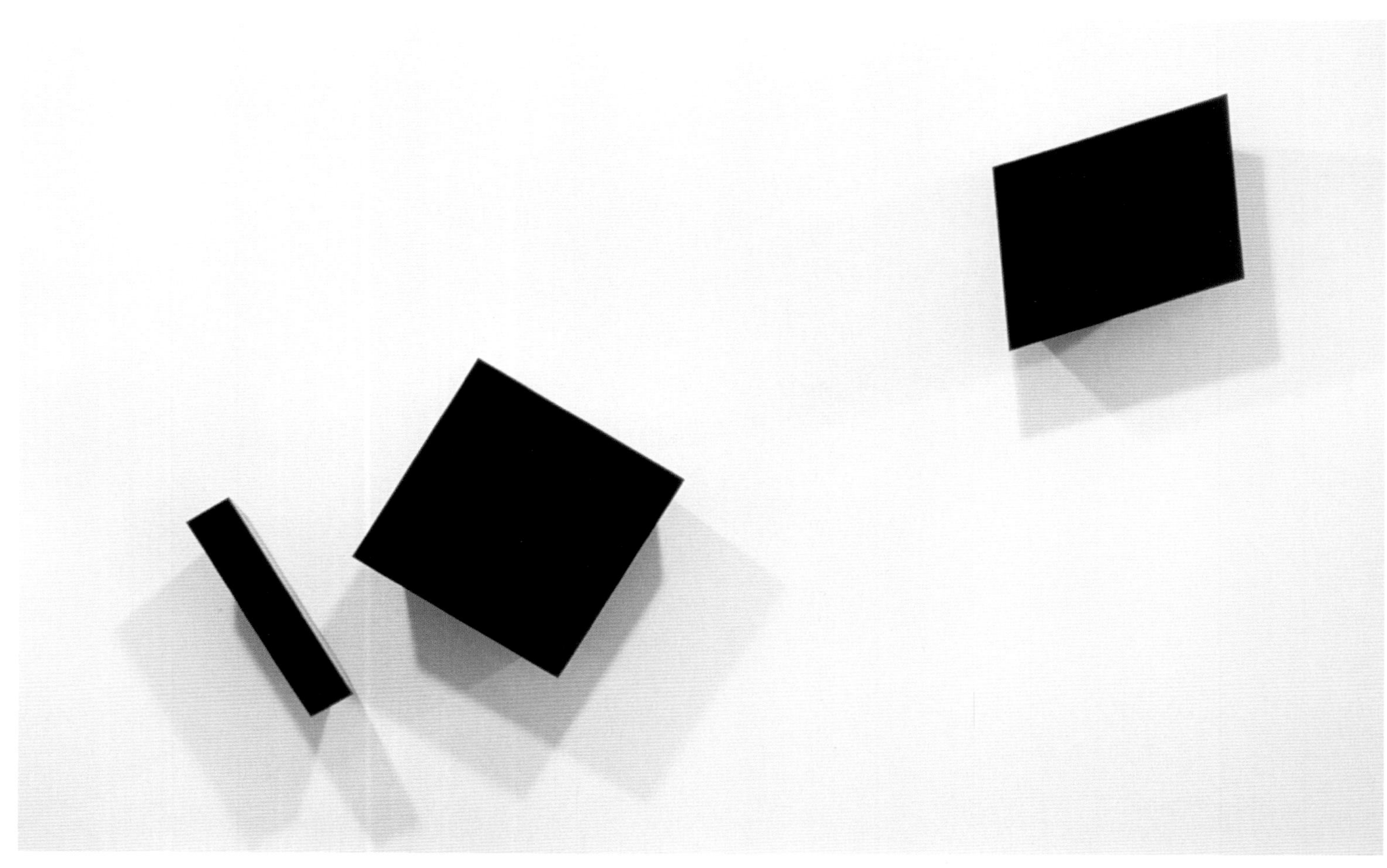

Rekonstruktion eines Zufalls vom 2. 3. 92, 1992
Reconstruction of a Coincidence from 3/2/92
Samt und Öl auf Beton, 30,5 × 6 × 14 cm,
30,5 × 30,5 × 14 cm, 30,5 × 22,8 × 14 cm
Velvet and oil on concrete

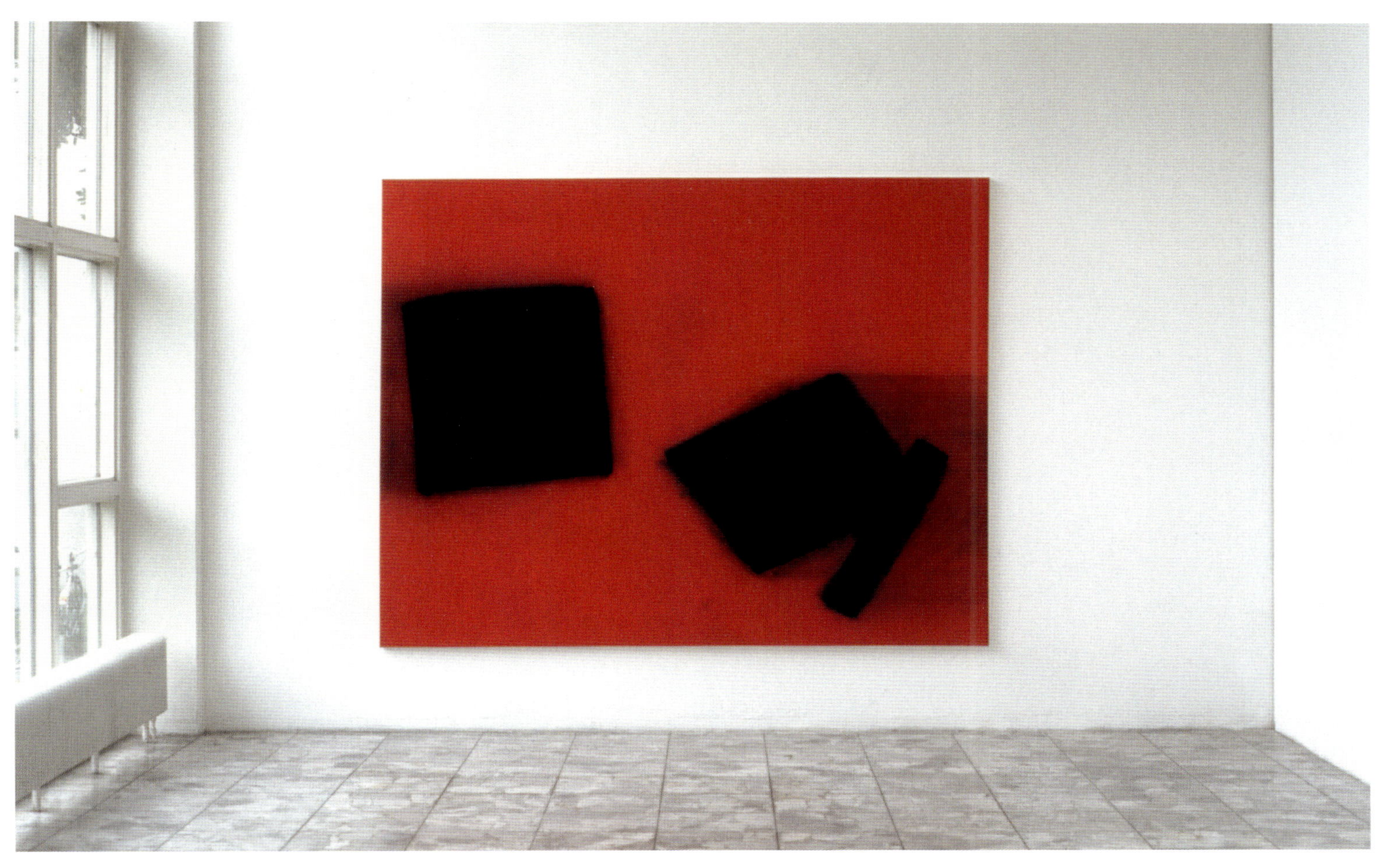

Rekonstruktion eines Zufalls vom 3. 7. 92, 1992
Reconstruction of a Coincidence from 7/3/92
Dispersion, Öl und Pigment auf Leinwand, 185 × 235 cm
Dispersion, oil and pigment on canvas

**Konstruktion mit Quadrat, Rechteck und
Parallelogramm (8.1.94),** 1994
*Construction With Square, Rectangle and
Parallelogram (1/8/94)*
Dispersion, Öl und Pigment auf Karton, 34 × 39 cm
Dispersion, oil and pigment on cardboard

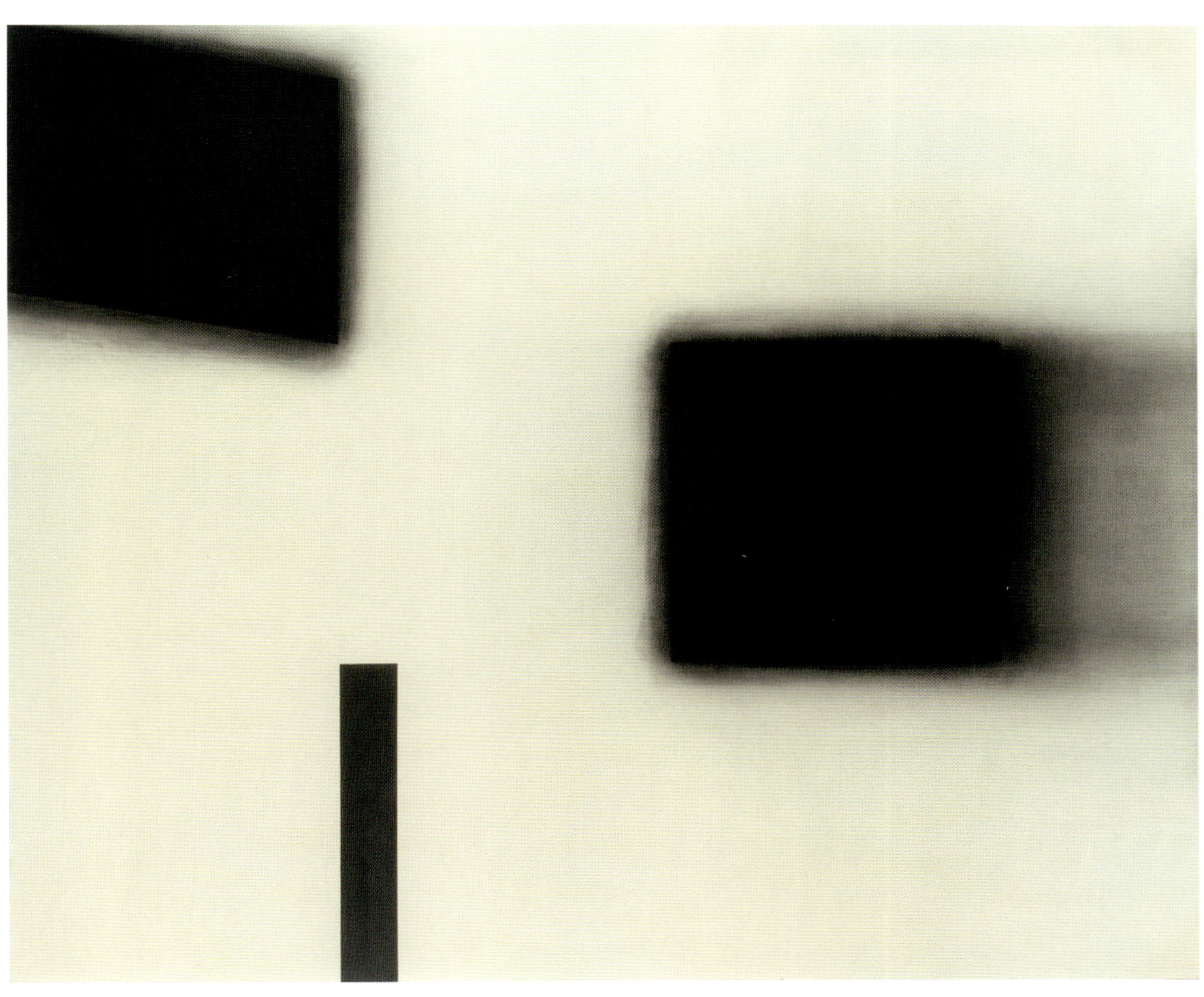

**Konstruktion mit Quadrat, Rechteck und
Parallelogramm (24. 3. 95),** 1995
*Construction With Square, Rectangle and
Parallelogram (3/24/95)*
Öl und Pigment auf Leinwand, 190 × 230 cm
Oil and pigment on canvas

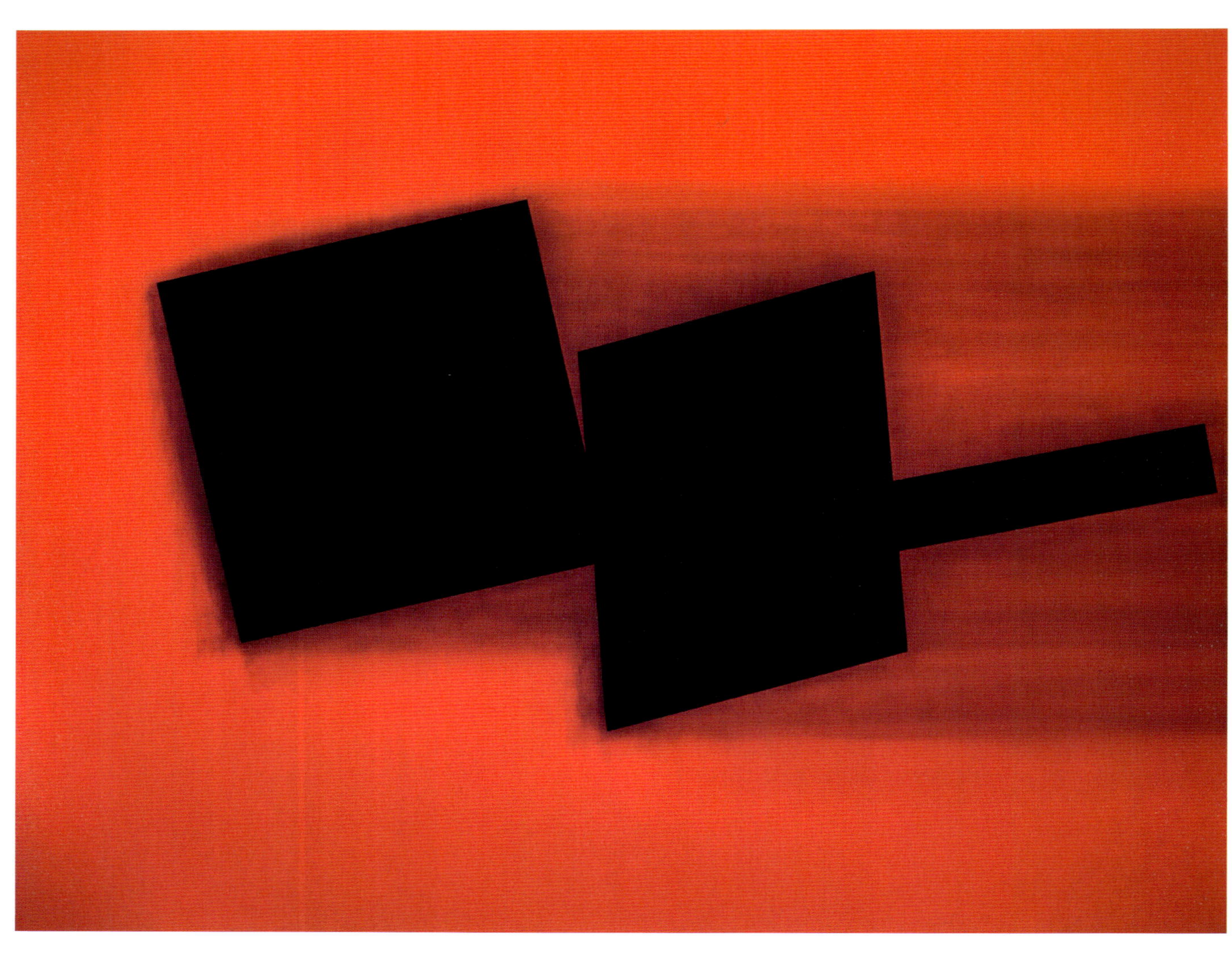

Komposition mit dem Zufall vom 17.11.93, 1993
Composition with Coincidence from 11/17/93
Dispersion, Öl und Pigment auf Leinwand, 205 × 265 cm
Dispersion, oil and pigment on canvas

Komposition mit dem Zufall vom 28.1.94, 1994
Composition with Coincidence from 1/28/94
Dispersion, Öl und Pigment auf Leinwand, 141 × 120 cm
Dispersion, oil and pigment on canvas

Rekonstruktion eines Zufalls vom 29. 8. 05, (W. N.), 2005
Reconstruction of a Coincidence from 8/29/05
Dispersion, Öl und Pigment auf Leinwand, 200 × 300 cm
Dispersion and pigment on canvas

Komposition mit dem Zufall vom 2.1.02, 2002
Composition with Coincidence from 1/2/02
Dispersion, Öl und Pigment auf Leinwand, 125 × 160 cm
Dispersion and pigment on canvas

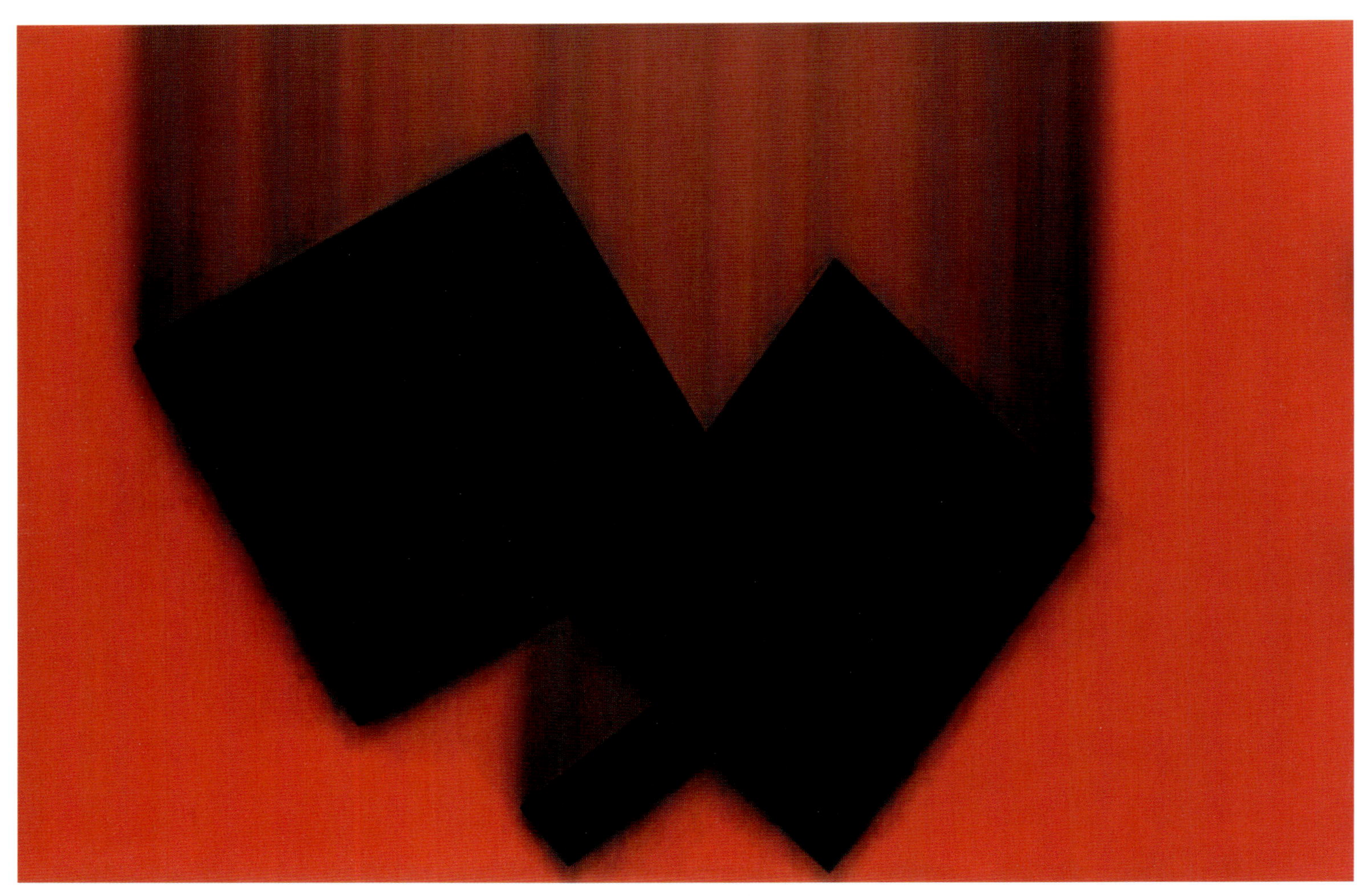

Rekonstruktion eines Zufalls vom 29. 8. 05 (Z. T.), 2005,
Reconstruction of a Coincidence from 8/29/05
Dispersion, Öl und Pigment auf Leinwand, 200 × 300 cm
Dispersion, oil and pigment on canvas

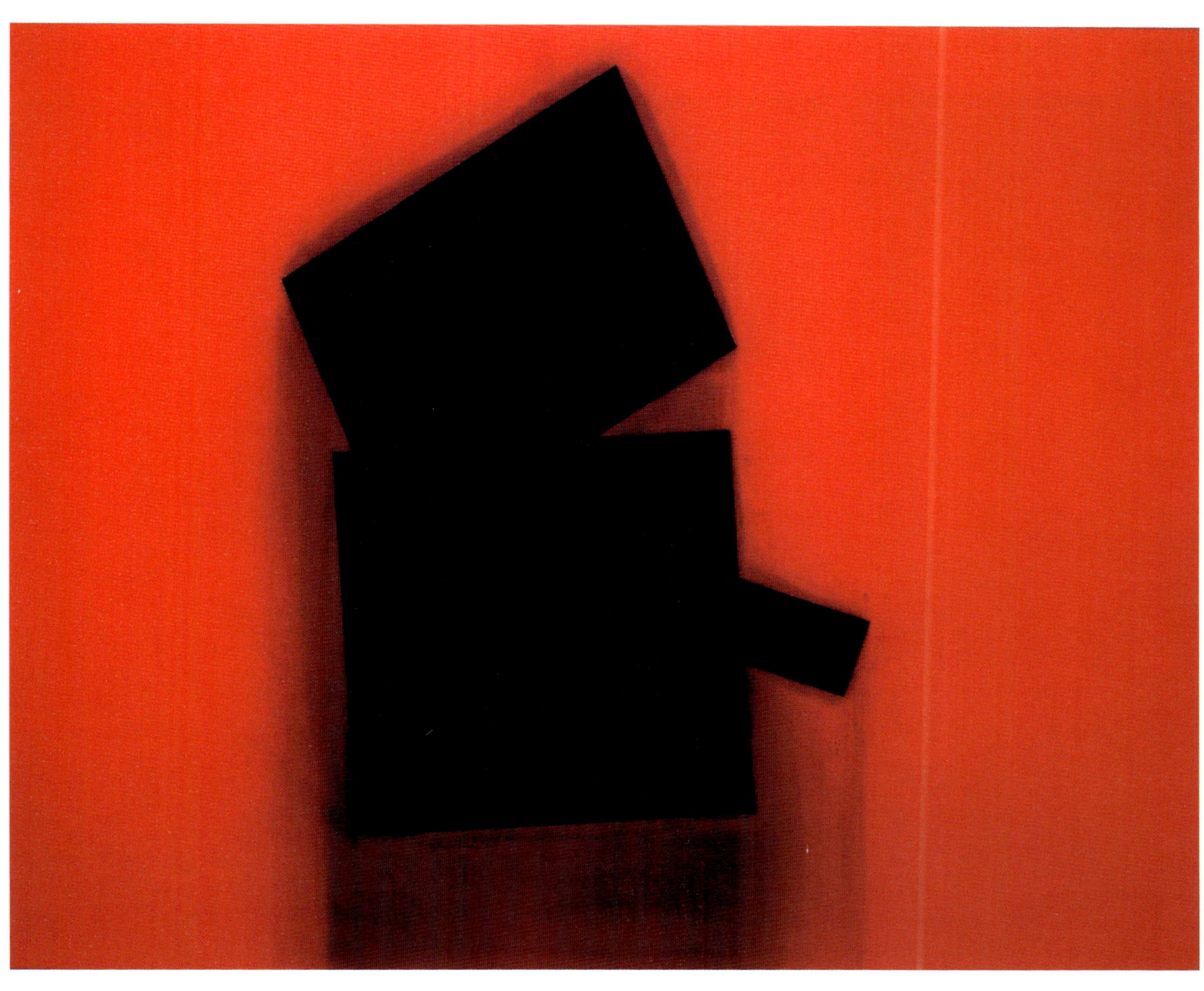

Komposition mit dem Zufall vom 28.10.95, 2004
Composition with Coincidence from 10/28/95
Dispersion, Öl und Pigment auf Leinwand, 140 × 115 cm
Dispersion, oil and pigment on canvas

**Konstruktion mit 4 aufeinander folgenden Fibonacci-
Zahlen bezogen auf das Format 91 × 70 cm,**
8 Blätter, progressiv, 2004
Construction with Four Serial Fibonacci Numbers,
based on the format 91 × 70 cm,
Eight sheets, progressive
Öl und Pigment auf Fabriano
Oil and pigment on Fabriano

Konstruktion mit der Telefonnummer 3 8 13 18, 1990
Construction with the Telephone Number 3 8 13 18
Öl und Pigment auf Leinwand, 200 × 160 cm
Oil and pigment on canvas

Konstruktion mit den aufeinander folgenden
Fibonacci-Zahlen 3.5.8.13 bezogen auf das
Format 200 × 105, 1991,
Construction with the Serial Fibonacci Numbers
3, 5, 8, 13, based on the format 200 × 105
Öl und Pigment auf Leinwand, 200 × 160 cm
Oil and pigment on canvas

Konstruktion mit den aufeinander folgenden
Fibonacci-Zahlen 3.5.8.13, 1991
Construction with the Serial Fibonacci Numbers 3, 5, 8, 13
Öl und Pigment auf Leinwand, 140 × 120 cm
Oil and pigment on canvas

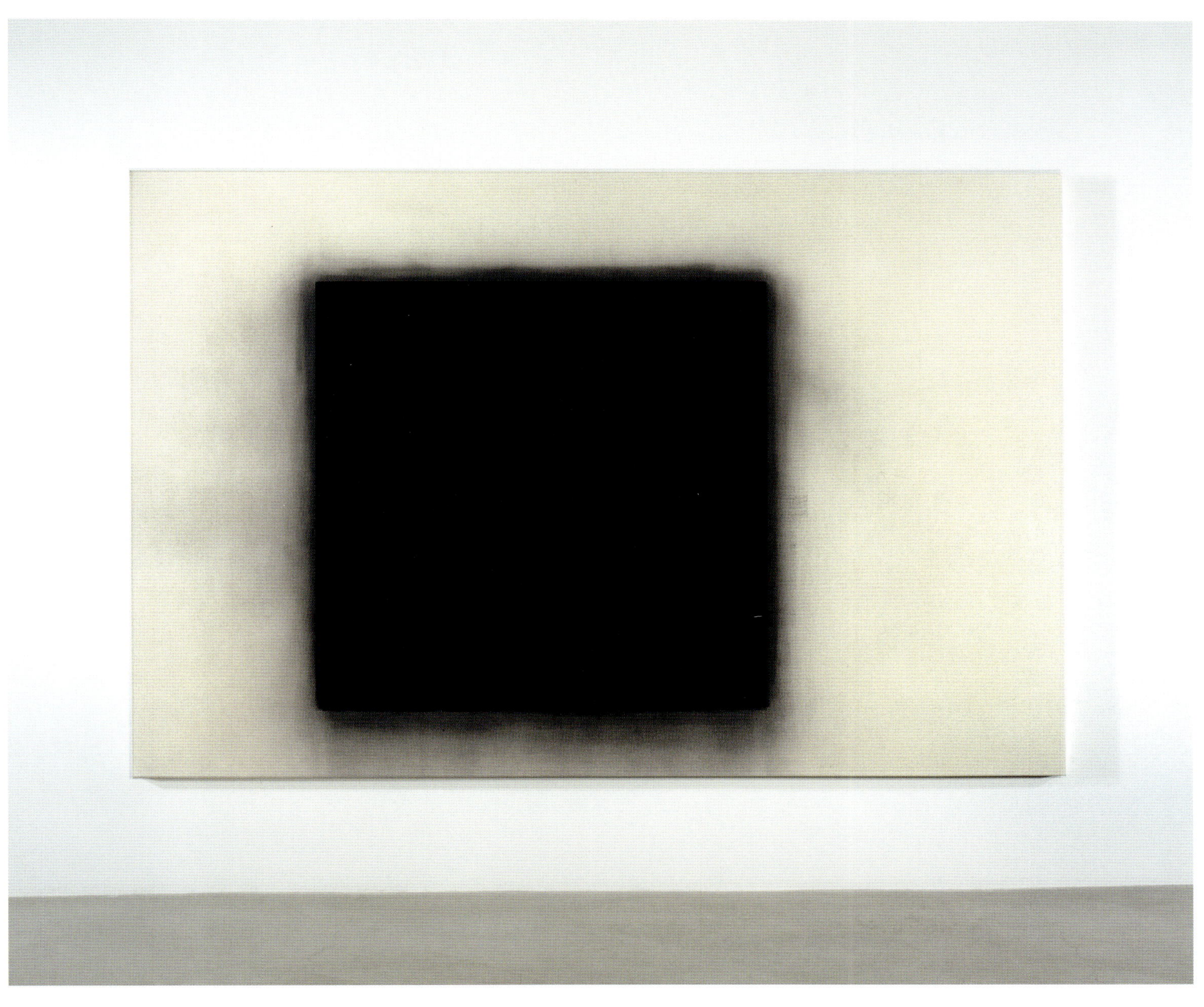

**Konstruktion mit den aufeinander folgenden
Fibonacci-Zahlen 34.55.89.144.233.377,** 1991
*Construction with the Serial Fibonacci Numbers
34, 55, 89, 144, 233, 377*
Öl und Pigment auf Leinwand, 233 × 377 cm
Oil and pigment on canvas

Konstruktion mit den aufeinander folgenden Fibonacci-Zahlen 21.34.55.89 bezogen auf das Format 289 × 200, I, 1991
Construction with the Serial Fibonacci Numbers 21, 34, 55, 89, based on the format 289 × 200, I
Öl und Pigment auf Leinwand, 289 × 200 cm
Oil and pigment on canvas

**Konstruktion mit den aufeinander folgenden
Fibonacci-Zahlen 21.34.55.89 bezogen auf das
Format 289 × 200, II,** 1991
*Construction with the Serial Fibonacci Numbers
21, 34, 55, 89, based on the format 289 × 200, II*
Öl und Pigment auf Leinwand, 289 × 200 cm
Oil and pigment on canvas

**Konstruktion mit den aufeinander folgenden
Fibonacci-Zahlen 5.8.13.21, 1,** 1994
*Construction with the Serial Fibonacci Numbers
5, 8, 13, 21, 1*
Dispersion, Öl und Pigment auf Leinwand,
200 × 160 cm
Dispersion, oil and pigment on canvas

**Konstruktion mit den aufeinander folgenden
Fibonacci-Zahlen 5.8.13.21, 11,** 1994
*Construction with the Serial Fibonacci Numbers
5, 8, 13, 21, 11*
Dispersion, Öl und Pigment auf Leinwand,
200 × 160 cm
Dispersion, oil and pigment on canvas

Konstruktion mit den aufeinander folgenden Fibonacci-
Zahlen 3.5.8.13 bezogen auf das Format 81 × 68, 1992
Construction with the Serial Fibonacci Numbers 3, 5, 8, 13,
based on the format 81 × 68
Dispersion, Öl und Pigment auf Leinwand, 68 × 81 cm
Dispersion, oil and pigment on canvas

**Konstruktion mit den aufeinander folgenden
Fibonacci-Zahlen 3.5.8.13,** 1993,
Construction with the Serial Fibonacci Numbers 3, 5, 8, 13
Dispersion, Öl und Pigment auf Leinwand, 141 × 120 cm
Dispersion, oil and pigment on canvas

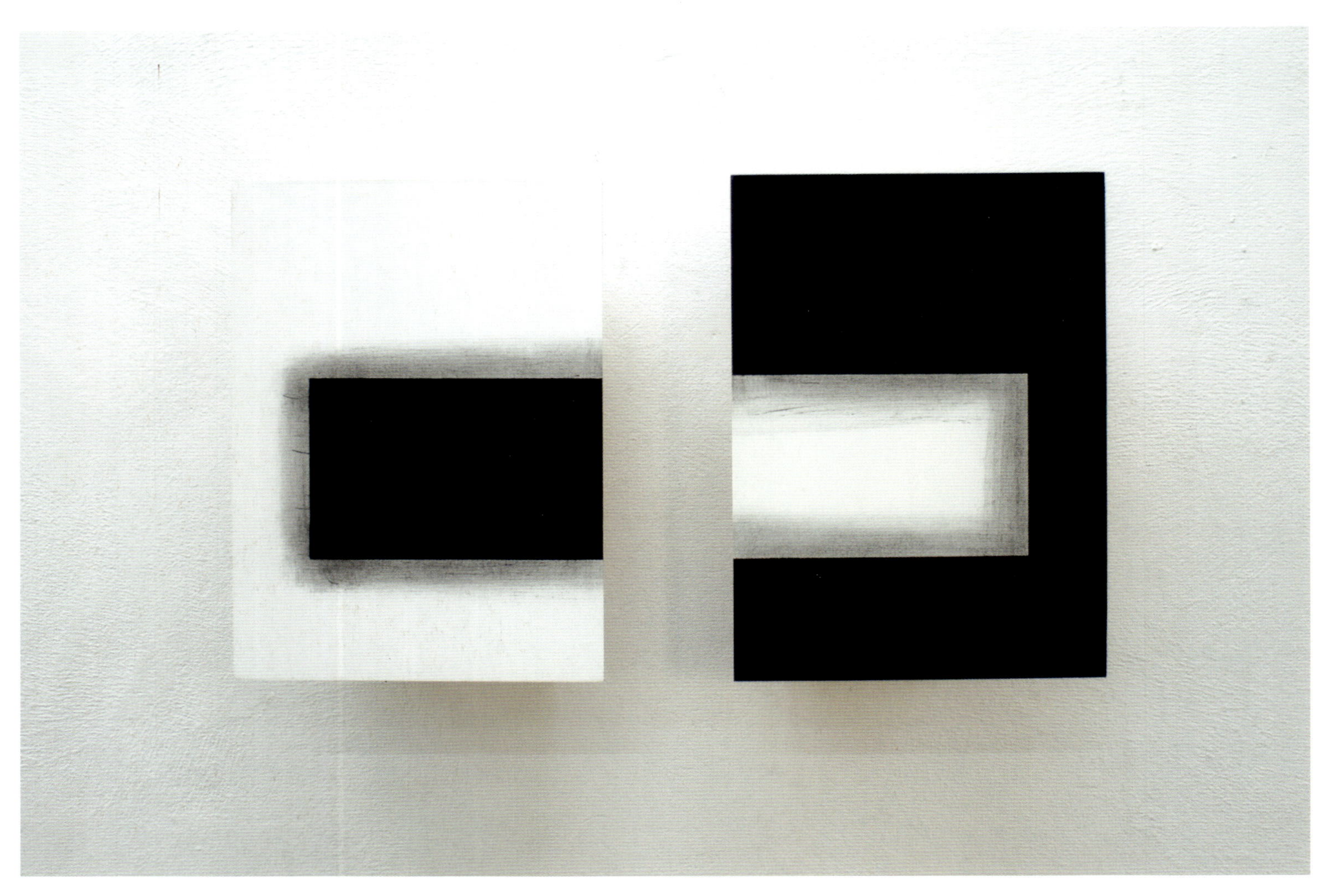

5.8.13. (hell und dunkel), 1992
5, 8, 13 (Light and Dark)
Öl und Pigment auf Karton auf Holz, je 33 × 24 × 15 cm
Oil and pigment on cardboard on wood

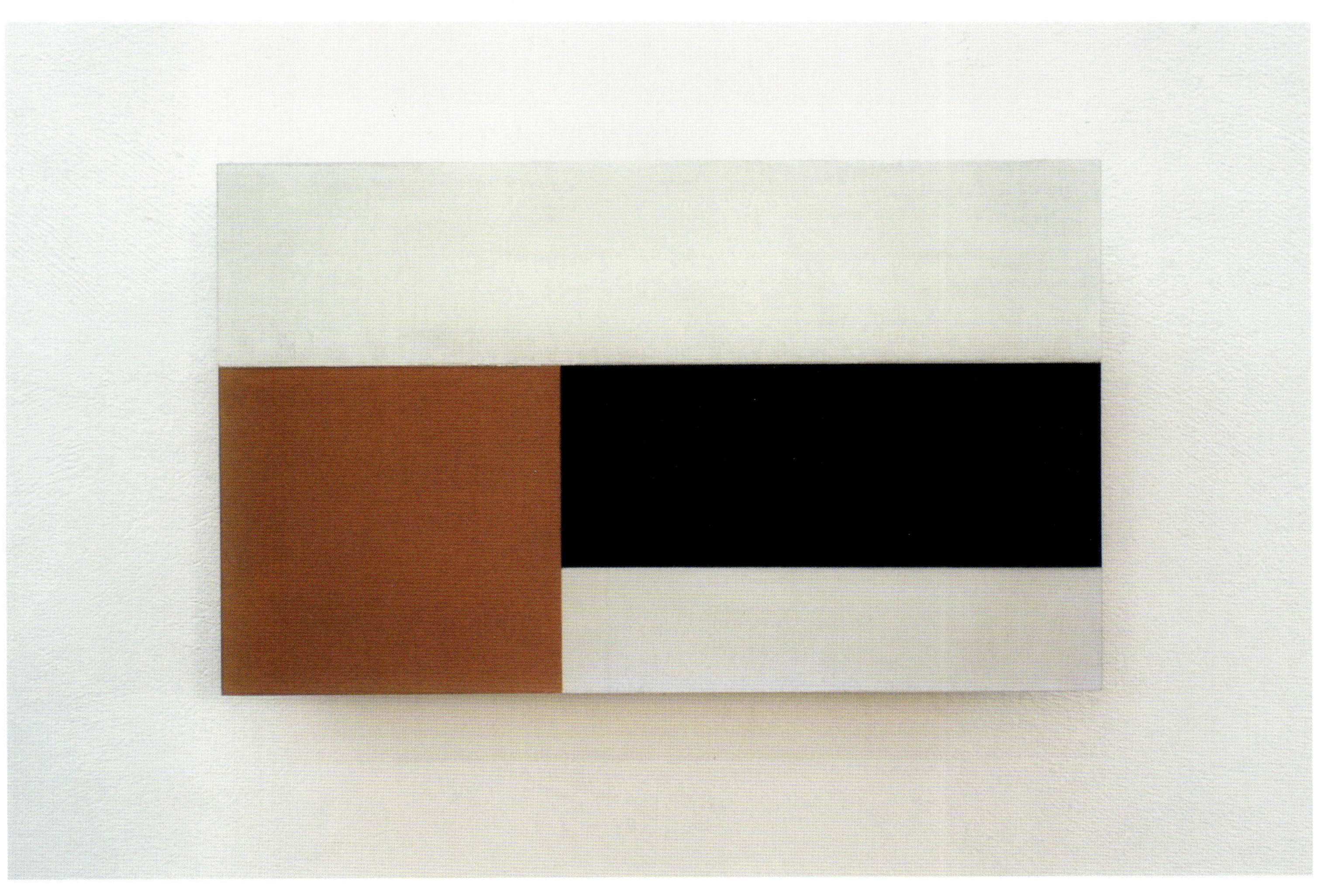

**Konstruktion mit den aufeinander folgenden
Fibonacci-Zahlen 8.13.21.34.55,** 1993
*Construction with the Serial Fibonacci Numbers
8, 13, 21, 34, 55*
Sand, Acryl, Öl und Pigment auf Holz, 34 × 55 × 11 cm
Sand, acrylic, oil and pigment on wood

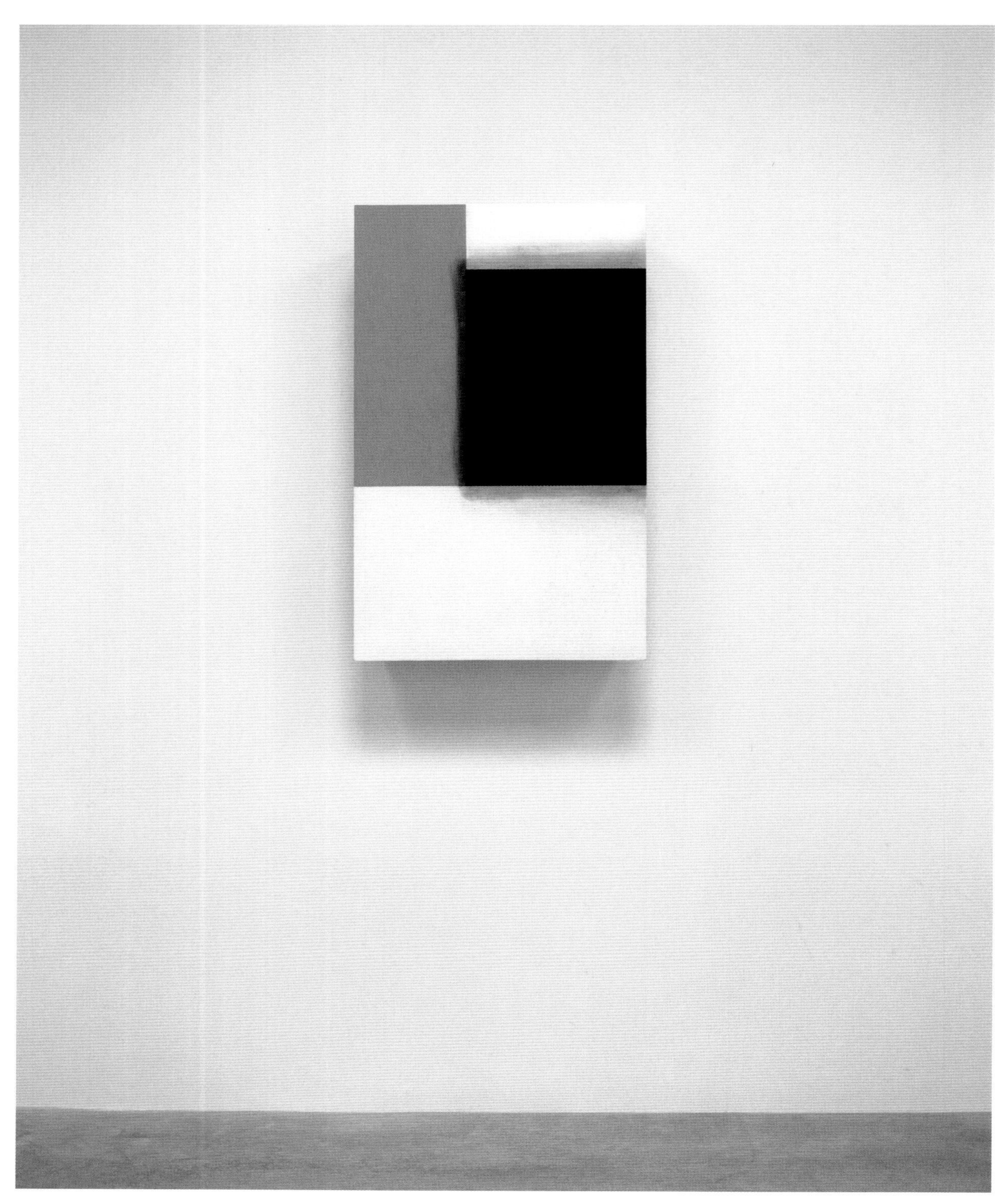

Konstruktion mit den aufeinander folgenden Fibonacci-Zahlen 13.21.34.55.89, 1993
Construction with the Serial Fibonacci Numbers
13, 21, 34, 55, 89
Acryl, Öl und Pigment auf Sperrholz, 89 × 55 × 12 cm
Acrylic, oil and pigment on plywood

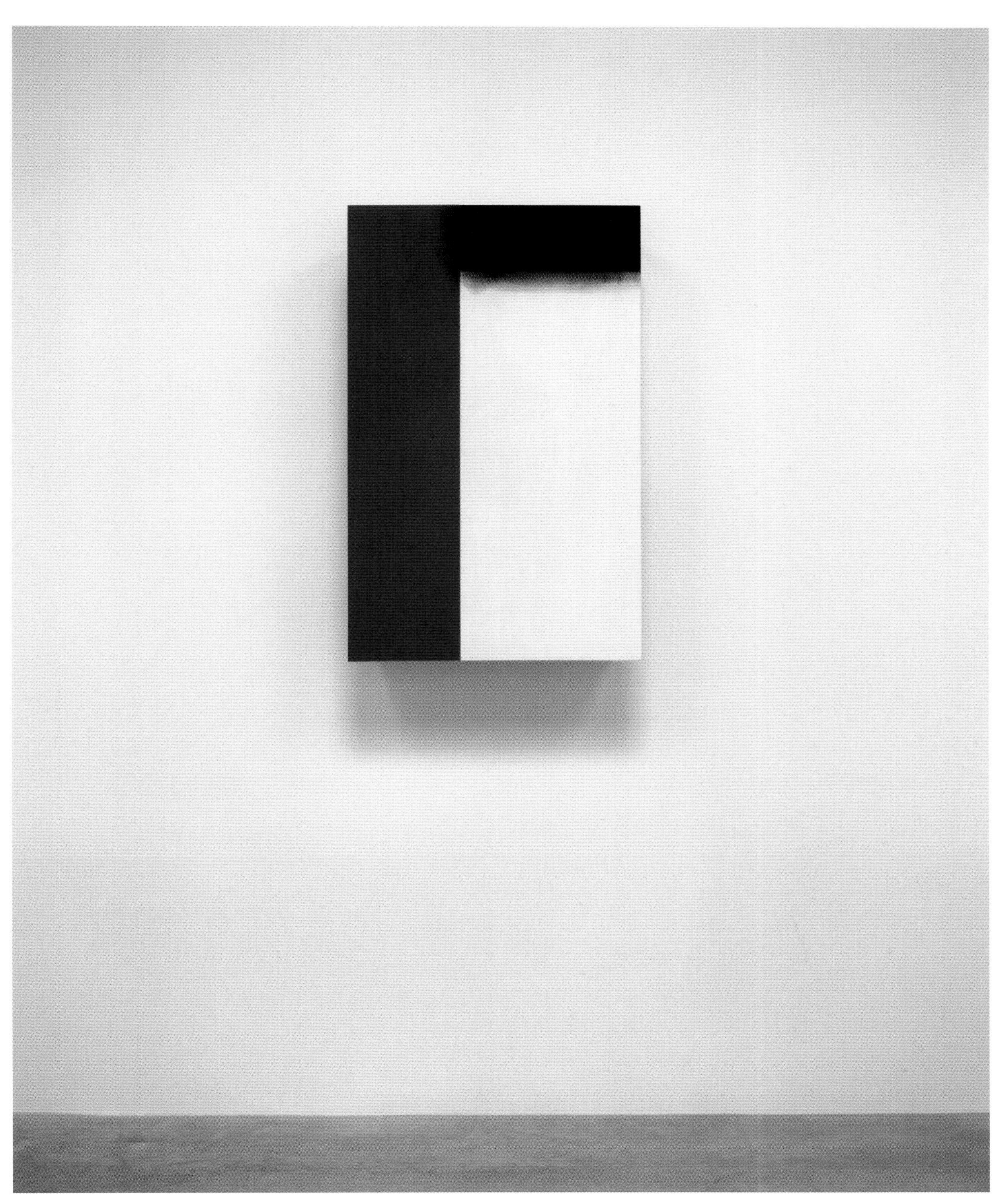

**Konstruktion mit den aufeinander folgenden
Fibonacci-Zahlen 13.21.34.55.89,** 1993
*Construction with the Serial Fibonacci Numbers
13, 21, 34, 55, 89*
Acryl, Öl und Pigment auf Sperrholz, 89 × 55 × 12 cm
Acrylic, oil and pigment on plywood

Drei Versuche der Annäherung an ein Fibonacci-Rechteck, 1994,
Three Attempts to Approach a Fibonacci Rectangle
Acryl, Öl und Pigment auf Leinwand, 104 × 123 cm
Acrylic, oil and pigment on canvas

148

**Komposition mit den aufeinander folgenden Fibonacci-
Zahlen 8.13.21.34 und mit drei Farbansätzen,** 1994
*Composition with the Serial Fibonacci Numbers 8, 13, 21,
34 and with three applications of paint*
Acryl, Öl und Pigment auf Leinwand, 141 × 175 cm
Acrylic, oil and pigment on canvas

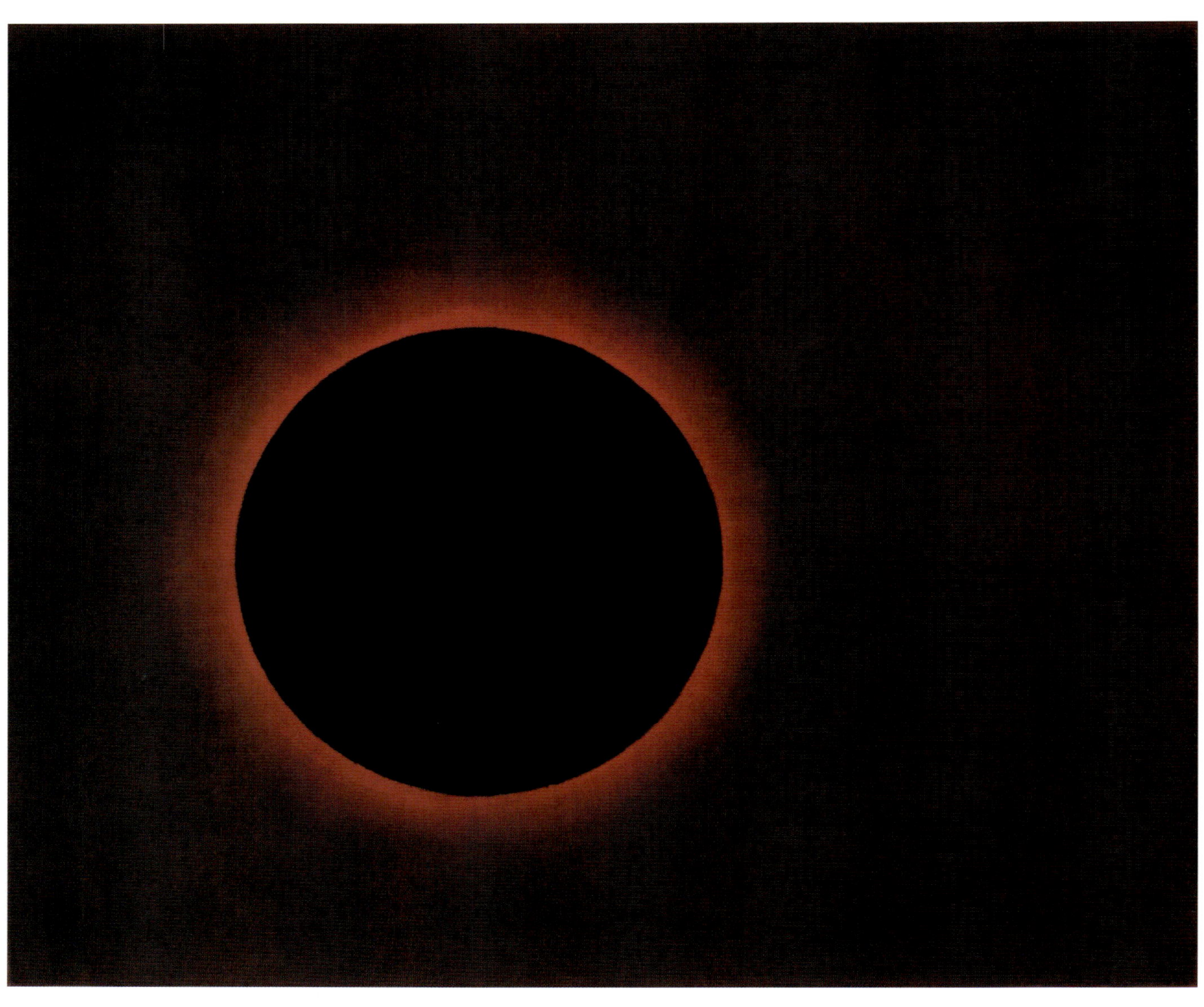

Aura, 1999
Aura
Dispersion, Öl und Pigment auf Leinwand, 75 × 90 cm
Dispersion, oil and pigment on canvas

Schwarzes Quadrat hinterleuchtet, 1999
Black Square Lit from Behind
Dispersion, Öl und Pigment auf Leinwand,
200 × 170 cm
Dispersion, oil and pigment on canvas

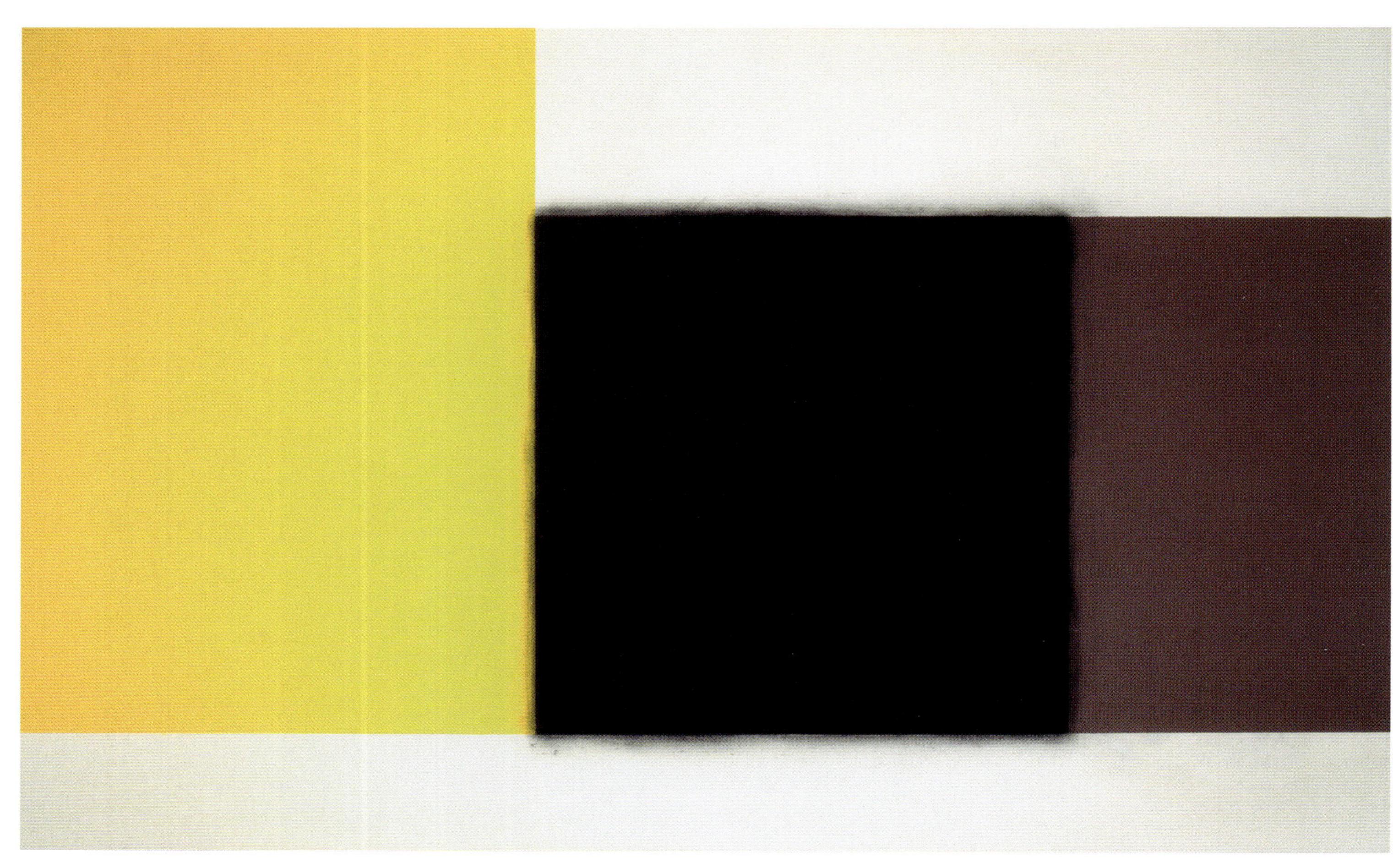

**Konstruktion mit den aufeinander folgenden
Fibonacci-Zahlen 21.34.55.89.144.233,** 1993
*Construction with the Serial Fibonacci Numbers
21, 34, 55, 89, 144, 233*
Acryl, Öl und Pigment auf Leinwand, 200 × 320 cm
Acrylic, oil and pigment on canvas

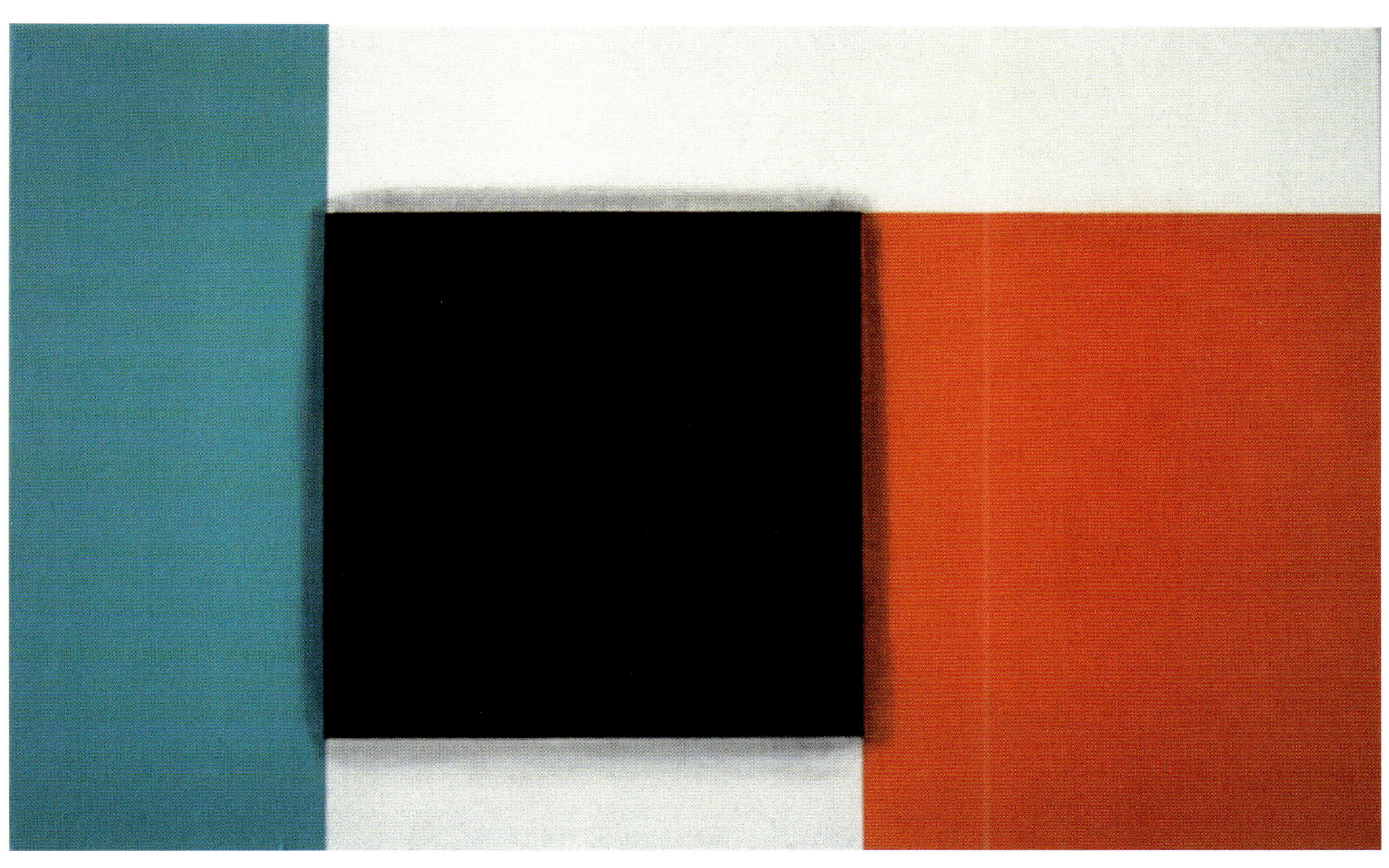

**Konstruktion mit den aufeinander folgenden Fibonacci-
Zahlen 8.13.21.34.55.89 (türkis-rot),** 1994
*Construction with the Serial Fibonacci Numbers 8, 13, 21,
34, 55, 89 (turquoise-red)*
Acryl, Öl und Pigment auf Leinwand, 89 × 55 cm
Acrylic, oil and pigment on canvas

**Konstruktion mit den aufeinander folgenden Fibonacci-
Zahlen 21.34.55.89.144.233 (grün-braun),** 1994
*Construction with the Serial Fibonacci Numbers 21, 34, 55,
89, 144, 233 (green-brown)*
Acryl, Öl und Pigment auf Leinwand, 144 × 233 cm
Acrylic, oil and pigment on canvas

Konstruktion mit den aufeinander folgenden Fibonacci-
Zahlen 21.34.55.89.144.233 (grau-gelb), 1994
Construction with the Serial Fibonacci Numbers 21, 34, 55,
89, 144, 233 (gray-yellow)
Acryl, Öl und Pigment auf Leinwand, 144 × 233 cm
Acrylic, oil and pigment on canvas

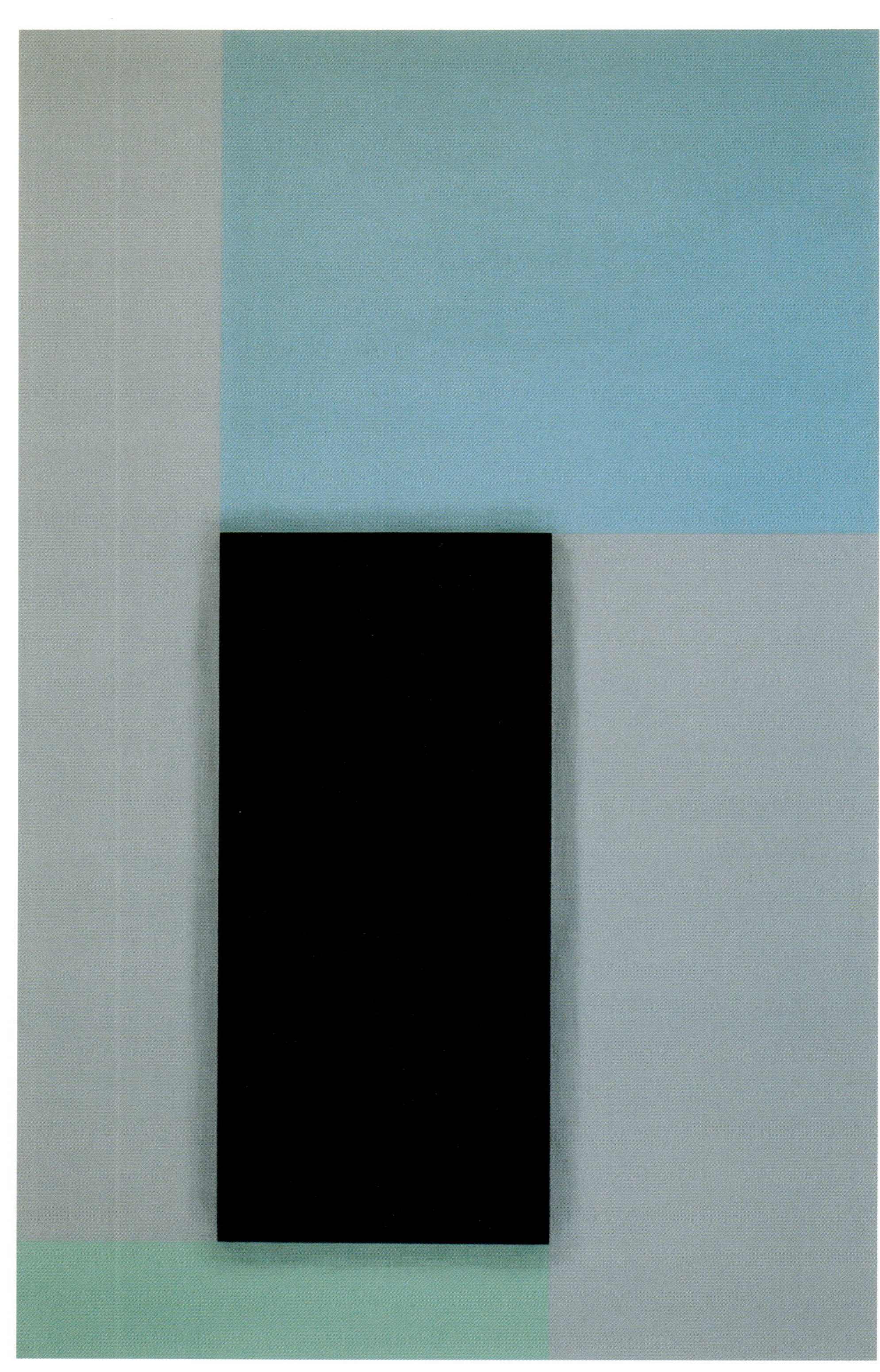

**Konstruktion mit den aufeinander folgenden
Fibonacci-Zahlen 21.34.55.89.144.233,** 1997
Construction with the Serial Fibonacci Numbers
21, 34, 55, 89, 144, 233
Acryl, Öl und Pigment auf Leinwand, 233 × 144 cm
Acrylic, oil and pigment on canvas

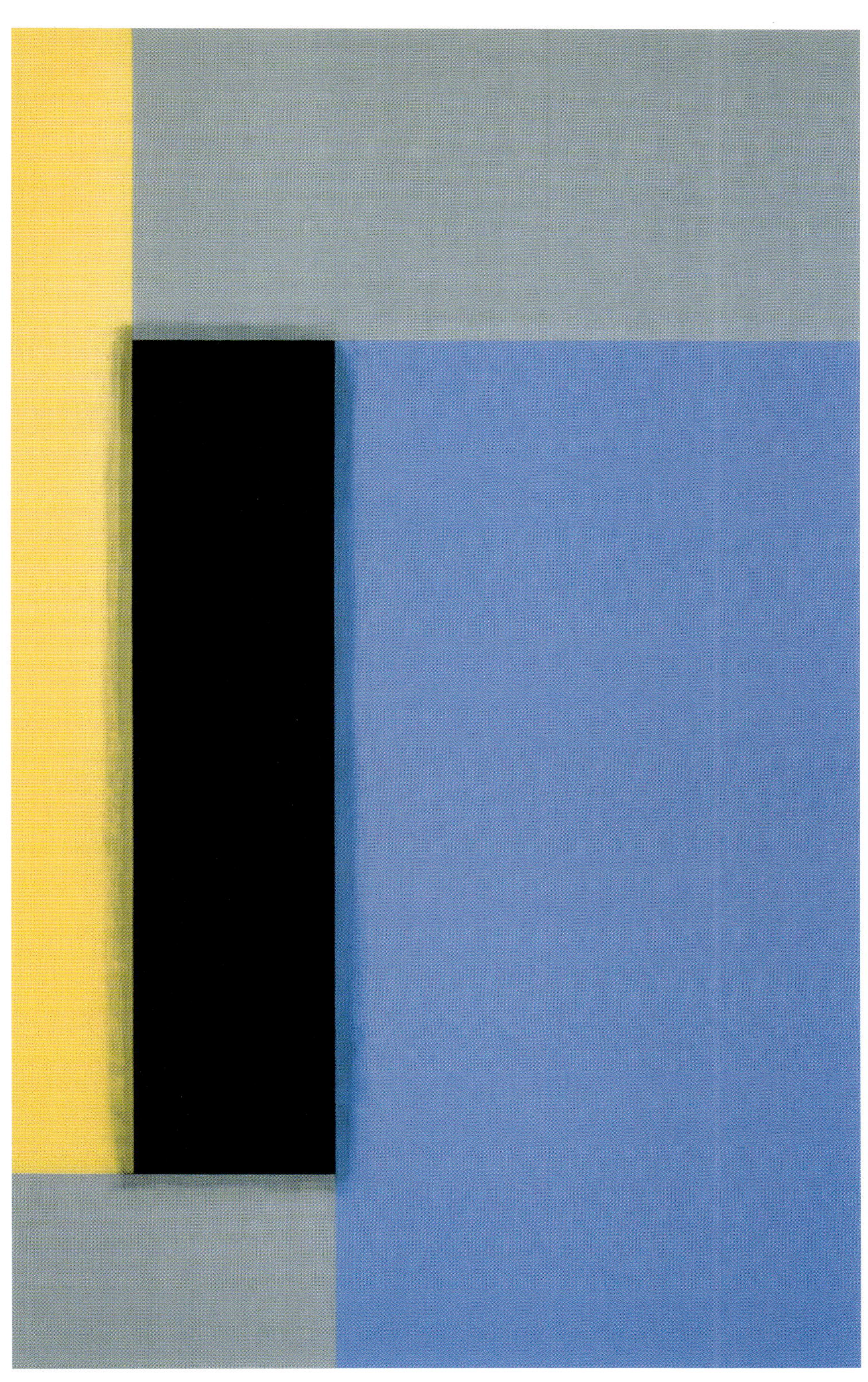

**Konstruktion mit den aufeinander folgenden
Fibonacci-Zahlen 21.34.55.89.144.233,** 1997
Construction with the Serial Fibonacci Numbers
21, 34, 55, 89, 144, 233
Acryl, Öl und Pigment auf Leinwand, 233 × 144 cm
Acrylic, oil and pigment on canvas

Konstruktion mit den aufeinander folgenden Fibonacci-Zahlen 21.34.55.89.144.233 (gelb-violett), 1998
Construction with the Serial Fibonacci Numbers 21, 34, 55, 89, 144, 233 (yellow-violet)
Acryl, Öl und Pigment auf Leinwand, 144 × 233 cm
Acrylic, oil and pigment on canvas

Konstruktion mit den aufeinander folgenden Fibonacci-Zahlen 21.34.55.89.144.233 (oliv-rot), 1998
Construction with the Serial Fibonacci Numbers 21, 34, 55, 89, 144, 233 (olive-red)
Acryl, Öl und Pigment auf Leinwand, 144 × 233 cm
Acrylic, oil and pigment on canvas

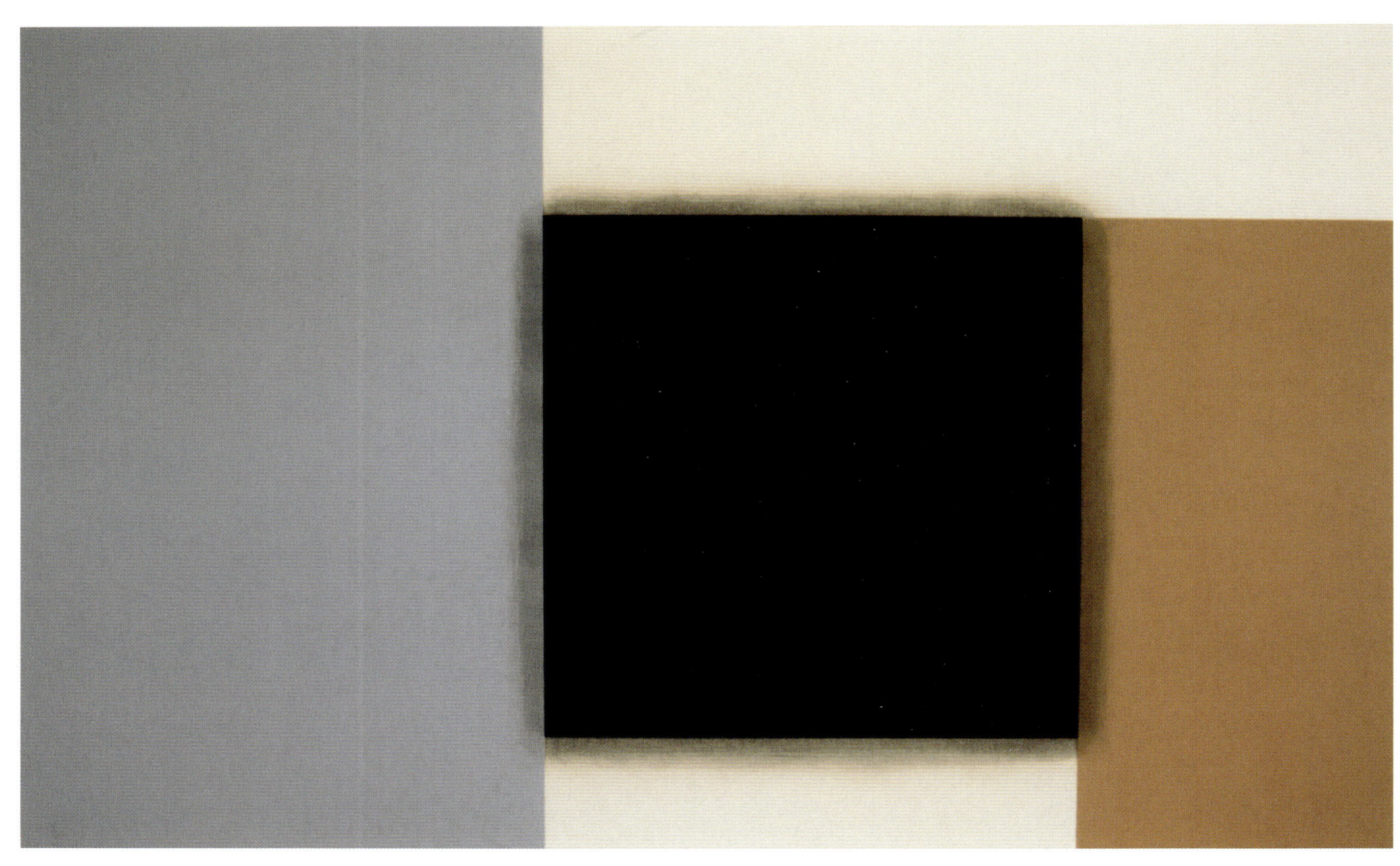

Konstruktion mit den aufeinander folgenden Fibonacci-Zahlen 21.34.55.89.144.233 (grau-braun), 1998
Construction with the Serial Fibonacci Numbers 21, 34, 55,
89, 144, 233 (gray-brown)
Acryl, Öl und Pigment auf Leinwand, 144 × 233 cm
Acrylic, oil and pigment on canvas

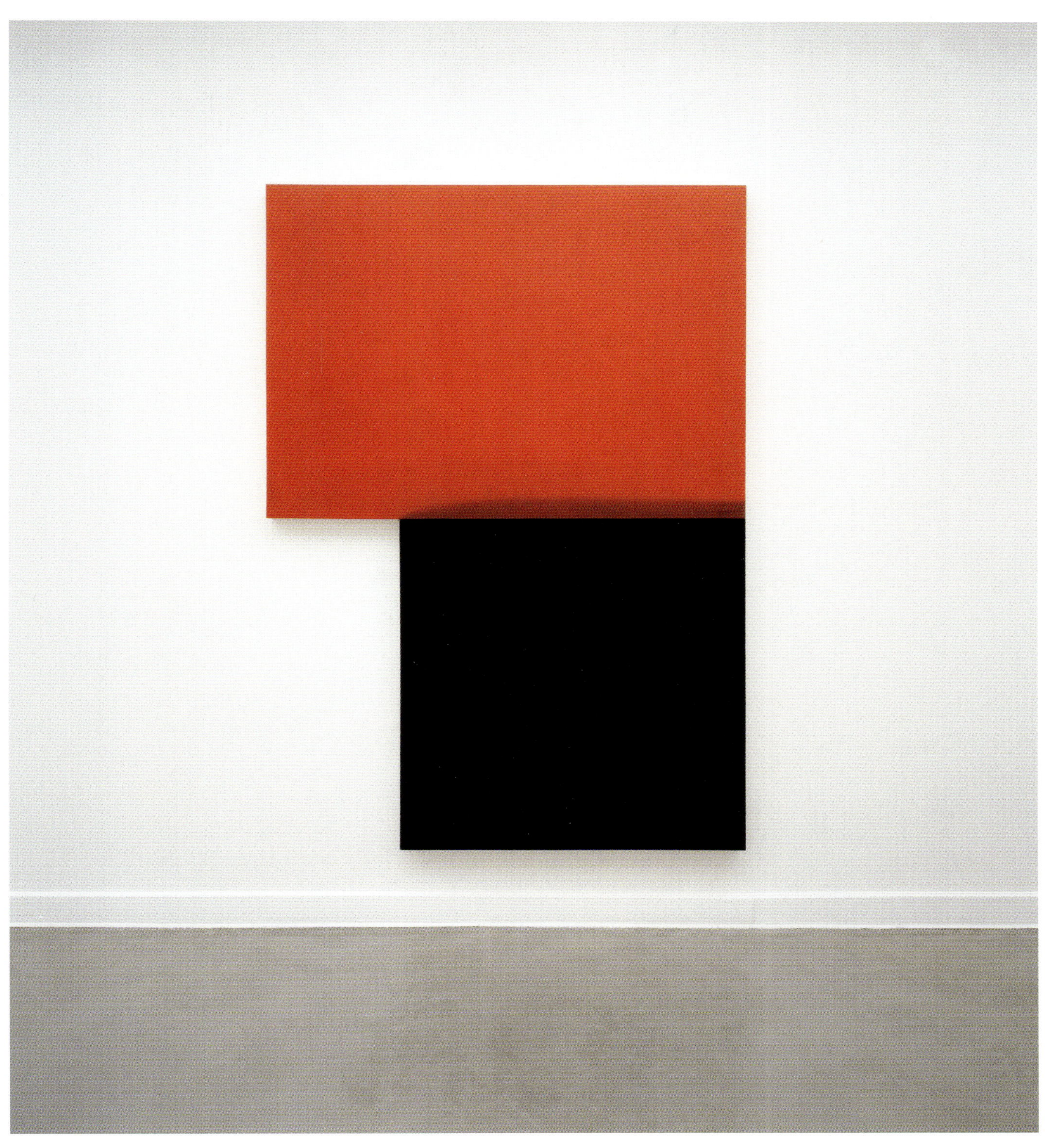

**Schwarz an Rot mit den aufeinander folgenden
Fibonacci-Zahlen 21.34.55.89.144.233,** 1996
*Black and Red with the Serial Fibonacci Numbers
21, 34, 55, 89, 144, 233*
Acryl, Öl und Pigment auf Holz, 288 × 199 cm
Acrylic, oil and pigment on wood

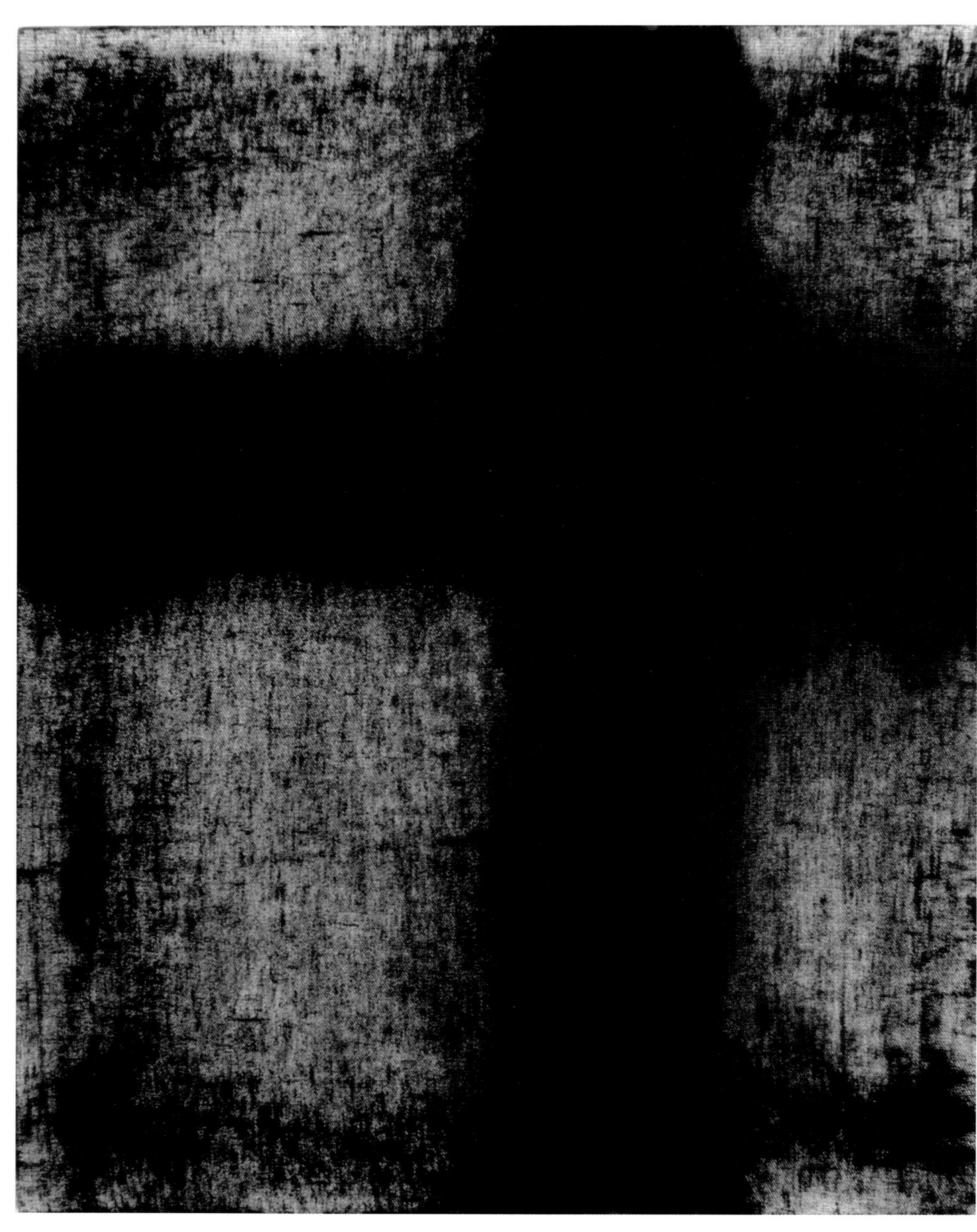

Versuch über den Goldenen Schnitt, 1993
Attempt at the Golden Cut
Öl und Pigment auf Leinwand, 57 × 44,5 cm
Oil and pigment on canvas

Zweimal Goldener Schnitt, 1993
Twice Golden Cut
Öl und Pigment auf Leinwand, 51 × 40,5 cm
Oil and pigment on canvas

Konstruktion mit 10 aufeinander folgenden Fibonacci-Zahlen, 8 Blätter, progressiv, 2005
Construction with Ten Serial Fibonacci Numbers,
Eight sheets, progressive
Öl und Pigment auf Fabriano, je 100 × 62 cm
Oil and pigment on Fabriano

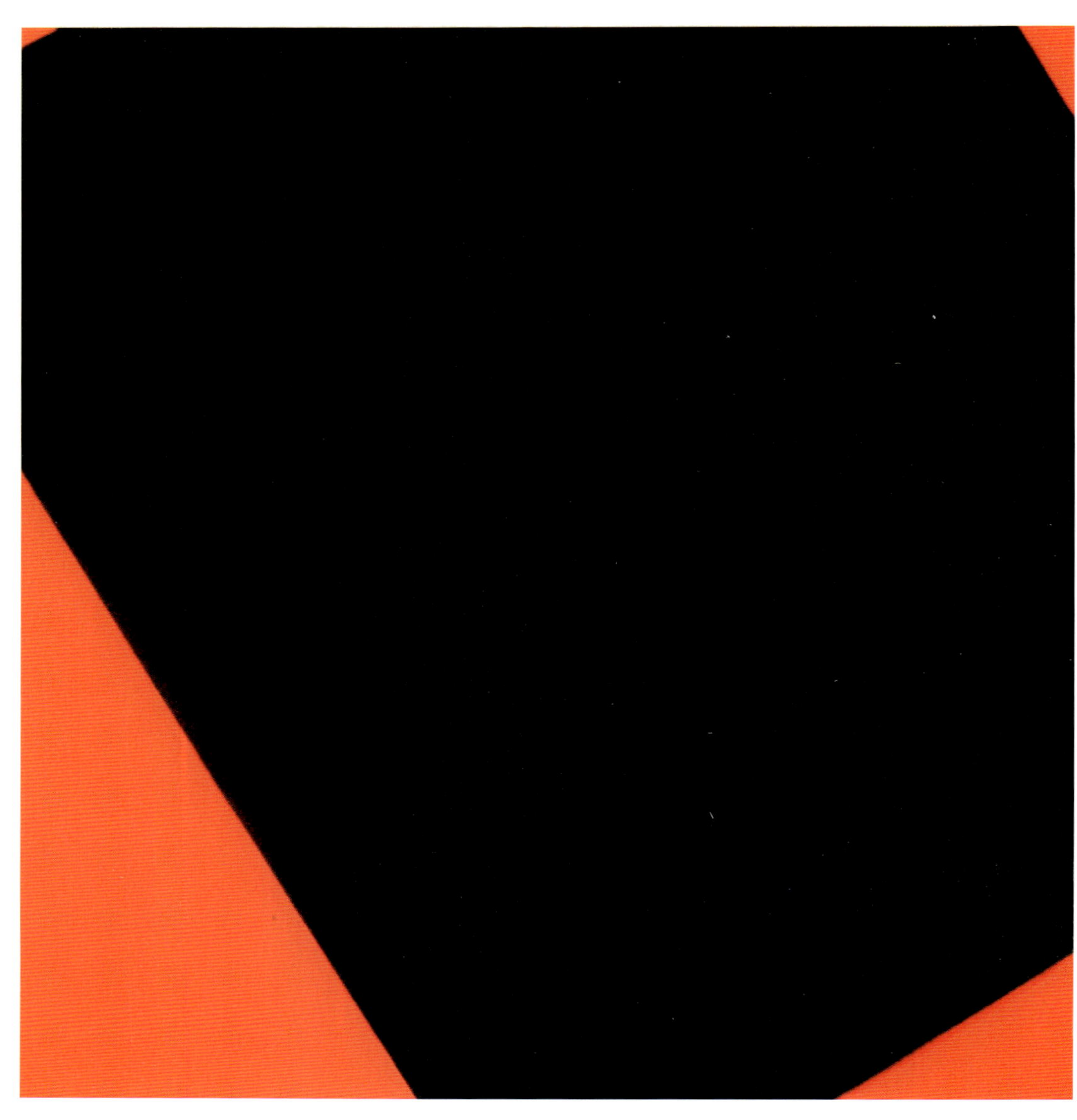

Zehn aufeinander folgende Fibonacci-Zahlen über Eck (rot), 2004
Ten Serial Fibonacci Numbers Diagonally Across (red)
Dispersion, Öl und Pigment auf Leinwand, 57 × 55 cm
Dispersion, oil and pigment on canvas

Zehn aufeinander folgende Fibonacci-Zahlen über Eck (grün), 2004
Ten Serial Fibonacci Numbers Diagonally Across (green)
Dispersion, Öl und Pigment auf Leinwand, 57 × 55 cm
Dispersion, oil and pigment on canvas

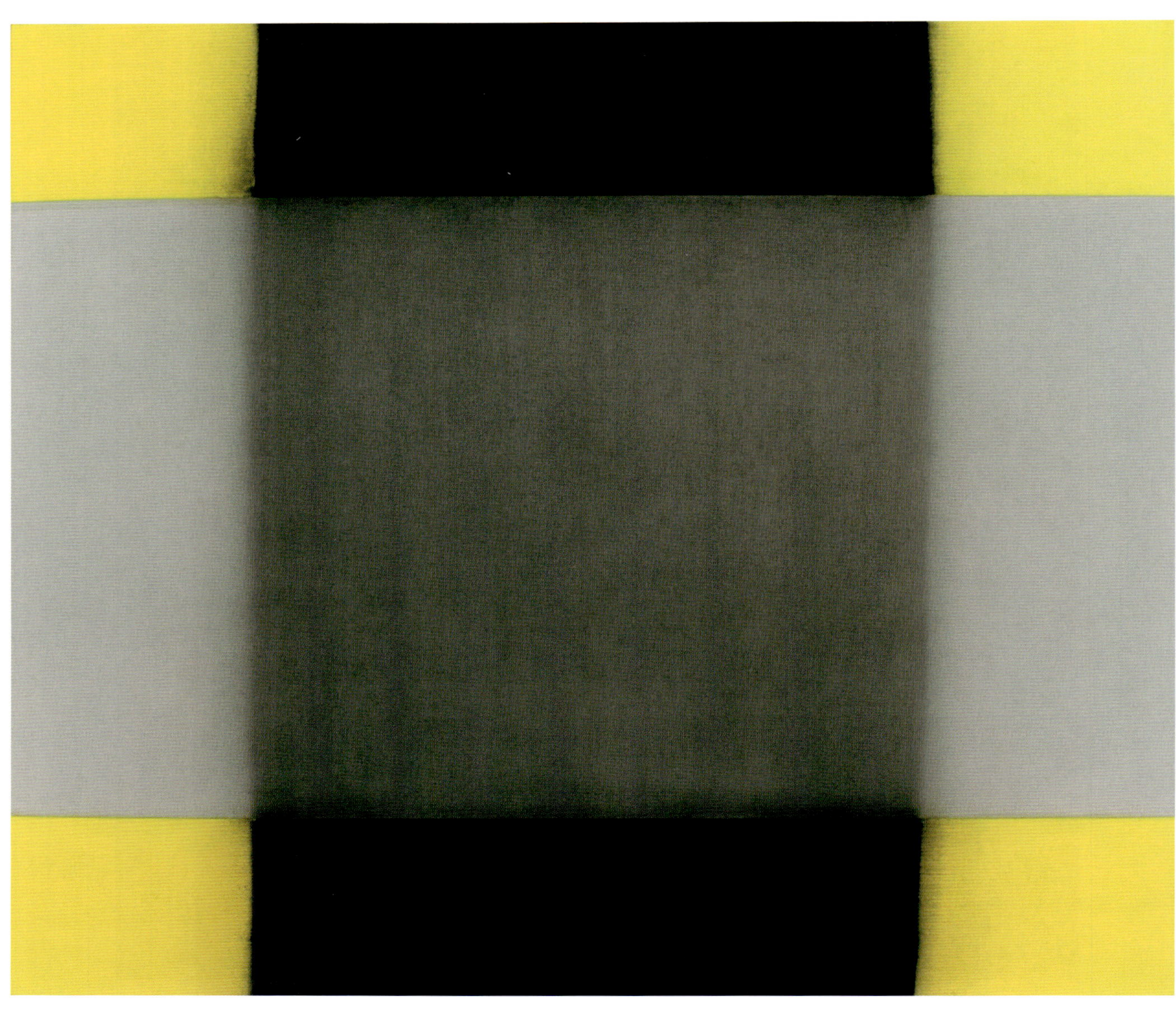

Fließendes Pigment über Gelb und Grau, 1995
Fluid Pigment over Yellow and Gray
Dispersion, Öl und Pigment auf Leinwand,
160 × 140 cm
Dispersion, oil and pigment on canvas

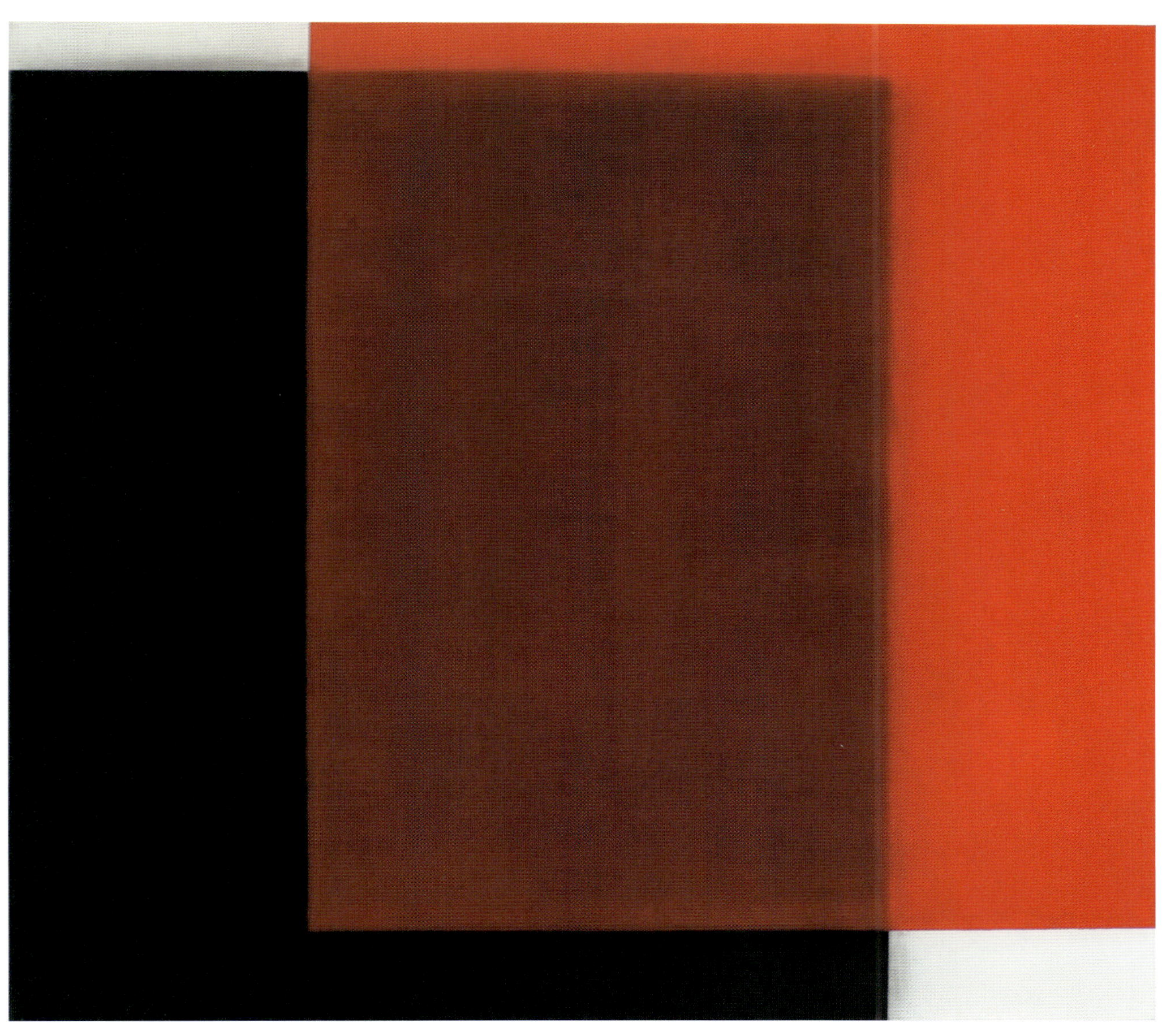

Rot und Schwarz auf Weiß, 1997
Red and Black on White
Dispersion, Öl und Pigment auf Leinwand, 100 × 90 cm
Dispersion, oil and pigment on canvas

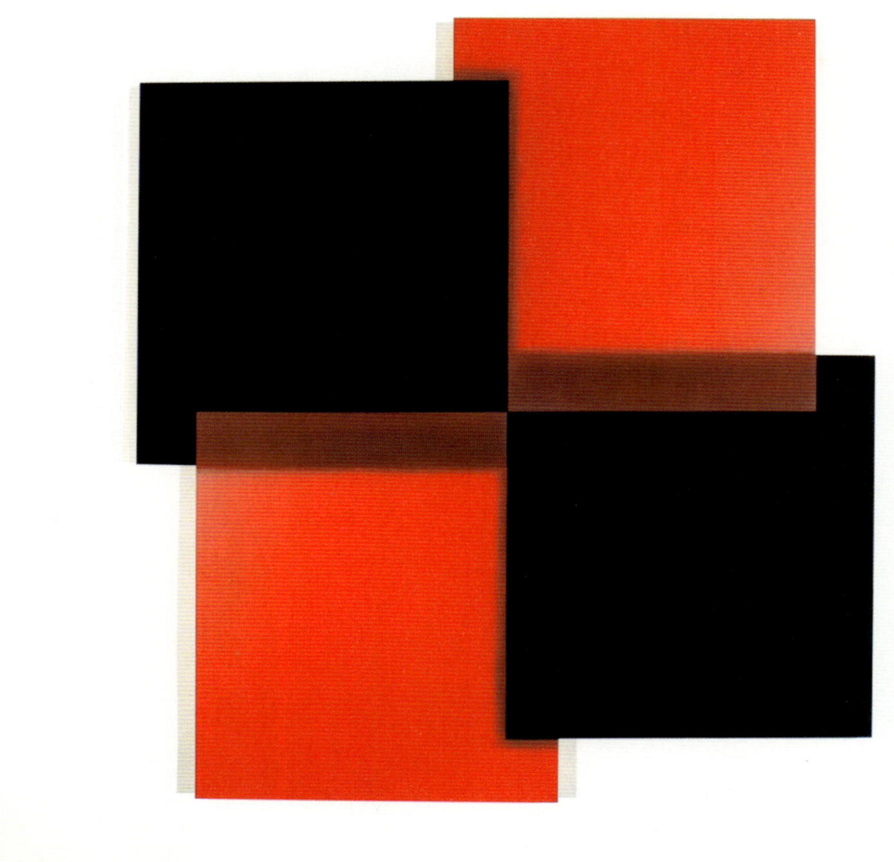

Vier Quadrate, 1997
Four Squares
Acryl, Öl und Pigment auf Holz, 160 × 160 cm
Acrylic, oil and pigment on wood

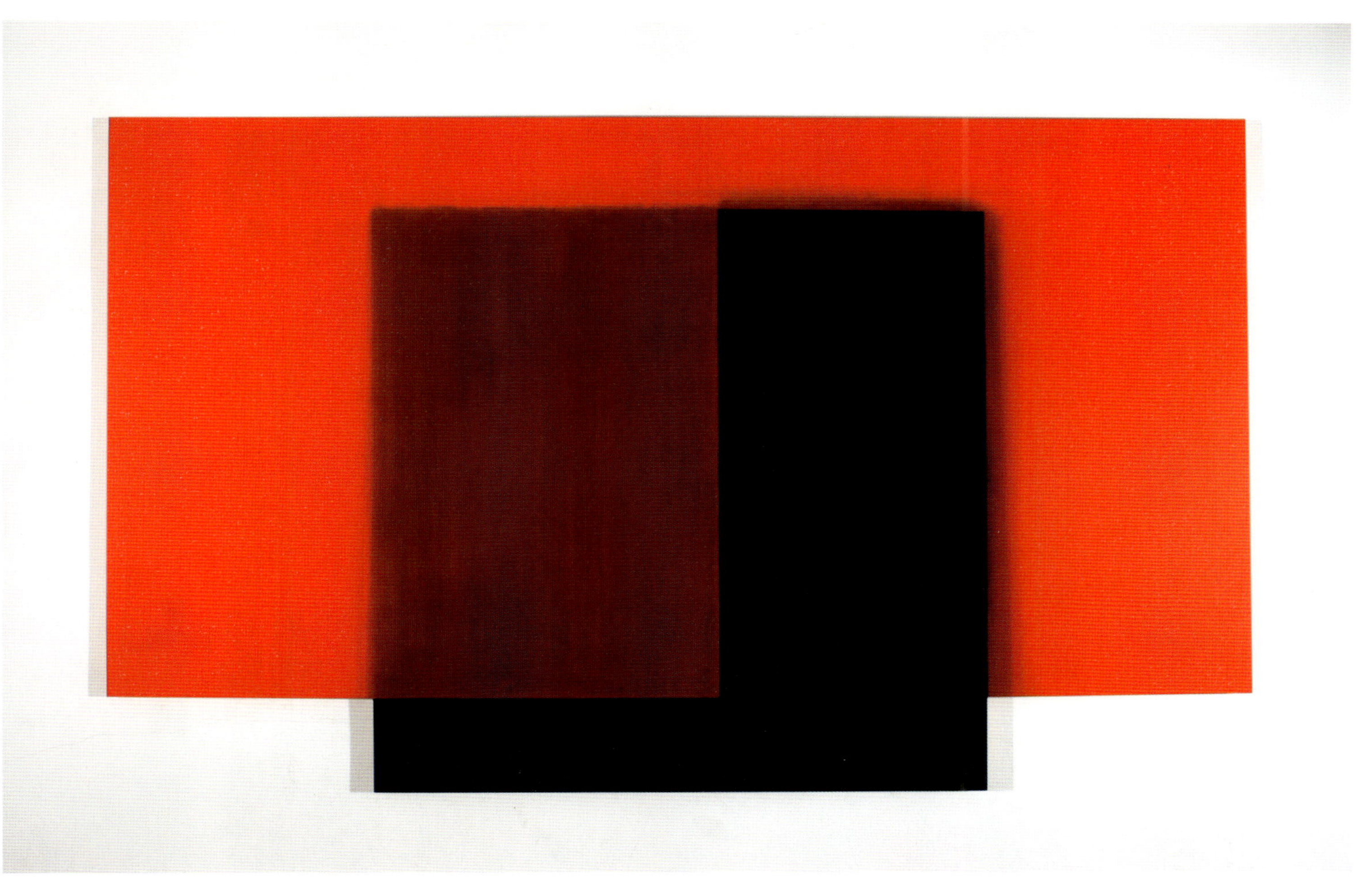

Drei Quadrate, 1997
Three Squares
Acryl, Öl und Pigment auf Holz, 155 × 250 cm
Acrylic, oil and pigment on wood

Zwei Quadrate sich überlagernd, 1998
Two Overlapping Squares
Öl und Pigment auf Beton, 40 × 44 × 13 cm
Oil and pigment on concrete

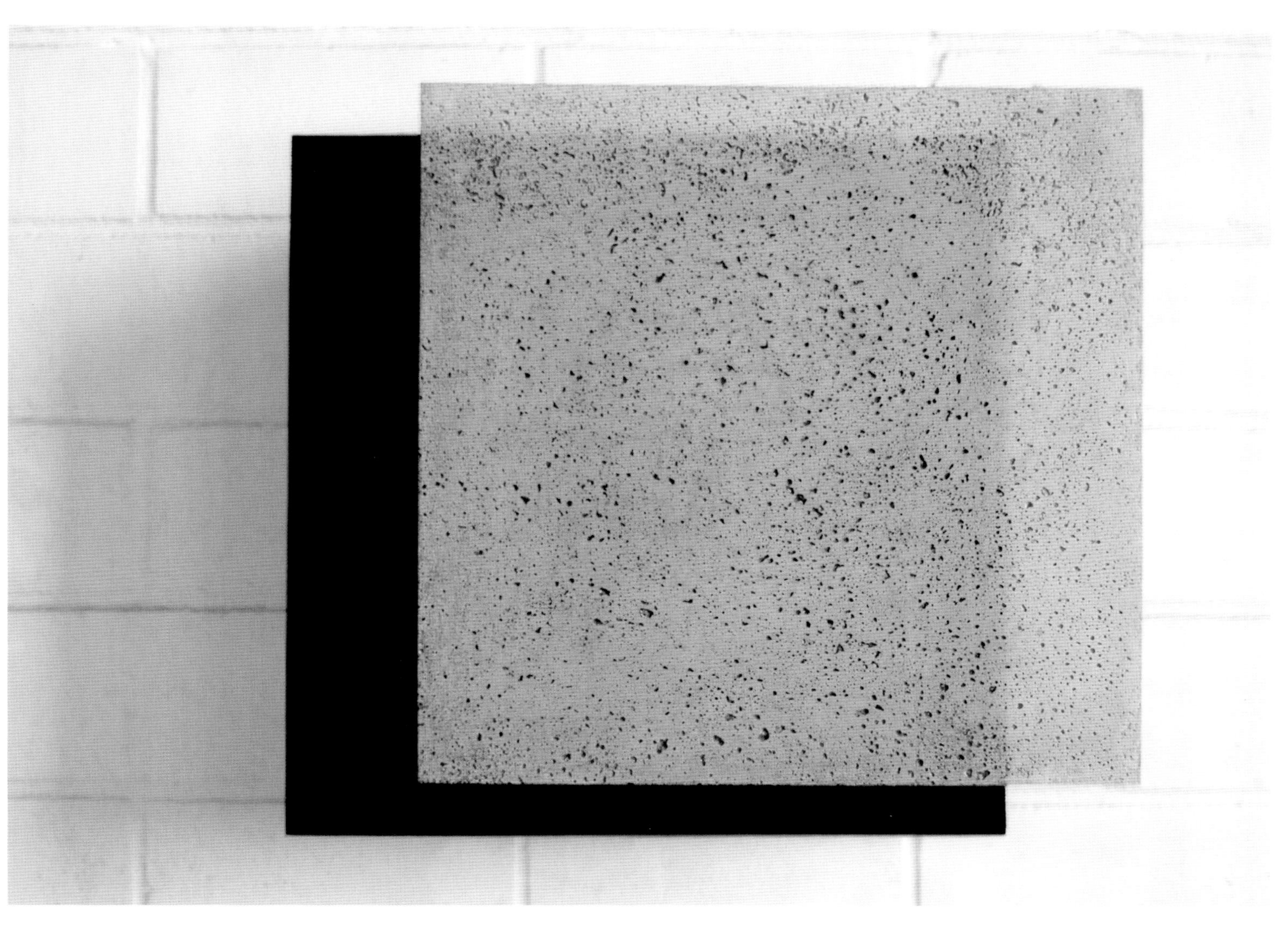

Zwei Quadrate sich überschneidend, 2004
Two Intersecting Squares
Öl und Pigment auf Beton, 49 × 44,5 × 13 cm
Oil and pigment on concrete

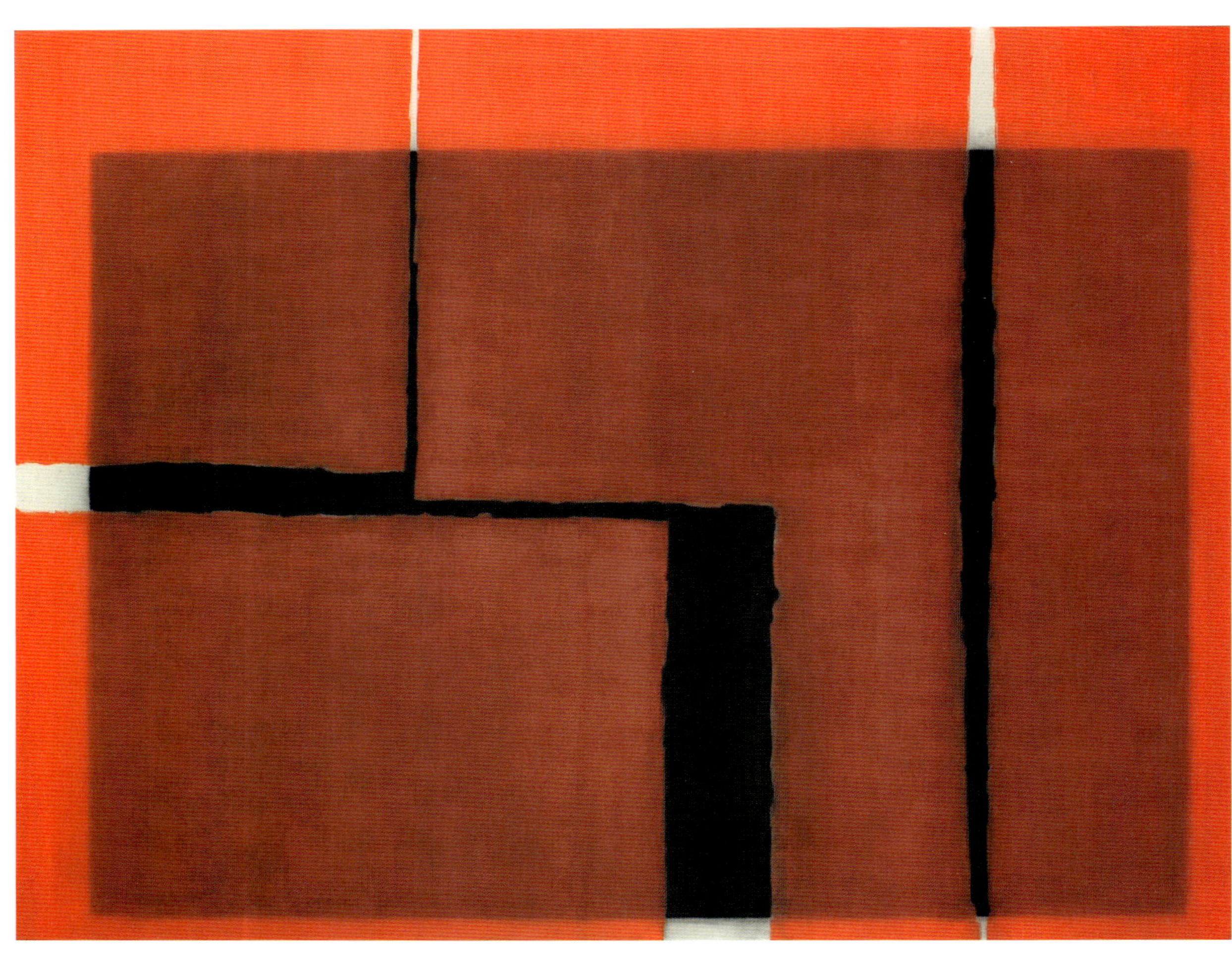

Schwarzes Pigment über zerteiltem Rot, 1999
Black Pigment over Divided Red
Acryl, Öl und Pigment auf Leinwand, 160 × 200 cm
Acrylic, oil and pigment on canvas

Schwarzes Pigment über zerteiltem Gelb, 1999
Black Pigment over Divided Yellow
Dispersion, Öl und Pigment auf Leinwand,
180 × 280 cm
Dispersion, oil and pigment on canvas

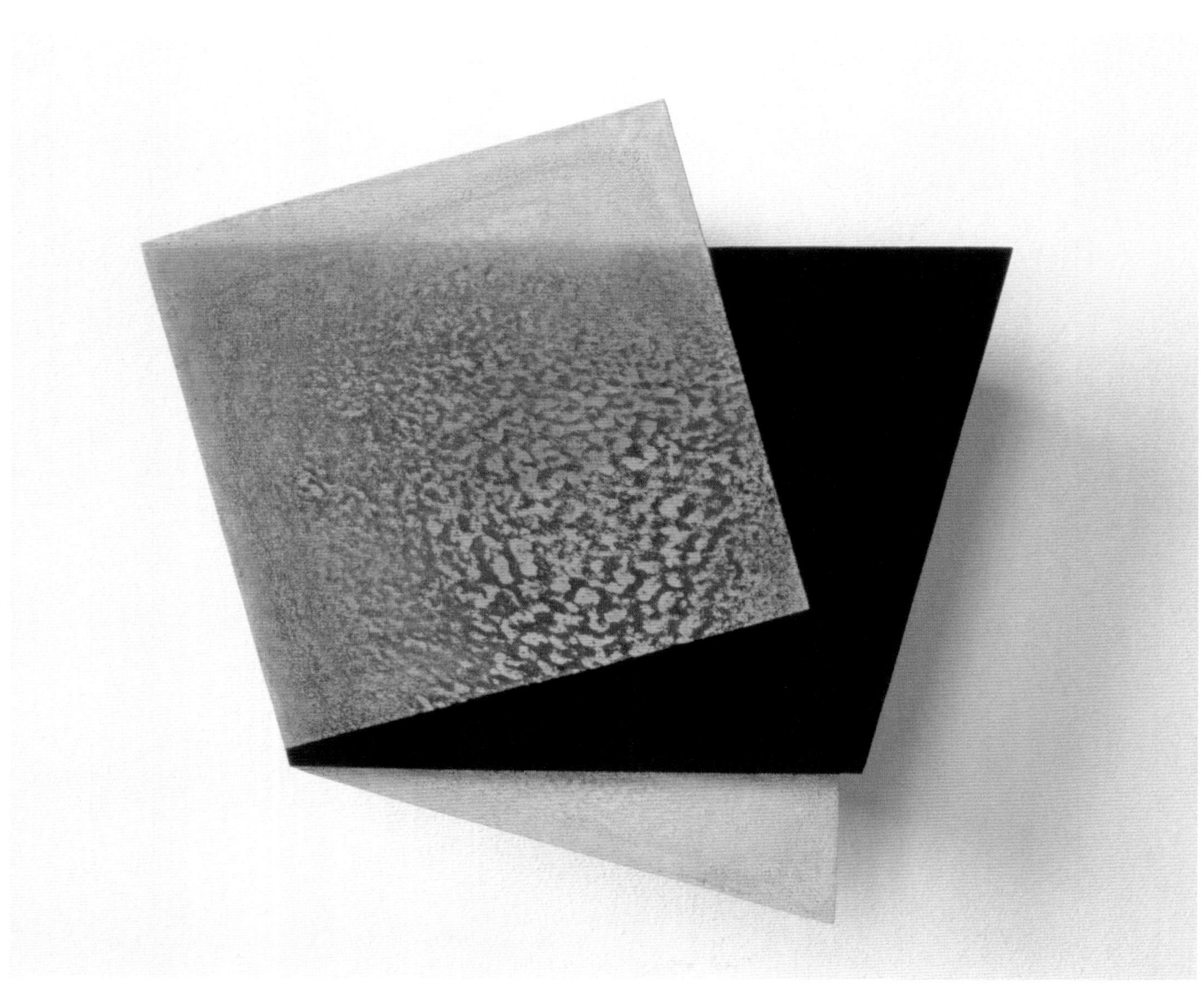

Zwei Schnitte in das suprematistische Rechteck, x/6,
1999
Two Cuts in the Suprermatist Rectangle, x/6
Öl und Pigment auf Beton, 40,5 × 41 × 14 cm
Oil and pigment on concrete

Quadrat und zwei Balken, 2000
Square and Two Bars
Zement, Öl und Pigment auf Leinwand, 82 × 61 cm
Cement, oil and pigment on canvas

179

Quadrat und Trapez, 1998
Square and Trapezoid
Öl und Pigment auf Beton, 42 × 44 × 13 cm
Oil and pigment on concrete

Wandgedächtnis, temporäres Wandbild in der Galerie
Art Studio 1, 1999
Wall Memory, temporary mural in the Galerie Art Studio 1
Schnur, Öl und Pigment auf Wand, für eine 6 m lange Wand
String, oil and pigment on wall, for a 6-m-long wall

Zement transparent, 1999
Cement Transparent
Zement, Öl und Pigment auf Leinwand, 160 × 200 cm
Cement, oil and pigment on canvas

Zwei Quadrate sich überschneidend, 1999
Two Intersecting Squares
Acryl, Öl und Pigment auf Holz, 50 × 70 × 12 cm
Acrylic, oil and pigment on wood

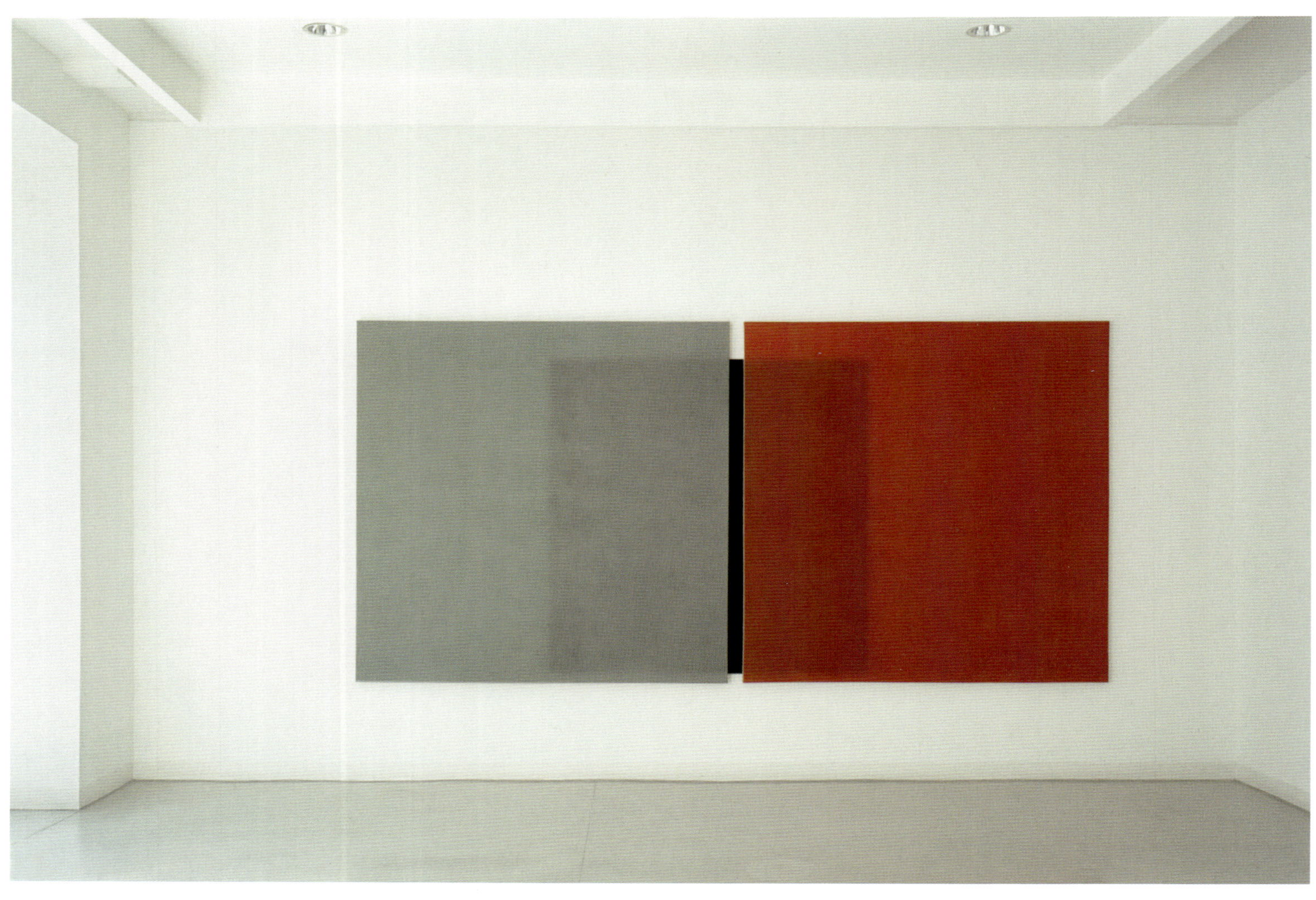

Drei Quadrate (dreiteilig), 2003
Four Squares (four-part)
Dispersion, Acryl und Pigment auf MDF und Leinwand,
180 × 370 cm
Dispersion, acrylic and pigment on MDF and canvas

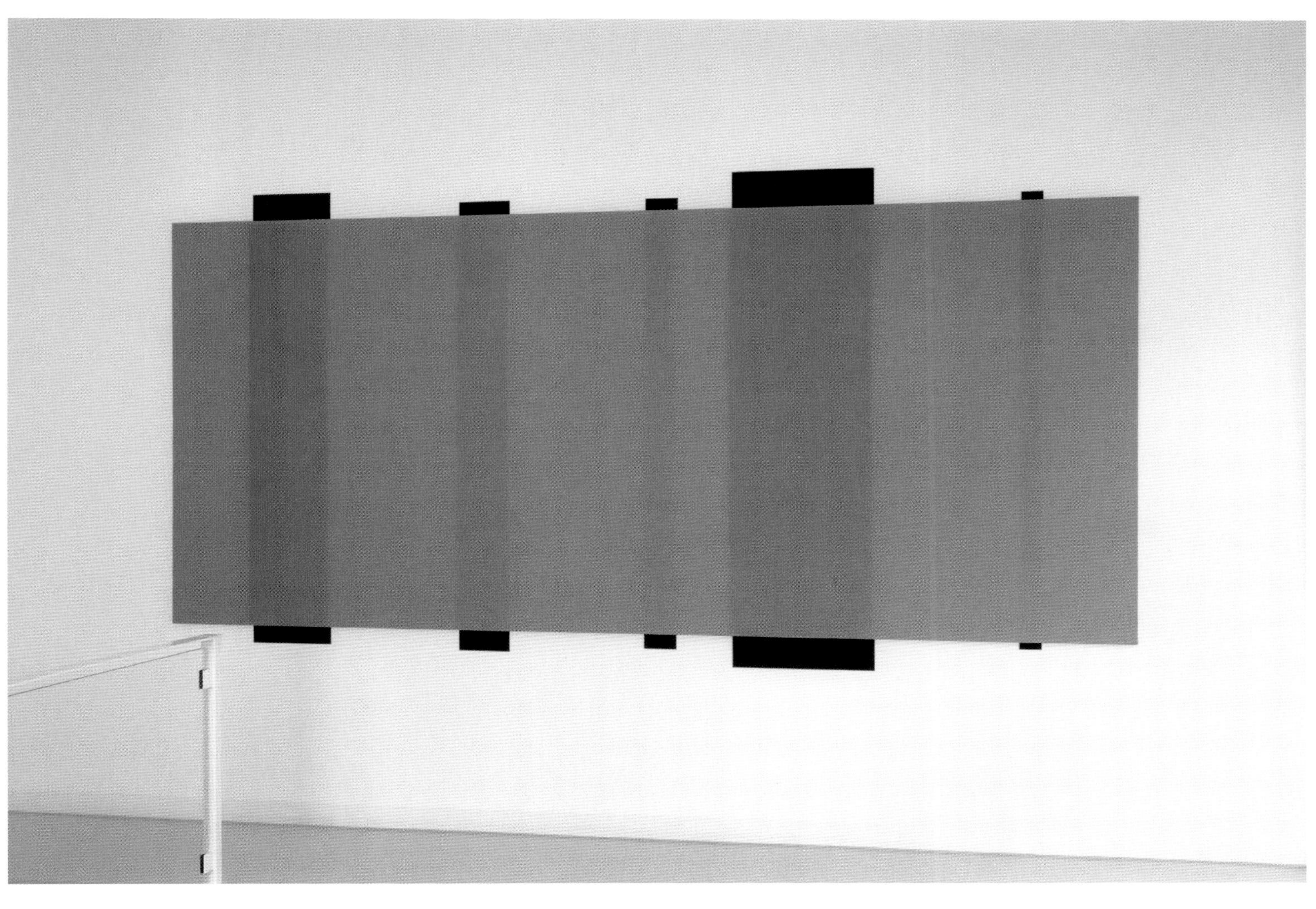

Fibonacci-Rhythmus, 2003
Fibonacci Rhythm
Dispersion, Acryl und Pigment auf MDF und Leinwand
180 × 360 cm
Dispersion, acrylic and pigment on MDF and canvas

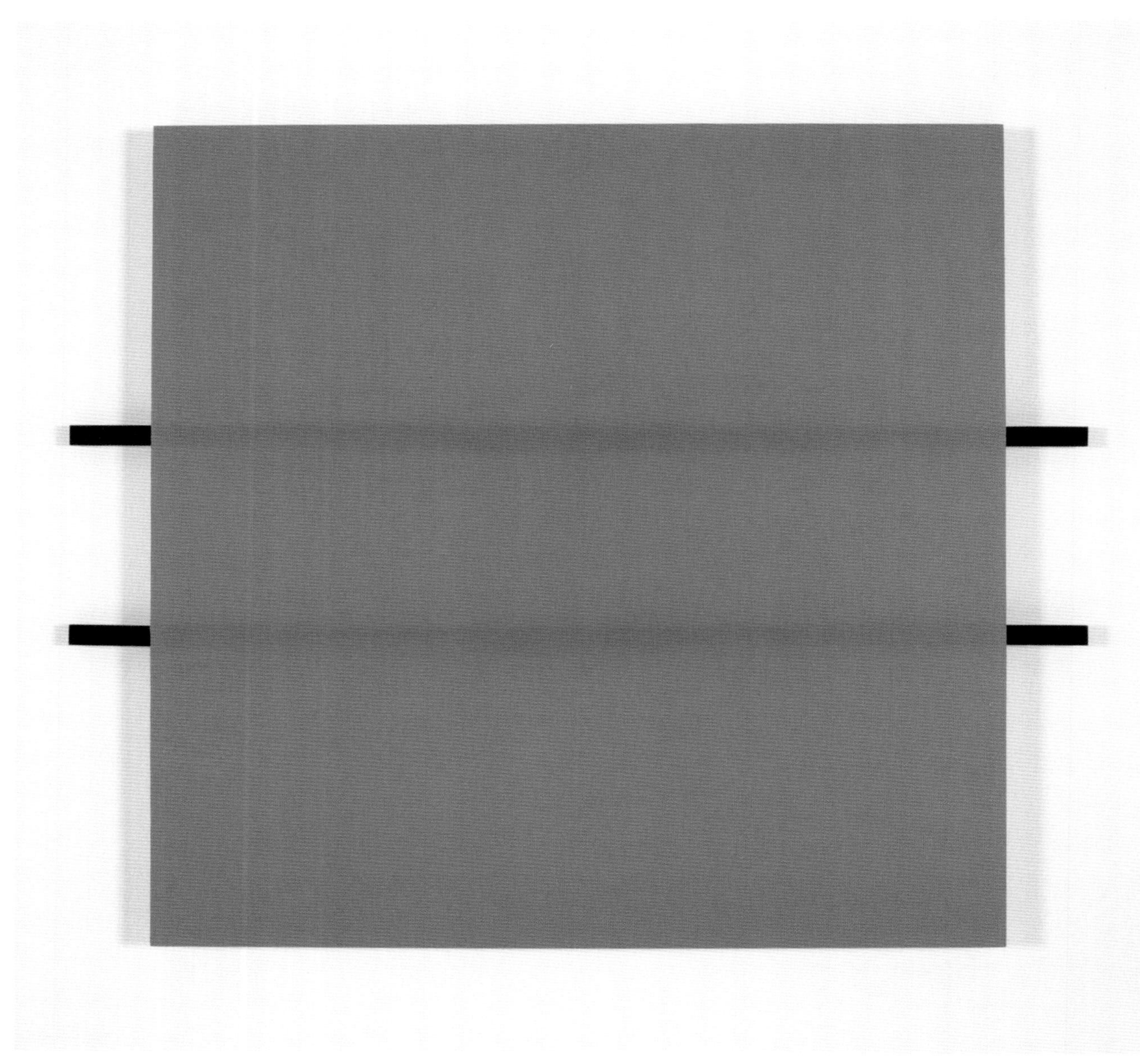

Quadrat und zwei Balken, 2003
Square with Two Bars
Dispersion, Acryl und Pigment auf Holz, 70 × 80 cm
Dispersion, acrylic and pigment on wood

Zwei Leinwände sich überschneidend II, 2002
Two Intersecting Canvases II
Dispersion, Acryl und Pigment auf 2 Leinwänden,
66 × 66 cm
Dispersion, acrylic and pigment on two canvases

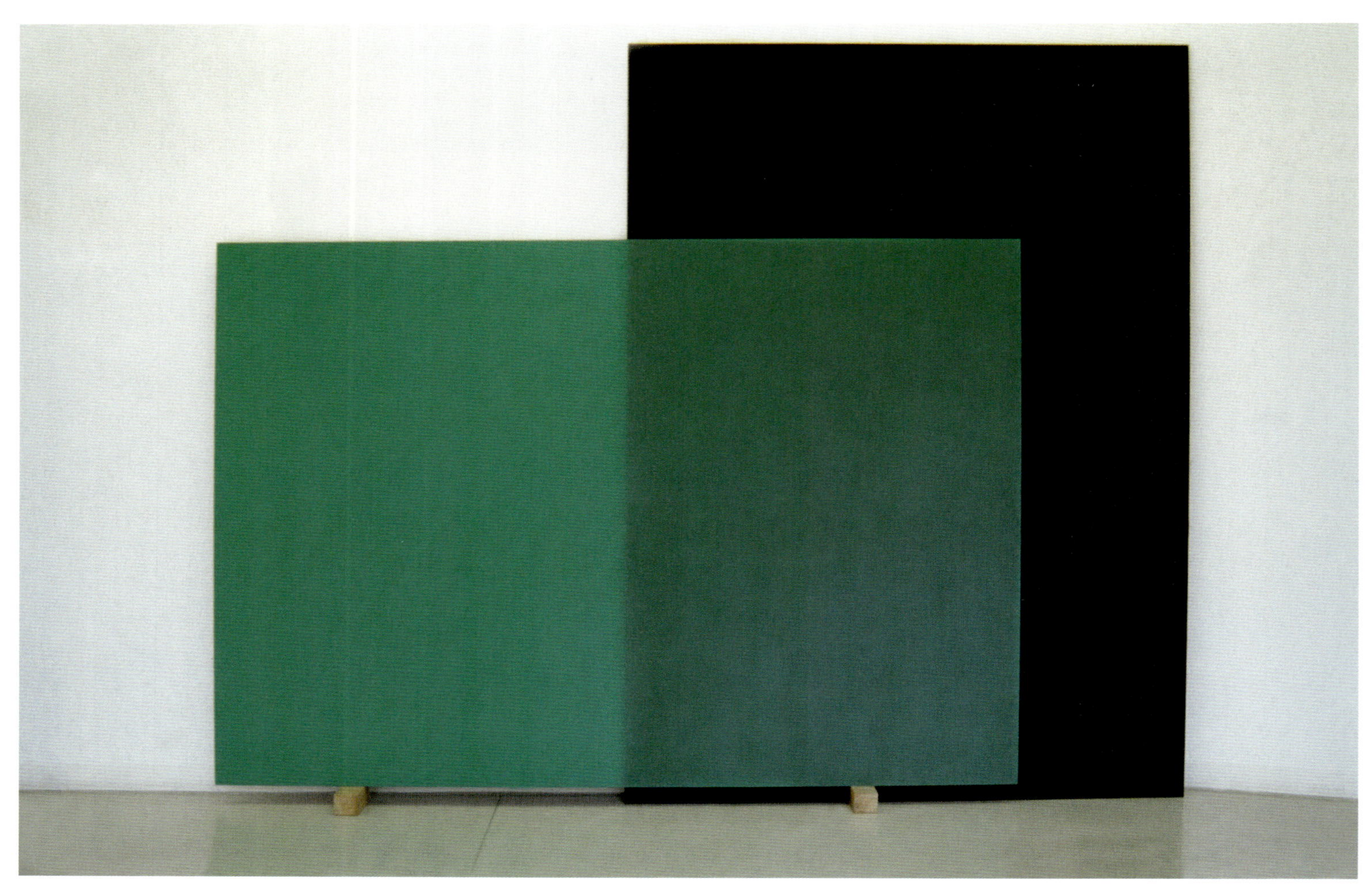

Grün vor Schwarz, 2002
Green Before Black
Acryl, Dispersion und Pigment auf zwei Holzplatten,
250 × 300 cm
Acrylic, dispersion and pigment on two wooden panels

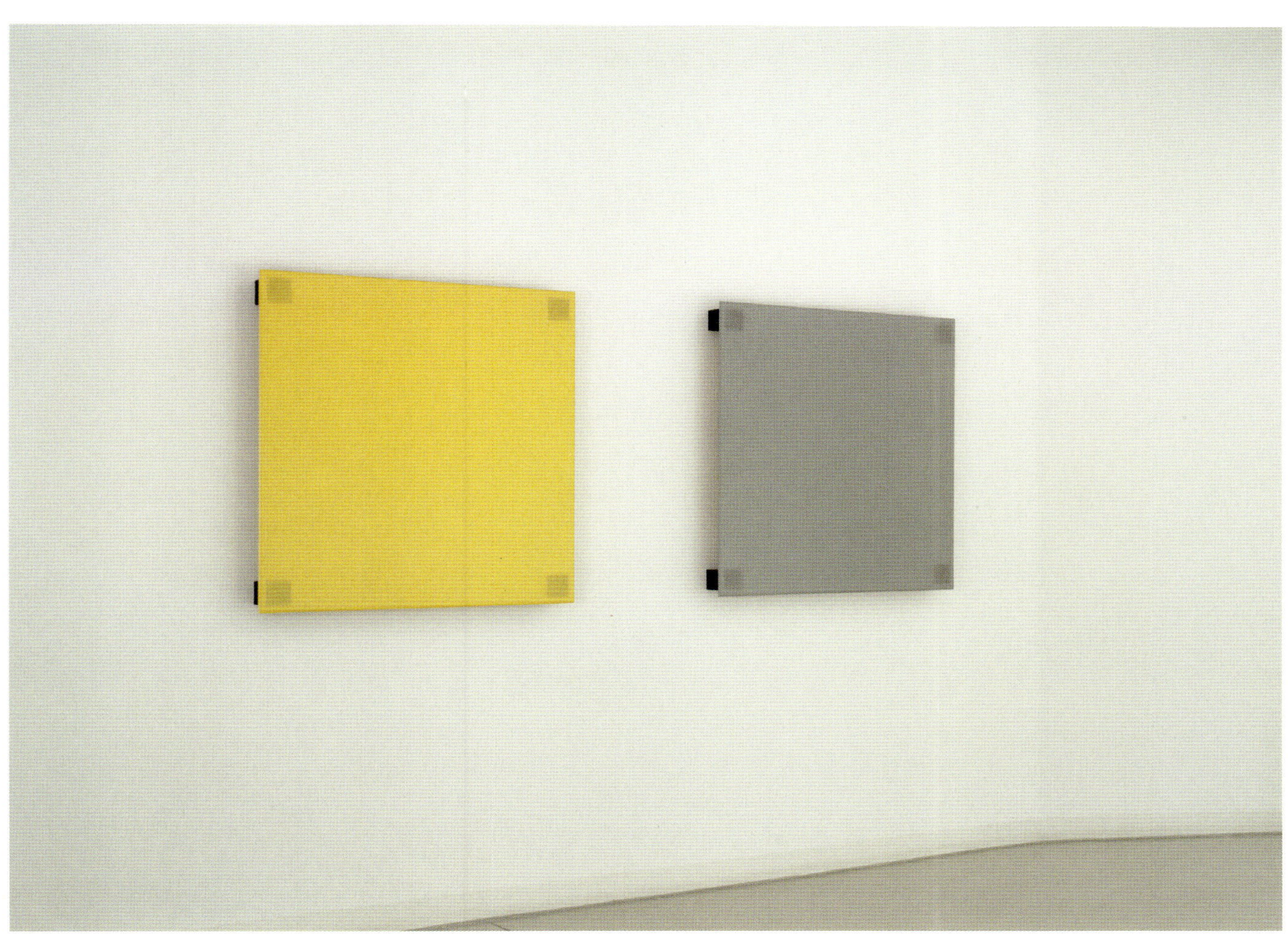

Vier Würfel, ein Quadrat (Doppelbild), 2003
Four Cubes, One Square (double picture)
Acryl und Pigment auf Holz, je 100 × 100 × 11 cm
Acrylic and pigment on wood

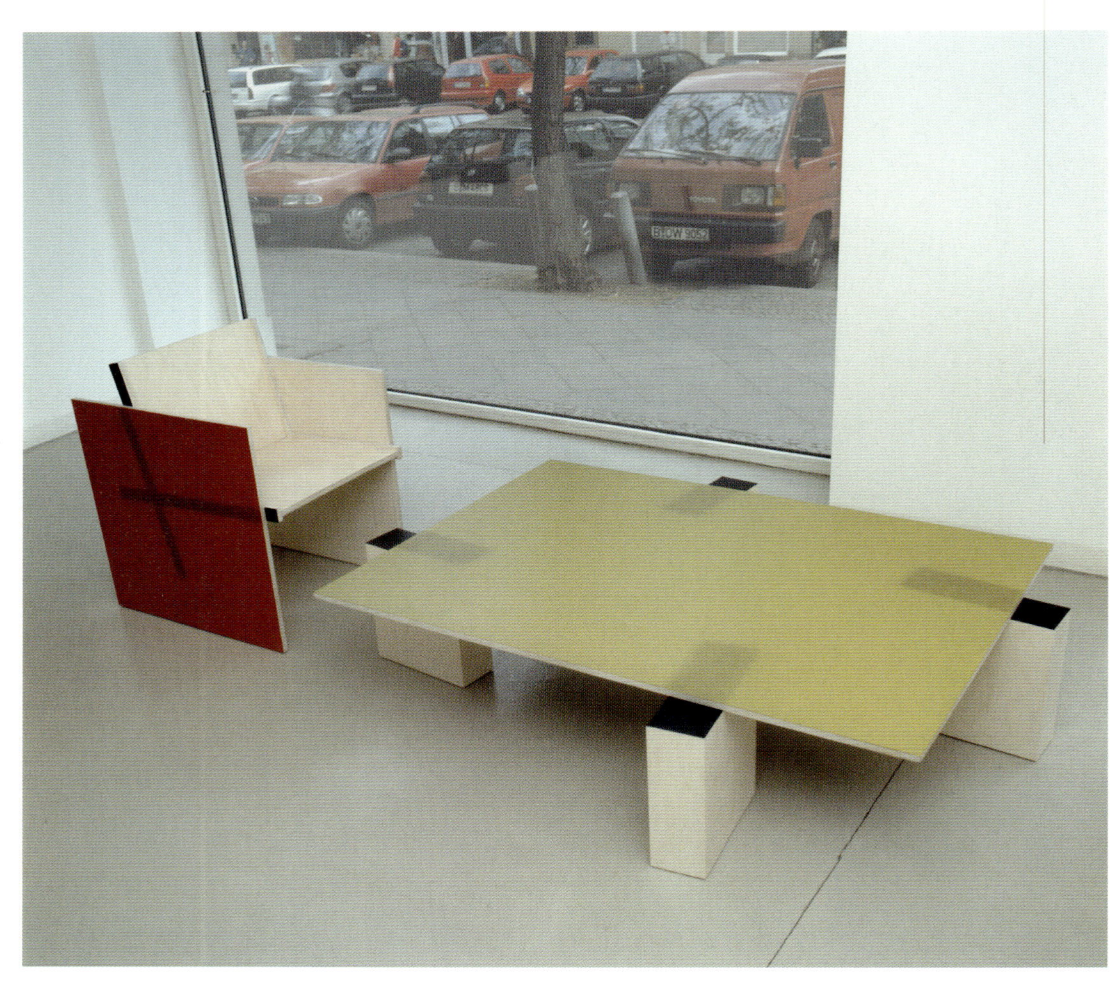

Tisch und Stuhl, 2003
Table and Chair
Acryl und Pigment auf Holz
Acrylic and pigment on wood

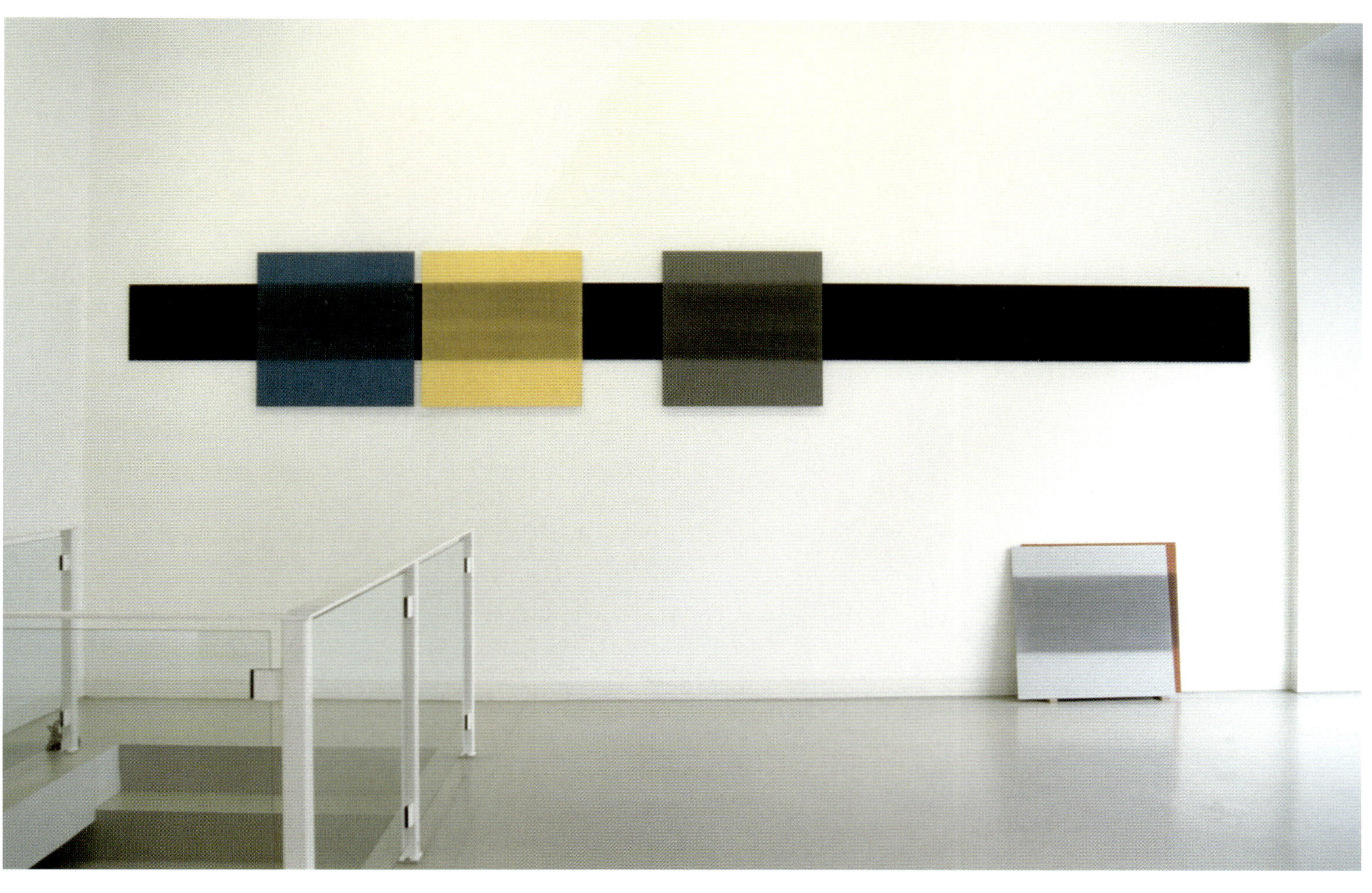

Fünf Quadrate und ein Balken, 2001
Five Squares and One Bar
Dispersion, Acryl, Öl und Pigment auf Holz,
75 × 500 cm
Dispersion, acrylic, oil and pigment on wood

Zweimal Grün, 2004
Twice Green
Acryl auf Holz, 84 × 84 × 5 cm
Acrylic on wood

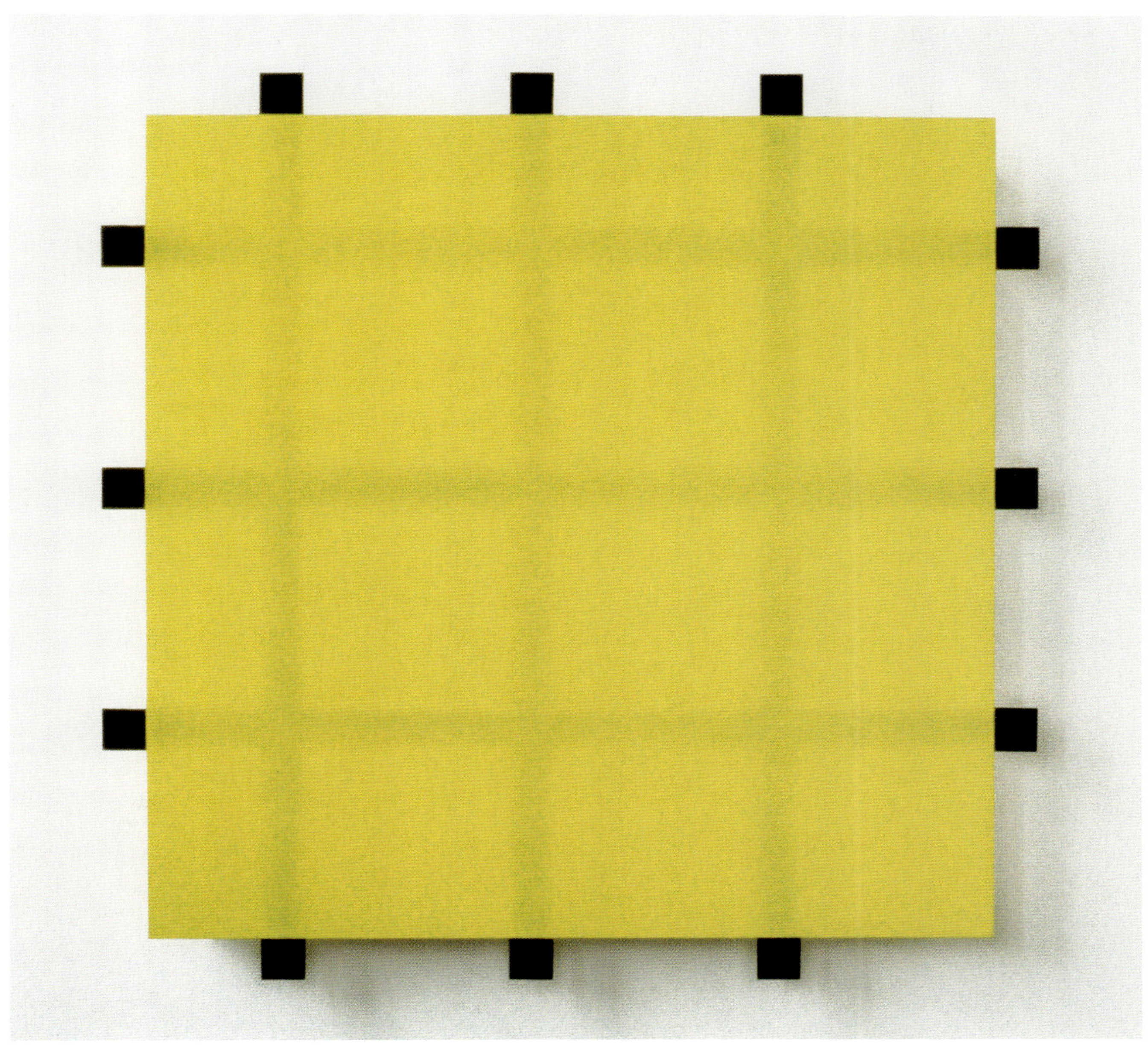

Leuchtendes Gelb, 2004
Radiating Yellow
Dispersion, Acryl und Pigment auf Holz, 83 × 83 × 5 cm
Dispersion, acrylic and pigment on wood

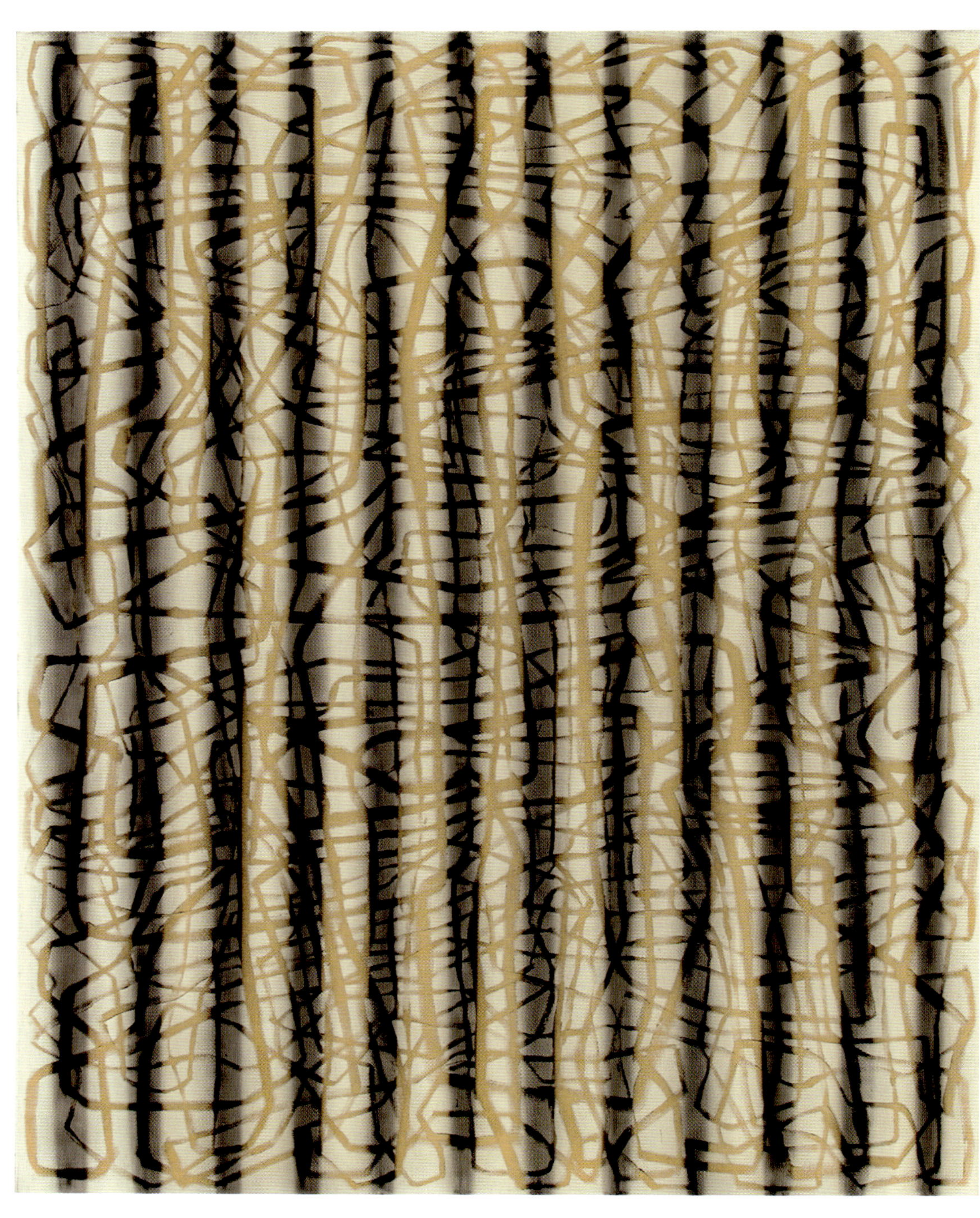

Fließendes Pigment über Ocker und Leinwand 1, 1995
Fluid Pigment over Ochre and Canvas 1
Öl und Pigment auf Leinwand, 200 × 160 cm
Oil and pigment on canvas

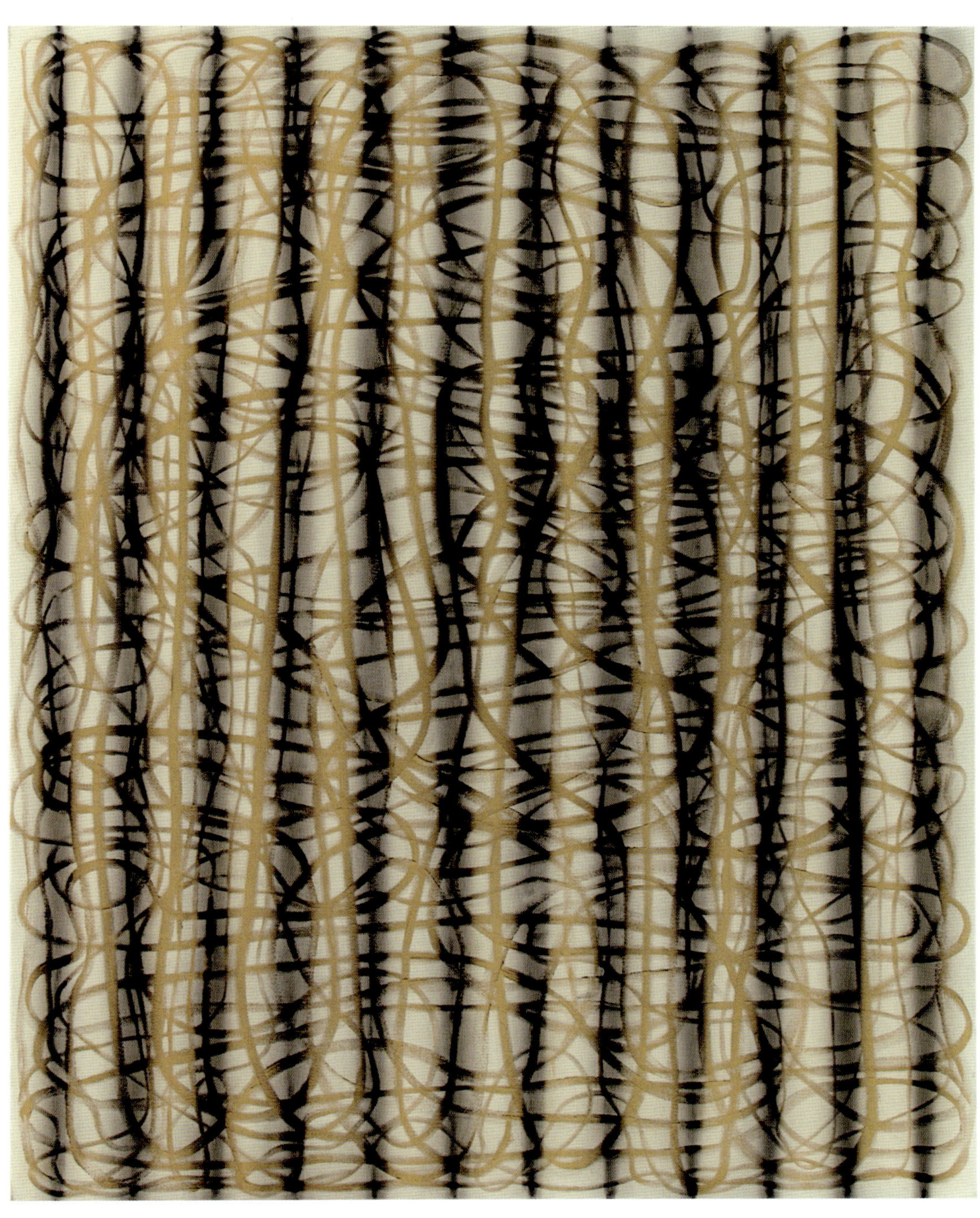

Fließendes Pigment über Ocker und Leinwand II, 1995
Fluid Pigment over Ochre and Canvas II
Öl und Pigment auf Leinwand, 200 × 160 cm
Oil and pigment on canvas

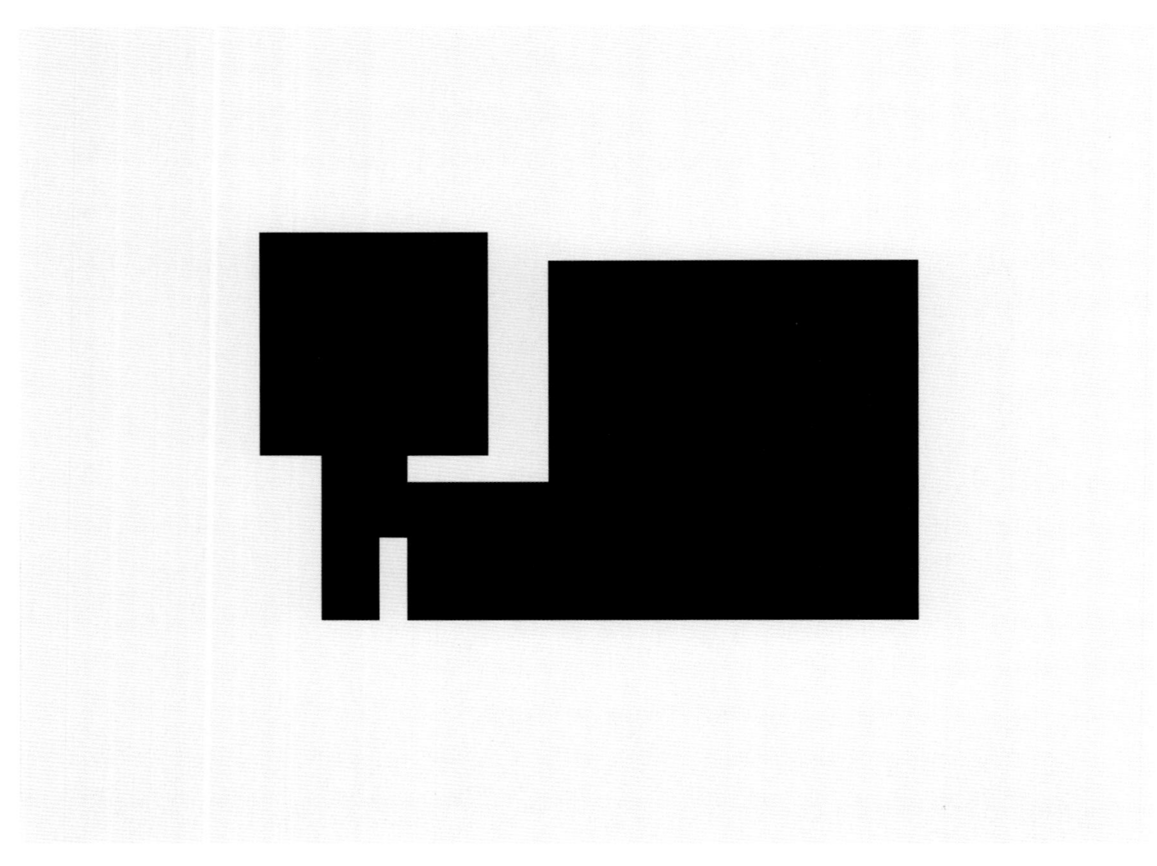

Sieben Fibonacci-Quadrate, Nr. 25, 2003
Seven Fibonacci Squares, No. 25
Computerdruck, 30 × 40 cm
Computer print-out

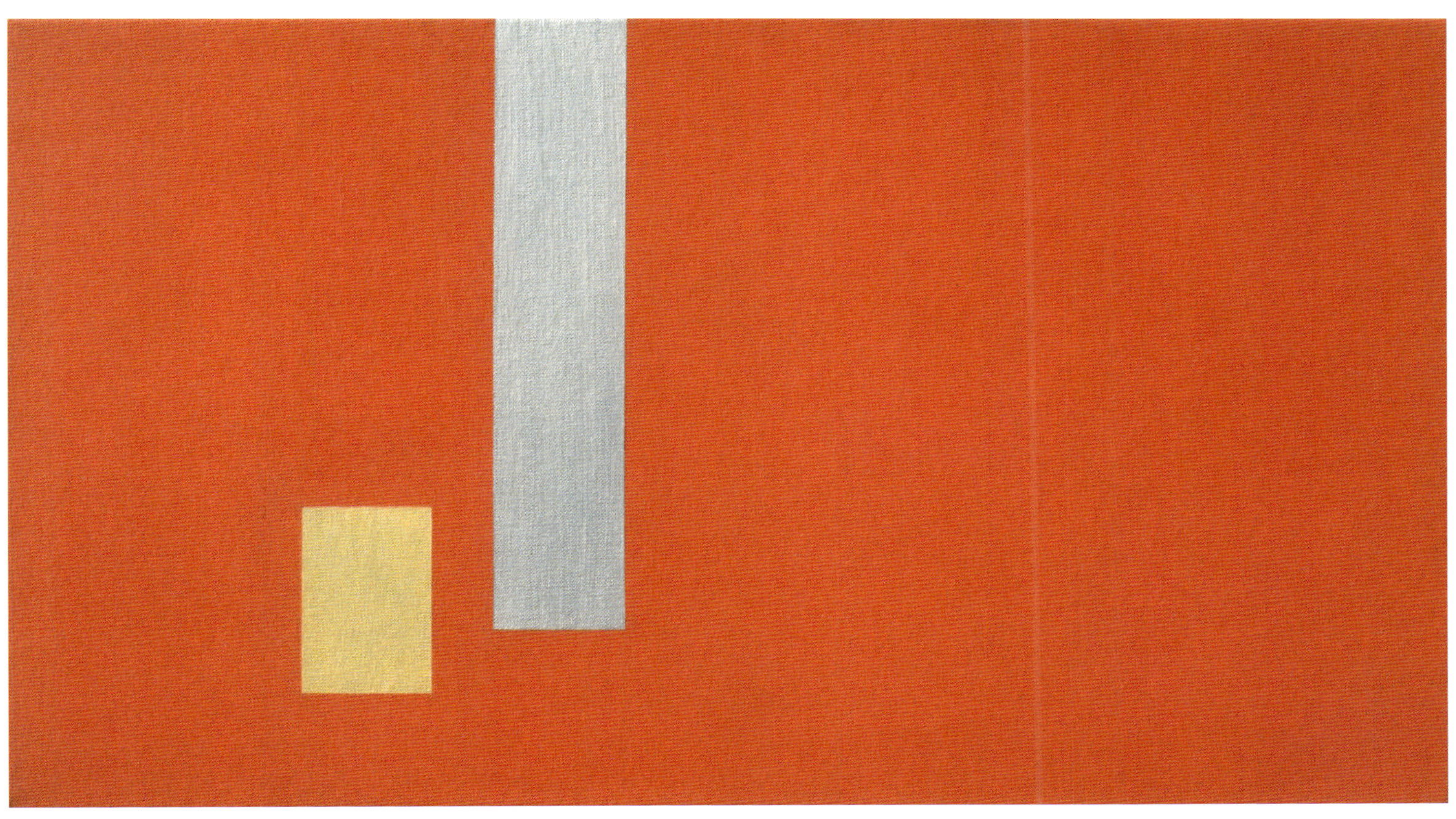

Sieben Fibonacci-Quadrate, Nr. 5, 2003
Seven Fibonacci Squares, No. 5
Acryl auf Leinwand, 39 × 69 cm
Acrylic on canvas

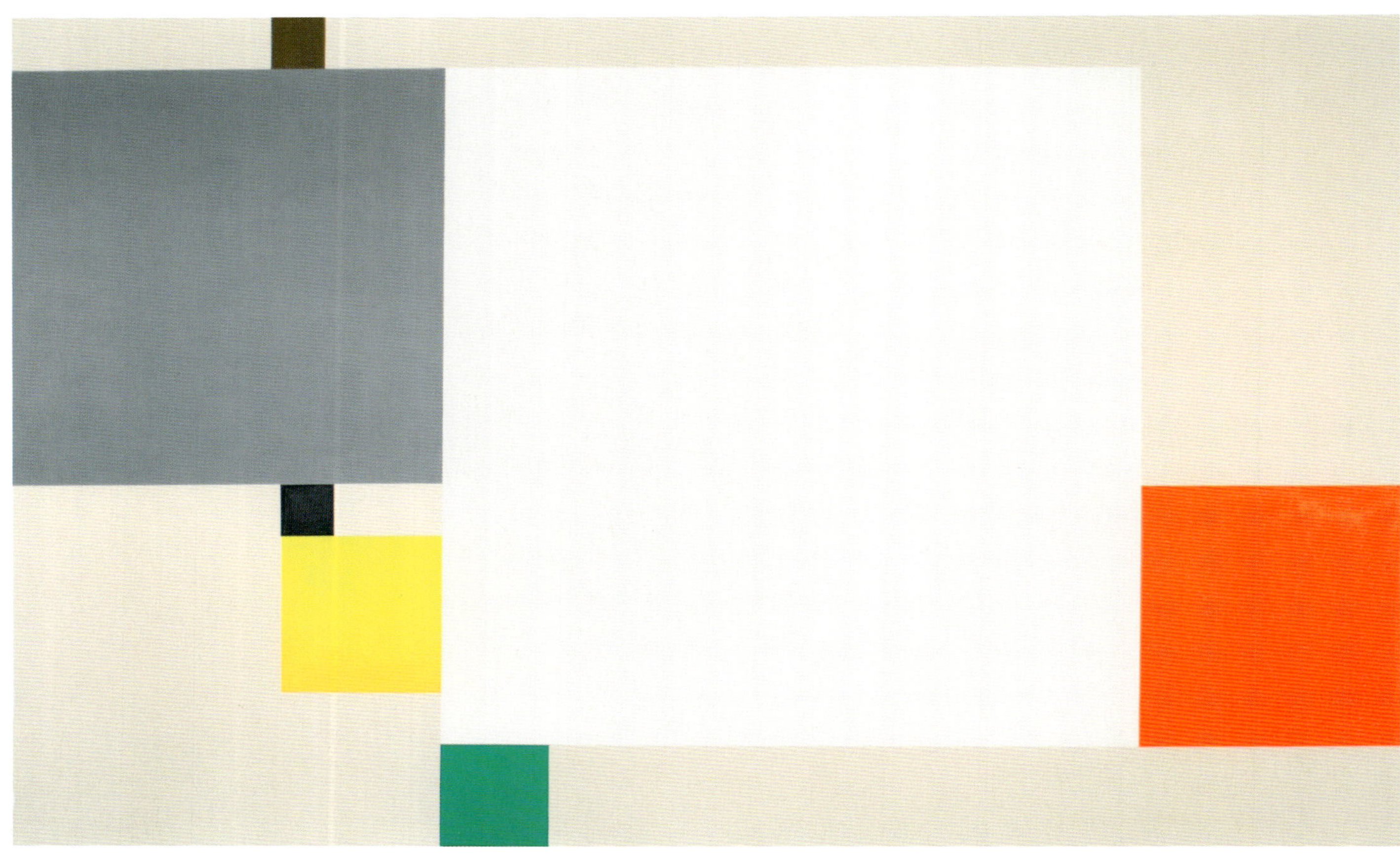

Sieben Fibonacci-Quadrate, Nr. 14, 2003
Seven Fibonacci Squares, No. 14
Acryl auf Leinwand, 200 × 300 cm
Acrylic on canvas

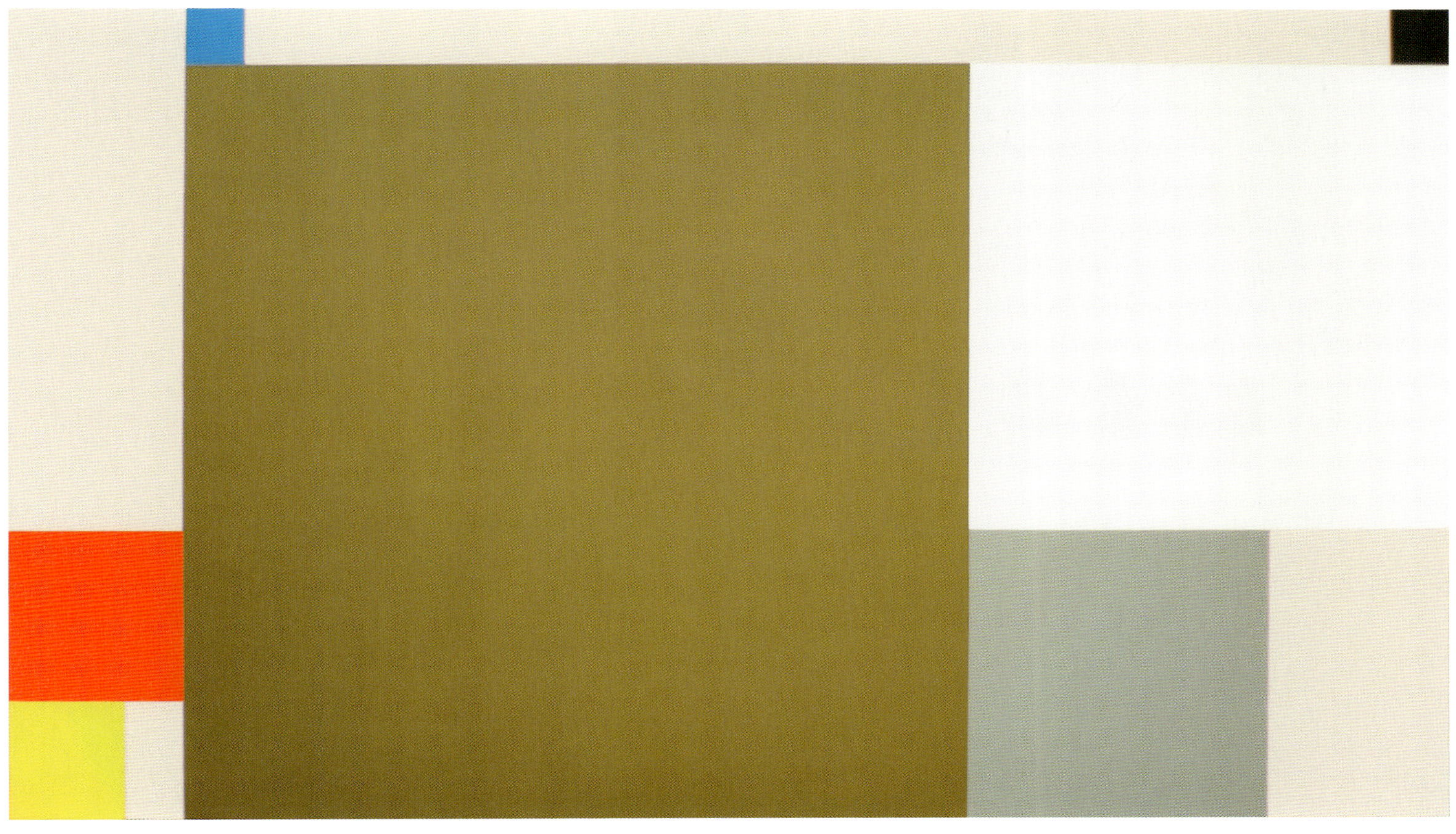

Sieben Fibonacci-Quadrate, Nr. 15, 2003
Seven Fibonacci Squares, No. 15
Acryl auf Leinwand, 200 × 300 cm
Acrylic on canvas

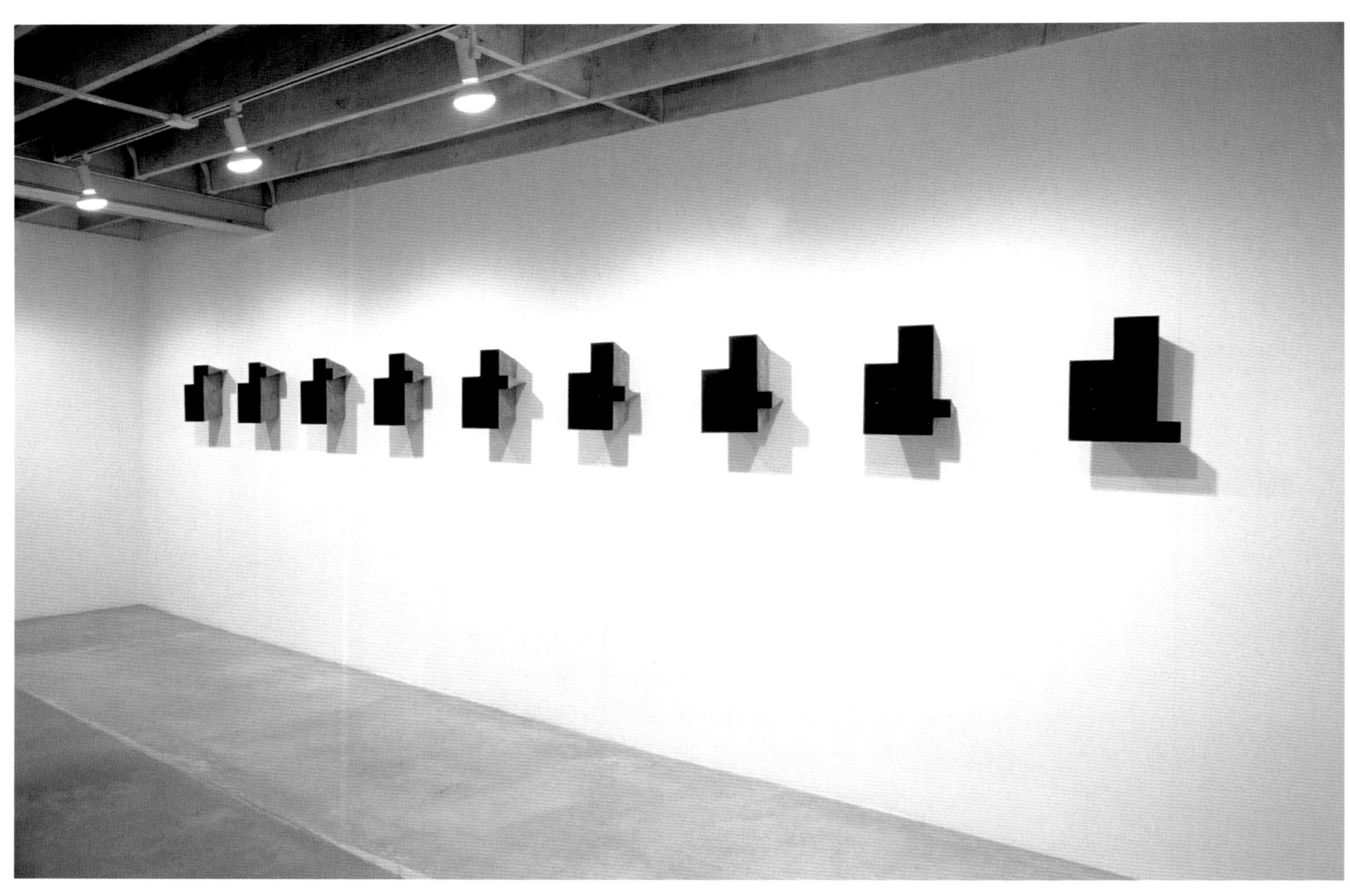

aus der Serie: **Drei Quadrate,** 1991
From the series: *Three Squares*
Samt und Öl auf Beton, je 37,5 × 31 × 16 cm
Velvet and oil on concrete

aus der Serie: **Drei Quadrate,** 1991
From the series: *Three Squares*
Öl und Pigment auf Fabriano, 33 × 24 cm
Oil and pigment on Fabriano

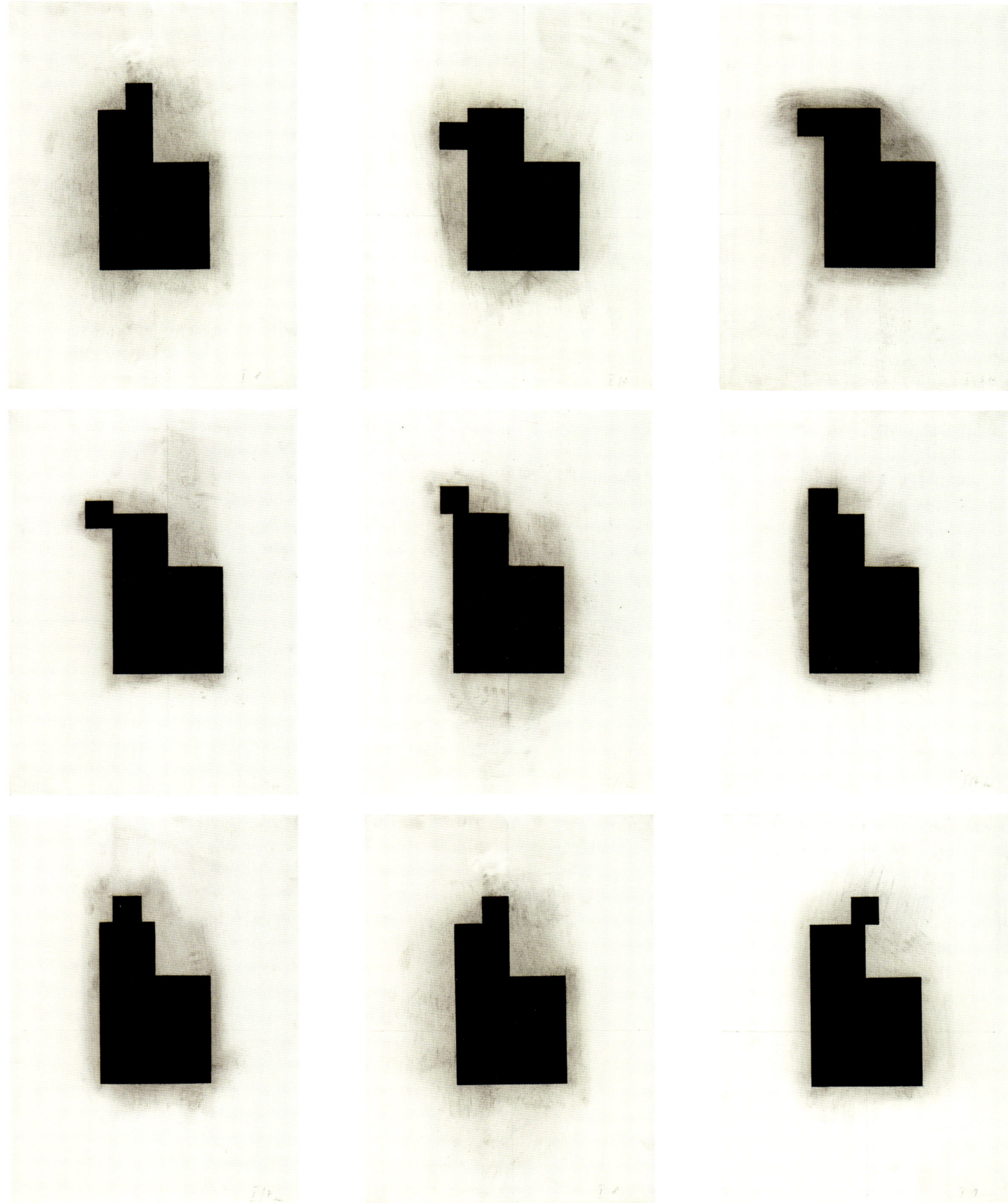

Drei Quadrate (schräg), 1992
Three Squares (oblique)
Öl auf Holz, 45 × 35,5 × 25,5 cm
Oil on wood

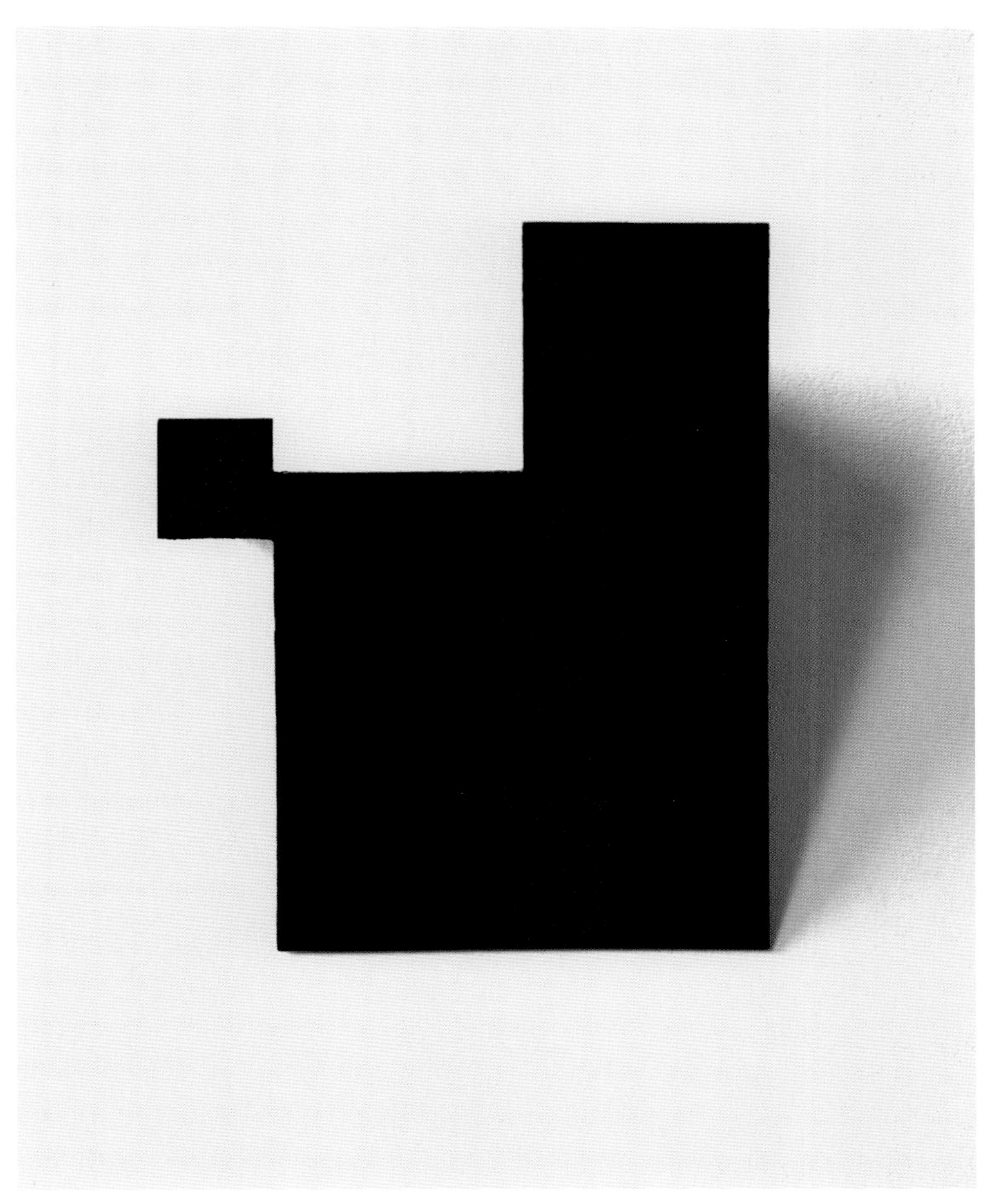

Drei Quadrate, 1992
Three Squares
Öl auf Holz, 28 × 45,5 × 28 cm
Oil on wood

1941 Geboren in Steterburg
Born in Steterburg
1962–63 Zunächst Wehrdienst ohne Waffe,
dann Ersatzdienst im Krankenhaus |
Unarmed military service, then non-mili-
tary service in a hospital
1964–67 Studium der Kunstpädigogik an der
Hochschule für Bildende Künste (HBK)
Braunschweig, Staatsexamen | Studied
art education at the HBK Braunschweig,
state examination
1967–69 Studium der Freien Malerei bei
Alfred Winter-Rust | Studied painting
with Alfred Winter-Rust
1969–70 DAAD-Stipendium für Paris | DAAD
scholarship for Paris
1969 Niedersächsischer Förderpreis | Spon-
sorship Award of Lower Saxony
1971 Preis *Neues Forum* prize, Bremen | *New
Forum* prize, Bremen
1972–79 Lehraufträge an der HBK Braun-
schweig | Lecturer at the HBK Braun-
schweig
seit | since 1972 Atelier in Lu Fraili, Sardinien |
Studio in Lu Fraili, Sardinia
1979 Preis der Villa Massimo, Rom | Villa
Massimo prize, Rome
seit | since 1979 Verheiratet mit Regine
Seemann; Kinder Johanna und Lukas |
Married to Regine Seemann; children
Johanna und Lukas
seit | since 1980 Professur an der HBK
Braunschweig | Professor at the HBK
Braunschweig

seit | since 1985 Längere Arbeitsaufenthalte
in Los Angeles | Extended working so-
journs in Los Angeles
1986 Niedersächsisches Künstlerstipendium
Artist's Scholarship of Lower Saxony
1997 Kunstpreis der SPD-Fraktion des Nieder-
sächsischen Landtages | Art prize from
the SDP faction of the State Parliament
of Lower Saxony
1999–2004 Vizepräsident der HBK Braun-
schweig | Vice-president of the HBK
Braunschweig
2005 Preis *Bildende Kunst* des Verbandes der
Deutschen Kritiker | *Fine Art* prize from
the Association of German Critics

1970 Galerie Langer, Braunschweig
1971 Frankfurter Kunstkabinett Hanna Bekker
vom Rath
Galerie Müller, Köln | Cologne
1972 Kunstverein Kreis Unna e. V., Unna
Neues Museum, Ulm (mit | with Rune
Mields und | and Alfred Hofkunst)
Studio des Kunstvereins Kassel
Galerie Brusberg, Hannover
1974 Oldenburger Kunstverein (mit | with
Hartmut Wiesner und | and Sigi Zahn)
1975 Galerie Langer, Braunschweig
Galerie Movie, Kassel
1981 Kunstverein Hannover (mit | with Roland
Dörfler und | and Malte Sartorius)
1984 Süd-West-Galerie, Karlsruhe
1985 Kunstverein Wolfenbüttel (mit | with Karl
Schaper und | and Peter Tuma)
1986 Galerie Mathea, Wolfenbüttel
1987 Angles Gallery, Santa Monica
Galerie Jöllenbeck, Köln | Cologne
Galerie kö 24, Hannover
1988 Angles Gallery, Santa Monica
1990 Galerie Schmücking, Braunschweig
1991 Kunstverein Gifhorn
Kunstverein Wolfenbüttel
Angles Gallery, Santa Monica
1992 Art Studio 1, Deinste
Galerie kö 24, Hannover
Mars Gallery, Tokio | Tokyo
Auchincloss Gallery, New York
1993 Zellermayer Galerie, Berlin
1994 Raab-Boukamel Gallery, London
1995 Gesellschaft für Kunst und Gestaltung,
Bonn
Kunstverein Salzgitter e. V.
Galerie Gudrun Spielvogel,
München | Munich

1996 Zellermayer Galerie, Berlin
Galerie kö 24, Hannover
Hirschwirtscheuer, Künzelsau
Zellermayer Galerie, Berlin
1997 Annemarie Taeger. Raum für Kunst,
Frankfurt am Main
Angles Gallery, Santa Monica
1998 Galerie Spielvogel, München | Munich
Art Studio 1, Deinste
1999 Galerie Kirchencampus, Wolfenbüttel
2001 Zellermeyer Galerie, Berlin
2002 Galerie Mathea, Braunschweig (mit | with
Siegfried Neuenhausen und | and Gerd
Winner)
Galerie Spielvogel, München | Munich
2003 Zellermeyer Galerie, Berlin
Art Studio 1, Deinste
2004 Marketing Management Institute, Braun-
schweig
Sparkasse, Goslar
Galerie Gudrun Tiedt, Goslar (mit | with
Siegfried Neuenhausen)
2005 St. Maternus, Köln-Südstadt | Cologne-
Südstadt

1969 *Junge Stadt sieht junge Kunst*, Städtische
Galerie Wolfsburg
Strenge Gestalter, Galerie Querschnitt,
Braunschweig
Herbstausstellung niedersächsischer
Künstler, Kunstverein Hannover
1970 *Six Jeunes Allemands à Paris*, Goethe-
Institut Paris
3. | 3rd Internationale der Zeichnung,
Darmstadt
10 Braunschweiger und 10 Wolfsburger,
Städtische Galerie Wolfsburg
Herbstausstellung niedersächsischer
Künstler, Kunstverein Hannover
Galerie Muchow, Freiburg
1971 *German Art Today*, Redfern Gallery,
London
*Aktiva '71. Kunst der jungen Generation
in Westdeutschland*, Münster
Septième Biennale de Paris. République
Fédérale Allemande, Paris
Deutscher Künstlerbund, Stuttgart
3. | 3rd Internationale Frühjahrsmesse,
Berlin
Art Cologne, Cologne
Junge Deutsche Künstler, Galerie Rothe,
Heidelberg
1972 *Deutsche Grafik*, Krakau | Cracow,
Warschau | Warsaw
Junge Künstler, Jahrhunderthalle Frank-
furt
14 × 14, Kunsthalle Baden-Baden
1973 2. | 2nd Biennale Internationale d´Epinal,
Epinal
Kunst nach Wirklichkeit, Hannover,
Milano | Milan, Rotterdam, Paris
Reale und irreale Räume, Galerie Falazik,
Neuenkirchen
Gegenwartskunst aus der BRD, Multiples
und Grafik, Mexico City
3 Deutsche, Goethe-Institut, Paris
Tyske Tendenser, Kunstmuseum, Åalborg
Räume, Paula-Modersohn-Haus, Bremen
Das weiße Bild, Galerie Querschnitt,
Braunschweig

1980 Ars '74, Ateneum, Helsinki
Deutsche Zeichner, Galerie Wilbrand,
Köln | Cologne
Biennale de Menton, Menton
Deutscher Künstlerbund, Mainz
*Amerikanische Hyperrealisten – Europä-
ische Realisten*, Museum Boymans-van-
Beuningen, Rotterdam
Herbstausstellung niedersächsischer
Künstler, Kunstverein Hannover
1975 *Internationale Zeichner*, Galerie Thelen,
Köln | Cologne
Deutscher Künstlerbund, Dortmund
Deutsche Zeichner, Kunsthalle Baden-
Baden
1976 *Menschenleere Räume*, Badischer Kunst-
verein, Karlsruhe
Deutscher Künstlerbund, Mannheim
Handzeichnungen, Baakscher Kun-
straum, Köln | Cologne
Plätze der Macht, Galerie Falazik, Neuen-
kirchen
6. | 6th Grafik Biennale, Krakau | Cracow
Hinterzeichnung – Arrière Dessin,
Steinkimmen-Angers
Gebackene Kunst, Kunstverein Hannover
1977 Deutscher Künstlerbund, Frankfurt
12 Norddeutsche Zeichner, Städtische
Galerie Nordhorn
Hommage à Schwitters, Kunstverein
Hannover
1978 *Deutsche Druckgrafik der 70er Jahre*,
Sindelfingen, Frechen
Herbstausstellung niedersächsischer
Künstler, Kunstverein Hannover
Deutscher Künstlerbund, Berlin
1979 *Nachbilder*, Kunstverein Hannover
Deutscher Künstlerbund, Stuttgart

1980 *5 Künstler der Villa Massimo*, Goethe-Institut Neapel | Naples
Jahresausstellung der Villa Massimo, Rom | Rome
Herbstausstellung niedersächsischer Künstler, Kunstverein Hannover
1981 Museumsverein, Herzog Anton Ulrich-Museum, Braunschweig
Deutscher Künstlerbund, Nürnberg
1982 *Sammlung aus Bundesankäufen*, Bonn
Herbstausstellung niedersächsischer Künstler, Kunstverein Hannover
Deutscher Künstlerbund, Düsseldorf
1983 *Villa Massimo-Stipendiaten 1978 – 82*, Karlsruhe, Kassel,
10 Zeichner – 10 Aspekte, Nassauischer Kunstverein, Wiesbaden
Deutscher Künstlerbund, Berlin
Neue Gruppe, Haus der Kunst, München | Munich
1984 *Kunstlandschaft BRD*, Gütersloh und | and Münster
Braunschweiger Konstruktivisten, Galerie S. B. Tautz, Braunschweig
Der Bestand, Museumsverein für zeitgenössische Kunst e. V., Braunschweig
Bradford Biennale, Bradford, West Yorkshire, England
Herbstausstellung niedersächsischer Künstler, Kunstverein Hannover
1985 *Ecken und Kanten*, Städtische Galerie, Lüdenscheid
Deutscher Künstlerbund, Hannover
Nationale der Zeichnung, Augsburg
Künstler als Initiatoren, Kunstverein Wolfenbüttel
1986 Herbstausstellung niedersächsischer Künstler, Kunstverein Hannover
Neue Gruppe, Haus der Kunst, München | Munich
1987 Deutscher Künstlerbund, Bremen
Profile – Impulse, Mönchehaus Museum, Goslar
25 Jahre HBK Braunschweig, Kunstverein Hannover

1988 *Künstler der Galerie*, Galerie kö 24, Hannover
Künstler der Galerie, Galerie Jöllenbeck, Köln | Cologne
Deutscher Künstlerbund, Stuttgart
Neue Gruppe, Haus der Kunst, München | Munich
Art Cologne, Köln | Cologne
Herbstausstellung niedersächsischer Künstler, Kunstverein Hannover
1989 Art Cologne, Köln | Cologne
Seven Artists, Angles Gallery, Santa Monica
Ankäufe des Landes Niedersachsen, Kunstverein Hannover
1990 *Neue Gruppe*, Haus der Kunst, München | Munich
Licht und Raum, Guehring Art und Technik, Frohnstetten
Referential Drawings, Angles Gallery, Santa Monica
Squaresville, Angles Gallery, Santa Monica
Artfair, Los Angeles
Deutscher Künstlerbund, Berlin
Raumklima, Herbstausstellung niedersächsischer Künstler, Kunstverein Hannover
1991 CeBit, Hannover
Salon Salder, Städtisches Museum Schloß Salder, Salzgitter
1992 *Art by Numbers*, Angles Gallery, Santa Monica
Lemberg Gallery, Birmingham, Michigan
Modern Surfaces, Auchincloss Gallery, New York
Leocosmo, Art Project Guidance II, Tokyo
Szene Hannover, Herbstausstellung niedersächsischer Künstler, Kunstverein Hannover

1993 Art Cologne, Köln | Cologne
Salon Salder, Städtisches Museum Schloß Salder, Salzgitter
1994 *Shape*, Auchincloss Gallery, New York
Künstler der Galerie, Galerie Spielvogel, München | Munich
1995 *Szene Hannover*, Herbstausstellung niedersächsischer Künstler, Kunstverein Hannover
1996 *Zeitströmungen*, Sprengel Museum Hannover
Wiedersehen, Herbstausstellung niedersächsischer Künstler, Kunstverein Hannover
Lehrer und Schüler, Städtisches Museum Schloß Salder, Salzgitter und andere Orte | and other locations
Kunst der Gegenwart aus Niedersachsen, Sendezentrum des ZDF-Studios
2001 *Vom Zufall und vom Glück*, Kubus Hannover und | and Galerie vom Zufall und vom Glück, Hannover
2002 *Abstrakte Positionen*, Sammlung Piepenbrock, Kulturgeschichtliches Museum, Felix Nussbaum-Haus, Osnabrück
Zwischen allen Stühlen, Art Studio 1, Deinste
Ad Infinitum, Wynn Kramarsky, New York
2004 *Infinite Possibilities; Serial Imagery in 20th-Century Drawings*, Davis Museum and Cultural Center Wellesley, Massachusetts
7 up, Galerie Schüppenhauser, Köln | Cologne
2005 *Merci. 50 Künstler für 50 Jahre*, Obernai
Hermann Waibel. Sein Werk im Kontext der konkreten Kunst, Städtische Galerie, Ravensburg
Square. Die Sammlung Marli Hoppe-Ritter, Museum Ritter, Waldenbuch
2005 *VIA unterwegs, Zeitgenössische Kunst in der Kirche Sankt Jakobus*, Goslar

Henrike Junge-Gent, „Über die Arbeiten Lienhard von Monkiewitschs. Fünf Versuche der Annäherung", in: *Lienhard von Monkiewitsch*, Ausst.-Kat. | exh. cat. Hirschwirtscheuer Künzelsau, München | Munich 1997, S. | pp. 5–9.

Gabriele Makus, „Varianten des Raumes", in: *Lienhard von Monkiewitsch. Malerei, Objekte*, Ausst.-Kat. | exh. cat. Annemarie Taeger. Raum für Kunst, Frankfurt am Main 1998, S. | pp. 5–7.

Heino R. Möller, *Innenräume—Außenwelten. Studien zur Darstellung bürgerlicher Privatheit in Kunst und Warenwerbung*, Gießen 1981, S. | pp. 208–211.

Heino R. Möller, „Lienhard von Monkiewitsch. Räume und Architekturen", in: Heino R. Möller, Ingeborg Bloth, *Studien zu Kunstwerken im Sprengel Museum Hannover*, Schriftenreihe der Hochschule für Bildende Künste Braunschweig Bd. | vol. 8, Braunschweig 1985, S. | pp. 151–181.

Lienhard von Monkiewitsch, in: *Kunststreifzüge*, Katalog zu | Catalogue accompanying Kultur im Norddeutschen Fernsehen N3, Hannover 1997, S. | p. 54.

Lienhard von Monkiewitsch, in: *Stolpersteine. Gibt es Regeln für die Bildgestaltung?*, hrsg. von | ed. Martin Scholz, Ute Helmbold, Wiesbaden 2004, S. | pp. 57–75.

Lienhard von Monkiewitsch, „Ideal geratener Zufall", in: *Künstler. Kritisches Lexikon der Gegenwartskunst*, Ausgabe | issue 68, H. | no. 27, 4 | 2004, S. | p. 14.

Lienhard von Monkiewitsch, „Gibt es Regeln für die Bildgestaltung?", in: *Künstler. Kritisches Lexikon der Gegenwartskunst*, Ausgabe | issue 68, H. | no. 27, 4/2004, S. | p. 15.

Juliane Roh, „Licht und Farbe", in: *Deutsche Kunst seit 1960. Druckgraphik*, München | Munich 1974, S. | pp. 83–84, S. | p. 203.

Lothar Romain, „Die Maler", in: *Einblicke. Sammlung Robert Simon im Bomann-Museum Celle*, Hannover 2000, S. | pp. 13–23, S. | pp. 52–53.

Willy Rotzler, *Konstruktive Konzepte. Eine Geschichte der konstruktiven Kunst vom Kubismus bis heute*, Zürich 1977, S. | p. 202.

Peter Sager, „Figurativer Realismus", in: *Neue Formen des Realismus. Kunst zwischen Illusion und Wirklichkeit*, Köln | Cologne 1973, S. | pp. 138–186.

Herbert Schober, Ingo Rentschler, *Das Bild als Schein der Wirklichkeit. Optische Täuschungen in Wissenschaft und Kunst*, München | Munich 1972, S. | p. 17, Abb. | illus. 95.

Michael Stoeber, „Lienhard von Monkiewitsch", in: *Lienhard von Monkiewitsch*, Ausst.-Kat. | exh. cat. Marketing Management Institute, Braunschweig 2004, o. S. | n. p.

Michael Stoeber, „Metamorphosen der Bildstruktur", in: *Künstler. Kritisches Lexikon der Gegenwartskunst*, Ausgabe | issue 68, H. | no. 27, 4/2004, S. | pp. 3–13.

Michael Schwarz, „Texte zu den römischen Bildern von Lienhard von Monkiewitsch", in: *Lienhard von Monkiewitsch, Bilder über Architektur*, Ausst.-Kat. | exh. cat. Kunstverein Hannover, Hannover 1981, S. | pp. 13–16.

Michael Schwarz, „Lienhard von Monkiewitsch", in: *Zeitströmungen. Kunst der Gegenwart aus der Sammlung der Niedersächsischen Sparkassenstiftung*, Hannover 1996, S. | pp. 172–175.

Walter Vitt, „Lienhard von Monkiewitsch. Kunst der Reduktion", in: *Lienhard von Monkiewitsch. Ölbilder, Farbstiftzeichnungen, Druckgrafik*, Ausst.-Kat. | exh. cat. Frankfurter Kunstkabinett Bekker vom Rath, Frankfurt am Main 1971, o. S. | n. p.

Walter Vitt, „Lienhard von Monkiewitsch", in: *Brusberg Berichte* Nr. | no. 15, Hannover 1973, S. | pp. 54–67.

Walter Vitt, „Lienhard von Monkiewitsch", in: *Menschenleere Räume*, Ausst.-Kat. | exh. cat. Badischer Kunstverein, Karlsruhe 1976, S. | pp. 44–48.

Walter Vitt, „Lienhard von Monkiewitsch. Die Untauglichkeit der Stil-Einordnungen", in: Walter Vitt, *Von strengen Gestaltern. Texte, Reden, Interviews und Briefe zur konstruktiven und konkreten Kunst*, Köln | Cologne 1982, S. | pp. 122–125.

Peter Winter, „Lienhard von Monkiewitsch. Koordinatenräume, Alpträume einer Putzfrau", in: *Das Kunstwerk* 4/xxviii, Stuttgart 1975, S. | pp. 36–37.

Ludwig Zerull, „Lienhard von Monkiewitsch", in: *Bestände. Sammlung der Landschaftlichen Brandkasse Hannover und der Provinzial Lebensversicherung Hannover*, Hannover 1995, S. | pp. 60–61

Ludwig Zerull, „Lienhard von Monkiewitsch", in: *Lehrer und Schüler*, Ausst.-Kat. | exh. cat. Niedersächsische Sparkassenstiftung, Hannover 1995, S. | pp. 6–9, S. | pp. 26–38.

Ludwig Zerull, „Licht in der Malerei", in: *Das erste 24-Stunden-Museum der Welt*, Kunst-Stiftung Celle, Hannover 1998, S. | pp. 58–77.

Ludwig Zerull, „Lienhard von Monkiewitsch", in: *Vom Zufall und vom Glück*, hrsg. von der | ed. Niedersächsische Lottostiftung, Hannover 2001, S. | pp. 32–37.

Ludwig Zerull, „Lienhard von Monkiewitsch", in: *Sammlung Sparkasse Stade – Altes Land*, Stade 2002, S. | pp. 44–45.

Herausgeber | Editor
  Michael Schwarz
Übersetzung | Translation
  Rebecca van Dyck
Lektorat | Copy-editing
  Kerber Verlag, Katrin Günther,
  sowie Ecke Issensee,
  Rebecca van Dyck
Fotos und Bildbearbeitung
Photographs and Image Editing
  Gerd Druwe, Erich Jorns,
  Winfried Mateyka, Lienhard von
  Monkiewitsch, Ivano Polastri,
  Thomas Steen, Reinhard Voigt,
Gestaltung | Design
  Andreas Koch, Bielefeld

Umschlagabbildung | Cover illustration
  Zement transparent, 1999 |
  Cement Transparent, Zement, Öl
  und Pigment auf Leinwand,
  160 × 200 cm | Cement, oil and
  pigment on canvas
Frontispiz | Frontispiece
  Konstruktion mit den aufeinander
  folgenden Fibonacci-Zahlen 3, 5,
  8, 13 bezogen auf das Format
  68 × 61, 1991 | Construction with
  the Serial Fibonacci Numbers 3, 5,
  8, 13, based on the format 68 × 61,
  Öl und Pigment auf Leinwand,
  68 × 61 cm | Oil and pigment on
  canvas

ISBN 3-938025-54-9

Printed in Germany

Verlag und Gesamtherstellung
Printed and published by
  Kerber Verlag, Bielefeld
  Windelsbleicher Straße 166–170
  D-33659 Bielefeld
  Telefon   +49 (0)5 21 / 9 50 08-10
  Fax   +49 (0)5 21 / 9 50 08-88
  E-Mail   info@kerberverlag.com
  Internet   www.kerberverlag.com
US Distribution
  D.A.P., Distributed Art Publishers
  Inc.
  155 Sixth Avenue 2nd Floor
  New York, N. Y. 10013
  Phone   001 212 6 27 19 99
  Fax   001 212 6 27 94 84